D0338850

A PRIVATE
FAMILY MATTER

A PRIVATE

FAMILY MATTER

A MEMOIR

Victor Rivas Rivers

ATRIA BOOKS
New York London Toronto Sydney

ATRIA BOOKS

1230 Avenue of the Americas
New York, NY 10020

All rights reserved, including the right to reproduce
this book or portions thereof in any form whatsoever.
For information address Atria Books, 1230 Avenue
of the Americas, New York, NY 10020

ISBN: 0-7434-8788-5

First Atria Books hardcover edition April 2005

10   9   8   7   6   5   4   3   2

ATRIA BOOKS is a trademark of Simon & Schuster, Inc.

Interior book design by Davina Mock

For information about special discounts for bulk purchases,
please contact Simon & Schuster Special Sales at
1-800-456-6798 or business@simonandschuster.com

Manufactured in the United States of America

Library of Congress Cataloging-in-Publication Data

Rivers, Victor, date.
A private family matter: a memoir/Victor Rivas Rivers—1st Atria Books hardcover ed.
p.   cm.
1. Rivers, Victor, date. 2. Adult child abuse victims—United States—Biography.
3. Adult children of dysfunctional families—United States—Biography. 4. Cuban-
American families—Case studies. 5. Actors—United States—Family
relationships—Case studies. 6. Actors—United States—Biography. I. Title.
HV6626.52.R58 2005
362.76'4'092—dc22   2004062253

For Mami, Tony, Ed, Barbie, and Carmen,
and
in loving memory of Robert Rivas

acknowledgments

First, I want to express my deepest gratitude to my spiritual and literary guide, my wife, Mim Eichler Rivas. Without you, my journey through this book, and more importantly, life, would not be as rich and evolved. To my son, Eli, whose wisdom and love have helped me to exorcise many of my demons, thank you. I love you both to infinity.

My gratitude extends to the angels who helped bring this book to life: Malaika Adero for your editorial insights; Judith Curr for your warmth and guidance; Justin Loeber and Michelle Hinkson for a stellar publicity campaign; and everyone at Atria books, it has been a pleasure. To my agent, Joe Regal, thanks for your literary contributions, your protection, and your nurturing camaraderie.

Finally, to Donna Edwards, Lynn Rosenthal, to the village that raised me, and to all the advocates that continue to save lives and rescue souls, *muchas gracias*.

I will try to pay it forward.

contents

author's note

This is a work of nonfiction. Events, actions, experiences, and their consequences have been faithfully retold herein as I have remembered them. Names and identifying characteristics of certain individuals have been changed.

Conversations presented in dialogue form have been re-created from my vivid memory of them but are not intended to represent word-for-word documentation; rather, they are meant to evoke the essence of what was actually said and the spirit in which it was spoken.

prologue:
the madman

THIS IS A STORY about how I was saved by love, at a time when most people considered me beyond rescue.

My journey from embattled boy to angry young man in need of rescue took place over a precise period of four days during the summer of 1970, in the predawn fog on a stretch of Interstate 10 near the town of Sierra Blanca, Texas. The exact moment was marked by our crossing of the road's graveled edge as our overloaded brown-gold '63 Impala station wagon sped out of control toward the dark, rocky ravine beyond the gravel. Besides the weight of four frightened kids and the driver, asleep at the wheel, the Impala was towing a cabin cruiser packed like a moving van, its tonnage adding to the momentum that would intensify the certainly fatal impact of our impending crash.

At age fourteen, kidnapped was not even a concept I would have known to use for what was happening to us, even though there had been warnings that something more dangerous than usual was in the works. The first inkling came four days earlier, in the morning, when three of my siblings and I were suddenly summoned to the kitchen by the bellow of my father's voice.

The Los Angeles day had broken dry, hot, and still. Earthquake weather. Other signals put me on guard—the tightness of the air, unpleasant smells of leftover night-blooming jasmine mixed with uncollected garbage, and the buzzing of insects on alert. But it was an absence that most alarmed me—my mother's.

Mami had not been at home for at least a day, with no comment or explanation from anyone about the fact that she was missing.

Bictor! rang out once more. Dad's pronunciation of my name still carried a trace of the Cuban *b* sound used for *v*. Certain words gave his accent away. Otherwise, he had mastered English, improving upon the start he'd gotten in his teenage years at a Georgia military school. He loved to brag about how my wealthy grandparents had been able to afford to send him there, hoping their troublesome youngest son—El Ciclón, as his friends called him—might be tamed.

But other than the meticulous military demeanor he retained from that time, there was never going to be anything tame about Antonio Rivas, or the Americanized Anthony, as he was known by now. To us he was Dad or Papi, and to my mother he was Tony.

Relieved that I wasn't being summoned alone to the kitchen, I hurried there to join my siblings and silently quoted my G.I. Joe motto. A few years before, in the heart of the sixties, Vietnam fresh in the news, a fluke of a season of good behavior earned me my wish of getting a talking G.I. Joe. Turned out to be defective. It was stuck on one phrase: "I've got a tough assignment." I learned to say it just like the G.I. Joe's recorded voice. Resolved, committed to a higher purpose. It became both my unspoken and spoken mantra, employed for facing whatever lurked in the next room.

In khakis and an ironed dark T-shirt, sleeves rolled precisely to show off his strong arms, Dad sat at the kitchen table. With a disarming smile on his face, he waited quietly, smoking a cigarette, drinking the last of his Cuban coffee—Café Bustelo, an espresso that he doused with sugar. The four of us, dressed in an assortment of Levi's cutoffs, T-shirts, and sneakers, lined up in front of him like soldiers during an inspection. At attention, not parade rest.

My brother Tony, sixteen, was going into his senior year of high school, while I was going into the tenth grade. We were only fifteen months apart but he was pretty much a genius and had skipped a year, in contrast to my school career as a troublemaker and screwup. My two younger siblings, Eddie and Barbie, nine and almost four, were both well behaved and bright, not like me at their ages. Though individuality was strictly discouraged in my father's army, we each had our own distinctive way of anticipating his moods. Tony—restrained and mature, with his knack of staying out of the fray—stood at the head of our line, outwardly calm and emotionless. Eddie was next to him, jittery, his lanky body starting to shake. Third in line was Barbie, an olive-skinned Kewpie doll with a head full of short dark curls. Girlie, sweet, innocent. But scared. She took a step just behind me, at the end.

As Dad put out his cigarette and stood up, I bristled and widened my stance, the muscles of my stomach, chest, and back clenching tight—a reflexive reaction to being in his presence as I readied myself for the tough assignment, paying attention to every little detail, as if recording history. This was my self-appointed role as family court reporter, my job of remembering everything to hold it up for judgment later, pleading my case to a judge and jury who existed only in my imagination.

"We're moving to Miami," Dad announced, still with his placid smile, "soon as we get packed, tomorrow or the next day."

At first, none of us said a word. We didn't exchange glances, we didn't respond enthusiastically or not. A move to southern Florida—where many Cuban émigrés lived, including most of our relatives—wasn't illogical; Dad had been floating the idea for some time. Then again, Dad floated all kinds of schemes and plans that never panned out.

Except for the stuttering tick of the stove clock, there was only silence, which I broke, at last, asking the obvious. "Where's Mami?"

He pretended not to have heard me and turned away. Suddenly he stopped in his tracks, the muscles in the backs of his arms twitching, and he whipped back around. Eyes narrowed, smile gone.

To look directly at me, Dad had the humiliating need to lift his chin up, to see the terrible truth—the fact that over the past year I had dared to grow several inches taller than him, on my way to my top height of six foot two. But in all my senses my father continued to tower over me. His presence was huge, filling the small kitchen with the force of his being, an invading army unto himself, conquering the air we were breathing, the ground we stood on. I looked straight back, my sight line topping all five feet ten and two hundred athletic pounds of him.

Papi had always appeared bigger than his actual dimensions, thanks to a large bone structure, his muscular upper torso, and massive thighs. We were all going to have them, the notorious "Rivas thighs." In spite of his bulk, however, Papi managed to move with unusual feline stealth. Not with blazing speed, but with the natural agility of an above-average athlete blessed with amazing hand-eye coordination. Or a cobra.

He looked away, contemplating whether or not to respond at all, and as I watched him turn in profile, I had a fleeting sense of admiration. At times Papi was dashingly handsome, like an old-time movie star, even though his features, when taken individually, were flawed—a wide nose with flared nostrils; an unremarkable mouth with a thin upper lip that opened to reveal a pronounced gap between his teeth; overly fair skin that freckled and burned easily; and most loathsome of all to him, a receding hairline and a head of graying, thinning auburn hair. Dad battled these shortcomings by altering his looks with pathological frequency—with rapid weight gain or loss, changes in hairstyle and color (he had been known to wear a Beatle wig), various guises of facial hair (or clean-shaven), and an assortment of fashion statements. Oddly enough, he pulled off these different looks quite successfully, like a spy from the Cold War, or so I thought, as if his ability to be convincing as a businessman one day or a hippie the next day was a matter of life and death.

But there was one constant: his eyes. They were unforgettable and captured his whole nature for me. They were hazel—a color I had inherited from him, though mine had become greener than his amber tint, which was almost inhuman in shade. His were not the large almond shape of my eyes, but were more reptilian, almost beady, their lethal appearance made more intense by his thinning short lashes and thinning eyebrows.

Dad turned back to meet my stare. He could intimidate, console, entrap, persuade, and terrify with his eyes alone.

He spoke casually. Mami had left us. The idea of her leaving him wasn't out of the question, but his answer sounded too simple. "She's not coming with us," he reiterated, and shrugged vaguely. "She doesn't wanna go. You kids can stay here with her, if that's your choice, but she doesn't want you." With that, he began to drill us, starting with my older brother. "So . . . *que quieres,* Tony? You wanna come to Florida with me, or stay here with your mother?"

Tony, dark, handsome, a star student and athlete the same height as Dad, quickly answered that he wanted to go to Miami.

"Eddie?" Dad asked my younger brother, whose voice shook as he said, "With you, Papi." Barbie echoed Eddie's answer.

My father saved me for last. "Vic?"

"I'm staying with Mami." I planted my feet firmly on California soil.

"No! You"—he pointed at a spot between my eyes—"you're going with me." My mother couldn't control me, he went on in Spanish, in the Cuban intonation that is flat, understated, rapid-fire. Not with my behavior. She couldn't control me, not with my lies, my stealing, my cursing, and my clowning. Fucking *bago* (lazy) cocksucker *idiota comermierda* (shit eater) *estupido* he proclaimed me to be. His bad kid. *Coño,* what I needed was discipline that only he could give me.

For a moment I'd been fooled into thinking I did have a choice.

"*Bueno*." He shifted tones, rubbing his hands together. "Now that we've decided, we have work to do."

Eddie and Barbie were charged with staying out of the way while Tony and I went to work hauling important items from the garage and taking them into the front yard. The two-car garage that had never held any of our cars was a separate structure behind the house that opened onto the alley. What it did hold was every kind of power tool known to a home workbench, two Chrysler Crown marine engines, and my father's lifetime of accumulated junk, swap-meet treasure he had tremendous plans for that never came to fruition.

Because the Impala station wagon—painted that unfortunate brownish gold by my father—would be full carrying the five of us, the plan was to take only what we could fit in the hull of the twenty-two-foot cabin cruiser. This boat, like all my father's boats—and there were many—had never been in a body of water.

The cabin cruiser sat conspicuously on the front lawn, propped on an old single-axle trailer that was covered in rust and corrosion. Whether the trailer was even functional, I doubted. It served more as a pedestal so my father could let everyone know we owned a boat.

"Bullshit!" I said out loud to myself, out of Dad's earshot, once we got started.

"What?" Tony asked.

"I don't buy it. That bullshit about Mami being fed up with us and leaving, and not wanting us. Where'd she go? Where is she?"

Tony looked intently at me, about to say something, and it seemed he knew the answer but that the penalty for telling would be far more painful than the effort to wipe it from his memory. He said nothing.

We had to take turns carrying items from the garage, in back, to the front, one running for the next armful as the other stood guard over the valuables at all times. We worked from midmorning until dusk without a break.

A vague smell of overripe peaches clung in the evening air, thick that night from a layer of fog that rolled in from the ocean before the sun went down. The peach tree in the back was a reminder of King, our terrified, terrifying German shepherd, banished two months earlier. King would shit everywhere underneath the tree, fertilizing the soil, from which the peaches were nurtured into miraculous size and health.

A tinny radio blared from inside the house, where Dad was deciding what few items he could take along for the move. He was a sound junkie, alternating between Latin music, AM Top 40, the Beatles, and even psychedelic rock like Jimi Hendrix—to which he'd swirl his hips and coo, "Groovy, groovy!" his *v*'s more like *b*'s. "Grooby, grooby! Outasight, outasight! Sock-it-to-meee!" As songs reached their peak, he had a habit of hiking his knee into the air, with his index finger circling over his head. For a native-born *cubano,* he demonstrated a shocking lack of rhythm.

When it grew too dark to see what we were doing, Dad emerged from the house to set up floodlights, clipping some to the roof, sticking others in the ground. The lights gave the front lawn the look of a night baseball game, with all the stuff from the garage lined up in careful rows like captive spectators. Much later, maybe around midnight, two unfamiliar men showed up, conferred with my father, and left with the two engines and some of the boating-related things.

In the middle of the night, Tony and I were allowed to go inside to get some sleep. An hour or two later, just before 5 A.M., Dad shook me to full attention and, with explicit urgency, told me to put on long pants and a sweatshirt and to meet him at the station wagon.

The darkness was made heavier by the fog, and the streets were empty, with only the occasional glow of streetlights punctuating the mist. Dad drove west, toward the ocean, twenty minutes later pulling into a parking lot near the boat hoist by the Redondo Beach pier. A popular spot for many commercial fishing boats, the hoist was used to lift about any size boat off a trailer and place it in the water, and vice versa.

More than two dozen cars with trailers were in the parking lot, evidence of the fishermen who usually went out well before daybreak and returned in the late afternoon.

Dad drove slowly through the parking lot with our headlights off, studying those parked cars. The lonely wail of a foghorn pierced the disappearing night. Flashes of James Bond and Cold War maneuvers proposed themselves as I scanned the dark for a faceless, trench-coated presence. This wasn't a far-fetched conclusion. After all, for the last five years Dad had worked at North American Rockwell, with top security clearance, handling secret computer files.

But it soon became clear that such an important mission was not at hand. With the first hint of daylight throwing gray streaks into the black, I saw that Dad had pulled the station wagon up alongside a white pickup truck with a matching white trailer. Agitated, he left our engine running and quickly slid out of the car, unhooked the trailer from the white pickup truck, and began to lug it into position behind us.

"Bic!" he called hoarsely, beckoning me to assist. I needed no instructions. The two of us took little time in attaching the white trailer to our hitch.

On the road heading toward home, day breaking overcast, less dry and less hot than the day before, Dad lit a cigarette, turned on a Top 40 radio station, and hummed along, out of tune, with a self-satisfied grin on his face, tapping his heavy gold ring on the steering wheel in a beat all his own.

Back in our neighborhood, we came down the alley and pulled up behind the garage. Staring straight ahead to scope out the alley, he told me to go get Tony and put the trailer in the garage.

My brother hurried out to help. As soon as we detached the trailer, Dad sped off down the alley. Tony pulled as I pushed until we maneuvered the trailer into the almost empty garage.

"Now what?" I asked my brother.

Tony gestured toward the open garage door, indicating that we ought to close it. We headed out into the alley, lowered the door, and started up toward the house.

Dad met us on the way in, arms folded, nostrils flared. "Where do you two think you're going?" Before we could answer, he informed us we were to return to work to clear out any remaining items from the garage. "Except the paint compressor," he said. "Leave that on the shelf."

We stumbled back toward the garage.

He called after us, "I'm leaving but I'll be back soon."

Tony's face, which until now had shown little emotion, was starting to reflect the bewilderment I was feeling. But we both knew better than to say anything, thinking as we did that Papi was omnipresent, that he knew the truth of our misdeeds, our words, and our thoughts, no matter what.

Carrying the last of the junk, we trudged back and forth from the garage to the front yard, and every time we passed by the white trailer that belonged to someone else, I couldn't stop thinking that my father had just stolen it and that I had helped him. Confusion, disappointment, and shame mixed with the resentment, exhaustion, and fear that had been building.

There were scars on my body I could identify and enumerate, a chronicle of my thefts—marks given to me at ages four, five, seven, eight, ten, and so on—because, I was told, I deserved to be punished. They were supposedly left to remind me what happens to those who take things that don't belong to them. Papi usually claimed afterward that he hated administering such punishment, but what else would teach me that no one would ever trust or want to be friends with a *ladrón,* a fucking thief?

What I now saw was that he was the *ladrón.* Not only did he have no remorse, but stealing the boat trailer seemed to have given him pleasure.

It still didn't dawn on me that he was stealing *us.*

Night fell before we were ready to leave. Time and images of our last day in Los Angeles became jumbled in sequence. At one point there was the sight of Papi in the garage, bent over the front of the white trailer, a lit cigarette in one hand, a metal sledgehammer in the other, and a small wooden box at his side that held what looked like drill bits.

"See," he explained proudly, "I'm retapping the serial numbers so they'll match the old trailer." The wooden box, it turned out, was actually a tapping kit. After retapping the serial number, he employed his handy paint compressor, a tool acquired for the purpose of spray-painting our white refrigerator an awful avocado green.

I remembered how Mami reacted when he presented the fridge to the family. Of course, my mother—tall, beautiful, once proud and passionate—had been deprived for years of her natural expressions. Papi forbade her to even hug and kiss her sons, sure it would make us weak and effeminate. Still, she and I had our own form of communication, an unspoken, unarticulated love, and the same sense of humor. When she beheld the paint job, I saw her quickly put her hand to her mouth to cover up an expression of surprised repulsion—our eyes making covert contact.

The paint job on the Impala turned out better, even though that brown-gold color was another vain attempt to show the world Anthony Rivas was somebody—a *gold car* driver—when in fact it looked more like metallic shit. He used the same color to repaint the stolen trailer.

Seeing the ease with which my father stole, retapped, and painted this trailer confirmed to me that he had done this before.

By the time we loaded up the car, Tony and I had gone without sleep for roughly thirty-six hours. The toughest challenge came earlier when Dad lay down for a rest, leaving me to stand guard out front. If I sat down, I knew that I would fall asleep, so I anchored myself by holding a tall rake and fought to keep my eyes open. But before I knew it, my brother's voice startled me. "Vic! Vic! Wake up!"

Snapping to, I cleared my sight to focus in on Tony.

When he was sure I was conscious, Tony whispered, "You were asleep standing up. You were snoring."

"Shit."

My eyes had been open, he said, wide open. That tired, that scared.

Tony's turn came when he went inside to make the coffee for Dad. This was routine by this era. We'd been schooled from our earliest years in the fine art of brewing Cuban coffee, bringing a cup of it to Papi's bedside, and performing our respective duties in raising him from the dead of sleep—an effort that could sometimes become a daylong undertaking for the whole family.

Waiting for Tony to let me know the coffee was ready, I propped myself more firmly with the rake and again fell asleep standing up with my eyes open, which I discovered when the resounding *KA-POWWW* of a small explosion jolted me back awake.

I raced inside to the kitchen. Tony was on the floor, a sixteen-year-old mound of jeans and sweatshirt seated and slumped over, hard asleep. High above the stove that held the capsized empty metal espresso maker, coffee and coffee grounds dripped from the ceiling.

I turned the burner off and woke Tony. Eyes rimmed red, he blinked and pointed at the clock. We were almost two hours late waking up Dad. The cause for the full-on freak-out came when he reported that he had just used the last of the Bustelo.

Unlike me—all passion, all emotion, in need of discipline and control—my brother rarely rebelled, never cried. But now he rubbed the wetness from his eyes. At Hawthorne High School, Tony would have been headed for a triumphant senior year—a football and wrestling star, an honors student who'd already skipped one year of school, a popular, great-looking guy with several girls vying for him. All of that would no longer be his. In Miami, he would probably have to start over, maybe not play sports, maybe give up the scholarships and other future gold he'd planned for.

What I now saw was that being taken away from here would be much harder on him. For me, it was almost a chance to start over, to shake off my reputation of being trouble. Because I had no way of predicting my own future, I convinced myself that as bad as things had gotten, they couldn't be any worse in Florida.

The main event of the afternoon had been a pageant of my father's flawed genius as he masterminded moving the cabin cruiser from the old, useless trailer to the new trailer. Plan A involved wooden blocks built as a brace to slide the boat from trailer to trailer. That failing, Plan B was to saw the old trailer in half, pull it out, and slide the new trailer under the boat. Plan C was required, which involved using the electric winch of the new trailer and the three of us to lift the cabin cruiser up a few inches off the old trailer.

These complications were no surprise to me. There was some moral justice being doled out by unseen forces, I sensed. Dad was a thief, I couldn't argue with that anymore, and it looked possible that he would get away with this legally, but not in God's eyes. Tony and I, despite our roles as accomplices, would be forgiven because, God knew, we had no real choice but to obey our father's orders.

In the flow and dance of these maneuvers, a warning thought— triggered by the creaking of the wooden blocks—skittered through my head. Like the robot from *Lost in Space* who droned, "Danger! Danger, Will Robinson!" it told me that his idea to simply winch the boat forward onto the new trailer was faulty. In the din of Dad barking directions, the *SCREEEECH* of the winch, and the *SCRAAAAPE* of fiberglass against metal, it occurred to me that the physics at hand didn't compute; the boat was not floating on the water but, rather, its back half rested on blocks on our front lawn—not the intended dynamics in this equation for what he had in mind.

At just the split second that this logic materialized, I looked down to see the front end of the boat landing on my right foot. There was no pain. In what seemed like minutes passing but was surely instantaneous, I grabbed the boat and, with a guttural yell from the bowels of my soul, pushed it up and off my foot.

To my own amazement, I not only lifted the two-ton cabin cruiser but felt no damage whatsoever to my foot. It should have been crushed. Papi only gawked at me, he and Tony almost nervous in their slack-jawed silence, as if they'd just seen Superman, or something more marvelous—the revenge of the saints my mother prayed to, her only trusted source of protection.

"*Coño,* you all right?" Dad cried, rushing to me.

"Yeah," I said, hopping on it to show him.

He pulled off my shoe and sock, examined my foot, and pronounced me unscathed and able to return to work. At last, with the winch and a lot of pushing and pulling on our part, we succeeded in getting the boat onto the other trailer.

An hour and a half later, our home and lawn bare, darkness having fallen, Dad got behind the wheel, Tony at his right in the front passenger seat, Eddie, Barbie, and I in the backseat. The cool, dry summer night air was not comforting. There were no neighbors out to wish us well or give us freshly baked goods for the trip. There were no friends to hug good-bye.

I rolled down the window, leaned my head out, and looked back in the direction of the abandoned house, half hoping and half expecting to see my mother running down the sidewalk, imagining her night-splitting cry that would stop the car and reunite us with her.

But for as long as I could still see behind us, Mami did not appear. A memory of her perfume and an echo of her laugh came into my senses as we accelerated up the ramp onto I-10, heading east. Once before she had disappeared for weeks, after almost dying and being taken to the hospital as a Jane Doe. Papi had blamed her for abandoning us then, calling her collapse some sort of melodramatic feint for attention. Her "little holiday," he had called it. Any number of things could have happened to her this time, none of the scenarios reassuring, and they ate at me as I gave in to sleep, comforting myself as I did that in Miami there were uncles and aunts who would help me find her and make sure she was safe.

There was another person somewhere in the city's sprawl that I needed to come back and search for. My brother Robert, born a year and a half after Eddie, a brother I barely knew, was still living—or so I believed—in the care of strangers.

Before I closed my eyes to sleep, we passed the spires of downtown Los Angeles and I turned around again for a last look at the land we were leaving. These last looks were to be markers, like bread crumbs left in the woods, so that I could find my way home again after the night, back to wherever my mother really was.

I woke to a fog around my head and the pulsating, strobelike effect of yellow flashing lights. Our car was standing still, shaking violently from the velocity of the heavy traffic that was whizzing by. An eighteen-wheeler's delayed back draft made it feel that we might become airborne.

Had we been pulled over? Had the police tracked Dad down for stealing the boat trailer? Had my mother contacted the authorities and told them that her children were missing? How long had we been gone? Since it was dark out, could I have slept from one night to the next? What state were we in?

A hard tug on the car drew my focus through the front windshield, where an enormous tow truck was hooking its tow to our car. We began to move slowly along the shoulder, then back into the flow of traffic, until I spotted an interstate sign with "California" written on the bottom border.

The ensuing twenty-four hours of delay—caused by the collapse of our station wagon's rear axle—came as a slight reprieve. Dad was unusually subdued, despite his frustration that the nearest Texaco with a mechanic on duty wasn't open until the morning, despite the expense that fixing it was going to entail, despite the cost of putting us up in a motel room.

At Denny's, where we went after checking into our room, he quietly explained to Tony why the car had broken down—how the added weight of the boat and trailer had snapped the axle—speaking, as he often did, as if I weren't there.

We ate, as always, in silence, until Barbie broke it, her tan pixie face crumpling into tears. "I want Mami. Where is she?" She didn't wait for answers or worry that, as was his custom, Papi might reach underneath the table and give her a hard pinch. "I want Mami," she repeated.

"*Sí, sí,* I know," he answered, nodding sadly. "What can we do? We'll get to Miami soon."

At the motel, not long before midnight, I leaned over to turn off the light and noticed a phone book on the bottom shelf of the nightstand. It was then that I learned we had come only ninety miles, when I saw our location on it in big bold letters: "San Bernardino."

It was another marker, another sign of how wrong it was to think that life had to get better because it couldn't get worse.

Another night fell before we got back on the road. We continued to head east on I-10, through Palm Springs and into Arizona, at Blythe, as Dad raged about the slow, costly work of the mechanics at the Texaco, his tone suggesting, per his habit, that it was our fault.

"We're just pulling too many pounds," he rasped. "You fat-asses need to lose some weight!" He grinned playfully. Tony and I shit-grinned back. Papi caught my look in the rearview mirror and returned it with a burning scowl.

Considering the ridiculous weight that the car was hauling, it seemed to be driving fine. But to make sure he didn't add to the strain, he instituted a no-air-conditioning policy.

Having the windows open helped take the edge off the heat that combined with the constant trail of cigarette smoke swirling through the car. Dad's rings and watch clicked relentlessly on the steering wheel, punctuating the songs on the radio that seemed to have special significance—"The Long and Winding Road," "Mama Told Me Not to Come," and "O-o-h Child" . . . *things are gonna get easier . . .*

My father pushed on, driving like a man possessed, stopping only for fuel, food, or the restroom, and usually all three at the same time because they could be found in one stop. Tony—who'd just gotten his learner's permit but wasn't allowed to drive—played the role of navigator, studying maps and gauging distances that we had traveled.

Dad drove straight through the night after we left San Bernardino, through morning, noon, into the late afternoon, when, declaring his exhaustion, he pulled into a large rest area somewhere in southeastern New Mexico. Five hours later, two of which were occupied by staying away from the car so he could sleep and three of which were required for us to try to wake him, we set off again. I imagined the truck drivers and solo travelers shaking their heads in suspicion, the normal families talking to one another about how weird we had appeared—two teenage boys trying to pull their father's limp, lifeless body out of the car.

As before, we left under the cover of night, as though we were in a race, against what or whom I didn't know. Things *weren't* going to get easier.

Phantom screams and thrashing by unseen hands reached into my dreams, jerking me awake enough to identify the sounds of rocks and gravel hitting the undercarriage of the car. In the right rear seat where I'd been resting my sleeping head against the window ever since we edged into the flat span of western Texas, I looked out and found no road extending from the right side of the car. What I did see was a forty-foot drop into a gully covered in brown grass and rocks. To my left, Eddie was asleep, leaning against the left rear door. Looking forward, I saw that Tony was in a deep sleep, with his chin on his chest and with Barbie curled up asleep in his lap, cradled in his arms. Behind the steering wheel, my dad was asleep with his hands firmly gripping the wheel.

Other than the sound of gravel beneath the car, the interior was dead silent. The car was drifting right, the sound of the gravel growing louder, all of us veering toward that downward plunge.

If I slapped my father to wake him up, I might die. But if I didn't hit him, we would all definitely die.

My choice wasn't difficult. It was simply a matter of adding up the many times my father had hit me in my face, a child of six, eight, eleven, twelve, even when I was sound asleep. Besides that, I realized that the primal act of getting to hit him back for the first time in my life was going to give me great pleasure.

part one

war zone

1

sancti spíritus

(1955–1957)

The multitude of palm trees of various forms, the highest and most beautiful I have ever met with, and an infinity of great and green trees; the birds in rich plumage and the verdure of the fields; render this country, most serene princes, of such marvellous beauty that it surpasses all others in charms and graces as the day doth the night in lustre. I have been so overwhelmed at the sight of so much beauty that I have not known how to relate it.

—Christopher Columbus, on Cuba,
to King Ferdinand and Queen Isabella, 1492

OLGA ANGELICA LOPEZ IBARRA was born prematurely on September 21, 1929, at 3 P.M. in a hospital in Havana. She was the size of a small Coca-Cola bottle, all of four pounds. With no neonatal units or incubators to nurture her into life, she began her existence much as she would live it—in struggle.

My mother, to me, was the embodiment of Cuba. She was a natural beauty, dark, exotic, proud, intelligent, opinionated, ironic with a sense of tragicomedy, but unspoiled; then later, like our island itself, conquered, exploited, oppressed. My father did his best to obliterate her; he broke her into many pieces, but she refused to be completely vanquished. She had native and Spaniard coloring but was a mix of other ethnicities, like Cuba, my homeland. Many of her memories and experiences were passed on in my cells, my DNA, or were told in fragments over the years, usually with her back to me as she bent over our various kitchen counters preparing countless numbers of meals,

19

often, if Papi wasn't around, while her beloved Cuban music played on scratchy records or obscure radio stations.

In public, my mother danced with an abandon and joy—whether slow or fast, *son* or *mambo*—that seemed to belong to someone else, but at home she wasn't allowed to dance, as though it might rouse her to counterrevolution against Papi. But music or not, she moved with a sensual grace to some internal Cuban beat, its core from African culture, with the rhythm of the claves—two thick wooden sticks about a foot long—keeping time.

My mother had another distinctive quality that she kept secret. She had the gift of sight. She could read omens and feel the presence of ghosts. Her energy produced heat and caused still water left in drinking glasses to bubble up as in a boiling cauldron. She had innate healing powers that, had she been free to direct her own destiny, might have led her to become a licensed medical professional. These powers may have been strengthened in her earliest days when she struggled between life and death, "all eyes and hair" as her parents described her at birth.

Pero con el ayudo de Dios—but with the help of God (Mami's favorite phrase)—baby Olga survived and was soon allowed to go home. Her father, a handsome, stern policeman by the name of Jose Manuel Lopez—known as Manolo—carried his firstborn out of the hospital in one of the oversized pockets of his suit jacket. In their modest home, her mother, Eladia Ibarra, a pretty young seamstress, sewed garments smaller than doll clothes to fit tiny Olga.

Other struggles ensued. Less than a month after she was born, the Wall Street crash plummeted Cuba into its worst economic crisis up until that time. Four years later, a second child, Carmita, was born to the Lopez family, just as the country teetered on civil war. In the atmosphere of uncertainty, President Gerardo Machado resigned before boarding a plane to Miami, and a youthful army sergeant named Fulgencio Batista took control of the island nation.

Despite her family's relative poverty and the national instability, love and protection were in abundance at home, such that Olga remembered her childhood as simple and quiet. She never thought of herself as a great beauty, she would say, but admitted later, "I had a certain look and knew how to win people over." Was she too modest? "Well, they used to tell me that I was friendly and funny. Perhaps, due to my good nature, I was showered with happy moments."

That charm, that positive, attractive energy drew her many suitors. After her diminutive start in life, she grew surprisingly tall—five foot six, taller than most Cuban girls of her generation; and with her milk-chocolate-colored eyes, thick long lashes, and a mane of wavy black hair, Olga Lopez, struggles notwithstanding, had the sparkle of one fated to be lucky in love. But then, through an unlucky series of circumstances, she met Antonio Rivas. Her gift of sight apparently fled her. For the rest of her days, Olga could not for the life of her recall what she had seen in him.

Nor could she fathom why she had recently broken off her engagement to Artemio, the true love of her life. Maybe it was partly because she had been only twelve years old when they met on the Havana city bus that she took to school (where her adored English teacher was Miss Amelie, who, as it so happened, went on to have a son named Andres, later to become famous as the actor Andy Garcia).

Aside from the fact that Artemio was nine years older and worked as a bus driver, he had qualities Olga liked. He was dark-haired, six feet tall, with a stylish thick mustache and a wonderful smile. Even though she was too young for suitors, he was a gentleman and very persistent, eventually earning her parents' permission to take her on chaperoned dates. They made a striking couple, everyone agreed. With her gentle but hawk-eyed mother at their side, Olga and her beau experienced the glittering, glamorous Havana nightlife of the late 1940s. Though she was only the daughter of a civil servant, and he was but a humble bus driver, they were the most popular couple on the dance floor. With his rich singing voice, Artemio also made her feel special when, on occasion, he was asked to join the orchestra to sing and dedicated his crooning to her.

The plan was for them to be married once Olga completed the teaching program in which she enrolled after graduating from high school with honors. This career path was not entirely of her choosing. When she had told Manolo that she intended to become a nurse, her father had said, "Absolutely not." A good man and a protective father, he was of the old-fashioned mind-set that nursing was not a respectable profession for an unmarried young lady. Why? "Because," he insisted, "doctors carry on affairs with their nurses, ruining their reputations."

Engaged to marry Artemio, in accordance with Manolo's wishes, she pursued her teaching curriculum, but without her father's knowledge and consent, she enrolled in nursing school at the same time. For three years, on top of her demanding studies to become a teacher, Olga secretly worked as a nurse's aide at a local hospital that treated police officers.

In her circle of friends, there was a general attitude that fine, educated young ladies ought to seek marriage above their station in life. At first, this did nothing to mar her feelings for Artemio, who had patiently, attentively watched her blossom from adolescence to womanhood, remaining respectful of her innocence all the while. Olga's friends agreed he was handsome and polite, but pointed out other concerns. Money and social status mattered, as did a prospective groom's family name, despite what the love songs said. In fact, in America front-page headlines blamed the escalating divorce rate on crooners who made romantic love seem so simple, when, as everyone with any sense knew, marriage was work, hard work.

Olga couldn't keep these notions out of her head. With what looked to be a life full of promise ahead of her, she broke off her engagement. The towels had already been monogrammed.

Only later did she come to regret ending her relationship with Artemio as the second worst decision of her life.

Meanwhile, after graduating with her teaching degree, Olga was preoccupied by an unexpected set of adventures and challenges that had come her way. Though she had assumed her first assignment would be in a school in Havana, she was instructed to pack her bags, as her job would be taking her out to classrooms across Cuba, in the underserved countryside. Almost like a young missionary, sometimes traveling on her own, she subsequently saw her island as few did, visiting every province of the land that lay beyond Havana—Baracoa, Santiago, Bayamo, Camagüey, Trinidad, and Sancti Spíritus. No doubt this turn of events worried her father, but she assured him that wherever she went, she was well treated.

Senorita Lopez taught students from all walks of life—from the families of wealthy ranchers and from the poorest of peasant families. She marveled at those who had little or nothing but managed to be very generous with whatever they did have. As she taught, she was also learning—picking up, for example, some of the folk medicine and healing rituals of Santeria, the white magic that combined African and native Caribbean spiritual beliefs, in addition to food recipes from the different regions.

Manolo had been a mess chef in the military and had taught both of his daughters to cook at an early age. By the time she was nine years old, Olga had been cooking most meals for her family. Now added to her repertoire were recipes she collected as she traveled across the countryside, yielding her versions of traditional Cuban dishes like *arroz con pollo* and *lechón* that were arguably among the best ever tasted, and eclectic creations without rival—like her Cuban fried rice, inspired by descendants of the Chinese traders who had once come to the island expecting to pass through but could never bring themselves to leave.

For a young woman who had been so sheltered, Olga Lopez became unusually independent—traveling in various modes of transportation not limited to boats, trains, and buses, but sometimes by *coche* (horse-drawn buggy) or even on the backs of horses and mules. She had many occasions to be fearful but managed to survive the ordeals of travel, until one of her assignments took her out into the countryside at night and she was caught in a torrential downpour, on horseback, while crossing a river whose banks had overflowed. Terror seized her. For an instant she panicked, pulling back on the horse's reins to turn him around as he pitched and reared, almost throwing her off into the turbulent water. She was sure she was going to die. Then she closed her eyes, allowing a calm to wash over her as she put herself in God's hands, asking him to guide her horse. Beneath her, the horse began to swim and she clung to his mane the whole way, finally ending up miles from her destination—wet, still terrified, but safe.

Beautiful, strong, a teacher and a nurse who happened to cook like an angel, and an exceptional dancer, Olga attracted many suitors, among them a doctor, a sugarcane engineer, and an officer in the military. Despite the fact that she was almost twenty-three—by many standards old not to be married yet—she was not in a hurry to become engaged, and enjoyed their attentions. That changed when Batista's minister of agriculture, Eduardo Suarez Rivas, began making unwanted advances toward her.

Minister Rivas first spotted her at a public art exhibit of her students' work in the city of Sancti Spíritus, the capital of the province of the same name. Olga had taught in various schools in the region that catered to the children whose parents toiled on the big sugarcane plantations, as well as to the children of plantation owners. She also continued to offer her nursing skills to the local populace when she could.

The city of Sancti Spíritus—or Holy Spirit—presented her with further history lessons regarding her country's early struggles. When the Spaniards first attempted to establish the city, a well-organized defense was staged by the area's native inhabitants—hordes of notorious stinging ants—which made life unbearable for the conquistadors. The city of Sancti Spíritus was then moved to a new location, which was subsequently burned to the ground, not once but twice, by pirates. Lost in the blazes was Cuba's first church, the Iglesia Parroquial Mayor del Espiritu Santo, built in 1522 and rebuilt later.

As a journalist riding with the Spanish army, a young Winston Churchill had visited the city in 1895. The region's lush beauty and its undercurrent of imminent danger were impressed upon Churchill

when he narrowly escaped death during a skirmish with Cuban independence fighters.

Senorita Lopez had no inkling of her imminent danger when the
head of the ministry of agriculture first laid eyes on her at the public
gathering to view the artwork of the students in the city. Aristocratic
and chivalrous, the elderly minister merely took note of her, masking
evidence that he was quite smitten. He may have turned and said
something to a younger man at his side, his twenty-two-year-old
nephew, Antonio Arturo Guillermo Rivas Garcia-Rubio—who also
bore an aristocratic, charming air—to find out who she was. Neither
said anything to her until another gathering in Sancti Spíritus provided an occasion for the minister to approach her, introduce himself,
and ask her where she was from, how she had come to teach in the
area, and who her family was. Innocently enough, Olga answered his
questions, volunteering that she was hoping to return to Havana
soon to see her family.

"Well, then," Minister Rivas declared, handing her his card, "you
must come to see me when you're in Havana." He promised that if
she did—and his desires were now clear—he might be able to arrange
for her to receive a promotion.

Since Olga was still in an apprentice program and had not
obtained her permanent teaching credentials, she badly wanted a promotion. But not if it meant submitting to the lust of a man older
than her father. When she didn't come to see him in Havana, the official continued to pursue her; she continued to fend off his advances.
Finally he threatened that unless she gave in to him, he would arrange
for her dismissal.

Distraught that all of her schooling and hard work would go to
waste because she hadn't fulfilled the fantasies of an old man, Olga,
when she happened to run into the minister's nephew, couldn't
refrain from confiding in him.

Antonio Rivas, or Tony, as his friends called him, listened empa-
thetically. "Don't worry," he told Olga, "my uncle will change his
mind. I'll see to it."

True to his word, he pulled the appropriate strings and she was able to keep her job, continuing, for the time being, to teach throughout the province of Sancti Spíritus. Olga felt indebted to Tony and appreciated how he had so gallantly extended himself on her behalf, without asking anything in return. Or so she thought.

What she didn't suspect was that perhaps Tony wanted to prove himself by snaring the unobtainable woman that even his powerful uncle couldn't obtain, not so much because he was smitten or in love, but almost as a kind of macho contest. Ironically, when he made occasional visits to see her at the schools where she taught, Olga assumed that his interest was only platonic. Of course, she wouldn't have minded if he had romantic intentions. With his white freckled skin, light reddish brown hair, and intense light eyes—not to mention that he wasn't so tall—he wasn't her type. But he was rich. Or so she thought.

Antonio Arturo Rivas Garcia-Rubio had been born into one of the most prominent families in Sancti Spíritus. His father, Victoriano Rivas, was locally revered as the magistrate of the province. The majority of the family wealth came from cattle ranching through the Garcia-Rubio lineage of Tony's mother, Maria Garcia-Rubio. The family owned and resided on a sprawling ranch called Las Minas— the Mines.

Yes, Olga had to admit that she was impressed by his pedigree, by his stylish, immaculate attire, by the articulate way he spoke—with his flair for drama—and most of all, by his flattering words about her generous spirit, which he witnessed in her classroom. Tony told her that it was obvious how much all the students loved their friendly, funny, and attractive teacher, and that he admired her infectious goodness, which made it so easy for her to win people over. He also expressed his shock and concern that she had to suffer working conditions that were unsanitary for both her and the children—without any form of ventilation or fans to relieve the monstrous tropical heat and humidity. He pledged to use his influence to help.

In this subtle, chaste way, he was pursuing her, Olga soon understood, not with any sexual overtures but with personal interest that was more than that of a kind friend, and that possibly—she may have secretly hoped—would lead to a marriage proposal. She waited coyly for a courtship to evolve. It never did. He did not ask to be her boyfriend, or invite her to elegant places to woo her. They didn't go dancing, never held hands, never kissed.

Instead, to her surprise, Antonio Rivas arrived at her parents' home unannounced during one of her visits to Havana, asking to have a conversation with her father.

"Senor Lopez," Tony began respectfully, "I don't want your daughter to work anymore. The conditions are unbearable. She shouldn't have to suffer such hardships."

Manolo was annoyed at the young man's presumption, aware that he was rich and couldn't fathom the fact that some people had no choice whether to work or not. Biting back his annoyance, he said, "Yes, that's true, but I do not approve of a single woman not having a legitimate job, with the implications that go along with that."

"I understand," countered Rivas. "In three months I intend to marry Olga. *Con su permisión,* of course."

"What? Three months, you say? Is there a reason for such a quick wedding date?" As a policeman, Manolo had been trained to control his anger. But he was clearly furious.

Tony apologized profusely for any misunderstanding, explaining that he wished to marry her as soon as possible in order for her to stop working so that she could take her rightful place in his home. "I would marry her tomorrow," he swore, "except that it will take a little time to organize a proper wedding, as she deserves. With my parents' help as well." His family would take care of the costs, he insisted.

Manolo was now impressed. Who was he to stand in the way of his daughter's marrying into a family of the stature of the Rivas Garcia-Rubios? Throwing off his earlier misgivings, he acquiesced to the plan. After Antonio left to return to Sancti Spíritus—pleased to have, in effect, just bought himself a beautiful, virtuous bride—Manolo presented the news to Olga.

She was overjoyed, even though it occurred to her, in passing, that she was sorry to give up her work—the teaching and especially the nursing. But this was a sacrifice she was willing to make, if it mattered to Tony, because other than that, the life she was about to begin seemed like a dream come true, a Cinderella story. Caught up in imagining a future married to the heir of a vast fortune, Olga didn't consider how little she really knew him. She didn't question how she really felt about him, assuming perhaps that she would grow to love him in time, and she ignored warnings that she would have otherwise heeded.

For example: in Havana, Tony Rivas had a reputation as a playboy and a troublemaker. He was a known member of a motorcycle club that raced in a pack across the island along the palm-tree-lined highways, wearing their black leather jackets and black leather-brimmed caps, with no political agenda other than following the drive of their testosterone. (Later photographs revealed his stark resemblance to Marlon Brando in *The Wild One*.) This was how Tony earned his nickname as El Ciclón—the Cyclone; he was at the center of the storm that roared into Havana to raise hell in the nightclubs before blowing out, back to the provinces.

Olga also didn't know that the reason Tony's parents had sent him to America to be educated at a Georgia military school was disturbing behavior in his childhood and youth that had given him, as the youngest of their three children, the role of black sheep in the family. She was aware that he was extremely smart, capable of attaining success in any number of professional capacities. But she dismissed clues that he had already squandered most of his inheritance and had no money of his own, and that one of the reasons his parents were eager for him to marry her was probably the hope that her responsible, upstanding nature would rub off on him.

Of course, none of that was suggested by his parents or siblings when they arrived in Havana a few weeks before the wedding. Unlike the Lopez family, which had more indigenous blood, the Rivas family members were essentially Spaniards in their appearance and attitudes.

Tony's father, Victoriano, a distinguished-looking gentleman with a head of well-coiffed white hair, carried himself with the stately air that went along with the office of a provincial magistrate—reminiscent of President Woodrow Wilson. Tony's mother was likewise elegant, gracious, and sweet, "a saint" in Olga's eyes. She was equally impressed by Tony's older brother, Jose Luis, who was tall and dashing, with a quiet intelligence, and their beauty of a sister, the fair-skinned, regal Maria Rosa.

In the midst of her unfolding fairy tale, only days away from the wedding—planned as a simple ceremony to be well attended—Olga was just too excited and busy to entertain second thoughts. But Manolo was not as blindsided. When he sat his daughter down for a talk, his face was grave as he began, "Don't marry this man."

Dumbfounded, she sat frozen until she could muster the courage to ask why her father had changed his mind about Antonio.

"Because," Manolo stated without reservation, "he is not a good man."

Was he forbidding her to get married? No, but he begged her to call the wedding off. "Mark my words," Manolo warned, "he is a mama's boy."

Olga saw her father's genuine worry. She knew he wanted only what was best for her, to protect her for as long as he could, and she also believed he was deeply perceptive, that he usually saw through the most adept of disguises—a quality she had inherited from him. So she deliberated carefully, weighing his concern against thoughts of how the invited guests would react if she called everything off, not to mention Tony's parents, who had taken care of all the expenses of the wedding and the lavish honeymoon, in addition to the house they had rented for the new bride and groom in Sancti Spíritus—complete with expensive furniture and all the necessary items for a couple to begin married life together. Ultimately, she decided that Manolo was just being overly protective, not so uncommon for any father about to give his daughter's hand away in marriage. No, he had to be mistaken about Tony. He would see.

On July 24, 1953, Olga Lopez married Antonio Rivas in a chapel in her hometown of Arroyo Narango, a suburb of Havana. She was radiant, the most stunningly beautiful bride any of the guests had ever seen, or so many repeated at the wedding reception—which, oddly enough, seemed to bother the groom after hearing it said with every "congratulations." Olga didn't notice that when they posed for family photographs, he was the only person in the wedding party who refused to smile for the camera.

On July 26, two days later, the theretofore little-known Fidel Castro and his band of revolutionaries attacked the army barracks of the Moncada garrison in Santiago. The coup was a total failure and those who survived, including Castro, were imprisoned on the Isla de los Pinos—the Isle of Pines. But it was not the last of Fidel or the revolution; rather it was the beginning of the end of everything Cuba had been before.

That same night, in her honeymoon suite, my mother's fairy tale was quickly unraveling. It was the end of everything she had been before, the beginning of the nightmare.

As I was growing up and hearing the different pieces of her story, Mami spared me the graphic details of how that first assault took place. She had a talent for understatement that way, always facetiously referring to Papi as "El Caballero": "the Gentleman."

Part of the picture I got was that, in Jekyll-Hyde fashion, he turned out to be one of those abusive men who believed that once he had married a woman and taken her virginity, she belonged to him—to beat as he pleased, as he might a horse he owned at the ranch, the way he mistreated servants. On a whim.

But there was something else, some weirdness in the bedroom that led to the violence when it erupted the first time. Later Mami said she thought it was jealousy underneath the rage that caused him to beat her senseless as he called her a whore and used a pair of scissors to ruin each of the lovely dresses that had been made or bought for her honeymoon, by slashing them and then cutting them up into hundreds of little pieces. Instead of being proud of her good looks, he was jealous of them, if that was possible, enraged by her beauty and by the way others found her attractive.

My mother locked herself in a hotel room, packed the remains of her clothing into her suitcase, and made the decision to leave the next morning and return to her parents. When morning came, she hesitated, remembering the sacred vows she had taken, feeling ashamed for not listening to her father, and not wanting to bring further shame to her family. But all her inner voices were telling her—leave, leave, leave!

My father showed up before she left, crying morosely and wringing his tear-streaked white handkerchief in his hands, begging for forgiveness. He assured her that an outburst like that would never happen again. He promised to replace the dresses. For the next few days he was his charming, considerate self, but when he brought the new dresses to her—several of them—she was mortified to discover that they were long and unflattering, severe, meant for older, matronly women.

Mami's gift of sight returned to her then. She prayed to her saints for protection and guidance to help her awful choice of a husband to improve, but she remained wary. For the time being Papi did improve. He tried to control his temper for the most part, at moments showing her warmth, affection, and even the fun, seductive side of El Ciclón. Unfortunately, this was a side of himself that he liked to show to others too. After Mami became pregnant, some three months following their marriage, she was informed, somehow, that the housemaid who had been working for her and Papi had paid a startling visit to Las Minas.

The maid asked to speak with my grandparents, whereupon she disclosed that she had been having an affair with their son Antonio and was pregnant with his child. Apparently the young woman had already learned that her employer had no money to give her, so she was appealing to his parents for financial support.

Victoriano—who may have dealt with similar appeals in the past—did not question whether she was telling the truth or not. But he did remind the unwed mother that she was of legal age and therefore the baby was her responsibility. He sent her away empty-handed.

Mami later heard that the maid gave birth to a girl, though the paternity was never verified. If Papi was the father, somewhere in the world there would be a half sister to my siblings and me, born roughly in July of 1954, around the same date that my mother went into labor with her baby and was rushed to La Clínica de Los Angeles.

During the excruciating hours that followed, Dr. Orizando eventually came to the conclusion that if he was able to save the baby, the mother, given her weakened state, would probably not survive the birth. The problem, so Mami explained, was that Antonio Arturo Rivas Jr., weighing over ten pounds, was obviously quite content to stay in her safe, warm, aquatic womb, and simply refused to come out. If it is true that prenatal babies can hear and sense the world that's waiting for them, that would make sense in my family's case.

When Tony was finally born, on July 9, Mami's vital signs were fading and she began to hemorrhage. She lost so much blood that Dr. Orizando was now certain that giving life to my brother was going to take hers. *Pero con el ayudo de Dios . . .* she survived. I later wondered if in that tunnel through which we are said to pass after death—the dark gauntlet with the glorious light at its end where Mami's saints would have been waiting to guide her to heaven—she didn't turn back and decide to return for her new infant and the other children to be born to her. She may have known how much we would need her.

My father undoubtedly was overjoyed to have a First Son, his namesake, almost as if Tony Jr.'s goodness and brilliance would redeem Papi's shortcomings. There was never a question in my young mind about his proud, loving feelings for my brother. In my role as Second Son I was cast in the position of always having to try harder to prove my worth, and I didn't always recognize the toll that Papi's expectations for perfection took on Tony, starting at an early age, in addition to the stigma he bore for being the baby Mami had almost died for when bringing him into the world.

My birth, fifteen months later, on October 1, 1955, at La Clínica de Los Angeles in the town and province of Sancti Spíritus (amid angels and holy spirits), was much less auspicious, except for the accidental fall Mami took on the last day of her ninth month when, during a visit from my Abuela Maria and Abuelo Chucho (our nickname for Victoriano), she tripped and landed awkwardly on the edge of a drawer with her huge belly. Maybe it was an omen that I was destined to withstand major physical onslaughts later on, accidental and otherwise.

When she was pregnant, Papi's violence tended to be restrained, so in a way she was fortunate to be as fertile as she was—although, considering the size of her babies, this was a mixed blessing. Thankfully my delivery was not the gargantuan struggle Tony's had been, but I was even bigger, weighing in at a hefty ten and a half pounds. "A beautiful baby!" Mami liked to say whenever remembering—except, well, there was one thing. The fingers. I had been born with six fingers on each hand, an ominous sign the meaning of which was never explained to me. The doctor snipped them off and preserved them in a jar for Mami, who kept them under lock and key, another family secret.

In honor of both my grandfathers, my parents named me Victor Manuel Remigio Rivas Garcia-Rubio Lopez. While Tony had my mother's darker coloring and features, from Papi's side I was fair skinned, with light eyes.

Back at home, Mami had two babies to nurse, one for each breast. At church and other community or family gatherings, we presented a handsome picture of a happy, loving, upper-class Cuban family. My father was a magician at striking the pose of normalcy. My mother's open smile became forced. She learned to keep more secrets.

Papi's roaming continued. Shortly after my birth, during a dash to and from Havana, he broke his leg in a motorcycle accident.

While he was in a cast, he volunteered to sleep on the living room sofa—so as not to disturb Mami's sleep and to avoid any accidental kicks from her.

She didn't object but was highly concerned at one point when she woke in the middle of the night to hear my father moaning and gasping, seemingly in a bout of horrendous pain. Mami hurried to the living room to help. The bedding on the sofa was in disarray and he wasn't there, as if he had tumbled out and dragged himself to the bathroom. With the volume of his moans escalating, she ran to the bathroom, imagining that he had slipped on the tile. He wasn't there either. Following the reverberation of what was starting to sound more like pleasure than agony, she made her way to the live-in housemaid's bedroom. After a moment's hesitation, she opened the door. There he was, leg cast and all, on top of the young woman, humping away. Mami closed the door, swallowed whatever outrage ought to have been hers into a silent, cold shield that was forming around her heart, and returned to her bedroom.

Manolo had been right. Antonio Rivas was a mama's boy: he saw what he liked and he took it, with a sense of entitlement that had nothing to do with how he was raised. But on a more encouraging note, Papi seemed to take seriously his role as a provider. When he and Mami were married, his father had gotten him a post with the Justice Department—the first job he had ever held—and though that hadn't lasted long, he struck on a better idea, announcing to Mami late in 1956 that he had decided he wanted to move to the United States. His days at the Georgia military school had left him with fond memories of the good life in America, and he assured her there would be plenty of professional opportunities there for which he was well suited.

Just three years later, the first great wave of Cuban exiles would begin migration to American shores, fleeing Castro's communist regime and all that it entailed. But our departure had nothing to do with the revolution, even though its roots were taking hold out in the provinces, partly in reaction to the growing decadence and corruption that flourished in Havana. Oblivious to the political winds that were blowing, my father, then as later, simply wanted to move somewhere else, somewhere better (perhaps away from the scrutiny or judgment of his parents and siblings), and made arrangements to do so as quickly as possible.

Because it would be easier to obtain the necessary paperwork in the capital, the four of us moved to Havana to stay with Mami's parents. Soon after that, Papi was granted his visa and went on ahead of us to search for work and housing. For almost a year, my mother waited for him to send for us. In the interim, she rarely heard from him and he never sent her any money, so both sets of grandparents supported us. Finally, not long after my second birthday, Papi called to say he was ready for us to join him.

On October 26, 1957, Mami, my brother, Tony, and I flew to the United States, leaving our tropical homeland officially for good. Only one submerged memory of my earliest childhood in Sancti Spíritus came with me. Other memories of Cuba were acquired a year and a half later, thankfully, when Abuelo Chucho and Abuela Maria sent for my brother and me in the summer of 1959 to come for a two-month visit.

Some of the grainier images stayed preserved, very generally, from what was my then almost four-year-old awareness, like bright, wide swipes of color—in multiple shades of green everywhere, in tropical, jungle shapes, in snaking narrow roads through expansive fields bursting with crops of different kinds, swatches of grazing land with contented livestock dining away, and air so thick with humidity it refracted all those colors like a prism. Other recollections were more vivid and specific, like the day that my grandparents took us to the famed beaches of Varadero, where the sand was so white and squeaky underneath my feet that it felt as if I were walking on talcum powder.

Our stay in Sancti Spíritus at Las Minas also left strong impressions: the long, unpaved driveway lined by towering palms that led to the opulent two-story main house, with gardeners, ranch hands, chauffeurs, cooks, valets, housekeepers, and other servants (apparently more populous than the number of actual residents), all of whom seemed to welcome our presence and cater to our wants. Most memorable was Moya, the head *cochero*—driver—who worked on the ranch with his wife.

Moya was one of the most striking men I had ever seen, with ebony black skin so dark he was almost blue in tone, and a royal demeanor that, in my perception, put him in my wealthy grandfather's league of importance. When he wasn't chauffeuring family members in a luxury car, Moya drove an old topless army jeep around the ranch, running errands, on which Tony and I volunteered to join him as often as he would have us.

That is, until the day we went out with him and he had to stop back at the ranch to get something. Moya turned off the motor, took his keys, and bounded into the house. Tony—who had just turned five—slid over to the driver's seat, placed his hands on the steering wheel, and pretended that he was driving.

Entertained, I laughed and said, "Let me try!"

Tony ignored me and instead studied the mechanics of the stick shift, jerking it hard enough to force it out of gear and into neutral. We could feel the jeep begin to roll slowly backward down the slight incline of the driveway as we exchanged big smiles. Magic!

Tony held the steering wheel straight as we began to pick up speed, at exactly the same moment we looked back to see Moya emerge from the house. Racing toward us, he waved both of his hands at us, screaming, *"Coño! Que estan haciendo?"* Our laughter turned to frightened hysteria as it became clear that the faster Moya ran after us, the farther away from him we were. Picking up speed, somehow the jeep—which fortunately did not have power steering—maintained a fairly straight reverse course. We flew backward down the entire length of the driveway and across the paved main road, careening into shrubbery so dense that it behaved like a latter-day air bag, cushioning our crash.

Moya's immediate concern was for our well-being, not the blame he was going to shoulder for our mishap. Seeing that we were uninjured, though traumatized, he told us we were extremely lucky that there had been no traffic on the main road and that we hadn't crashed or tipped over into a roadside canal. Moya's message had another implication for me, which was that a protective adult would do anything in his power to make sure children in his care were not hurt. My father's messages from this era told me something else.

When we visited my mother's parents in Havana, they too made us feel safe and loved unconditionally. Even though I have only a dim recollection of their home and lifestyle from this visit, I later wondered if the feeling of safety that I associated with Abuelo Manolo and Abuela Muñeca (she was affectionately nicknamed "Doll") had come from our earlier, yearlong stay with them when Papi had already left for the United States.

When Tony and I left Cuba at the end of the summer of 1959, we said good-bye to my mother's parents not knowing that we would never see them again.

Only three months after we left, Fidel Castro's New Year's Eve coup toppled Batista's regime in Havana and flooded the country with fatigue-wearing revolutionaries. There was no mention in our household of why it was happening, what it meant, or how this might impact us or our relatives. Certainly, the prospect that we would never see our homeland again was not suggested.

As other events and challenges occupied my attention, the soil from which I first grew became more and more distant in my sensibilities, and my early years all but faded from conscious memory. Many years later, I had a strange dream in which I was a toddler, maybe a little over one year old, that I eventually recounted for Mami, as usual when she was busy in the kitchen, this time while doing dishes.

In the dream, I told her, I was wearing a diaper and had the terrifying, helpless sensation of falling backward, as though in slow motion, attached somehow to a high chair.

With her back to me as I described the odd emotion of shame that accompanied my fall in the dream, I saw her suddenly freeze.

Her shoulders hunched over the sink and began to shake involuntarily. She was crying.

Without turning around, Mami said, *"Ay, hijo, como tu te puedes acorda te ese momento? Tu tenias meno de dos anos."* How can you remember that moment? You were less than two years old.

What I hadn't recovered in my dream was that just before the fall I took in the high chair that day in Sancti Spíritus, she had, innocently enough, told Papi that she had found me in my high chair with my hands down the front of my diaper—obviously having discovered my penis and the primal pleasure that came from touching it—and she hadn't known what to do to discourage such behavior.

For Mami, there was a lesson to emerge from this episode, making it the first and the last time that she asked El Caballero to resolve a situation involving her children that she could handle on her own. For me, the lesson filtered into later years, bringing with it the idea that whatever punishment I received, I deserved.

The moment Papi heard what his fifteen-month-old Second Son had been doing, he walked over and gazed down at me, and then, without a second thought, gave me a stinging backhand slap. The force of the blow not only sent the high chair and me toppling over backward, but threw me out of my chair so that I hit the back of my head on the coffee table.

All that came to me in the dream at a later age, however, was the sensation of free-falling backward, my first memory in life, one of my few memories of Sancti Spíritus.

2
chicago
(1957–1964)

You're not bad, just badly raised.
    —"Romantic Comedy," Stars, from the album *Heart*

THERE WAS A BATTLE being waged for my soul.

By the time I began kindergarten at the first parochial school I attended in Chicago, two months before I was to turn five, that message had started to become clear. That the world inside our home was akin to a war zone was still a harsh reality, one I resisted accepting, as though convinced that the rugged terrain of childhood into which I had parachuted—by mistake, I might add—was only a training ground to prepare me for my real destiny. It was either that—an elaborate test with a prize at the end—or a joke.

Survival lesson number one: Maintain a sense of irony.

In an abstract way, it was actually hilarious that of all the places in the United States where Papi could have chosen for us to begin our life in America, he picked Chicago. Or "Shhee-cogoh" as I pronounced it in my accented English. I went from the balmy tropics, where my attire had been basically a diaper, to the subzero temperatures of the Windy City, where, as anyone who has lived through a Chicago winter can attest, multiple layers of clothing are required to insulate against the lacerating winds that whip off Lake Michigan and barrel through the corridors of city blocks. Trudging to school and back in snowsuit, overpants and long underwear, shirts, sweaters, boots, mittens, hat, and scarf, I could lean my entire body weight into the wind and feel as if I wasn't moving at all. Just the ordeal of dressing and undressing could be trying, especially when I had to use the bathroom, which demanded that I artfully peel off every single layer of clothing in a race not to wet myself. Sometimes I lost.

Mami had certainly struggled to maintain her sense of irony on the snowy night in late October 1957 when she arrived with us— Tony age three, me age two—at O'Hare Airport, none of us dressed for the plummeting temperatures. Papi was nowhere to be seen. Since the plane had been delayed, Mami assumed he would have found extra time to park his car and meet us at the gate, but when he didn't show, she led us, shivering and tired, down to the baggage claim, collected our suitcases and boxes, and managed to assemble everything and us—wrapped together in her lightweight shawl—on the curb to wait for Papi. Finally, unable to bear our whimpering as the wind and wet buffeted us, she flagged a taxi and gave the cabbie my father's address.

When Mami rang the apartment buzzer, we were let in by an elderly couple who seemed to have no idea where Mr. Rivas, their new tenant, was. But seeing our condition, they immediately ushered us into their apartment and brought out several blankets to swaddle Tony and me in, a steaming cup of coffee for Mami, and warm milk and cookies for us. My mother spoke no English but was somehow able to express her appreciation.

Survival lesson number two: Accept the kindness of strangers.

At 5 A.M. the next morning, Papi burst into the apartment, fuming about the toll that the double work shifts as a city bus driver were taking on him. It was not his fault that he wasn't at the gate to meet our plane, because he had been at the airport, after all, waiting dutifully. Early! But because of his exhaustion he had leaned back against his seat and fallen asleep. "You should have looked for me," he whispered, so as not to wake his landlord and landlady. "If you weren't so stupid, you would have!"

Several days later, Papi located an apartment for us while he and Mami spent the rest of their money on a few items of furniture and, more important, warm clothing for all of us to weather the Shheecogoh weather, which was intensifying. My mother, after having had to quit her job as a schoolteacher because my father had insisted that no wife of his was going to work out of the home, now had to search for any kind of employment she could find that was within walking distance. That turned out to be an assembly-line position at a nearby plastics factory, where she earned $1.25 an hour, though she soon rose to a senior-level job at what was then the maximum pay, $1.45 an hour.

Mami didn't complain about the hard work or the walks to and from the factory; she was becoming La Luchadora, the wrestler or struggler, and she was more than willing to do whatever she could to contribute to our welfare. She did complain, however, after the fact, about her difficulty adapting to such a drastic difference in culture and weather, and even the American food. She claimed that she intended to learn English, but because the majority of her fellow employees were from our mostly Italian neighborhood, she ended up learning Italian.

In my father's defense, he was not the only crazy tropical islander to venture north past Miami into the hinterlands of the States. There was actually a vibrant if small Cuban community in Chicago that congregated frequently at the Club Madrid—we called it *El Club Cubano*—a loud, smoky dance hall and social club where the likes of Celia Cruz and Tito Puente performed, turning winter into summer and Chicago into home.

Here is where the visual memory of my childhood first came into focus and where—between the ages of three and nine—I observed the charismatic El Ciclón in action. Who was he, this man with the different moods and faces? Here at El Club Cubano he could make an entrance, survey the scene, cool and disinterested, but then—why not?—decide to become the life of the party, joking and storytelling with the other men as my mother huddled with the ladies, and while Tony and I ran off to play in the spacious hall with other kids.

Papi was in his element, verbally jousting with the men, flirting safely with some of the married women, like the petite blond *cubana* Mecca, whose children, Charlie and Elena—ironically much later to become our stepbrother and stepsister—were in the mix playing with Tony and me. Usually Mami didn't dance with Papi watching but swayed in place, smiling because this was *her* music, as it reverberated off the walls.

There was one special night, however, when my mother stole the show, much to Papi's displeasure. The guest artist that night was Miguelito "Mr. Babalu" Valdez, a very famous, handsome, tall mulatto singer from Cuba, and Club Madrid was really hopping. With the help of Mecca (short for "America"), who was a hairdresser, Mami had her hair done platinum blond and had worn a tight off-the-shoulder black cocktail dress. When Mecca's artist friend Cascara, all ninety-eight pounds of him, escorted my mother onto the dance floor, Papi didn't seem to mind, except that everyone stopped to watch her fabulous moves. The next thing Mami knew, Mr. Babalu himself came to cut in, asking Cascara if he didn't mind.

Cascara said, "This is a married woman. You'll have to ask her husband." He pointed my father out over by the bar.

Papi shrugged. Sure, why not?

Olga Lopez Rivas and Miguelito Valdez cleared the dance floor. All eyes were on their perfectly synchronized sambas, mambos, meringues, and cha-chas. The whole of El Club Cubano came to a standstill as Mami and the Cuban singer moved across the dance floor with steps that drew applause and cheers. Even though she would pay for it later from Papi, it was one of my mother's shining glories.

Whenever we went to El Club Cubano, there was a great amount of pontificating and gesturing in the way that both Cubans and

Chicagoans are wont to do. The city, of course, had been nicknamed the Windy City not only because of the force of the air but from the backroom politics of Chicago's early days, when plenty of hot-winded conversations and boastfulness prevailed. Its other nickname, the Second City, was from that long-towering shadow cast over it by New York City, which seemed to make Chicagoans, native or not, appear to try that much harder and talk that much louder.

By the end of the night, the hall was so humid from the body heat that the walls were sweating. But instead of a walk out into a balmy tropical night, a stop at the coatroom was an instant reminder of where we really lived. Papi never had to come and tell us that it was time to go; we could feel his eyes on us, like trained pets, and knew to hurry and get dressed. But no sooner had we gone through the process of pulling, yanking, and zipping ourselves into our multiple layers than someone would offer Papi another *cafecito,* another cocktail, another joke, and with a shrug he would accept, leaving Mami to stand by silently, as Tony and I lingered like miniature abominable snowmen, sweat drenching every bit of our clothes and bodies within our self-contained saunas.

This was the Cuban good-bye. The routine could go on all night. And to complain—well, by kindergarten I knew better than that.

I was in enough trouble as it was that winter, with punishments and warnings on the rise. As a result, when we weren't in public, Papi's presence at home created a looming tension, a feeling that at any moment he could strike. He was on me like a hawk, I felt, watching for any minor mistake that required disciplining—usually a hand spanking or a good smack on my behind, but if I was really out of line, he would take off his belt and whip me across my bare *culo.* To make sure I felt the fear and pain intended, he had a habit of folding the belt over and then snapping it a few times. The sound made me that much more afraid. His bus driver's belt—three inches wide with a huge buckle—was usually his weapon of choice. He left many a handprint and belt slash on my butt.

As Christmas approached, Papi did acknowledge my effort to be on my best behavior, noting that if I stuck to it, there would be a reward for me under the Christmas tree.

"Listen to your father," Mami encouraged me each morning. "Be a good boy."

We still spoke only Spanish at home, even though Tony and I had been learning English at the nearby Catholic school, where I had attended nursery school the year before. Little by little, I'd begun to communicate in broken English, learning to ask the nuns for different items of food like cheese and milk. I learned the Lord's Prayer, the Hail Mary, and the Pledge of Allegiance. By the next year, with Tony in first grade and me in kindergarten, we were bilingual. Accented but bilingual.

"Good boy," Mami said on a morning in late November, smiling approvingly, rooting for me, believing in me, as I arrived at the breakfast table, washed and dressed in my standard Catholic school uniform— white shirt, clip-on tie, dark pants, and black shoes—to find Tony almost finished eating.

"Eat." Mami handed me the simple meal that was the same breakfast we ate for many years—*pan de flauta* (a soft Cuban bread) with butter and jelly, and a cup of *café con leche,* espresso with steamed milk and lots of sugar. The hot beverage was intended to warm our bellies for the cold day ahead. It never occurred to my parents that maybe the reason that the nuns kept reporting that I was unusually boisterous at school had something to do with the human jet fuel I was drinking every morning.

"Mami, you're getting fat," I said suddenly, noticing her protruding belly for the first time.

"Yes, I know, I'm going to have a baby soon. You're going to have a little brother or sister."

"I am?" This was wonderful, but confusing. "How? Why?"

"Because God wants me to."

The concept fascinated me, toying with my brain as I poured myself into my winter gear, stumbled outside, and shuffled after Tony for our walk to school, neither of us saying a word so as not to get a

blast of cold air into our throats. The mystery of babies was perplex-
ing but a good distraction from the mocking calls of "Little Fidel!"
and "Communist!" sent across the street from a group of older neighborhood boys who taunted us with names we were starting to hear
more regularly. Whatever that meant, I knew it was bad and began to
turn around to say, "Jou chutt op!" but Tony, in his quick, stoic fashion, caught my arm and tugged me along after him.

At school, Tony sped off toward his first-grade class, leaving me in
the kindergarten area, which was at enough of a distance that, except
for mass, we rarely saw each other through the course of the day.

"Goo morneeeng," I greeted the sister who was my teacher before
waddling off to the coatroom to remove my winter gear. Still struggling with my new language, I was nonetheless improving.

The world outside of our home, as I understood it, was where I
could be a child, except that it was ruled by nuns, who apparently
were in league with Papi in the effort to rid me of my innate wicked-
ness. They were also responsible for all matters pertaining to the classroom, providing both academic and religious instruction.

This morning, as every morning, we attended mass at school, celebrated by the same priests who led Sunday mass, which we were
required to attend as well. Another puzzle to me was that while Tony
and I went to church every Sunday, neither of my parents, for
unknown reasons, attended. My five-year-old brain tossed that
thought around as we filed into mass, past the glowering Mother
Superior. Though I was aware that in the church hierarchy she was
not as powerful as our parish priests, she seemed to have special status
over all, because the nuns answered to her as a headmistress, and I
reflexively skulked past her.

During this mass, we engaged in the various Catholic prayer rituals—genuflecting, kneeling, standing, and making the sign of the
cross. Our Kindergarten Sister prodded us throughout the hour with
her cricket, a small bug-shaped tin device held between the thumb
and forefinger that, when pressed, made a two-toned clicking sound.
Click-*CLICK*. Every nun carried a cricket. There was a code of

cricket language to learn on top of English. One click of the cricket meant *stand;* two clicks, *genuflect;* three clicks, *kneel;* and four, *make the sign of the cross.* The entire school attended the morning mass, and with all of the nuns clicking in unison, it struck me this particular morning that there was a kind of music filling the church as it echoed with the strange chorus of chirping, metallic crickets.

If I closed my eyes and rocked on my heels, I could almost make it sound like the music at El Club Cubano, which in turn reminded me of the previous summer, when my father's parents had come to visit us in Chicago and we'd all gone out to the social club.

The presence of Abuelo Chucho and Abuela Maria for two weeks brightened our household beyond recognition because Papi, as when we were out in public, put on his best show for his parents, his perpetual ridiculing of my mother kept to a minimum. Instead of total silence at the dinner table punctuated by a barked "Salt!" or other brusque command to Mami—who never sat at the table with Papi to eat, but waited on us like a servant—he made a grand to-do of having her sit down and even complimenting her cooking. Our spankings and punishments were almost nonexistent. Better yet, I was allowed to accompany my grandparents on sightseeing outings to many of the parks and museums along the shoreline of Lake Michigan. There was Lincoln Park, with its popular zoo, and my favorite, Grant Park, with its famous Buckingham Fountain, which on summer nights was lit by multicolored lights.

No matter where we went, my grandparents were impeccably dressed—Abuela Maria with her elegant dresses, expensive jewelry, and subtle perfume, Abuelo Victoriano in his tailored suits and spit-shined shoes—and I walked proudly between them, my chest puffed up to be related to such a handsome couple, aware of the admiring looks they received. Best of all was the physical and verbal affection they showered on us, spoiling Tony and me with gifts and treats.

Click-*CLICK!* The sound of the cricket jerked me back into the present, as I stood on cue. But a memory lulled me away again, just as fast, as I remembered how I had misbehaved with Abuela by being stubborn about not wanting to take my nap and how she had handled it.

"Here," she offered, holding out a shiny new quarter, "take your nap and I'll give you this."

With my eyes wide, I looked at her, at her fair smooth skin, her brown hair neatly coiffed, and at her sparkling eyes, and watched as she placed the quarter in my hand. "Now, be a good boy and go take your nap." She smiled.

Two bits! That's what they called it in Shhee-cogoh. You could buy about a hundred pieces of candy for that, as far as I knew. Not saying one word, I dashed gleefully down the hall to the bedroom I shared with Tony, leapt into the twin bed, and clamped shut my eyes. I tightened my hand into a fist around the coin, and tried my hardest to fall asleep. Visions of candy treasure danced on my inner eyelids. Jawbreakers, Good & Plenty, Bazooka bubble gum. Chocolate candy bars! Who could sleep in an exciting moment like this? What I really wanted to do was jump up and down for joy. So I did. But then, as I stood up on my bed and started to bounce, it occurred to me that I might drop my beloved new quarter. Where to put it, though? Of course, I knew, I should put it in my mouth! Safe and secure, the quarter tucked into my cheek, I began to bounce away, drawing my sturdy thighs up toward my chest, as I transformed into a ball.

Then the inevitable happened. A high jarring bounce made me gasp for air as the quarter slipped out of my cheek and lodged itself firmly in my throat. My airway was totally blocked off. I tried screaming for help but nothing came out. Within seconds, I was in a complete panic and I was beginning to lose consciousness. In my desperation, I threw myself against the wall, hoping that someone would hear the impact on the wall. In fact, the impact caused the coin to dislodge, but I promptly swallowed it.

Help arrived in the form of Mami and my *abuela*. They found me gasping for air and crying. In between sobs, I confessed my actions and the loss of my quarter. "Now I'll never see it again," I cried, almost hyperventilating. "It's gone and it's all my fault!"

My grandmother comforted me and said with a very mysterious look on her face, "You will see your coin again, I am very sure of it."

"How?"

Mami had left the room, but even so Abuela Maria leaned over and whispered, "Tell me the next time you make a *caca*. But don't flush. Then I'll tell you how."

The next morning, no doubt soon after *café con leche,* I stuck my head out of the bathroom and called for my *abuela* to come. She came in and closed the door, directing me to stand aside so she could examine the contents of the toilet bowl. Her face was somewhat disappointed as she bent down looking, but then broke into a satisfied smile. "There." She pointed. "Look!"

To my astonishment, I could see something shiny in the water. Magic! She fished the quarter out with a plastic cup, sanitized it, and returned it to me.

Another survival lesson: Sometimes you have to dig through shit to retrieve lost treasure.

My *abuela* may have been sending me other messages, maybe just that she loved me and didn't want to see me so upset. This was a woman, at least at the time, who could very easily have just given me another quarter. But this was my coin and she had promised to get it back for me. What should have been a most distasteful and unpleasant situation turned out to be a loving lesson and one of my fondest memories of her.

With deep regret to see my grandparents go, I was reassured by Abuelo Chucho that after they returned to Cuba they would plan on moving to the United States, so they would see me before I knew it. But with the ban on Cuban immigration that was soon put in place, it would be several years before I saw him again. As for my *abuela,* our good-bye after the quarter incident was the last time I ever saw her.

"Victor Rivas!" The Kindergarten Sister hissed my name into my ears in a sharp rebuke, snapping me out of my daydream once more and back into mass. She narrowed her eyes in a warning. My eyes

pleaded back. I was a good boy, really, and I would try harder. I
promised!

There was a standing threat at school that if a student's misbehavior was serious, parents were to be informed. Fortunately, as the
Christmas break came, there had been no reports to Papi about any
trouble at school and I became cautiously optimistic about presents
for me under the tree.

On the much anticipated day, still dressed in my long underwear that
doubled as pajamas, I made it to the living room seconds before
Tony, to discover that in fact there was a small pile of wrapped gifts—
most of which contained more long underwear, socks, and winter
clothes—but there was a fire truck for me and, for both Tony and me
to share, the Lincoln Logs we had been asking for. *Feliz Navidad!*

We tore off the wrapping at the same time. Tony and I were
known to fight over games and toys, our two different personalities
coming at odds mainly over rules and process. At age six, he was
strictly a law-and-order, by-the-book kind of guy, one of those kids
who always read all the instructions before beginning any new game
or project. My approach, then and later, was usually to unceremoni-
ously rip open the package, throw the pieces on the floor, and begin.
Baptism by fire was more my style.

"Wait! Wait!" Tony cried, unfolding the paper insert and starting
to read, as I dumped out the load of notched, redwood-stained logs
of variable lengths, and the flat green slats typically used for building
the roof of the cabin.

Ignoring him, I began stacking the smallest logs on top of one
another. I managed, after a few failed attempts, to balance the logs
into a two-foot vertical tower.

Tony had barely finished reading about the venerable history of
Lincoln Logs and was about to begin studying the intricate diagrams
with building instructions when I pronounced my project completed, proudly singing out, "Look at my ranger station!"

Unimpressed, Tony picked up a small log and heaved it at my creation. A direct hit! The ranger station toppled.

"Jerk!" I shrieked. Our dialogue at home was in Spanish except for an occasional smattering of American slang. My brother's mean-spirited action prompted me to tears.

Tony grinned and began to chuckle, which infuriated me, and it maddened me even more to see him nonchalantly go back to his precious instructions, as if nothing had happened. Picking up a log from my fallen tower, I flung it at him. A direct hit! Square in his right eye.

Tony let out a howl that carried throughout the apartment, triggering the sound of Papi's footsteps, which came from the back bedroom and grew closer.

My brother went silent midhowl. We exchanged looks of horror. No more Lincoln Logs for a few days.

"What the hell is going on?" Papi, dressed and groomed, roared down at us, his crime-scene investigative technique surveying evidence that centered on Tony's already swelling right eye.

We knew better than to answer. That would come in the interrogation process, my father's method for getting to the bottom of things, as he liked to say, which involved separate interviews. Standard police procedure. That way, each suspect was never sure what the other person had said about the same incident and couldn't lie to protect the other. By virtue of his status as First Son and because of his injury, Tony was interrogated first.

After several minutes, my brother returned holding a bag of ice on his eye. That and my father's grim face as he came up behind Tony, glaring in my direction, were enough to tell me that there would be no interrogation for me. I had been convicted without taking the stand. Unfair. Unfair.

"Go to your room," Papi ordered me. But calmly, matter-of-factly.

Dutifully, I scrambled to my feet and hurried down the hall, tensing my stocky little body for the unseen slap or punch from behind. To my surprise, none came. Maybe I would get to tell my side of the story. Or maybe Papi sided with me from hearing Tony's version, agreeing that I had only been acting in self-defense, or defense of my property.

When we arrived at the bedroom that Tony and I shared, my father nodded in the direction of the closet door, saying, "Open it."

Not sure where we were headed with this, I quickly obeyed.

"Now," he said, "pick out your favorite belt."

My belt? Were we going to go out somewhere? Did he want to make sure I dressed to his liking? My favorite was a very thin plastic cowboy belt. "That one," I said, reaching for it.

My father helped, taking it off the hook, saying as he did, "Turn around."

Obviously, we were not going out. I assumed the familiar position to receive my spanking, bent over with my hands on my knees. Papi pulled the back of my long underwear down and gave me a first lashing. The pain was acute, biting against my skin as if with his very rage. I gasped and tears fell.

"No crying!" he commanded. "How many times do I have to tell you?"

How many times he whipped me I didn't remember, focused impossibly as I was on not crying. The more I cried, the harder and longer he beat me. But I could remember a warm, wet feeling that started to trickle down my leg.

Finally, Mami—who was rapidly approaching her due date and slower than usual on her feet—walked into the room and begged him, please, to stop.

To the shock of both of us, he did. The sight of blood tended to snap him out of his frenzy. Almost glad to be given a reprieve from the hard task of disciplining me, he cheerily put the belt away and headed for the door. But just at the moment that I pulled up my long underwear and Mami went to give me a comforting embrace, he whipped around and held up his index finger as a warning.

By now Papi had forbidden her to hug or kiss me and Tony, because, he believed, "you pamper them and they'll turn into a couple of *maricónes*"—slang for homosexuals—"or sissies."

Mami didn't argue as she stalled, feigning the need to sit down. She smoothed her maternity dress and patted her big tummy, waiting for him to leave the room. Then she rose from the bed, put her hand on my shoulder, and walked with me to the bathroom to inspect the damage. The blood had soaked through the back side of my long underwear, which stuck to my buttocks and the backs of my legs, letting me know that the rear view of me was not a pretty sight.

"*Ay,*" she said in an undertone of disgust and pulled out some first-aid items from the medicine cabinet, including my mother's cure-all: Mercurochrome. She placed everything on the lowered toilet seat and perched herself on the edge of the bathtub, gently cleaning my injuries and doing the healing work she knew how to do. The pain was significant enough that it was difficult to sit down for the next few days, but I also had to run around with a red butt.

While Mami was still doctoring me, Papi appeared in the doorway. Now he asked for my version of the story. "Why? Why did you throw a Lincoln Log at your brother's eye?"

With the sting of the alcohol Mami used before the Mercurochrome making me catch my breath, I pled my case, explaining that Tony had started it by knocking down my tower.

"Tony!" Papi bellowed and sent him to the bedroom.

Three quick blows reached my ears. *Whack, whack, whack!* Then came the sound of Tony crying. And that was it.

Whatever Tony had first told my father in his version of the story, I never knew, but my beef wasn't with him. At fault was Papi's injustice.

Another cold survival lesson: Every man for himself.

Four days later, a very different mood filled the apartment as my father roused us from sleep early in the morning with wonderful news. The previous night Mami had gone to the hospital and given birth. His Third Son, Edward Alexander Rivas, had arrived.

He had broken out one of his best cigars, a big fat proud one, which he puffed on in the heated car as we drove slowly over the icy streets to the hospital. The prospect of being an older brother was exciting. Papi was in such a happy mood that I cared for this new family member already, not having even seen him yet.

At the third-floor maternity ward of the massive hospital—where nurses, orderlies, and doctors were dashing about this way and that at breakneck speed—my father stopped at the nurses' station to ask for directions. The perfect gentleman, he politely bowed to a nurse, who pointed down the hall to the observation window.

From a distance, the room appeared to contain a bizarre collection of medium-sized white boxes on stilts. As we got closer, it looked like the rows and rows of boxes contained small dolls, their colors varying from pink to yellow to brown and many shades in between. They were all bundled up, probably for going outside, but since they were dolls they didn't have to really worry about getting cold. Suddenly, all by itself, a doll opened its mouth. Several others did too. They appeared to be crying, but no sound could be heard.

Standing now in front of the window, I was horrified by a realization that made me take two steps backward. These dolls were not dolls at all, but tiny babies, many the size of one of my arms. Their faces scared me the most. Many looked deformed and some were even monstrous. I stood staring with my mouth open, ready to run if any of them tried to escape their little boxes.

"Excuse me!" Papi called to the nurse on the other side of the glass, tapping on the window. When she seemed not to hear him, he began to yell, *"Rivas! Rivas!"* She glanced up, saw him, then continued her rounds. With an opened palm, my father banged insistently on the window. Not to be intimidated, the nurse turned around again and held up her hand in a signal for him to hold on a minute. Several minutes later, she closed the notepad she was writing in and headed for the back door, disappearing from view.

Within the blink of an eye, the same nurse was standing at Papi's side. "What is it? What do you want?" she asked.

With a cavalier smile, my father put a hand on my shoulder and on Tony's. "I want to see my new son. They want to see their baby brother."

"Yes?"

"We can't seem to find him. Could you perhaps hold him up so we can get a better look at him?"

She inquired as to which baby that would be.

"The Rivas child." Papi pronounced our last name in that context eloquently, like a line of poetry.

Her stern demeanor collapsed and, obviously unable to keep herself from cracking up, she laughingly said, "Just look for the baby that doesn't fit." She turned and walked away, still chuckling.

Papi, Tony, and I pressed our noses to the glass and began scanning the cribs. Tony noticed that each crib had an information card taped to the front. Each card had a name, a time, and a date. As I was looking down the right side of the window, I was amazed and frozen by what I saw. Barely contained in one of the far cribs was a dark hairy ball of flesh. Tony noticed this about the same time and began reading the information on the card aloud: "Edward Alexander Rivas, 3:20 A.M., 12-29-60."

As we looked closer, we realized that there was more writing on the lower left-hand side of the crib. What Tony read seemed to affect only my father: "Thirteen and one half pounds. Twenty-four inches."

Mami cried for several days after she returned home, no less caring toward her blessing from God than she would have been to any baby, even though she may have secretly worried that his little body, which was covered with a fine layer of dark hair, was part primate. He also had the extra finger on each hand that I was born with; they too were promptly removed. The hair soon fell off and Eddie no longer looked like a monkey. Either way, I was still thrilled to have a little brother of my own. Early on, I made it my job to keep an eye out for him, to protect him if I could, even when I couldn't protect myself. Because that's what Tony tried to do for me and what a big brother was supposed to do. That's what people did who loved each other.

* * *

My understanding of love was remote, full of contradictions. Romantic love, of course, was totally over my head. I had never seen my parents kiss or hug, so I was doubly intrigued by the kissing in the movies from the forties that played on our black-and-white television. There was nothing to inform me that five-year-old little boys couldn't sweep five-year-old little girls into an embrace and plant kisses on their lips.

Sure, some of the boys in kindergarten said girls were icky. Girls were rumored to have cooties, which was a bug or a germ that sounded made up if you asked me. As early as the spring of 1961, toward the end of kindergarten, I was already interested in girls. They were like exotic foreigners, with their alien girl culture, elfin and magical. The most interesting girl of all to me was a petite blond-haired girl in my class with electric blue eyes. Not knowing the proper procedure for letting her know that I had a crush on her, I decided to do it the movie way and give her a kiss. Baptism by fire.

Approaching her unabashedly, I leaned forward with my prominent head—the Charlie Brown proportion of body to head did not go unnoticed in my younger years—as I closed my eyes and puckered up my lips.

Nothing happened. I opened my eyes and saw her staring back in confusion. "I want jou to kees me," I explained.

The Blue-Eyed Girl scrunched her face as if smelling something foul.

"Jou kees me," I repeated eagerly. And again, more emphatic, "Jou kees me!"

"No!" she answered firmly.

How could she say no? What had I done to deserve a no? "Jou better kees me," I told her, and, noticing that I had her backed up into the corner, added, "or I wheel push jou head in da wall." Couldn't she see that I wanted to compliment her by getting a kiss?

She tried to push her way past me and I pushed her back. It was never my intention to hurt her, but I shoved her so hard that she crashed headfirst into the corner of the wall. Her piercing wail of pain brought the class to a standstill.

The Kindergarten Sister came striding over, pushed me aside, and picked up the Blue-Eyed Girl to comfort her. It was then that we both saw the damage. No mere bump. Her face was streaked with blood, which was seeping into her blond hair and turning it red.

As though on the cue of a cricket, the entire class, in unison, screamed to holy hell. *AGGGHHHHHH!!!!!!!* And again. *AGGGHH-HHH!!!!!!!!*

Frozen with fear and shame, I stood in the middle of the room while my classmates whispered and pointed, and several other sisters flocked into the room, brought there by the screaming. The Kindergarten Sister handed me off to one of the other nuns, who grabbed a hunk of skin at the nape of my neck and marched me out of the classroom.

"God will punish you for what you've done," she scolded, shoving me down the hall toward the main office.

I was less concerned about him than about what my father would do to me when I got home.

In the waiting area of the main office, she sat me in a small chair facing the wall, and disappeared into the Mother Superior's office. No one had to tell me that my father was being called.

As I sat waiting for him to arrive, my head swam with images of the beating I would get and the knowledge that I would probably be punished for most of my summer vacation, which was only days away.

When Papi got to the office, I turned away from the wall, sincerely remorseful, but he didn't say a word; he just looked at me with beady eyes and pursed lips. The Mother Superior came out and frowned in my direction with a more glowering expression than ever. Papi followed her back into her office.

Some time passed and the door opened. My father stood in her doorway and thanked her. He turned to me and said, "*Venga.*" Come.

He used *venga* frequently. It became especially significant when he combined it with *aca:* come here. He usually emphasized *venaca* with a finger that pointed to a spot in front of him. My training was to come but then to stop within an arm's length of him. Not good enough. His game was to keep repeating *venaca* and gesturing, menacingly, with his finger to a spot just in front of his feet. Wherever this took place, I would inch in until I could see what hole his belt was cinched in at, close enough to be blanketed by the scent of his body.

Fastidious in every way, not just in his appearance, but in his breath and body odor, even though he was a two-pack-a-day smoker, Papi always smelled fresh and clean.

That was the scent that filled the car as we drove home in silence. No radio and no conversation. Then: "*Venaca.*"

From the backseat, I could see his unblinking eyes in the rearview mirror. Moving forward, I leaned my head over the front seat, knowing a hard backhand slap was coming. My focus was not to flinch before the hit because if he missed or made minimal contact, I would have to lean forward again. I took the hit, which drove me into the backseat, where I cried quietly, knowing there was more to come, praying that there wouldn't be.

When we got home, the aroma of food cooking in the kitchen assured me that my mother was back from the factory. Papi sent me to the bedroom. At the door, he directed me to sit on the bed, which was to become my designated punishment area for years to come. "*Esperame,*" he said. Wait for me.

Thoughts of the impending pain clashed with my concern for the Blue-Eyed Girl and the sense that I deserved to be reprimanded. In another part of the apartment, Papi was speaking to my mother, though his words weren't audible. Mami did respond a couple of times with "*Ay Dios mio!*" but the routine sounds of silverware on ceramic as Papi and Tony ate dinner fooled me into thinking that the incident might pass without terrible repercussions.

Then I heard a chair being pushed back. He was coming.

My father took the punishment he had given me on Christmas morning up to another level. This time I did not choose my favorite belt. And instead of standing up, I was told to lie down on my stomach on the bed.

Leaning in the doorway of my room in his sleeveless undershirt, which showed off his bulky upper torso, he looked like he was readying for a prizefight, drawing out his bus driver's belt with a terrifying resolve. The initial slashes elicited shrieks from the depths of my chest. But with blow after blow of leather and metal landing on skin, the pain changed. A vague warmth began to wash over my buttocks and thighs, almost numbing the hurt as my lower body pulsated slowly.

At some point Mami threw the door open and screamed, "*Ya, Tony!*" Enough.

My father stopped hitting me. I propped myself up on my elbows and turned back to see him lift the belt as if to strike her with it. She stared back, scared but resolved. He moved toward her. She didn't flinch. Finally, he pushed past her and left the room.

The tears that I had held down unleashed themselves. Sobs racked my body. Mami helped me stand, her sad brown eyes, bloodshot and swelling with tears, looking into mine. There was nothing she could say. She began to take off my uniform. When my pants were off, she turned me around. *"Ay, mijo,"* she said softly. I could tell she was crying by the vibration in her voice.

"Leave him alone." My father's voice startled us. He dismissed her, talking now to me from the doorway. "Put on your pajamas, pee, and go to sleep!"

This was not the way it happened in the movies.

The word "Help?" was called by a small voice as a kick ball from a nearby game came rolling into the middle of my dodgeball game on a sunny, crisp Chicago fall day in 1961.

Just turned six, I was back at the same Catholic school after Papi had masterfully convinced the Mother Superior that I had been rehabilitated over the summer.

Absolutely, I agreed. After long hours spent in my room with the curtains drawn—for three months of gritty, grueling, hot Chicago days, in which the buildings that served as wind tunnels in the winter maniacally acted as heating coils in the days before everyone had air-conditioning—with no hopes for going to the pool, or for ice cream, or playing whatsoever, I had borne the weight of my wrongdoing. There was no chance that I would ever try to kiss a nonconsenting girl again. Or at all. From time to time, I did wonder how another father might have dealt with the situation, thinking perhaps that men like my grandfathers or Moya might not have been so harsh.

President Kennedy might have given me a stern talking-to, or sent me to my room to write an essay, but that would have been the end of it. John Fitzgerald Kennedy was my mental prototype of an ideal father—noble, brave, strong—and I thought of him as though we were personally connected, drawing out elaborate fantasies in which I was adopted by Jack and Jackie and brought to live at the White House. Many Cubans, I later learned, saw red at the mere mention of JFK, especially after the Bay of Pigs. But I didn't understand any of those ramifications until I was older, and had spent so many hours feeling related to the first family that I would never lose my love and admiration for our thirty-fifth president.

Elvis, however, was my true idol. To fantasize that I could be his son seemed almost sacrilegious, too much of a stretch even for my rich imaginary world. But I did entertain myself with my very young Elvis imitations, playing my air guitar, swinging my hips, and singing Cuban-inflected versions of "Jou ain't notting bot a hound dog" and "Har-brake Hotel."

When Mami was home and my father not there, my isolation was alleviated by the view I had from my bedroom door into the adjacent kitchen, and I could watch her cooking and cleaning, noting what ingredients she chopped to season the black beans in the pressure cooker, how she pounded the skirt steaks with the meat tenderizer and breaded them just right for *bistec empanizado* (my favorite), and the proper way to fry plantains. With one foot in the kitchen and one foot in my bedroom—not breaking the rules, only bending them slightly—I couldn't keep myself from engaging her in conversation.

She warned me, "You know you're supposed to be sitting on your bed. If Papi comes home . . ." Mami didn't have to finish the sentence. Still, she seemed to enjoy our innocent conspiracy, telling me stories that took us both out of our less than favorable circumstances, at least temporarily.

The school year couldn't arrive fast enough for my liking, not only to get me out of house arrest and to have the much needed outlet of fun and self-expression lacking at home, but also because I sincerely wanted to prove that I could be a good boy. The rules were now very clear and I was confident that first grade would be very different from kindergarten.

Even clearer was the fact that the sisters of this parochial school were an extremely physical bunch of women. Some of the nuns grabbed us by the napes of our necks, others pulled our ears or forced our arms above our heads. And then there were the nuns who liked to swing the lumber. If you were caught talking or daydreaming some would use rulers to rap you over the knuckles or on the top of your head. And others were straightforward paddlers.

To make sure that I was under the strictest of supervision, Mother Superior may have been instrumental in assigning me to the first-grade class taught by Sister Ernestine Marie, considered to be the hardest-hitting nun at the school. She was known to us as "Sister Ernie Banks," a nickname given to her in honor of the Chicago Cubs first baseman and future Hall of Famer for her major windup swings and for the number of yardsticks she had broken over students' behinds.

Sister Ernie Banks saved the yardstick for the bigger offenses. Off to a rocky start, I seemed to have an uncontrollable knack for daydreaming, clowning, and rabble-rousing, whatever that was, and was summoned frequently to the classroom coat closet, where more than a few yardsticks were broken over my butt. Fortunately, she maintained the rule that if we took our punishment in class, our parents weren't called.

Unfortunately, Papi had created a new demand on my second-grade brother, Tony, to report directly to him about any instance of my bad behavior at school, home, or anywhere. "You are my extra set of eyes," he had said, wagging his finger at Tony. If Tony failed to report my misdeeds to him, he would be beaten and punished.

That gave me very little margin of error, except during recess and lunch, the breaks during the day when daydreaming, clowning, and playing were not against the rules. I could go from game to game at will, lost in the sea of kids ranging from the first grade up to sixth grade. Freedom, sweet freedom.

"Could you help?" There was that voice again as the kick ball rolled toward me. I stopped it with my foot and turned around to discover the source of the voice was a little kid with dorky glasses, gesturing to me to retrieve his ball for him.

Happy to help, I reared back with my right foot. My foot hit the ball perfectly and the ball shot forward, as if it was fired out of a cannon. The boy had his arms outstretched, but I knew, immediately, because the ball was traveling too fast and he was too small, that he had no chance to catch it. Worse, the ball hit him squarely in the face, knocking him off his feet. On the ground, his glasses hanging off one ear, he widened his mouth into a silent scream that, like a siren, exploded after a beat into a long, loud wail. Before I could apologize or help him, he scrambled up from the ground and ran away.

Resuming my game, I heard his voice again minutes later shouting, "There he is! That's him!"

The kid with the glasses was pointing at me and with him were three older, bigger boys glaring angrily.

"Lemme splain," I began. "Eet was an accident. I try to help."

The bigger boys stepped closer, surrounding me, moving in like a scene between the Jets and the Sharks in *West Side Story.* For a second I thought they were bluffing, but with no nun or big brother in sight to come to my rescue, my next move was to run like hell, weaving through the several games on the asphalt blacktop, disrupting them, but not losing the group of boys chasing me.

I tore around the side of the school building only to realize, as they rounded the bend, that I was trapped. Cornered. Looking around, I noticed a small rise of stairs that led to a door. Please, please let it be unlocked, I prayed, dashing up the steps and grabbing hold of the door handle. The door was locked.

My pursuers approached the stairs. They had stopped running and were walking slowly, threateningly.

One of them, probably the little kid's older brother, snarled, "You're dead."

They moved up the steps. I took a step backward, they took a step up. I took another step back, they moved up another step. On my next step backward, the ground disappeared and I lost my balance. Arcing backward, my arms flailing, I looked skyward, with an oddly familiar feeling of free-falling in slow motion, and I began to brace for the impact. Instead of slamming into asphalt, I bounced into a soft, powdery cushion, heard a distinct *POOF,* and everything turned black.

Some sort of dark fluffy substance engulfed me while I thrust my way to the surface, gasping for air. With burning lungs and nostrils, I coughed several times, emitting a little black cloud with every cough.

From above me I could hear laughter. Now towering over me at the top of the stairs, the bigger boys and the little kid with glasses were bent over pointing and howling, calling, "Look at the tar baby!"

That was the clue to me that the three-feet-deep bin of powdered tar into which I had fallen had turned me black. Every inch of me. The bell rang, signifying the end of recess, and the boys ran off holding their sides. My attempt to dust off the black powder covering my body and clothes was fruitless. It only made things worse, sending up small black clouds that hovered around me. Charlie Brown no more, now I was Pigpen, the misfit that I always felt sorry for. Now I was feeling sorry for me, and began to cry forlornly as I made my way to the main doors of the school.

The playground was emptying of kids, but one of the stragglers happened to be Tony. He gawked openmouthed, blinking, as if he was wiping the image out of his mind so he wouldn't have to report it to Papi.

To the credit of a group of younger nuns, who held a brief conference about my predicament, I was treated with a great degree of kindness that afternoon as two of the sisters arrived with some clean clothes and some towels and led me to the girls' bathroom.

Once inside, they helped me undress—an excruciatingly humiliating moment, but necessary so that they could scrub me down with the towels and hand soap. They comforted me throughout the ordeal, a gesture so thoughtful that I cried even harder.

When I was dry and as clean as I could get without a proper bath, they helped me put on the clothes they had brought—a long-sleeved white shirt and what was to pass as pants, of a color that can best be described as lime green. The shirt fit fine but the pants were very tight on my Rivas thighs and my butt, and didn't want to zip up. (At Sears, Roebuck, I was already classified as a Husky.) It took me and both nuns to pull, tug, and eventually get the zipper zipped up. The lime color was punishment enough but the discomfort around my crotch area, when I tried to walk or sit down, was hard to bear.

Sister Ernie Banks was also unusually sympathetic when I returned to class, although there was some snickering from my classmates. Walking home by myself, so as to avoid Tony, I hung my head, realizing only then that these incredibly ugly pants were also very short, sitting just above the ankles. The thought of Papi being home early from work ate at me. How would I live this down with him?

Pero con el ayudo de Dios . . . my father never knew anything about the tar baby incident. It may have been the talk of our school but Tony pretended to be oblivious to the entire story. Besides the gentle treatment I received from the nuns, the other light note was the laugh I gave Mami. With Eddie on her hip, cooking in the kitchen, she did a classic double take when I came walking in and told her my tale of woe. Then, as she examined me, she began to laugh uproariously, as I had rarely heard her laugh. Ten-month-old Eddie, joining in the mirth, started to laugh too. After having been the brunt of laughter all day long, I would have had my feelings hurt if Mami hadn't explained that the lime green pants were girls' pants with a side zipper. Somehow the nuns and I had managed to move the zipper to the front, which explained the difficulty I had walking. Now, from relief and exhaustion, I joined in the laughter with my mother and baby brother.

It would be a long, long time before I heard Mami laugh like that again.

A survival mechanism born around this time was inspired by a popular ad from the early sixties for Charles Atlas's Dynamic-Tension, which ran in all the comic books I devoured hungrily. The superheroes and the soldiers were my favorites, and most of them ran the Charles Atlas ad that explained, through a series of illustrations, how he had studied the movement and constant muscular tension of tigers to develop his theories of Dynamic-Tension. To learn this technique, all I had to do was send my money in and he would send me his secret training regimen. But I didn't have any money or any way to get any.

Instead, I tried a do-it-yourself approach and began to study tigers on my own, looking them up in books and magazines, or gluing myself to *The Ed Sullivan Show* when he had a famous lion-and-tiger tamer on. The lions were impressive, but the power and grace of the tigers were what captivated me. I watched the subtle changes in their bodies when they were stalking prey or angered by the whip of their tamer. Tigers were tensed and ready to pounce or flee at all times.

Asleep at night, I began to travel in my dreams as a tiger. I would begin the dream as myself, in my own body, and then slowly transform into a tiger as danger presented itself. My night vision was superhuman, and the eyes of the tiger I was becoming were my own hazel-colored eyes. My body moved gracefully, low to the ground, powerful and quick. My tiger never attacked or killed prey; it only protected other creatures in peril and then disappeared into the night.

* * *

Two other survival mechanisms developed in this time frame: lying and stealing. The lying was an outgrowth of the stealing, which began for me as a necessity and then became a habit. The cycle started with the Good Humor man. In the warmer months, the ringing of his bell or the sight of his white truck moving slowly down the street bearing its bounty of Nutty Buddies, push-ups, rainbow pops, and other frozen treats set off a reaction of salivation and desire in me as if I were Pavlov's dog. But because it was Papi, not Mami, who was the Lord of the Change, I was never sure if he would give me the money or not for the ice cream. Therefore, with the behavioral response of salivating came a nervous uncertainty and eventual fear, even loathing, in a physical sensation that I experienced not as butterflies in my gut as some people do, but as a tingling in my testicles, as if I had to pee.

In a fair-weather mood, Papi did reward me by grinning, exposing that familiar gap between his two top front teeth, and flipping me a quarter. But if he wasn't there or if I was being punished, the sound of the Good Humor truck to the ears of the penniless six-year-old that I was started a primal stress reaction from my groin to my brain. This convinced me that if I didn't find a way to get some ice cream, I certainly was going to starve and possibly die.

Only such a primal threat to my existence could have prompted me to start sneaking coins off Papi's dresser, where he unloaded his pockets at the end of the day into an assortment of change, extra keys, matches, and other items that men typically carried in their pockets. The first time I did it threw me into such a panic that I only kept the quarter for a few days and then put it back again without buying ice cream. But when Papi made no mention of missing a quarter, I figured he wasn't counting his change, and so I swiped another quarter, this time making it to the Good Humor truck, furtively devouring my Nutty Buddy, and going back inside unnoticed by Mami or Tony.

"Bictor," Papi called to me several days later, asking me to come to his room. In his matter-of-fact detective voice he asked if I knew who was taking money off his dresser.

"*Yo no se.*" My answer came fast, with a shrug, as I stressed the "*yo*" of the response. *I* didn't know. Lying to Papi—the all-knowing master of the Rivas kingdom—was one of the scarier acts I had committed, and I knew it was bad to lie. But the words flew from my mouth before I could consider an alternative.

"Well, somebody around here is," Papi said, scrutinizing me up and down. "And sooner or later, I'll catch the fucking *ladrón.*"

My escape from punishment was lucky, except that, having gotten away with petty thievery, I tumbled next into the harder stuff and began sneaking into his room and sifting through his other stashes of what I assumed were overlooked coins. There was a dish that held a tie clasp, a ring, and two large silver coins. In my logic, Papi would be much more inclined to miss the shinier, newer coins spread out on his dresser than either of these dull, faded, and rather clunky coins in the dish. Not sure that it was even worth anything, I snagged the bigger of the two coins, unimpressed by the year of its origin that I read on it: 1894.

The Good Humor man was impressed but seemed wary about taking it. "Where'd you get this?"

"I found it."

Not only did he take the coin but I got three quarters back.

A day and a half later, Papi called me into his bedroom. This time: "Bictor, *venaca.*"

Standing by the dresser he calmly inquired, "Did you take something off my dresser?"

"N-n-no. We-eh-well, I don't think so," I stuttered. The Good Humor man's reaction had been a clue that the big dull coin might have been something of value after all.

"I'm going to ask you again. Did you take something?"

"No." My lie had to sound more convincing. But it wasn't. His hand swung back and then at me, striking me with the first slap.

"Before you answer," Papi warned, "remember: I already know the answer. So be careful."

"I don't know who took the money. It wasn't me."

"Who said anything about money?" Papi asked, as the second slap knocked me down.

"You did. You said someone took some money off the dresser." What madness made me argue with him I didn't know. But I picked myself up off the floor anyway, not able to keep myself from crying.

"What I said was, did you take something off my dresser?"

"Oh. I wasn't in here, so it couldn't have been me." He was right about me. Besides being a thief and a liar now, I was stupid.

He reached for his belt buckle, unhooked it, and with one tug pulled it off his pants, folded it over, and began snapping it. "I'll give you one more chance. Did you take something off the dresser?"

A true dilemma. Recant, confess, and be beaten? Or stick to my original statement and be beaten? The thought did occur to me that if I was going to steal or lie in the future I would have to learn to do a better job of it. For the meantime, I repeated my fib: "I don't know what was taken, but I didn't do it."

"Fine. Turn around." In the whipping that ensued, he ranted, promising not to stop until I confessed, shouting, "That was an 1894 silver dollar. It's worth a lot more than that. I can't believe you're stupid enough to stuff your fat ass with ice cream using that coin!"

The fact that he knew I'd used the coin for ice cream, whether or not the Good Humor man turned out to be another one of his informants, made me know without a doubt that Papi was as omniscient as he professed to be. Even so, I refused to back down, preferring that tiny, illogical satisfaction of not giving him what he wanted, despite the knowledge that he was hitting me that much harder and longer because I wouldn't concede my patch of ground, lie though it was. More logically, I decided that he was going to tire eventually and he would already have disciplined me once. If I changed my answer now, it would start all over again.

This was obviously flawed judgment on my part, but nowhere near the idiotic, defiant act I committed a week later when I went against his most explicit of orders never to take any toy or other belonging to school. For my previous birthday, I had received a small red rubber ball that I treasured and, without thinking, tucked it into my school satchel that morning, maybe just to know it was there or to show to my classmates. With Sister Ernie Banks, I wouldn't dare to take it out to play with it, so there was practically no chance of losing it or having it stolen.

As it so happened, when I arrived at school and went to class, I discovered that Sister Ernie Banks was taking a sick day and that we had been given a substitute. This sister was one of the oldest nuns I'd ever seen, a member of the staff that I'd noticed occasionally at mass or shuffling through the halls, but never teaching.

At my desk in the very last row at the back of the class—where Sister Ernie had placed me after my chronic disruptions—I joined with most of my classmates in the age-old ritual of confusing the substitute by answering to different names during roll call. Hard of hearing and sight, if the thickness of her glasses was any indication, the Old Nun was not much of a challenge to confuse. She was a tiny wisp of a woman, her stature made smaller by the curvature of her spine, and her speaking voice was not much more than a mumble. In the high-ceilinged classroom with the tall thin windows towering along one side, she seemed that much frailer.

I tested her hearing by making funny noises. The farts and burps produced the best responses from the other students but were apparently inaudible to her. Perhaps ignoring me and the other trouble-makers, the Old Nun made it through much of the morning. With only our math lesson to go until recess, she stood at the chalkboard and covered it with a mural of math questions that she proceeded to answer herself in a flow of unintelligible mumbles.

Temptation, terrible temptation like the devil himself, whispered to me from my book satchel in the red rubber ball language that only a bored, mischievous six-year-old could understand. Maybe I could just feel it, make sure it was still there. That went well. Maybe I could just take it out and hold it until recess. No problem. I looked at the Old Nun, lost in her chalk and math, and rolled my ball around in my left hand and then my right. I tossed it in the air with one hand and caught it with the other.

Before long, I was mesmerized by the ball, which took on a will of its own, begging to be bounced off the hard tile floor, its hollow innards making a *boiinnggg* sound whenever it rebounded off the floor or the walls. Building from smaller bounces to larger ones, I kept checking for the Old Nun's reaction, but she was utterly oblivious.

Some of my classmates egged me on while others urged me to stop. Either way, the attention, positive or negative, was thrilling. With each throw, the ball got closer to the ceiling. To generate enough force to reach the ceiling, I stood up, slammed it onto the tile, and watched it ascend all the way to the top of the classroom, rebounding downward. But before it could bounce off the floor again, on its downward flight, the ball was intercepted in midair. With a palm facing up, a hand cupped my red rubber ball. An old hand with bent, knobby fingers. I looked up from the hand into the thick lenses of the Old Nun.

Without a word, she went to her desk, opened a drawer, dropped the ball into it, and closed the drawer. She returned to the chalkboard and her mathematical mumbling.

The rest of the day passed without incident. As the day was coming to a close, the Old Nun gave out our homework assignments and asked, "Are there any questions?"

Mine was the only hand that shot into the air.

"Yes. What is it, young man?"

"Can I have my rubber ball back?" I asked. My English was getting much better, though still accented.

"Yes, you may . . ." In that pause of a breath, I quickly headed toward the front of the class to retrieve my ball, when she said, ". . . at the end of the school year."

"But it's only April."

"That's too bad, young man. You should have thought about that before you brought that ball to school."

"I won't bring it again!" I promised.

Her mumbling was suddenly very clear and well pronounced as she countered that there wasn't going to be any ball for me to bring until the end of the year.

"But I want my rubber ball back now!"

"No. Sit down, young man."

"Give me my rubber ball. Right now!" This was what was known as a tantrum, and I was about to have one.

The Old Nun saw it coming. "That's it. You're going to the Mother Superior."

The mere mention of the glowering Mother Superior was enough to bring me to a standstill, knowing the call to my father would come next. Begging for forgiveness, I told the Old Nun she could keep the ball forever, and I would just go sit down in my place and be no bother at all. There was no negotiating with her. We were going to the main office and that was that.

Desperation set in. "Please, I'm sorry, I'm sorry," I cried. "I won't do it again. I'll sit down and be quiet."

"Too late. You're going and that's that." With no idea of the carnage that would be waged on my body by the inevitable call to my father, she grabbed me by the arm and started dragging me to the door.

Determined not to go, I dug my heels in and pulled back, which resulted in a tug-of-war between me, stocky and strong for my age, and the feeble Old Nun, in her late sixties or older. We pulled back and forth as my paralyzed classmates sat and watched. With one final pull of desperation, I yanked as hard as I could, precipitating the worst possible outcome, which unfolded in horror-movie slow motion, this last tug throwing the Old Nun off her balance, forward, as she came crashing against my body, only to be tripped by my extended leg. The class inhaled in unison into a clenched *GASSSPPPP* as she tumbled onto the hard tile floor, landing there on all fours. Her habit had flipped over her head, veiling her face, giving her the appearance of a downed, winged bird. Then she lifted her head and let go a bloodcurdling SCREAM.

Her screams were unending, which induced screaming from some of my classmates. *Ay, Dios mio!* What had I done, what had I done? Other nuns began arriving to lend assistance to their fallen comrade. The floor actually felt as though it were rising and falling, as if it were going to crack open wide and suck me down into the abyss of hell where I belonged, even though it had been nothing but an accident.

The Mother Superior arrived moments before the paramedics and needed no instruction as to who the culprit was. She pinched my earlobe and dragged me by it out of the classroom and into the hall, hustling me to her office as the distant screams of the Old Nun echoed throughout the halls of the school.

Because she was unable to reach my father, after paddling me herself—the three hard swats from the paddle were appropriate—the Mother Superior employed another notification process by typing out a note on her old Underwood typewriter, sealing it in an envelope, and pinning that to my uniform blazer with a long straight pin. "Do not touch this," she glowered. "Go straight home and show it to your father."

The walk home was nightmarish. My vision was blurred by tears streaming from my eyes down my face as I stumbled over sidewalk cracks. God may have known that it had been an accident but I prayed with all my heart for him to forgive me for the pain and suffering I caused the Old Nun, also putting in an extra plea that he protect me from Papi's wrath. The four-block walk home took me over an hour.

There was no relief to be had in discovering that Papi wasn't home from work when I walked through the door. Putting myself on punishment, I went directly to my bed and sat down. But when I looked down at the floor, all I could see was the envelope on the left side of my chest, like a clown's misaligned bow tie. Both Tony and Mami came in to ask me why I had an envelope pinned to my chest and what had happened at school. All I could do was cry. Mami asked, *"Ay, mijo, que hisiste?"*

Too ashamed to tell her, I cried harder. She tried to feed me but the idea of eating or being comforted was not right, not while the Old Nun was suffering.

The jingling of Papi's keys at the front door sent jolts of fear through me, touching off that panicked tingling in my testicles. His wing tips clomped down the hall in my direction.

As beatings went, this one was different—not that Papi liked to repeat himself—since clearly the punishments he had been giving me weren't working. One difference, before he slapped me across the face with one hand and ripped the note off my chest with the other, was that before the blows started this time I was already priming my muscles, like a tiger, in my own version of the Charles Atlas Dynamic-Tension technique, tightening them in the area where I could expect that the blows would land. But the other difference was that Papi seemed to sense my attempts to mount a defensive resistance—once he carefully tore open the end of the envelope, blew a quick breath into it, and reached in to retrieve the letter, which he read in the few blinks of an eye, that put him in a rage the measure of which I had never seen.

"Parate." Stand up, he ordered. Before I was fully on my feet, my muscles tensing across the front of my body, he back-fisted me in the chest, which lifted me up and onto my bed.

"Parate."

I couldn't stand. Gasping for air, I was paralyzed on the bed—the wind knocked out of me—in that limbo land that feels like you'll never breathe again. As my muscles strove to tighten to prepare for the next hit, he parried and went another direction, grabbing me by my uniform top and throwing me down onto the floor. I landed hard, which drove the air back into my body.

Everything became a blur, with my brain unable to accept what was happening but my muscles figuring it out, knowing that instead of tightening they needed to go as loose as possible to allow for the least amount of impact as Papi tossed me around the room like a rag doll. Bouncing and careening off the floor and walls and furniture—the bed, the dresser, the toy box—I tried to be more like a tiger than a red rubber ball, an effort that took away from the awareness of pain occurring from head to toe. With a tremendous jerk up and flight down, his last throw landed me face-first on the rounded end of the bedpost.

As my vision came back into focus, I saw Papi standing over me. Mami was in the doorway. "Olga, get some ice," he told her, and after she was gone from sight, he turned back to me. *"Parate."*

With one last effort, I stumbled to my feet, trying to tense my body, but found no energy left. He pointed to the bed. I walked past him, keeping my eye on him in case he made a move. I climbed up on the bed and sat facing him. Mami arrived with the ice; he walked out. She laid me down with my head on the pillow. The washrag ice pack went on my eye, which was throbbing and quickly closing up. Mami looked at me. Under her breath, she said, *"Hijo de puta."* Son of a bitch.

"Que?" Papi was standing in the doorway, smoking a cigarette. He told her what the note had said, what I had done at school. Mami cringed with disbelief, giving me a look of "Why?" that hurt me more than my eye.

After the many times I had witnessed Papi beating and degrading her, often when she was trying to protect Tony, Eddie, and me, I had much earlier come to the conclusion that hitting a woman was wrong. The shame that I felt for hurting the helpless Old Nun made me unable to look at my mother.

That night I fell asleep praying, as I would daily for weeks to come, that God in his mercy could forgive me. It didn't occur to me to ask for forgiveness for Papi, because I was, after all, at fault. At the same time, I was aware that my father had physically assaulted me as never before; he had attacked me like a man hitting another man in a street fight. But I wasn't angry at him. Not yet.

A period of calm followed, as though after a storm. Maybe Papi regretted being excessive or maybe it was another part of the test, to trip me up again. Just as Mami had stayed home from work when Papi had given her a black eye or some other visible bruise or injury, I was kept home from school for a few days to allow my eye to heal.

In this interlude, the Mother Superior called my father to inform us that my assault on the Old Nun had broken her kneecap. A decision had been made, the Mother Superior announced to Papi, that I would be allowed to finish the school year but would not be invited back the following year.

When I returned to Sister Ernie Banks's class to finish out the last month of first grade, the other kids tended to keep their distance from me, suggesting to me they had been warned by their parents and others that I was a bad boy, and not to get mixed up with the likes of me.

Maybe it wasn't so terrible that I was changing schools. Until then, summer was almost here and I was fully resolved to behave. Maybe I could enjoy my vacation for a change.

Regrettably, there were some weeks in the months to come when I was punished and kept inside for ridiculous infractions like accidentally tearing my pants or for being two minutes late coming home from playing. For the most part, however, the summer of 1962 brought with it moments of great fun and even a few enjoyable outings shared with Papi.

There were many things that impressed me about my father, but I was especially proud of the fact that he was an amazing diver. Wherever we lived, he loved going to the local municipal swimming pools and demonstrating his impeccable dives, from springboards or high platforms, perfectly executing his showstopper, a one-and-a-half somersault in a tuck or pike position. He could throw a twist into the same dive or do a swan dive with incredible grace. Watching the kids at these various pools marvel at his dives, I was proud to let them know that the muscular man on the diving board was my very own father. "In Cuba, he competed as a diver for the Olympics," I exaggerated, assuming they'd never know that it wasn't exactly true.

And then there was the security factor of being in public with

Papi, besides the native island boy in me that loved being in or around any body of water. Tony and I had been taught to swim very young at the local Boys Club. The one thing that I didn't understand was that at this Boys Club you had to swim naked. You would wear your swimsuit to the pool, but before you jumped in, you had to take it off. This included the big hairy Italian lifeguard.

Swimming, especially underwater, gliding just beneath the surface, dangling my legs like a tiger, was a temporary escape into a tranquil world. Hearing the muted sounds of the people above me, I could pretend to be on a mission to save someone, connecting to my good self, loving the freedom, safety, and peace.

Something else that Papi did was distinctively cool in my eyes. Papi could *smoke* a cigarette. He wasn't a nervous smoker or an ashes-falling-everywhere smoker. He was rather soulful as a smoker. A little cocky. Manly. He could have been a rugged outdoorsman smoker, like the Marlboro man, even though, at least early in my life, he smoked nonfiltered Pall Malls or Lucky Strikes. There was no shame in smoking in the 1960s, when cigarette ads were plastered on billboards and buses and in magazines. On television, most of the stars smoked on camera, including Desi Arnaz, our fellow *cubano*, and Frank Sinatra.

Like a ballplayer going through an elaborate ritual in his game, Papi had a certain way that he lit up. First, he took his pack of smokes and tapped down both ends of the pack. Then he pulled the cellophane string that released the outer wrapper, and sometimes he used the string as dental floss. Next, ever so precisely, he tore off one corner of the silver inner wrapper and tapped the pack gently until one cigarette poked its head out. With his teeth, he eased that cigarette out from the pack and held it between his lips at the same time that he magically produced one of his lighters as if out of thin air, and lit his cigarette. He smoked it slowly, concentrating, as if smoking made him a better thinker. Papi tapped the ash off the end with his index finger, sometimes rolling the red hot end on the edge of the ashtray. He never smoked it to the very end.

A few months before my seventh birthday, toward the end of the summer, in an attempt to be cool like Papi, I tried to smoke my first cigarette. On a weekend morning, after Papi had left the house, presumably for the rest of the day, I took a few stolen Blue Tip matches—which I loved lighting on abrasive surfaces—and went out hunting for discarded cigarette butts. I located several right away, including a couple of relatively unsmoked butts that weren't too dirty or mashed from being in the street.

Getting the butt lit was no challenge, but when I took a long deep drag like I'd seen my father do countless times, my body instantly let me know this was a big mistake. Expelling the smoke as I might hurl poisonous food, I hacked and huffed. White foam dribbled out of my mouth. Dizzy and clammy, I stumbled onto all fours desperately trying to extinguish the fire in my chest. It was at that point, when I heard a car idling behind me, that I realized I was in the middle of the street. I rotated my head around slowly and recognized the car. It was the silver convertible Valiant with the red interior belonging to Tony Rivas Sr., my father.

Papi sat behind the wheel, nonchalantly smoking his cigarette, a half smile on his face as he pointed to the house. Instead of using my bedroom as his court of law, he called me to the kitchen and pulled up a chair for us to sit next to each other at the faux marble kitchenette table.

"So," he said, in an eerily calm voice, "you wanna smoke?"

"No, Papi," I answered.

He pulled out his pack of Pall Malls from his shirt pocket and reached into his pants for his lighter, and placed both of them in front of me on the table.

"Go ahead. Smoke."

I was sorry, I said, so sorry. I didn't want to smoke ever again. "It was a mistake."

"No? You seemed like such a big guy out there smoking." He held out his pack. "Here, smoke one now."

"I don't want to, Papi." The tears had begun.

"Ah, but you see, you're going to." Not a speck of anger marred his cool.

He took a cigarette out of his pack and lit it. He tried to put the cigarette in my mouth, but I wouldn't open. I closed my lips down as tight as I could. He made several attempts but I wouldn't open my mouth. That was when, with just the hint of annoyance, and a shrug that said, "Okay, have it your way," he grabbed my jaw tightly with one hand and with the other stabbed the burning end of the cigarette onto my lips, holding it there for the count of three before he removed it.

My confused senses tried to separate the pain from the smell of smoke and charred flesh.

My father looked at me, concentrating, and took a long drag off the cigarette. He pressed it into the ashtray, putting it out.

My tiger's tension released as I prepared to go to my room. Earlier on the street I had learned that I couldn't handle the taste or the effects of smoking; my father had definitely reinforced that lesson. Before I stood, he said, reaching for a second cigarette, "Let's have another one."

This time after he lit it and grabbed my jaw, I pulled back, maddening him noticeably. He repeated the lesson on another section of my upper lip. Papi continued burning me with more cigarettes until both my upper and lower lips were burned.

He put out the last cigarette and got up and left the kitchen, returning moments later with a washcloth and a jar of Vaseline. In dread, I watched him make an ice pack with the washcloth and a handful of ice cubes. With two fingers covered by a glob of petroleum jelly, he dabbed at my blistering lips as I stared back into his yellow, short-lashed eyes with what he must have recognized as disbelief and the first glimmers of anger, which to my bewilderment seemed to give him a sense of satisfaction.

Warmly, caringly, Papi handed me the ice pack and instructed me, "Go lay down and keep the ice on your lips."

I did as I was told.

* * *

Mami got fat again. God wanted her to have another baby. Papi made plenty of digs about her size, ordering her to wear girdles to "hide your big ass."

This was going to be her fourth child. A new brother or sister was almost here. By August, with the end of summer upon us and the beginning of the new school year days away, I noticed that her stomach was massive and other parts of her body looked unusually swollen.

Mami rarely laughed or smiled anymore. Even my antics when we talked didn't lighten her very much. She had a new job, working at Zenith assembling radios, still full-time, and was responsible for cooking, cleaning, and child care. During the summer, when she was at work, she dropped off Tony, Eddie, and me at a babysitter, which helped, but the heat and her pregnancy combined with everything else had been exhausting.

One afternoon when she picked us up at the sitter's, she informed me and my brothers that Papi was taking us out for dinner that night so she didn't have to cook. Tony and I were to wash up and watch Eddie so that she and Papi could get ready.

At home, we did as she'd asked and waited in the living room. The sound of Papi's voice thundered from their bedroom as he yelled about what I couldn't decipher. His voice kept getting louder and angrier until I heard her scream with the sound of terror I'd never heard before. Like more of a shriek.

I inched down the hallway and stood outside the door, afraid and uncertain as to what I could or should do. When I heard the resounding thud of a body hitting the floor and Mami's moans of *"Ay, ay!"*—despite my terror of what I might find on the other side of the door—I opened it anyway.

The image of what I saw next burned me far worse than the cigarettes. Mami was prone on the floor, spread-eagle, clothed in a bra, panty hose, and a girdle that rode over her gigantic belly. Papi was fully dressed with his back to me. In the boots that he was wearing, he planted one foot on the floor, like a field goal kicker, and as I watched in sickening horror because I knew what he was about to do, he kicked her in the stomach. Then he reared back and did it again. Not done. He wasn't done. There was more. Moving in on Mami, Papi leaned down over her and his hands reached toward her to punch or choke her, at the same time that I ran the short distance from the doorway and hurled my almost seven-year-old body onto his back. I wrapped my arms around his neck and tried to pull him off, yelling, "*Ya,* Papi!"

Not human, not even animal, but like a programmed robot or machine, he snapped his head around and looked at me from the corner of his eye, the computer of his consciousness assessing the moment. It worked. I was now the target. Papi stood up, grabbed my arms, and whipped me around and let go of me, catapulting me into the wall, where I slid down and crumpled to the floor.

His hair disheveled and nostrils flared, he looked down at me, his son, cowering and crying on the floor, waiting for his wrath to fall on me. As he continued to stare at me, something changed in his eyes. He snorted, smoothed back his hair, half smiled at me, and walked out of the room.

I went to Mami, who was sitting up on the floor. I didn't want to look at her, because she was in her undergarments, a sight I had never seen. After I helped her stand up, Mami said, with tremendous effort, "Go to your room, and try to stay out of his way."

Consciously, I was not aware that a threshold to a more dangerous existence had been crossed. But on some level I sensed that what had been minor or not so minor skirmishing in our home was about to turn into full-scale battles with life-and-death scenarios. Later Mami wrote about this time period, saying with a certain understatement, "My husband began treating me in a harsher manner, and our marital relationship worsened," and she remembered this night as the turning point.

More time needed to pass before I was old enough to understand the connection between what I'd witnessed and the complications that occurred with the birth of my brother Robert David Rivas, born two weeks later on September 6, 1962.

He was a big, beautiful baby, as Mami allowed herself to recall later on, weighing in at nine and a half pounds. She knew immediately that my father's assault two weeks earlier had damaged the baby's head. The doctors diagnosed his condition as microcephaly, a developmental disorder. She was told that his small head lacked the soft spot that babies were supposed to have. He suffered from other maladies the doctors predicted would get worse.

When Mami and Robert came home after a few days in the hospital the atmosphere at home was desolate. That much I knew. Advised by the doctor not to breast-feed, Mami suffered increasingly over my brother's lack of development. She cried constantly, later admitting that she almost lost her mind. For the first time in her life, Mami started smoking. When Papi forbade it, she continued to do so covertly. Sometimes I ran to the store to buy cigarettes for her; other times, when Papi interrogated me about whether I'd seen her smoking, I lied adeptly to cover for her. Mami and I were now a conspiracy.

When my father began explaining that Robert was retarded, something he pointed out "is very common in large families," she and I knew that wasn't the full truth. There were other stories he told in years to come—that Robert had been born with the cord wrapped around his neck, and so on—but I never bought it.

Robert lived with us for a month. After my parents met with a series of specialists, they were advised to institutionalize him. Mami protested, adamantly disagreeing, but these doctors were insistent that his special needs would be better addressed with specially trained doctors and nurses. "Mrs. Rivas," said one of the specialists to her, "these types of children are not capable of understanding the absence of love."

She argued, pointing out that Robert certainly understood the presence of love. He was a sweet-natured, smiling, innocent baby. Who were they to tell her he would not feel the absence of love?

She was then told that children with Robert's afflictions were mentally little less than animals. And besides, the demands of taking care of him would make her unable to care for her other children.

Mami finally gave in, allowing Robert to be placed in a group home facility in the suburbs outside of Chicago.

The first time we went together as a family to go visit Robert, Papi announced in the car to me and Tony, "You're going to see some very strange children here. I'm warning you."

Mami held Eddie in her arms and stared off.

On this first visit, as on the others, I found Robert's crib in a corner and went to say hello. He beamed back at me with his infectious smile, like a little angel. Aside from his small head, he seemed fine to me. With his light skin and light eyes, he looked more like me than my other two siblings.

As a family, we visited him on three separate occasions over the next year, each time causing my mother such despair that she could barely speak for days afterward. After the third visit, Papi said that was it, we wouldn't go visit Robert anymore. Mami attempted to argue, saying she would go on her own, but he forbade it. My father tore up the one picture of Robert that she had, and then went about tearing up any records of the address and phone number of the group home.

A second-grade survival lesson: Adversity doesn't always breed character. And later: If the shoes don't fit, don't wear them.

The Mother Superior at my new parochial school had the same glowering expression as her counterpart at my former school, but allowed a glint of zeal, like cockeyed optimism, to show through as she lectured me upon my arrival in the fall. She was apparently well aware of my reputation but seemed to be prepared with a plan of action should I continue to be a troublemaker. The Second-Grade Sister whose class I was assigned to had this same no-nonsense approach, placing me on my first day of school in the last row, with the advisory "Behave."

Except for a couple of times when she caught me clowning around at mass—which resulted in a couple of swats of the yard-stick—I managed for a few weeks to stay out of trouble. There were advantages and disadvantages in not having Tony going to the same school as I did anymore. To my regret, he and I no longer had the fellowship of riding the bus together to and from school, and I also didn't have his steadying presence in the event that I needed an older brother to look out for me on the playground. On the other hand, even though I didn't plan to misbehave, it was comforting to know that if I did, Tony wouldn't have to tell Papi.

Had Tony been there, I might not have lost my cool during a recess in late September when a particularly belligerent kid, from another class, called me "Little Fidel!" and "Communist!" one too many times.

"I'm no communist!" I yelled back at him, balling my hands into fists and getting in his face.

"Oh, yeah? You're a Cuban, arncha?"

It was the way he sneered as he said "Cuban" that made me start the fistfight, which ended up with me punching him and bloodying his nose. Feeling no remorse, I was held back by some of his friends before I could hit him again.

The Mother Superior greeted me with her paddle ready and an expression that said she was not surprised to see me. After the paddling was over, she pointed to the chair outside of her office, saying, "You may wait there until your father gets here."

"Don't call my father, please!" I begged as she picked up the phone. "I'll be good, I promise, I'll do better. No more fighting. I'm sorry, please?"

Perhaps it was the sincerity of my plea that made her stop dialing the telephone, as she offered me an alternative. "Have you ever thought of becoming an altar boy?"

"Not really," I answered. It went without saying that I had never considered myself a suitable candidate. But the Mother Superior saw this as a ripe opportunity to save my seven-year-old soul, and when she gave me the choice of becoming an altar boy or having her call Papi, I put on my most eager choir-boy face and chose: "Oh, altar boy, yes, thank you, Mother Superior."

"You were invited to be an altar boy?" Papi was impressed. "That will be good for you, Bictor, it will build character." And then came the best part, spoken as he ran a hand through my hair and smiled: "I'm very proud of you."

Somewhat nervous about being so close to the holy altar—where, we were told, the body and blood of Christ were contained—I joined the group of altar boys already in training as we were taught the various responsibilities required to assist the priest during mass. Among the jobs were carrying a candle, holding the plate at communion, assisting the priest at the altar, and ringing bells, all of which I would be called upon to master. Though I was one of the youngest boys in our group, I felt confident that I could be as good an altar boy as any one of them. As it turned out, despite the angelic appearance that our vestments gave us, in our group the invitation to become an altar boy was typically given to troublemakers. All the while that we performed our duties to the satisfaction of the priests, our other undeclared mission was to crack one another up or cause one another to fumble. We raised our level of deceptive screwing around to an art form.

My stint as a candle carrier was so successful that I was promoted to the challenging task of carrying the plate (called a paten) that was held under the chins of communicants when the priest gave communion. If the communion wafer dropped, the paten would prevent it from falling to the floor. The difficulty for me was to maintain a straight face as I held the plate under the chins of the adults, who, when kneeling to take communion, were at my eye level, while the priest held out the Eucharist, intoning, "Body of Christ," and placed the wafer on the extended tongue of the worshiper. My view into the mouths of countless adults was hilarious enough, but their expressions as they slid their tongues out at me and rolled their eyes heavenward made me literally bite my lip to keep from laughing hysterically. The urge to stick my tongue out back at them was almost uncontrollable.

Bell ringing was where my creativity soared. At certain points in the mass, the bell ringer was supposed to ring his bells, sometimes in a series of three rings, to signal solemnity; some congregants would softly beat their breasts three times. Occasionally, as on one of my last days as an altar boy, I experimented with adding a fourth ring, and then watched with mirth out of the corner of my eye as confusion spread among the congregants, and the other altar boys snickered outright. The first few times the priest looked over, I gave him my best shrug to indicate it was an accident as I mouthed the word "Sorry," and that sufficed. But eventually, after having served as a good boy in training for almost six months, I was not invited to continue on and returned to bad boy status.

My intention was not to be bad, of course, but to avoid what was worse: being *nothing*. Somehow I had to find a way to distinguish myself, to hold my head up and walk proud of something nobody else had. In mid-February of 1963, days after I was dismissed from being an altar boy, I found that very something tucked away in my parents' closet. Mami's cowboy boots. Perfecto. With pointed toes and three-inch heels, white swirly stitching on the yellow-brown shiny leather, they were several sizes too big for me, causing me to wobble and wiggle after I tugged them on to see how they fit. Images of John Wayne and Elvis came to mind.

"Victor!" Mami's voice called from the kitchen, beckoning me to hurry and put on the rest of my winter gear before we left for the bus. With the frozen city newly plowed after the last snow, the extra layers weren't an option. I started to put the boots back into the closet, but then stuffed them into my book satchel, certain they'd impress someone.

The plan wasn't necessarily to wear them at school, but once I was in the coatroom that thought presented itself. Why not? For the rest of the morning, I clodded up and down the halls, my legs bowed like a real cowboy. You bet I was walking tall, three inches taller, in fact, than my regular above-average height.

Nobody noticed until we hit the playground, an expanse of solid, aging asphalt. The only green ever seen out here came from weeds shooting through the cracks, though now they too were covered by a sheet of ice overlaid by crusty sludge, a pseudo–ice rink, over which my *zapatos* performed like well-waxed skis.

"Neat!" said one of my classmates, a playground-organizer-type kid, as others joined in with admiring remarks and laughter. When teams were chosen for a game of Red Rover, the Organizer picked me first. My Red Rover reputation wasn't bad, since I was a naturally strong kid, notorious for almost always breaking through a group of kids with linked hands and bringing them toppling to the ground with me whenever "Red Rover, Red Rover, send Victor over" was called out.

This day, Mami's boots gave me added momentum and speed, and as I powered from my team's line toward the opposition like a giant racing bowling ball, knowing I could plow through the other second-graders like flimsy pins, I had my first taste ever of the euphoria of athletic competition. It was life-altering—not only the thrill of the moment in the actual contest, but also that flicker of something that might make me somebody after all. After the first two times my name was called, my teammates were celebrating our imminent victory and sending me awed looks.

The third time my name was called, after the other team took a surprise time-out, I was aware as I began my stampede and slide toward them that they were all wearing odd smiles as if they'd figured out how to stop me. Not a chance. With adrenaline and icy speed fueling me, I flew so hard and fast toward them that I closed my eyes right before breaking the link, waiting for the impact to knock them all down along with me. But there was no impact. At least, not for several seconds.

Opening my eyes in horror, before my brain could register the fact that they had purposely unlinked arms to let me hurtle through— against the rules!—I realized that I was hurtling perilously toward the school yard fence, made of rebar, the tall, reinforced, thin steel bars, with a width of eight inches between each bar, built for durability and security to keep strangers out and schoolchildren in. *Ay, Dios mio.* What had I done? With my arms outstretched to brace my collision, I again closed my eyes, only to miss pushing against the fence. Instead, in a twist of almost impossible mechanics that could have made a listing in *Ripley's Believe It or Not,* my arms slipped right through the spaces between the bars, and my big Charlie Brown head somehow managed to do the same and traveled through to the other side, wedging me just behind the jawline and ears. Though I was conscious and not in a lot of pain, my jaw instantly began to swell.

There I was, in Mami's cowboy boots, stuck facing out to the city traffic for all the world to see, with uproarious laughter from my classmates coming from behind me. Moments later the bell rang, and as they all receded from the range of my hearing, no doubt filing back into the cozy confines of our orderly parochial school, I was left to my tears and my panic, and the darkening, freezing day, which threatened more snow. And not long after that, the sound of the Mother Superior's voice asking me how on earth I had gotten myself into such a position. My tears broke into sobs, and taking pity on me, she called for help from two school janitors.

The Mother Superior went outside the fence to face me as the two janitors each grabbed hold of a leg and began to pull backward. Rather than give me that half-glowering, half-zealous look, or trying to scold me, the Mother Superior reached into her frock and pulled out a beautifully hand-embroidered handkerchief. She very tenderly began to dry my tears and runny nose—which helped to relieve some of my embarrassment, despite the janitors' consensus that outside help was required.

Forty-five minutes later, my ears, nose, and mouth frozen numb, the help arrived in the form of a panel truck, out of which stepped a guy bearing a large tank and wearing a full face shield with a dark rectangle where his eyes should be. He had an inanimate demeanor that reminded me of Gort, the robot from the movie *The Day the Earth Stood Still,* that was not diminished as he unsheathed his gunlike flamethrower and lit it up.

The Mother Superior held my hand through the bars as Gort approached with the high blue flame and draped my head with a protective cloth. Blubbering quietly to myself, I smelled the rotten odor of burning iron and began to pray with tigerlike intensity to be liberated from my cage. In the universal scheme of things I understood, obviously, that I might not have deserved to have my prayers heard. But then again, the Mother Superior, as close to God as could be, was praying for me too.

She got through, thankfully, and I was free, bruised and humiliated but otherwise unscathed. Papi never found out, because if he had known, he would have whipped me good for losing at Red Rover. Just to settle the score with the members of the opposing team for setting me up, I did make a point the next day of seeking them out individually and kind of bumping into them, making sure each landed in a pile of slushy snow.

I felt for some weeks after this episode that the Mother Superior and I had a warm, close bond. But then, in late March, it snapped.

On the way to school that morning, at the family-owned corner market where I had intended to buy some candy, I had instead avoided the long line at the counter by shoplifting a bag of Oreos and stashing it in my book satchel. The cookies stayed there all day until our afternoon study period, when the Second-Grade Sister announced she was going to the office and would be right back. My cue to have an Oreo. With my seat in the back row, I'd have time to anticipate our teacher's return, I figured.

"Can I have one?" said a boy to my right. "Me too?" asked another. "Cookies?" came a chorus from the front.

"Nope," I answered everybody, until the request came from the Aloof Girl to my left. The fact that she never talked to me except to tease or make fun of me hadn't stopped me from having a crush on her. When she asked for an Oreo, I obliged, and took another one for myself. The Aloof Girl ate hers in two chomps, swallowed, and then held out her hand for another cookie.

"No, one's enough."

"I'll do something if you give me another one," she said, less aloof than before, but not quite friendly.

"What?"

"I'll lift up my skirt and show you my panties."

Fair enough. After she flashed me, I handed her a second cookie. She held out her hand again. We did this exchange a couple more times. When she asked for a fifth cookie I shrugged. "Nah, I've seen enough."

Determined, she leaned closer and whispered, "I'll pull my panties down and show you my thing."

"Okay." I craned my neck as she followed through on her offer, during which other students sitting nearby either giggled or groaned in disgust. Then, grasping an Oreo, I extended it across the aisle, and as she reached out her hand to take it, a third hand wrapped around both of ours. The sister had returned. With a dour expression, she pointed me to the front of the room to wait, and escorted the Aloof Girl out of class to the office. Minutes later the sister returned, looking even more dour, followed by the arrival of a scowling Mother Superior. The same saintly woman who weeks earlier had dried my tears with her own embroidered handkerchief now pointed her index finger at me and hooked it back toward herself, beckoning me to follow her.

Once outside the classroom, she grabbed me by the ear and dragged me down the hallway until we got to the swinging door of the boys' bathroom, which she threw open and then pushed me inside.

In front of a row of urinals, the red-faced Mother Superior shocked me by saying, "I want you to show me what you were doing with that little girl."

As my tears started to fall, I protested, "No, I can't! I'm not gonna tell you!"

"Oh, yes you are!"

"I can't!"

"Do it!"

The moment I tried to explain that I didn't have my cookies and that the girl wasn't there to lift up her skirt and show me her panties and her thing, the Mother Superior exploded. "Don't lie to me, young man! I know what you were doing. She was giving you the cookies and you were pulling out your peepee. Pull it out. Show me what you were doing."

Shock and revulsion stopped my tears. Obviously, the girl had turned the story around, which I attempted to explain to the Mother Superior, but she wasn't buying it in the least. She kept demanding that I show her what I did. After refusing several direct orders that I show her my penis, I was dragged by the Mother Superior out of the bathroom by my ear and into her office, where she typed a letter to my father, sealed it in an envelope, and pinned it to my uniform top. Another school, another Mother Superior, the same drastic measure that was going to result in the same excruciating consequences once I got home.

As a send-off, the Mother Superior pronounced in ominous tones, "Do not come back to school without your father."

On the bus traveling back to our neighborhood, I thought about running away from home. The menacing note pinned to my uniform top brought back such horrible memories from the last time that when I got off the bus, I ripped the envelope from my chest and tore it up into little pieces, throwing them in an alley trash bin three blocks from our building. At home, keeping to myself and avoiding eye contact with everyone, I went to bed early but didn't sleep as I racked my brain over what to do.

By morning my plan presented itself. After breakfast, I put on my uniform, grabbed my book satchel and my lunch, and walked out the door. A block from our apartment on the way to the bus, I climbed through a broken window into the basement of an apartment house where a kid I knew kept his army stuff. There were little jeeps and trucks and soldiers set up on a dirt battlefield that his father had built him. For the next four days, I maintained this routine, leaving as if going to school in the morning, playing all day alone in the basement with hundreds of green plastic soldiers, some with bazookas, some with rifles, some poised on the battlefield, some fallen. At the end of the school day, when I spotted the shoes of other schoolkids traipsing home past the basement window and heard their voices, I cleaned up, put my uniform top and my clip-on tie back on, took my book satchel, climbed back out the window, and walked home.

On the fourth day, as I turned onto my block, I saw that the street was lined with several police cars. Suddenly a man in a sports coat and tie was at my side, holding a school photo of me. "Are you Victor Rivas?" he asked, bending over and staring at my terrified face.

With his hand on my shoulder, I was guided home, so frightened that I crapped my pants.

Mami helped me into a bath, too relieved to see me alive to be mad. She heard my side of the story and then told me how she had figured out that I'd been playing hooky after the Mother Superior had called her at work to ask if I was sick.

"Does Papi know?" I asked with dread.

She nodded yes, sadly.

Oddly, the next few days of prolonged punishment, with not one but a few beatings, were not especially memorable. But what I could never forget was the sight of the police cars on our block and crapping in my pants.

I never returned to that Catholic school or any other Catholic school, though I did continue going to church, and continued to pray for guidance, protection, and forgiveness.

By 1963, Christmas had become a foreboding holiday. For the past few years I'd been punished and had received only the customary underwear and winter clothes. By now it was my habit to pretend to be sick on most Christmas mornings so I didn't have to suffer the indignity of not getting any toys. But this year was very different. After weeks of trepidation, I woke up to find that there were several gifts for me, including a Mousetrap game and a brand new Radio Flyer sled. Tony and Eddie, who was about to turn three, both had lots of presents too.

"You see what happens when you work hard?" my father was quick to point out, flashing his gap-toothed smile that looked like approval to my eight-year-old eyes.

It was true that I had made an impressive comeback from early-onset juvenile delinquency, even though there were some rough patches after my expulsion from my second parochial school and subsequent transfer to Bateman Elementary, where I had to finish second grade in a class for kids who made me and my former group of altar boys look like, well, altar boys. Tony—who had transferred to Bateman back in the fall and had been moved up from the third grade to fourth because of his advanced abilities—was once again required to be Papi's eyes and ears on campus and to report any inklings of my misbehavior back to him.

My father had actually escorted me to Bateman my first day, dropping me off at the door of my classroom after having a private conversation with the young, pretty teacher in charge of this group of wayward second-graders.

"Class, I'd like to introduce the new boy . . ." she began, her voice drowned out by the talking of the students. "Class," she continued when a pushing and shoving match in the back interrupted her again. "Class!" she finally yelled as the room more or less quieted down. "This is the new boy, Victor Rivas," she told them as I tried a half-friendly smile.

"Yeah, so what?" called one voice.

"Who cares?" called another.

My half smile vanished. She glanced at me and then, brightly, asked who wanted to help me get the materials I'd need.

The next heckler said loudly, "Why don't you, you're the teacher!"

The sarcastic and rude comments went on throughout the day, some students refusing to do what they were told. One of the boys even took a pointer off the teacher's desk, and when she went to the chalkboard with her back to us, he used the pointer to lift up the back of her dress.

Compared to most of these kids, I was a model student. At first, however, as I tried to fit in, my behavior deteriorated further, causing me to get in more trouble at school and at home. One of the worst incidents happened after school when my naughty love of lighting Blue Tip matches led to my accidentally catching my bedroom curtains on fire when nobody was home. Rather than use a bucket, which I overlooked, I tried to put out the fire by filling a drinking glass with water and racing back and forth to the kitchen to refill it. The curtains burned away completely and the walls and ceiling around it were scorched.

Tony arrived home just after the damage was done and found me in the living room packing a small suitcase.

"What are you doing?" he asked.

"I'm leaving."

"Why?"

I nodded toward the bedroom without saying a word. Tony sped off to investigate and when he returned, he nodded toward the suitcase and said, "Let me help you."

Before I could make my escape, Papi arrived home early from work. Ever since he had stopped driving a bus and had started working as a computer programmer, he seemed to be in a better state of mind generally. But not when he saw the blackened bedroom. At the same time, he didn't lose his cool as he calmly administered a severe beating, and grounded me for two months.

Perhaps the worst thing I ever did in this time period was to wear Mami's beautiful gold watch—a present to her from Papi's mother, Abuela Maria—to school. On the playground, I told some of the kids that it was made of pure gold and had been given to me by my rich grandparents in Cuba. An older Bully Kid snorted and made a snide remark about me being a communist if I was from Cuba. That made me furious. To be honest, I was starting to want to hide my Cuban background and wished that I could get rid of the hint of the accent I had left. Anything other than Cuban would have been preferable. Ideally, Irish would have been my chosen ethnicity, as a long-lost son of President and Mrs. Kennedy. Steaming mad, if I hadn't been wearing Mami's watch, I would have gotten into a fight with the Bully Kid.

That would have been better than what I did. I let him hold the watch. The second he took it, he sauntered off, declaring that it was his. Hysterical, I chased after him, yelling and crying that he'd better give it back, which prompted him to swivel around. "You want it?" he asked. "Go get it." And he threw it up into the air. Diving for it, I missed and watched Mami's prize gold watch crash onto the asphalt, the crystal shattering and the hands breaking off. The teacher in charge of recess helped me pick up the broken pieces and put them in an envelope for Mami, enclosing a note that explained what had happened. Because I was too ashamed to give the envelope to Mami, I hid it in the space between the stove and the wall.

My mother found it a couple of months later and reacted by giving me the only physical beating she had or would ever give me. She used a belt on me as I stood naked in the bathtub, screaming from pain and shock and shame. In the past, Papi had tried to say that what he was doing hurt him more than it did me, though I never believed it. In this case, even though Mami didn't say it, I knew that inflicting physical punishment on me hurt her far more than it did me. From then on, I was grounded or denied privileges, but that was the last time she ever lifted a finger to punish me again.

In our unspoken form of communication, we forgave each other, as if we knew not to blame each other for my misbehavior and for her frustration. For the rest, we seemed to resolve without words to not allow each other, or Tony and even Eddie, to be divided and conquered. After our last visit to see Robert, around this time, Mami started physically intervening more and more when Papi became overly threatening with any of us three boys. And when he was threatening her or my brothers, I developed the habit of trying to cause a distraction, something that was turning out to be my area of expertise, for better and for worse.

In early summer, Papi gave me a break from punishment to go with him and Tony one night to see the Ringling Bros. circus. My excitement about the outing was over the minute Papi stopped to pick up a woman he introduced as his "friend" and her obnoxious little boy, about my age. It was clear to me, young and generally unaware though I was, that this woman was his girlfriend, which made the circus of minimal interest. Worse was the obvious expectation that I was supposed to buddy up with this whiny kid while Papi pawed at her in front of us. Not willing to play along, I ended up punching the kid in the nose.

"*Coño!* What are you thinking!" Papi roared at me over the circus crowd, as the boy screamed and the woman rushed to stop her son's nose from bleeding.

I had no remorse. Needless to say, that was the end of that date, but the beginning of a few days' worth of being disciplined and punished all over again. On one of those afternoons when I should have been in my room, seated on the bed, feet on the floor, I crept out and into the kitchen, where I broke the news to Mami that Papi had a girlfriend. She gave me a look that said either that she knew already or that his carousing was the least of her worries. Saying nothing, she shrugged and sighed, then walked away.

By midsummer, I had managed to survive my various punishments and shown enough initiative—Papi's favorite word—that I was allowed to go away for two weeks with Tony to the Boys Club camp in Salem, Wisconsin. We were free in a way that we had never been before. Tony didn't have to live up to being perfect all the time and I didn't have to wear my troublemaking mantle all the time. We got to be kids.

Toward the end of the two weeks, a counselor informed Tony and me that we were wanted in the camp director's cabin. When we arrived, standing side by side, the director asked us to have a seat. He had some news from home that he needed to tell us. Soberly, Tony and I took our seats and waited, swinging our muscular, tan Rivas thighs in our white camp shorts to cover our nervousness. We were trained to be stoics.

The director looked prepared to comfort us, as though his news was bad, but when he went on to say, "Your father called and he needs you to stay another week," his expression changed to surprise at our elated faces. Whatever the opposite of homesickness is called, that's what we felt and we couldn't hide it. The only time we had regrets was after the three weeks were over and Papi came to pick us up.

Back home in Chicago, I felt different somehow, renewed and grateful to have been away. The city itself seemed different to me, too, and I appreciated it in ways I hadn't before. As the Second Son, who had to try harder, I related to the Second City, which also tried harder, to the mix of different ethnicities and passions of Shhee-cogoh, and to the resilient personality of a town whose fans never lost hope on ball teams that rarely won. All of the American sports inter-ested me, but the Church of Baseball prevailed in our home, with Papi preaching the gospel of what made great and not-so-great play-ers. My brothers and I didn't start Little League until later, but between Papi's opinions and my devotion to "da Cubs," I was well versed in baseball knowledge long before I swung my first bat.

So in the spirit of being willing to try harder, I was given a chance to spend third grade in the regular class, no longer in the "class for delinquents," as Papi called it, and stayed out of trouble, except on the playground, where I had the reputation of being a fighter. My own self-image was that I was a mean kid and not so smart. This was reinforced no doubt by my father, who held up Tony's academic achievements against mine and often stood over me as I did my math homework, which was not as easy for me as spelling or penmanship, where I did well. The effort to concentrate with him breathing down my neck was clearly a challenge, and if I got a math problem wrong, which I did inevitably because of my nervousness, he was sure to try to motivate me with a *pescozón*—a slap on the back of my head—that reminded me I could never be as smart as Tony. But in the special brand of Anthony Rivas Sr. justice, I was bequeathed a title of superi-ority to Tony in one area. Papi had decided, in spite of my infinite shortcomings, that I had a quality of generosity. According to our father, Tony was selfish.

A Rivas survival lesson: Don't argue with praise, but don't trust it either.

My lowest point in the school year was not related to any trouble I caused or to problems at home. It was in response to the event that brought the world to a standstill on the afternoon of November 22, 1963—the assassination of President John Kennedy. My third-grade teacher wept openly when she announced that the president had been shot, and as I walked home, people in the street were wailing and huddling outside in the cold around televisions in storefront windows. Word spread on the street that he was dead. John Fitzgerald Kennedy was dead. No, no, no, I couldn't believe it. In convulsive sobs when I got home, I pushed Mami aside as she came to comfort me.

"You're not my mother!" I cried. "My mother is Jackie Kennedy!"

Mami seemed to understand that I didn't mean it, but her own sorrow was such that when she turned away from me, her shoulders hunched forward and her body quivered in what I recognized was her silent way of crying. Later that night, I apologized. Of course she was my mother.

For the next several days, televisions were on constantly, even in the classroom, on a cart that had been rolled in so that we could watch the funeral together with the rest of the nation. Along with many of my classmates and my teacher, I cried openly during the funeral, especially at the moment when John-John saluted his father's coffin as it passed him on its way to Arlington National Cemetery.

After Christmas, a month later, I was reminded of John-John and what I imagined he, Caroline, and Mrs. Kennedy were going through in trying to grieve the loss of a father and husband while the whole world watched their every move. G.I. Joe's motto was right. Getting through this time was a tough assignment for everyone.

Because we had our own war zone that made us increasingly isolated from others, we lived in a kind of vacuum, in which the other changes swirling around us rarely registered on Papi's radar. Even with the turmoil surrounding JFK's assassination, the building civil rights struggle, the ongoing Cold War, and an escalating war in Vietnam, he seemed fairly oblivious. But then, on the evening of Sunday, February 9, 1964, my father embraced a historic moment and in a surprising fit of leniency called me out of my bedroom—where I was being punished for some reason—to share in the experience: "Bictor! *Venaca*."

In the living room he and the rest of the family were sitting around the TV. Papi pointed to the television screen as I observed what looked like a young Moe from the Three Stooges holding a guitar and singing. There were four young Moes and they could barely be heard over the frenzied screaming of the girls in the audience. This was the Beatles' Ed Sullivan debut, and without a word being said, I understood it was a history-making moment, the birth of a pop-culture phenomenon. We could all feel it. That I was able to preserve it in my memory as a witness to the beginning of the British Invasion and the dawn of the sixties was amazing, but what meant even more was that for this night we were a real American family, gathered around the glowing tube together. For the rest of the hour, we stayed that way. The dark fearful shadow that Papi's presence always cast over our family shrank back in the bright melodies of John, Paul, George, and Ringo. Things felt safe and normal.

The peace was short-lived. By the next morning, the shadow was back and we all went about our routines, walking over land mines, not sure what or where they were. Then, in the spring of that year, Papi laid a bombshell on us. In a replay of the move he had made to the United States from Cuba to seek a better standard of living, he was going to move us to California, where he already had a computer programming job with North American Rockwell, an aerospace company. Here was the best part: he was leaving at once, while the rest of us remained in Chicago so Tony and I could finish out the school year.

Suddenly it was camp again. Freedom, sweet freedom. The ever-present tension in our home fled right along with Papi on the plane that took him thousands of miles away. Mami relaxed almost all the rules at home so we could each breathe and just enjoy ourselves. As long as my homework was done, I could go and play daily, without fear of being literally slapped down if I was a minute or five minutes late getting home. But like a convict on early parole, I immediately overdid everything, ignoring or defying boundaries of safety and common sense.

Mami never knew about one of the things that happened, and with my record as a tall-tale teller, nobody else I told believed me either. First of all, I shouldn't have been walking home from school through the alleyways anyway, except that in my imaginary game of being a tiger prowling through the jungle, the alleys provided a better backdrop than the busy Shhee-cogoh streets. As I crept along, tensing and relaxing my muscles with feline control, a bolt of adrenaline shot through me when all of a sudden someone grabbed me from behind.

Hairy, smelly, and breathing heavily, he looked to me, as I twisted my neck to look back at him, like the kind of wolf that stalked Little Red Riding Hood on her way to Grandmother's house. Only he wasn't a wolf. He was a gigantic, mangy German shepherd, standing upright on his two back paws with his two front paws balanced on my shoulders.

"Never panic if a dog is being aggressive," Papi had told me before. "They can smell fear. And whatever you do, don't run."

Walking slowly now, barely inching forward, I tried to pose as being unafraid and waited for the shepherd to get down, but he stayed right up on my back, pushing on me as though to move or scoot me along. After giving me one final push, just as I got to our back gate, the dog released me, went back down on all fours, and sauntered off. By the time my breathing returned to normal and I started the climb to our apartment, I realized that the back of my shirt was sticky and wet. The reality that I had just been humped and come on by a German shepherd was too much to grasp at the age of eight and a half, though it did gross me out enough that I took an immediate shower. When I told Tony and some of my friends, they all agreed it was too absurd to be true. Their disbelief insulted me, even though I might have sensed that, as in the story of the boy who cried wolf, some of my earlier exaggerations might have been to blame.

Mami did hear from school about some other incidents, including one that required her to come to the principal's office, where I too had been summoned from class. Standing next to my mother, I kept my focus on my feet as the army-general-styled principal slid a small stack of checks across his desk toward Mami. "Mrs. Rivas, are you aware that your son has been forging his father's signature and writing checks for, ahem, large amounts, and distributing them among the students?"

Mami glanced over at me. She knew about the day that I wore an old pair of Papi's tortoiseshell prescription glasses to school and told everyone they were mine; she also knew that while rummaging around drawers at home I had found enough change to make a habit of buying candy and ice cream for other kids. But this was news to her. She held up the checks written on one of my father's old accounts. Her face went from displeased to appalled as she reviewed the different amounts: $200, $1,000, $10,000, $250,000.

The Army-General Principal asked her if he needed to contact my father. And how would he go about doing that?

"No, no," Mami said in her broken English. "I take care of Victor. He get puneesh."

She was not happy with me but let me off easy, with only a week of being grounded. Whether or not she understood that the checks and the made-up stories were all part of my desire to be liked and to have attention, my mother never indicated. But when I did something that was really unacceptable, she put her foot down, like the day that I came riding home on a beautiful brand-new bike with tassels on the ends of the shiny chrome handlebars.

Mami was out in the back of our apartment house working in the small garden she had started back there, Tony at her side helping, when I came riding up.

"Whose bicycle is that?" she asked suspiciously.

"Oh, this kid in the park let me borrow it. He said I could keep it for a week." The truth was that I had begged a kid in the park to let me ride it and he did—against his father's rules—and I had jumped on it, ridden it around in circles, and then sped off.

Mami knew a lie when she heard it and instructed Tony to return the bike to the kid in the park immediately. An hour later he returned, out of breath and furious with me, telling how he had almost been attacked by a group of older boys. Just as they were about to start pummeling him, the kid, happy to have his bike back, told his henchmen that Tony was not the same person who had stolen the bike. Being grounded again was a drag but having Mami and Tony mad at me really made me feel ashamed. When we got to California—I swore to myself, and God as my witness—I was turning over a new leaf.

Repeating another pattern from before, Papi never sent Mami any money or tickets for our move. La Luchadora, she made do anyway. Piece by piece, she sold our furniture and winter clothes and even her ironing board. All this she managed to accomplish with three boys aged ten, eight, and three, and her full-time job at Zenith. Mami kept her despair over leaving Robert in his group home somewhere deep inside her, in a private buried place, not forgotten but a hurt too terrible to think about often. Maybe I understood this, and for unknown reasons, I appointed myself the keeper of the secret that Robert David Rivas was becoming, starting with the attack on Mami that I had witnessed.

During the time that we were packing up to go, if my mother did think about the possibility of just not going to California, and trying to stake out life on her own, all of us free from Papi, the biggest obstacle she would have faced was the fact that she had not yet received U.S. citizen status. She knew that to get herself and her kids to safety, she had to first become a citizen, and the next step to that end was to join my father in California, and hope for the best.

In August of 1964, Mami, Tony, Eddie, and I boarded a train—the most economical way to travel—for a four-day ride cross-country from Chicago to Los Angeles. The trip between cities was spectacular, with ever-changing scenery and a driving motion, clickety-clack, clickety-clack, like the beat of the claves, lulling us with its happy, passionate rhythm.

"We have to do this again soon," Mami said on the last day, as we saw the spires of downtown Los Angeles poking up into brown, smoggy skies. When we disembarked at Union Station, we saw that this time, Papi was waiting for us.

3
hawthorne
(1964–1970)

Sixty-seven percent of boys between the ages of 12 and 18 incarcerated for murder are there for killing their mother's abuser.
—1999 statistic from
Men Ending Violence

FOR THE NEXT SIX YEARS, the only survival lesson that I learned was that none of the other lessons I had learned counted for much. There was no order in the universe that we inhabited except for that which Anthony Rivas Sr. decreed, when he decreed it. We were foot soldiers in his army; we were also the enemy. And these rules changed from moment to moment. We each learned to cope as best we could, even in matters of primal survival like eating and sleeping, which felt to me like catch as catch can, on the run, with a need to be on constant alert.

The tiger I had been in my night and daydreams seldom appeared; now I became more like the series of dogs, mainly German shepherds, that Papi, or Dad, as we called him now, brought home to terrorize along with us. This was also the era that brought me my defective talking G.I. Joe whose only phrase—I learned after several pulls of the string—was "I've got a tough assignment," the mission statement I adopted for life in the war zone.

With his reddish, thinning hair that had begun to show a bald spot on top, there was a losing battle being waged inside my father, as the part of him that was good, or wanted to be good, gave way, increasingly, to his demons. To my knowledge, his violence wasn't set off by drinking or drugs. If that had been the case, it might have been easier to predict his behavior and to stay out of his way when he was on a bender. Though I didn't have the psychological or criminal expertise to analyze him, I had plenty of clues that he was crazy, but that knowledge didn't help when the bullets started to fly. Part of his craziness, I started to suspect, was an act he put on to keep us all off balance. He was always in control, even after some of the worst explosions when he cried big elephant tears and wrung his handkerchief, begging for forgiveness for having lost control. Of course, he could and would explode with rage. But Dad was the most dangerous and deviant when he was in an almost Zenlike state, carrying out his every move with cold, methodical planning. To try to predict what he would do was folly. Even stupider was to try to humor or placate him.

This was evident at dinner one evening, not long after we had gotten to California, when, to our surprise, Dad was in a jovial mood, telling jokes and letting me and Tony chime in with laughter and our own funny remarks.

There was lots of humorous material in our new neighborhood of Hawthorne, a suburb of Los Angeles that was about five miles east of the Pacific Ocean, and close to Dad's job at North American Rockwell, including the characters who inhabited the six-unit pink building where our apartment was.

Our resident manager, Mr. Hyler, with the best comb-over I ever saw, was the king of offbeat characters, and had the bizarre habit of opening the door to our apartment without knocking, stepping inside, and then knocking on the door he had just entered through, as he asked, "Okay if I come in?" He drove a big white station wagon with a whip antenna that was attached at the back bumper, traveled the length of the car, and was secured to the front fender. Long before the era of car phones, Mr. Hyler pretended to talk on a pink Princess telephone that he kept on the floor of the passenger side. Weird.

"Stay away from that guy next door," Dad had warned us about our neighbor who claimed to own the apartment building. "He's a drunk." That was our father, protecting us from the unsavory neighbors.

Once when Tony stopped by to collect money for washing the next door neighbor's white Chevy El Camino, he found the guy standing at his kitchen counter eating a stick of butter. Our neighbor told Tony, "Coats the stomach for drinking."

Besides the characters we were getting to know, we started to develop friendships, something that we didn't have in Chicago, other than our occasional visits to El Club Cubano. In Hawthorne, our first friends were the Colemans—Jack and Lillian, from Argentina, and their two strawberry blond and freckle-faced kids Carol and Ronnie— who lived upstairs from us. Mami and Lillian Coleman struck up a lasting friendship, while Ronnie, Carol, Tony, Eddie, and I spent all of our free hours playing together, minus the time that I was on punishment.

Of all the friends and neighbors who must have heard the sounds coming from our apartment and suspected what was going on, the Colemans were the only ones who eventually tried to help Mami and us. Some of the sounds were misleading; the night that we were cutting up with Dad, our laughter probably made it seem like we were a happy, loving family.

Mami finished cooking and began serving us, starting as always with Dad's dinner. She came in from the kitchen carrying his plate, which had some sort of long, stinky vegetables that made Tony and me grimace and pinch our noses, cracking up.

Dad asked, "What's so funny? Why are you holding your noses?"

I said, "Those things on your plate are funny looking and they smell like a fart."

Tony and I sputtered into more laughter.

My father turned to the kitchen and barked, "Olga, bring me a couple of cans of asparagus and the can opener."

Dad opened the cans and put a can in front of me and one in front of Tony. "Eat."

"Sorry," I offered, "I shouldn't have made fun of your vegetables." No apology could have been more sincere.

"Let's go, smart-asses, pick up your forks."

We did as we were told and each spiked the first stalk out of the can. I took a bite and started gagging.

"If you guys throw it up, you'll eat that, too." There was to be no water to wash the slimy, waxy spears down and no other food to disguise the taste of cold canned asparagus. Smugly, Dad sat in his chair and watched us struggle. It wasn't the last time he forced me to eat asparagus, but it was the last time I tripped and fell on the trick of thinking it was okay to laugh and joke along with him. Tony and I did get into trouble at some point for smiling about something. When he barked, "Wipe those silly *greens* off your face," in one of his humorous mispronunciations, we lost it and laughed hysterically, subsequently paying the price.

On another night after dinner, in a much more restrained atmosphere after the three of us boys helped Mami clear the table and we all retired to the living room to watch TV, there was an authoritative knock at our door.

My father went to open it while the rest of us, without moving from where we sat, waited to see who it was. Dad bristled at the sight of a man and woman standing outside the door, the same couple who ran the group foster home near Chicago where Robert had been left. There was no mistaking the two-year-old child that the man was holding. My brother Robert, undoubtedly a Rivas, had the same angelic appearance but with more of a faraway look in his eye. Dad stood there, not saying anything, as the man said to him, "Did you forget something?"

Mami sat paralyzed, her eyes wide with shock, and when she stood up and started over, Dad quickly stepped outside and closed the door behind him. My mother held on to the wall to steady herself, hiding her face from us. When my father came back inside, some fifteen or so minutes later, no one dared ask what had happened and what was to become of Robert. At nine years old, I didn't put it together yet that Papi had skipped on the bills and legal responsibility he had for keeping my brother in private care, but I was old enough to recognize an abandoned child being held in that man's arms.

Later, Mami and my brothers couldn't recall that image, but I was tormented by it. My only solace was to tell myself that someday I would find him. Two weeks later a letter arrived that was addressed to "The Parents of Robert David Rivas," with the return address of Fairview State Hospital printed in blue and a picture of the institution embossed in blue. No one told me what was in the letter. But that name became a touchstone in the years to come that reminded me of one of my tough assignments.

Principal Blake of York Elementary School—where I was enrolled in fourth grade and Tony was in sixth grade—must have been tutored by Sister Ernie Banks in Chicago. His paddle was Paul Bunyan–sized and he did not believe in sparing it.

My reputation had been established in the early weeks of school as I worked my way to the top of the fourth-grade heap in tetherball and handball. With my virtually unreturnable slider in handball, I started taking on fifth and sixth graders. When a sixth grader moved in front of me to try to return my slider at one recess, I accidentally hooked my thumb in his pressed Oxford shirt, tearing off several buttons. For that, he knocked me back onto the blacktop and started punching me. Covering my face, I couldn't push him off me and in my desperation I called "TONY!" as loud as I could. Luckily, Tony was on the other side of the wall playing handball and flew to my rescue, lifting the kid off me and pinning back his arms. Swinging wildly, I got a couple of body shots in before Tony yelled, "Victor! Stop!"

By the time Mr. Blake arrived, the incident was over and nobody was pointing any fingers. Nonetheless, he let me know he had his eye on me. The sixth grader so happened to be considered the toughest kid in school. He never bothered me or Tony after that day, and for the most part, neither did other kids. Don't mess with those Rivas boys, I could imagine them saying, because if you mess with one you have to fight the other. The feeling wasn't a bad one.

My fourth-grade teacher decided that my playground reputation meant that I could not be a good student, despite my genuine effort and the interest I had developed in the newly instituted SRA reading program. In this color-coded system, students could advance to higher levels by reading one side of the card and answering questions on the other side. I moved through the colors quickly and was very proud and boastful about my accomplishments. When I reached the top level color, my teacher asked to see me at her desk. Thinking that she might present me with a ribbon or a medal, I was floored when she asked, "Victor, you've been cheating and looking at the key card, haven't you?"

"I have not!" I stomped my foot.

She asked me to reread a color card several levels below my current level and then she would give me the test. I refused. She asked me again and I refused again. She warned me that she was going to send me to the principal's office. Furious that she wouldn't believe me, I wouldn't budge.

Mr. Blake was waiting for me with a system of his own. He walked me into his office, sat down, and pulled out a three-by-five card. He rolled the card into his typewriter and wrote a few sentences. He got up and walked over to the wall and pulled down his paddle. I received three hard swats and was sent back to class, knowing full well that a visit to his office meant a call to my father.

That night Dad began by asking why I had cheated on the SRA program.

"I didn't cheat! I did the work and answered the questions on my own."

"You're lying, Bictor, and you know why? Because you're not mentally capable of doing the work you say you did. So now you're an *estupido* and a liar." Before I could argue, he knocked me around the room long enough to shut me up. Then he said, "Tomorrow, you'll start SRA over again at the lowest color."

Dad also had unpredictable, though fleeting, moments of compassion, like the night he came home after Tony and I had tussled over who was going to wipe Eddie's butt and who was going to wash the dishes. Dad had gone out somewhere while Mami, looking thinner and weaker than I had seen her before, had gone to bed after cooking dinner. She was getting a cold, she thought, or a flu, and had let us decide who would do which chore. In a footrace to the kitchen, Tony and I got tangled up and he, being bigger and stronger, pushed me aside, accidentally shoving me into a corner that whacked a gash in the back of my head. When I went in to see Mami and lay down on her bed, the blood gushed onto the sheets. Mami sat bolt upright. *"Ay Dios mio!"*

She ran to get supplies, soon succeeding in slowing the blood flow with a homemade ice pack. She then carefully applied Mercurochrome to the back of my head.

Dad arrived home a short time later. Assessing the damage, he calmly said, "We need to get to the emergency room."

The two of us took the short drive to the hospital. I needed nine stitches to close the cut on the back of my head. On the way home, Dad drove me to Clark Drugs and bought me a hand-packed ice-cream cone. We sat outside licking our cones.

When we got back to our apartment, he summoned Tony. He scolded him for the damage he had caused me and then slapped him. He turned and punched me in the stomach. He marched into his bedroom, closed the door, and pummeled Mami off and on for hours.

The rules changed, and I could sense that the world inside our apartment was growing darker. We rarely if ever had anyone over for dinner; our friends weren't allowed to play inside with us. Dad compensated for the thin walls that allowed us to hear our neighbors talking in their apartments as if they were having loud discussions by ordering us, all of us, to stand in front of him and endure beatings without making a sound. When we were incapable of doing this, he tied a gag over our mouths.

In one instance, Dad attacked Mami with a vicious karate chop to her throat that literally prevented her from speaking for a month. When her voice came back, it was no longer the melodic clear sound it had once been; from then on she spoke with a raspy and sometimes wheezy sound.

Dad's presence in the two-bedroom apartment made me learn to move quietly, speaking only when necessary. As soon as he left, I erupted, usually violating whatever punishment I was on and putting Tony in the uncomfortable position of having to report my actions to our father when he returned.

But just to keep us off-kilter, every now and then Dad suddenly became human—accessible, affectionate, even protective. "Go out and have some fun," he told me when summer arrived with the news that I had worked my way back up in the SRA reading program and passed. At first, I did so tentatively, but soon let go and enjoyed trips to the Hawthorne municipal pool, learning to skateboard on home-made boards, body surfing in the Pacific at nearby Manhattan Beach, and building and tearing down a series of tree forts on our apartment building's property. My brothers and I, along with Carol and Ronnie Coleman, invented our own version of the Slip 'N' Slide by watering down our oil-slicked carport. After rigorous play that often ended up with us ruining our clothes in the oil, we snuck over to our neighbors' plum tree and devoured every single plum.

The year 1965 also brought a slip 'n' slide of rock 'n' roll with more great hits from Elvis like "Crying in the Chapel" and hit after hit from the Beatles, who dominated airplay: "Ticket to Ride," "Eight Days a Week," and "Help!" were all released within a five-month period. Our anthems of this era, however, were anything recorded by the Beach Boys, hometown heroes who were

Hawthorne's only claim to fame. Their earlier hit "Be True to Your School" had special significance for me since I eventually attended the same three schools—elementary, junior, and senior high school— that the Wilson brothers had. This summer I couldn't get enough of "Do You Wanna Dance?" and "Help Me Rhonda" and "California Girls," songs that transported me through melody and beat to a place of safety and self-esteem that I didn't have the rest of the time.

Ironically, there was one week in August when, for the first time ever, home became safer than the world outside, according to Papi, after riots broke out in nearby Watts on August 11. A routine traffic stop triggered a literal firestorm of protest in the poor and oppressed African-American community as rioters took to the streets, looting and burning. From up in the trees in our backyard where we were playing, we could already see black plumes of smoke shooting up into the sky when Dad called, "You kids come inside, all of you."

Watching the news coverage that night, my father paced the floor, yelled back at the TV, and let us know we were not to go back outside until it was over. He warned us, "*These* people will kill you if they get a chance."

When nobody was looking, I snuck into the kitchen and confiscated a sharp knife that I placed under my pillow each night for the rest of the week as I tried to sleep with the constant wail of sirens traveling down Imperial Highway toward Watts. When it was over, there were thirty-four people dead, thousands more injured or arrested, and most of the buildings of the inner city were destroyed. In spite of the fear I had felt, there was another part of me that empathized with the rioters. At almost ten years old, I didn't connect to the issues of poverty, joblessness, or the lack of adequate housing and schools that had fed the flames of anger. But I did already have a bubbling sense of outrage over what felt like injustice to me, when those in power oppressed the powerless. Obviously, there was some kind of riot stirring up inside me.

For the time being, those impulses found their way into playground scraps. I began a habit of being a sort of reverse bully, keeping bullies in check. Since Tony moved to Hawthorne Intermediate to start seventh grade, and I was still in fifth at York Elementary, I was freer to act out without worrying that the reports would get back to Dad. My other outlet besides playground sports and fighting was finding ways to make people laugh. My clowning included lots of physical comedy, like the bit I borrowed from Larry of the Three Stooges for art class when I stuck a pair of scissors in the electrical outlet to see if I could get my hair to stand on end. The jolt of electricity *ZZZAPPPED* me all the way to the other side of the room. Or there was the lunch period when I leapt onto a bench and held up my Scooter Pie, advertised on TV to contain "eleven heavenly bites," and announced to one and all, "Wanna see me eat a Scooter Pie in one bite?"

Amid scoffing and cheering, I unhinged my jaw like a cobra and stuffed the pie into my mouth, raising my arms in triumph and chewing with full-body motion. The two circular graham crackers covered in chocolate and stuffed with a marshmallow core became, all at once, a giant sticky dry ball in my mouth, which I managed to swallow, but only halfway down my throat, where it expanded dramatically, cutting off my air supply. Still with my audience mesmerized, I jumped down from the bench and staggered toward my milk carton. Finding that I'd finished it already, I went from student to student, guzzling their milk cartons in desperation. Finally, the Scooter Pie dropped from my throat into my stomach. The sight of everybody laughing uproariously and applauding inspired me to leap back up onto the bench, and with milk dripping off my chin I again raised my arms in victory.

By the end of fifth grade, Principal Blake had a thick stack of three-by-five cards chronicling my misdeeds. Between getting paddled by him at school and what I was getting from Dad at home, my level of pain tolerance increased significantly. Mr. Blake never indicated that he suspected anything about my father's excessive force at home. That, after all, wasn't his job. On the other hand, he occasionally gave me a break and didn't call Dad after I'd gotten into trouble.

But in those instances, Mr. Blake also made sure I remembered the whacks he'd given me. Whenever I walked back into class after a visit to his office, my classmates turned to inspect my state to see whether or not I was crying. It became a contest for me to appear unscathed, even to smile. My bad-boy and clowning track records notwithstanding, I finished out the school year with passing grades, a report card that warranted only minimal punishment from Dad.

The end of the school year was followed by a move to a new apartment, a two-story affair with three bedrooms and a fireplace. Although we missed not having the Colemans upstairs, it was a vast improvement, what Mami considered the best place we had lived in. And with the help of God, I proceeded to earn the privilege of participating that summer in two lifesaving outlets, Little League and Boy Scouts.

Baseball was not only a sport I loved to play, it was also something I was very good at, giving me a sense of pride I honored with reverence for every aspect of the game. This was apparent, from the way I oiled my glove and shaped my hat to the impeccable way I wore the uniform. Before every game, I ironed my jersey and my pants. My sanitary socks had to be bright white; the exterior stirrup socks had to be high and perfectly taut. My secret tactic for accomplishing this was to sew a one-inch piece of elastic to the stirrup of the sock and then Scotch tape the rolled sanitary and exterior sock just under the kneecap. On one of the teams I later played for, the Colts, we wore white shoes like the Oakland Athletics. White baseball cleats were impossible to find at that time, so once a week without fail, I meticulously spray-painted my black cleats white.

"Thattaboy, Vic," Coach Leon Groshon said to me after one of our first practices when I made an adjustment he liked. No one had ever called me Vic before. Balding, with an easy smile and slight Southern inflection, Coach Groshon encouraged each of the thirteen players on the Orioles, including his son Jody, to feel special. I liked hearing him say my new nickname, which even my family members started calling me. Hearing "Thattaboy, Vic" was even better.

My field position that summer was at first base. Though I was left-handed and pitched as a southpaw, I batted right-handed. This was due to the fact that Dad made me learn to hold a fork with my right hand and taught me all sports as if I were right-handed. I boxed like a right-hander and kicked right-footed, which made me close to ambidextrous as an athlete. Being tall and big boned, with my unavoidable heavy Rivas thighs, I had the advantage of added power and torque with the bat. Early on, I had a tendency to overswing and I frequently struck out, but when I made contact it was usually a home run.

Once I learned not to pull my head in the direction of the swing, as Coach Groshon kept urging me, I became a pretty consistent power hitter.

"Bictor," Dad said to me after the end of that first summer season, nodding with approval, his yellowish eyes looking almost dreamy, "you could be a major league player one day."

Was he kidding me? Nope, he insisted. With my instinctual talent and that cannon for an arm that I was developing, he could see me going all the way. The compliment made me dizzy. Even though Tony was a great all-around athlete and also played Little League, on a different team, for once I didn't have to live up to his superiority. And for once Dad had given me a compliment that he didn't take back.

Boy Scouts was another saving grace. Our troop was well organized but not too militaristic, thanks to our scoutmaster, Mr. Casiano, a plumber by trade, who was a good-natured man with a terrific sense of humor. Some of our fellow scouts took themselves too seriously, but most of us were in it for the fun and camaraderie of the camping trips and jamborees. In the fall of 1966, shortly after I had started back at York Elementary for the sixth grade, our troop was getting ready to leave for a jamboree bringing hundreds of Boy Scouts together for a weekend of sports and other competitive and festive activities.

The week before, something I said or did wrong had caused Dad to air out an old phrase he liked to use with us. Putting the side of his hand just below his hairline, he said, "I've had it up to here with your bullshit. No jamboree!"

That meant I had to glumly watch Tony pack and get ready to go. As Dad headed out the door to go pay a visit to a neighbor, Tony with him, a benevolent whim struck my father. "You can go, Bictor, if you can get ready on time."

Overjoyed, I rushed around packing at the last minute. But I was in such a hurry that after I took off my underwear, instead of putting on a clean pair, I pulled on my Boy Scout uniform pants and tragically got my dick stuck in my zipper.

"*AYYYYYYYYYY!*" I screamed at full volume in a high-pitched, girly scream that brought Eddie, almost six years old now, running up the stairs to the bathroom to see what was wrong. "Vic, you okay?" he asked from outside the door.

"Go get Papi," I told Eddie. "Tell him to come home. It's an emergency."

The more I tried to unzip the zipper, the deeper my penis mashed into its teeth.

"Papi said he'll be over in a little while," Eddie called through the door when he got back.

"Go back and tell him that my dick is stuck!"

Moments later Dad arrived in the upstairs bathroom. He bent down for an inspection and said, "*Oooo.* You did a number on yourself, didn't you?"

I helplessly nodded yes as my father went to work yanking and pulling, causing my screams to grow louder and louder. The zipper wouldn't budge. A light came into Dad's eyes as he reached into the medicine cabinet and pulled out a double-edged razor blade.

My eyes must have looked ready to pop out of my head. Did I dare trust him?

"Now hold still and don't move, if you want to remain a man," he said in a reassuring tone of voice, carefully cutting away at the outside stitching of the zipper until he was able to peel the zipper open like a banana. My dick was bruised and cut, but free. Right then, he was my best friend in the whole world.

A very pregnant Mami had by now arrived home from the store and made it up to the bathroom in time to take over with her traditional role of applying medication. With my eleventh birthday having passed five days before, I had reached the age at which I wasn't comfortable letting my mother see me naked or exposed. But before I could do or say anything about it, Mami had Mercurochromed my dick. I spent the next few days at the jamboree peeing discreetly so I wouldn't have to explain myself.

"Victor, Tony," Mami greeted us at the end of the weekend, smiling over the head of a new infant at her breast, "this is your sister, Olga Barbara Rivas. Come and meet her."

Eddie stood by proudly and protectively, already well acquainted with the beautiful little girl, and First Daughter, who had arrived the same night that we left for the jamboree.

Mami noticed my bruised face and swollen eye. She had gotten a phone call from Daniel Freeman Hospital after I got stomped on by another scout's hiking boot during a rousing game of King of the Hill. Mami said her heart had almost stopped beating when the nurse first asked, "Do you have a son named Victor Rivas?" She had just come home from delivering her new child and thought in those horrifying seconds that she had lost a child. Much relieved that it was a scouting injury sustained in fun, she wasn't thrilled to see it now.

"I'm fine, Mami," I said, almost proud of the shiner. "Can I hold her?" I approached to meet Olguita, as we first called her before we switched to Barbie. Even though she weighed over nine pounds at birth, she seemed so small and vulnerable as Mami placed her in my arms. Tony had his turn next. Without Dad in our midst, an unspoken but certain feeling of love underlay our laughter and smiles at the pretty little blessing that God had wanted Mami to have.

Of course, a year later, in seventh-grade sex education and phys ed,

I found out that the process was a little more involved than that. Mami tried at one point to describe in writing what this period had been like for her—working eight hours a day at a factory, caring for three active boys, mourning the disabled fourth son she was not allowed to see, and suffering at the hands of my father—and she described how her fifth child had come into being. She said that she never knew if Dad was "sick in the head, sadistic, or simply a bastard" for the "randomly executed hitting, punishments, and torture that the kids and I endured." Mami said that if she were to write of each and every incident, she would surely run out of paper. But then she went on to say:

> He would publicly embarrass Tony and Victor, even hitting them in front of others. In the privacy of our home it was much worse, with Victor taking the brunt of the violence. He would hit this child as if hitting another adult, and he was a strong adult. He would hit me in my chest and on my stomach, which would knock the wind out of me. Also, he would hit me on my back, around my ribs. He would also hit me across the face and arms and so I began to wear dark glasses and long-sleeve shirts. I would tell my coworkers that I had tripped and fallen. . . . I became pregnant again, this time with Barbie. I was forced to continue having sex with him because he was a pervert and did not care whether I wanted to or not. I spent the entire pregnancy worrying about the child and whether it would be born healthy. I put myself in the hands of God and Saint Barbara, and thanks to them, a healthy baby girl was born in the Harbor Hospital. She was baptized in the old Mission of Santa Barbara in California.

Lillian Coleman had been trying to convince Mami for some time to go to the police. Not long after my sister was born, my mother must have called Lillian, who came immediately to pick her up and take her to the police station. Lillian, who spoke fluent English, translated for Mami. They both wanted to have my father arrested. The officers on duty informed them they could fill out a complaint, but beyond that there was nothing more that they could do. Lillian persuaded Mami to show them some of the bruising on her body beneath her clothing. The police still said, "We regret that there's nothing we can do; we have to catch him in the act."

The police actually told her, "Call us next time he's beating you."

In an otherwise dark and murky landscape of preadolescence, lit occasionally by siblings and baseball and Boy Scouts, a beacon of light known as Genie Hotez appeared in my life in the sixth grade.

My teacher that year, Mrs. Brooks, a pale-skinned woman with shocking red hair that she hairsprayed into a perfect helmet, never tired of comparing me to Tony, who had been in her class two years before. "Your brother was such a good student, so studious and quiet," she commented repeatedly. "Why can't you be more like him?" Sometimes I wondered if Dad had coached her to say that so they could chip away my individuality and self-esteem altogether.

Thank God for Genie Hotez. A transplant to California from somewhere cool like New York or New Jersey, she was a knockout, with brown hair, brown eyes, and brown skin. She had a deep raspy voice and a dazzling smile. But it was her body that made me weak-kneed in her presence. She had fully developed breasts and hips, with gorgeous legs that were enhanced by miniskirts and go-go boots. Athletic and competitive, Genie played endless games of tetherball with me on the playground, and though I snapped many a ball from its tether that went flying out onto Prairie Avenue, just to impress her with my strength, she won her share of the matches.

Because of my previous missteps with girls and because Dad was certainly no male role model, I had no idea how to tell Genie how I really felt; instead, I sat a few rows behind her in class and stared at the back of her head with secret infatuation.

As it turned out, our scoutmaster, Mr. Casiano, was Genie's uncle. That was the reason, as it so happened, that when Tony went on an outing with the Casianos to the Los Angeles County Fair—an adventure I couldn't attend because I was on punishment—when I looked outside, there was Genie Hotez sitting in Mr. Casiano's car.

"So, what did Genie say about me?" I asked the instant Tony got home, very late that night.

"Nothing." My quiet, studious, handsome brother shrugged.

"Nothing?"

"Well, it was, you know, a date. With me. Mr. Casiano set it up."

No one even knew that I liked Genie, but I was so furious with Tony and my scoutmaster and especially her that they were all traitors in my eyes. Beside myself, the next day at school I wrote and passed a nasty note to Genie, who promptly turned it over to Mrs. Brooks.

Betrayed again! Mrs. Brooks unfolded the note, read it, and threw me a dirty look as she sped out the door. None to my surprise, she reappeared moments later with Principal Blake, who walked directly toward me and snapped me up by the nape of my neck. Dragging me out of class and down the hall to his office, he finally turned and with a flustered, pained expression demanded to know, "Where on earth did you learn such a word?"

"What word do you mean?" I asked back.

"Kotex."

Instead of writing Hotez, to make fun of her because she had chosen my brother over me and had played me for a fool, I had used a word that I'd seen on a box of napkins that Mami kept under the bathroom sink. "I was looking for toilet paper and saw it one day and thought it sort of rhymed with Hotez, that's all!" I told Mr. Blake.

"You are a dirty little boy," he seethed and grabbed his paddle, whacking me so hard that I went back to class crying.

Genie wouldn't even look at me.

Heartbroken and confused, I had no idea why everyone was so outraged by the mention of the word "Kotex." This was not the first time I had gotten in trouble for using a word whose definition I didn't know. Earlier in the year, Mr. Blake had been standing right behind me when a couple of annoying girls were chasing me and I wanted them to stop. So I turned around and used, in English, a word Papi said all the time in Spanish, *puta,* a reference I understood only as an unrespectable woman. "Leave me alone, you whores!" I said assertively. Before I could gauge their reactions, Principal Blake hiked me up by my neck and dragged me into his office.

These words would also eventually be clarified for me in sex education class.

For the time being, I decided to swear off girls until I found something that made me as cool and irresistible as Davy Jones, or any of the other Monkees. Knowing that Dad would never let me take music lessons, because, as he said, "Baseball is your ticket to a better life, Bictor," the thought of actually pursuing an interest in music was too far-fetched. But suddenly that changed when I found myself staring up at a poster advertising a talent show that was being sponsored by a youth group at Saint Joseph's Catholic Church.

What could I do? What talent did I have? The question plagued me every time I passed the poster at church, where I regularly attended catechism class and mass in preparation for my confirmation. The prospect of being confirmed was meaningful to me mainly because it would give me a chance to honor my new idealized father figure, Gregory Peck. During one of my punishments, when Dad wasn't around, I had snuck downstairs and managed to watch all of *To Kill a Mockingbird,* which mesmerized me from start to finish. Relating to anything that confronted injustice, I was deeply moved by the story of a black man accused of a crime he didn't commit. The emotion and truth of the acting overwhelmed me, and the portrayal of Atticus Finch by Peck left an indelible impression on me. Finch's heroism in standing up for truth and righteousness was equaled by his devotion to his kids, Jeb and Scout. In my ongoing talks to God, I started praying to make Dad just a little bit like Gregory Peck. But even if that couldn't happen, I was going to take Gregory as my confirmation name.

"So what are you going to do at the talent show?" one of the kids at Saint Joseph's asked after I went ahead and signed up without specifying a talent.

The show was in a couple of weeks and I had to come up with something. Flashing for a second on our neighbor who had a huge rock 'n' roll record collection and several guitars, both electric and acoustic, I blurted those words out, "Electric guitar."

"You don't know how to play."

"Yeah I do."

A group of other kids gathered around and started laughing at my claims. One girl taunted, "You don't play and you don't own a guitar."

"I do too," I said calmly. "You'll see." I had not one clue as to how I was going to borrow a guitar from our neighbor, much less how I would play it.

Miraculously, he did loan me one of his electric guitars and a small amp. And at the appointed hour, much to the astonishment of the kid skeptics, I arrived at the parish hall with my rock gear, looking and acting very professional. Everyone appeared to be impressed, which threw me into a silent panic. Backstage waiting for my turn, I listened to a variety of talented youth—mostly singers and musicians—not knowing what I was going to do when it was my turn.

"Put your hands together for Victor Rivas!" the MC announced over the loudspeaker to a packed parish hall as I walked onstage with the guitar and amp. I was about to plug in to the little amp when a member of the rock band that was performing after the show called out from the audience, "Hey man, use our big amp!" Frozen and unable to respond, I stood facing the crowd. Someone yelled out, "Come on!"

After plugging in to one of the gigantic amplifiers, I tested the blaring sound by strumming an atonal chord. Making a bad face, I stopped and pretended to tune the guitar. BOOOOS and HISSES started slowly and then built as I did this several times. "Uh, sorry," I finally said, leaning up to a mike, "my guitar's out of tune," and I raced off the stage.

Unable to look anyone in the eye, I left and hurried home, crying and cursing myself all the way there. In general, I talked out loud to myself as a coping mechanism, just to keep myself company during stretches of isolation. The problem, I now understood, was that I was somebody special only in my vivid daydreams, the same imaginary world in which my father took me on outings every weekend—fishing trips, for example, during which we would have memorable father-and-son moments. These fantasies were so real I could smell the sea air and hear the waves lapping on the side of the boat. And when that possibility became too remote to dream about, I'd tricked myself into thinking I could turn my guitar-playing fantasy into a reality. The talent show disaster took me a long time to live down.

My redemption in the spring of 1967 was a discovery Coach Groshon made after practice at the start of my second season with the Orioles. "If anyone thinks they might want to pitch," he had announced, "stick around and miss the water break."

I was the only player who did.

Here too was another fantasy, of pitching like my great idol Sandy Koufax, the extraordinary southpaw of the Los Angeles Dodgers. Whenever the Dodgers were playing and Dad was out, I turned on the radio and listened intently as the incomparable Vin Scully called the game. When Koufax was on the mound, I stood in my room, imagining myself in his shoes, emulating him pitch for pitch. My setup was between our twin beds, with Tony's drafting T square as the pitching rubber, and a pair of socks transformed into a rosin bag and a baseball. Firing the balled-up sock into the side of the dresser, I pitched for as many innings as Sandy did, or unless Dad came home early to interrogate me about my day.

Oddly enough, when I took to a real mound for the first time that day upon Coach Groshon's suggestion, I had a feeling of familiarity, almost déjà vu. With each pitch, I became more confident. As a result, my pitching motion became more fluid and the catcher's mitt got bigger until that was all I could see. And with each pop of the glove and each "Jesus! Thattaboy, Vic!" I became more certain that I might have found my true position.

Coach Groshon got permission from Dad for me to come over to his house—where he had built a regulation pitching mound out back—so I could practice pitching with his son Jody. Training together, Jody and I could really bring the heat. Jody could throw a curveball along with his blazing fastball. I never threw a curveball in my entire pitching career but if I changed my grip, I had a natural slider and a rising fastball. But my fastball was nearly unhittable. Whenever Coach Groshon or Dad caught me, they would insert a hard sponge inside the catcher's mitt to protect their palms.

My velocity and occasional wildness had most Little Leaguers intimidated. I either struck you out or beaned you with a pitch. This would keep most batters off the plate. It was not uncommon for me to average twelve to fifteen strikeouts a game. With Jody and me alternating at pitcher, the Orioles became a tough team to beat.

My accomplishments as an athlete helped me salvage what remained of my self-esteem after I eked out only passing grades by the end of the school year. This was followed by an event of pride for Mami that summer when she became an American citizen. The accomplishment may have emboldened her to begin imagining an escape plan for her and us. But in the meantime, she filled out the necessary citizenship applications for Tony and me.

La Luchadora, she managed to accomplish this despite Dad's control of money, documents, and every single aspect that affected our family status. A few months shy of my twelfth birthday, I too could proudly say, "I'm an American citizen," and I had the official document to prove it.

A real American kid with serious potential as a pitcher, I rekindled a flame of hope inside myself that I would earn not only my father's praise, but his determination that I was worthy of something more important: his love. Maybe this was not a conscious goal, only a feeling that erupted in me after something happened to suggest that maybe he did love me, after all.

Dad had been unusually quiet on this summer late afternoon when, as he often had me do, I helped to wash and shine his motorcycles. Naturally, El Ciclón had to own at least a couple of bikes, and in this period he had both a Triumph and a BSA. My job, primarily, was to polish the spokes of the wheels with chrome cleaner, steel wool, and a soft cloth. Instead of his normal barrage of "*Idiota,* you missed a spot!" or "If you're going to do something, do it right!" he had only nodded with a "Not bad" as I went to put away the cleaning products.

"Wanna go for a ride?" he asked offhandedly when my back was turned to him.

I turned around to see if he was talking to me. "On the motorcycle?"

"Yeah."

"Sure!"

Galloping inside to take a quick shower, I passed Mami in the kitchen and danced gleefully, announcing, "Papi's taking me for a motorcycle ride!"

Mami shrugged her shoulders, started to say something, and then thought better of it, only rolling her eyes.

After I put on a pair of tight jeans and a white T-shirt, thinking I didn't look so bad, I heard Dad calling me to his room, "Bictor, *venga.*"

Nervous fear returned. He had obviously changed his mind. I had done something wrong. Some punishment awaited me. Dutifully, I walked into my parents' bedroom. In his hands, Dad held a black motorcycle jacket. "Put this on," he told me.

In awe, I slid into the jacket, checking myself out in his dresser mirror. Pretty cool, I'd say! Maybe even a little like Elvis.

"*Bueno,*" Dad asserted, throwing on a brown leather jacket as he said, "Let's go." But before I could get out the door, he stopped me. "*Bictor!*" Fear shot through me again. I turned back to him and in his hands were a pair of amber-tinted aviator sunglasses. "Put these on." He smiled.

Dad gave me a brief lesson on riding as a passenger on a motor-cycle. The most important thing to remember was to lean with him on the turns; if not, we would probably take a spill. He handed me a helmet, which I strapped on for the ride while he straddled the BSA, flipped out the kick starter, and jumped down on it a couple of times before it roared to life. After putting the back pegs down, he shouted above the engine roar, "Climb on! Keep your feet on the pegs." Then he pulled the clutch in, stepped down on the gearshift, and slowly released the clutch while he twisted back on the throttle. At last, we were moving.

Scanning the street, I wished desperately that someone I knew would be passing by and see me riding on the back of the BSA with my father, who, just as we pulled out of the driveway, said, "Wrap your arms around my waist."

We made a hard right out of the driveway and I, in my shock at this unprecedented experience, forgot what he had said and leaned left. "No, no, lean with me!" he yelled.

I nodded back in agreement and didn't make the same mistake again.

We drove through Hawthorne and were soon flying down the Harbor Freeway toward downtown Los Angeles. The vibration of the engine between my thighs, along with the wind pressing against my face, gave me a feeling I'd never had before. In a delayed reaction, I looked down and realized that in fact my arms were tightly wrapped around my father's waist. In spite of the shock of touching in a way that we never had in my life, I felt completely safe leaning against him, knowing he would protect me. I closed my eyes for a moment and felt free.

We blew past downtown and ended up in Pasadena, where we walked around, saying little but enjoying the quaint shops in the older section of town. Dad bought me an ice-cream cone and patiently waited as I savored it before we got back on the motorcycle and roared home as night fell and the glittering lights of Los Angeles twinkled as though just for me.

Rather than shutting my eyes and trying to steal sleep, as was my habit, I allowed myself to drift off this night. In my half-awake dreams, I saw our father-son relationship as changed. The future lay before me full of possibilities and adventures in which the two of us would shun work and school and go off together, riding around to different towns, maybe even different states; he would teach me to drive the motorcycle, and trust me enough to let me drive, as he sat behind me, holding on with his arms wrapped around my waist.

I woke up to my reality. Things had changed all right. They were worse. Much worse. Dad was shifting his tactics, getting ready to bring out heavy artillery. There was a new edict, implicit and explicit: Tell and you'll be killed.

We made another change in residence, leaving behind the nicer three-bedroom apartment and moving next door, to a small, dirty house with weeds six feet tall in the backyard. Before we moved in, Tony and I helped Dad clear out the weeds and paint the interior of the house, colors only someone with a Jekyll-and-Hyde personality, like our father, could have chosen. The room I shared with Tony had lavender walls and a black ceiling. The other rooms were either in the bright and festive purple family or dark and brooding in black and earth tones.

When we were cleaning out the backyard, Tony and I discovered a mechanic's pit, encased in cement and covered by a piece of plywood. A shallow well, made for a mechanic to be able to slide under a car and work on the engine from that angle, this pit was possibly the remnant of a gas station or garage, or perhaps had belonged to someone who worked on rebuilding cars. Since Dad was starting to dabble in rebuilding cars and boats, he appeared excited about our discovery, even though he preferred to use the carport alongside the house for his automotive projects. Tony and I were supposedly his mechanics in training, but what we mostly did was to hold the work light so he could see what he was doing. We also were required to put up with getting punched and having tools thrown at us if either of us accidentally allowed the light to spill onto his face and blind him or just missed the spot that he wanted illuminated. After all, goddamnit, if he was operating on a patient, one wrong slip of the wrench could be deadly.

Dad was a fairly impressive mechanic. Not surprisingly, while I knew how to identify the different parts of the engine, I learned very little about fixing them because of my hyper focus on properly aiming the light, while "Goddamnit, *idiota!* There!" was shouted at me. Inside, I was also chafing over the fact that the light had a hook on it that most people hung from the opened car hood. For several weeks in our newly painted psychedelic shack, Dad didn't see fit to use the mechanic's pit until one weekend when he decided to break it in. But not for its intended purpose.

The problem with being punished with such frequency was that I often forgot what I was being punished for. Sometimes when I was accused of doing something I hadn't done, I'd admit to doing it, knowing I would get pummeled anyway. The one thing I couldn't do was fall for the trick of agreeing that something was true when it was a falsehood known to the rest of the world. The more Dad pointed to the sky and insisted it was green, the more I argued that it was blue, and the more furious he would get. On the day in question, because I wouldn't agree with some crazy comment, he decided that I was to be punished while he took the rest of the family to Clark Drugs for ice cream. When I was younger Dad had left me in closets but as I got older and no one else was home to report on whether I'd strayed from my appointed cell, he had taken to finding ways to lock me inside. Once he tied me to a tree in the backyard, where our dog, Young King, was also bound.

This day, he had a better idea. Marching me to the backyard, he removed the plywood covering from the mechanic's pit and gestured inside. "Get in."

Refusing to show him how terrified I was, I obeyed his order. He replaced the other covering with a large piece of plywood that had several holes drilled into it for air. "Don't move," he barked, leaving for a

few minutes as I tested the lid. Once he was gone, I could easily lift it
and get out. But the next thing I knew, he had started up an old car he
was rebuilding and as the sound came closer, I realized that he was
going to drive it over the plywood that covered the mechanic's pit.

For the next several hours, I stayed in the pitch-black darkness, at
first quelling my terror by talking to myself, even having an imaginary conversation and yelling back at him, telling him what a piece of
shit he was and how much I hated him. Then I prayed and apologized for cursing, before asking God to send help soon.

That previous summer we had been visited by my father's older
brother, Jose Luis, his wife, his entire family of six kids, and an older
cousin from Spain. Uncle Jose Luis, a sugarcane engineer for C&H
Sugar, was being transferred to the island of Kauai in Hawaii and had
decided to stop off in California and visit us before making the move.
He and my aunt stayed in a hotel while all our cousins stayed with us.
They were all fun, intelligent, and attractive, especially my cousins
Maria and Carmen. I knew that nothing serious could happen with
first cousins but I had crushes on them, and did try to get in some
hugs that let me appreciate their buxom figures. They both seemed to
think I was cute and gave me some of the extra attention I so craved.

Dad took off a week of work to entertain our guests, picking up
the tab for everything and spending money like I'd never seen him
do. He was the consummate host, charming, fun, and easygoing. If I
had hoped that our relatives might find out what he had been doing
to us, Dad's award-winning acting ended those hopes. Of course, I
was taken off all punishment with the proviso that he would be keeping a close watch on me. We went to all of the local attractions;
Disneyland, Knott's Berry Farm, the Los Angeles Zoo, and the beach.
Only Mami was excluded from the festivities, because of work and
taking care of Barbie.

There would be a subsequent visit from my dad's cousin, a handsome young Catholic priest named Father Ernesto, who was a teacher
at Pace Catholic High School in Miami. At that time, my father had
been floating the idea of moving to Florida, and Ernesto, having

probably sensed that things were somewhat off in our house, suggested that he take Tony and me to Miami with him to get us enrolled at his school. Much to my disappointment, Dad thanked him but declined his offer.

In my isolation in the mechanic's pit, I remembered trying to hint to Uncle Jose Luis that I *really would like to get away from home sometime SOON* and visit them in Hawaii. Unfortunately that was never going to happen, but the mental images of escaping to Hawaii were so comforting they helped me curl up and go to sleep until Dad came home and let me out of the dungeon.

He may have apologized. He may have pulled out his handkerchief and wiped his brow as he explained that he was only trying to teach me, to make me better and stronger in the long run. My problem, he went on, wasn't just that I was stupid but that I was lazy. In fact, instead of asking him for money to pay for sports equipment, it was about time I got a fucking job.

A week later, I started delivering newspapers for the *Los Angeles Herald Examiner.* Every day, I rose early and rode my sturdy all-chrome bike a few blocks to a storefront. Several other sleepy-eyed boys joined me there as we folded papers. Then we loaded the papers into bags for our respective routes and took off. At the end of each month, I spent a weekend afternoon going door to door to collect from customers, receiving tips at pretty much every door.

"Bictor, it's good to see you taking some initiative," Dad congratulated me and presented me with a clear plastic bank he had gotten from his bank.

My clear plastic bank had columns for various coins, from pennies all the way up to half dollars, and in the back was a slot for paper currency. I could literally see my money growing. After almost filling it, I returned from school one day and found my bank empty. There was a piece of paper folded in the paper currency slot. Using the key that I kept in a secret hiding place in my dresser drawer, I opened the bank and retrieved the note. It read: *"I owe you $26.50, Dad."*

Shit! Talking to the wall, I confided in no one at all, aloud: "He took my money and he kept a key without telling me." Unfair, unfair! It happened again and again. Every time I filled up the bank, it would be emptied with IOU notes left behind. By the time he owed me close to a hundred dollars, money I seriously doubted I'd ever see, I decided to do something about it.

Unbeknownst to Dad, I went to my manager and begged him for a second paper route.

"Got to have parental permission," he warned.

"Well," I lied, "that, uh, would ruin the surprise. My Dad's birthday's coming up and I wanna buy him something real nice."

"Okay," he said. "You can have the second route on a trial basis. Make sure your deliveries are on time."

Every morning, I had to work twice as fast as before. I double-loaded my bike, draping one bag on the handlebars and another on the back book rack. During the week I could handle the extra weight, but it was tough to balance both bags on Sundays. Refusing to give up, I made my deliveries on time and my manager agreed to let me keep the second route.

To make sure Dad didn't suspect anything, I put the money from my first route in the plastic bank, which he emptied periodically. The money from the secret paper route I kept hidden between the mattress and box spring of my bed. When the house was empty, I would lift the mattress up and count my money. When I had gotten over a hundred dollars, it occurred to me that whatever I bought would have to be explained to Dad. But that didn't bother me because it was mine, and since it was a secret, he couldn't take it without permission.

One very hefty Sunday newspaper run almost did me in. It was my habit to pull a modest wheelie coming off the curbs, so that both wheels would land on the street together, lessening the impact. I had just left the storefront with both bags fully loaded when I came to the first curb. Pulling up and back, I saw my front wheel release from the bike and go rolling down the street. For a second, as if in a freeze-frame, suspended in air, my brain registered the sight of the wheel rolling away as I remained upright, teetering on the rear wheel. Then the front of my bike lurched forward and the front fork dug into the asphalt, launching me off the bike. I crashed into the street, tumbling head over heels. When I came to a stop, with a bleeding scrape on one elbow, I looked up and saw my papers everywhere. How was I going to wriggle out of this predicament? By hauling ass, I decided, as I ran down the street, retrieved my front wheel, repacked my papers, hand-tightened the loosened nuts and bolts, and kept on pedaling.

Toward the end of seventh grade, I came home from school one afternoon and found Dad, home early from work again, repainting our room. Nobody else was at home. Except for the furniture that had been piled to one side, the room was covered in plastic. Our twin beds were leaning against the wall. With a sinking feeling in the pit of my stomach and prickles of fear in my groin, I said, "Hey, Dad."

He turned with a cigarette in his mouth and paint roller in his hand. He just stared at me, with the slits of his eyes getting smaller by the moment and his lips getting tighter around the cigarette. Dad put his roller down and reached into his pocket. He pulled out a small wad of bills. "Where did this come from?"

I tried telling him the same story that I gave the paper route manager about wanting to surprise him with a special gift. But before I even finished the sentence he dropped me with a body punch. An eternity passed before I took my next breath. I stood up and began to tighten the muscles of my body for the next blow. "Follow me," he said, in a voice devoid of emotion.

We went into the kitchen. He pulled out a chair for me at the table and nodded toward it. "Sit there and don't move." He left the room as my ears followed his footsteps into his bedroom and heard his closet door open and close. When he returned, Dad was carrying a handful of neckties. He used two of them to twist and tie my left arm tightly behind me to the back of the chair. He took my right hand and strapped it down to the top of the table by my wrist.

A battle took place inside me between the terror I felt at not knowing what he was about to do and my will to steel myself and take whatever he had to dish out. My stomach, bowels, and very cells cringed, as though I could imagine the worst. But nothing prepared me to see him return to the table holding the meat tenderizer that Mami used to pound the skirt steaks.

Laying it down on the table, he sat and lit another cigarette. "One way or another we're gonna get to the bottom of this."

Fully ready to tell the truth, I opened my mouth, but before I could say a word, he whipped the meat tenderizer into the air and smashed it down onto the knuckles of my right hand. My reflexive scream made him reach over and clamp his hand over my mouth. "Keep quiet or this will get even worse."

I swallowed my pain and stared down, observing several small slits along my knuckles that had begun to bleed.

"Now tell me where the money came from," Dad asked, and then quickly added his familiar line. "Before you answer, just know, I already know the answer."

I told him the truth about the second paper route. "I did it because I was tired of you taking the money I earned." To acknowledge that was what he already knew, my father smashed my hand a couple of more times and left me sobbing quietly in the kitchen.

Dad returned in a few minutes with cotton balls, sterile gauze, white tape, and a bottle of rubbing alcohol. He poured the alcohol over my damaged hand. The alcohol hurt almost as badly as the blows that had caused the cuts that he was now disinfecting. He untied me and wrapped my hand in gauze and tape. He warned me not to tell anyone what had transpired in the kitchen or there would be hell to pay. "Go sit in the living room. I have to finish painting," he grunted.

The television had an old black-and-white Western on it, the rhythm and sound somehow comforting as it wrapped me in its flickering embrace. A short while later, Dad came in and announced, "That's it. You're forbidden to deliver papers anymore."

He never repaid me any of my money.

* * *

Every now and then, my survival sense of irony returned long enough for me to relish a contradiction that amused me, even if it did no one else. For example, at Hawthorne Intermediate, a large school consisting of only the seventh and eighth grades that combined the population of several area elementary schools, homage to the Beach Boys was so pronounced that we made boogie boards in shop class, for credit. Not bad. There was also a blind teacher who taught, of all things, typing. This struck me as hilarious at first, but my progress in his class demonstrated that I had learned to type by feel, not by looking.

With my reputation as a fighter established back at York, I was avoided by most of the tougher kids, who might have seen me as a threat. But in early 1968, I had a heated exchange with a large, gruff kid who usually kept to himself and sat in the back of typing class. We started to square off when our blind teacher put an end to it. We returned to our typewriters. As we left class, he walked over. He wasn't done with me and I wasn't backing down.

"I'll see you after school," I ventured. This was stupid. No one had told me what this kid had done in the past, or even what school he had come from. As most fighters can attest, knowledge of the enemy is helpful.

"Fine, I'll be there."

The bell rang, announcing the end of another school day. As I walked out of school, I could hear the shuffling of feet behind me. Word had somehow spread about the fight, and a large throng of students had elected to follow me around the corner to the designated parking lot. Just as we spilled across the asphalt, I could see my opponent coming around the other corner with his followers. For an ironic moment, I couldn't help but think of *West Side Story* (as I had back in Chicago with my tar-baby episode) and how the rumbles between the Jets and the Sharks always involved fistfights interspersed with fancy ballet moves. But that being neither here nor there for this tough assignment, I set my books down and walked into the middle of the circle of the students. My rival stepped into the circle too.

Unlike the fights that were sometimes only a war of words, ours began instantly. As he charged me wildly and I took a step forward to throw a left jab, my front foot slipped on the asphalt. Besides a growth spurt that put me eye to eye with Tony and with Dad, my feet had grown ludicrously large, to a men's size thirteen, which meant I had to wear men's dress shoes with leather soles. So as my leg slipped and then buckled backward, he tackled me around the waist and slammed me to the ground. Before I could react or recover, he climbed up my body, placed his knees on my shoulders, and pinned me to the ground, where I took a barrage of punches to my head. A couple of good hits to my mouth made it fill up with blood.

Something happened to me once I swallowed the blood and detected the iron aftertaste. Rage ignited through my body, powering me into an explosion. Letting him have it with both hands, I threw him off me and put him on his back, banging away in rapid fire, dripping blood from my lower lip all over my fallen opponent. Having wearied, he put up little resistance.

Like a gladiator, or so I imagined, I lifted my head to the crowd, waiting for the emperor to signal life or death with the flipping of a thumb. Several boys rushed me and pulled me off, saying, "That's enough, you won."

After I staggered to the bike rack and got onto my bike to ride home, I realized that my lower lip was so swollen it was touching my nose. Knots all over my head were popping up. Somewhat faint, I rode home slowly.

When the house came within view, I saw guess-who out watering the lawn, home early from work in what was becoming an almost everyday occurrence.

I sucked in my lip and clamped my upper row of teeth on it.

Dad wasn't fooled. He looked at me quizzically and said, "What happened to you?"

I opened my mouth to answer him and my swollen lip fell out of my mouth. "I was riding home on my bike and some little kids chased a ball into the street in front of me. I crashed my bike into a parked car, trying not to run them over."

Without any reaction, Dad dashed inside to get his keys and wallet and took me to the emergency room.

It took twenty-two stitches to repair the damage to my lip. Dad drove us to Clark Drugs to have ice-cream cones.

When we got home, and he closed the door behind us, he reeled around and said, "Bullshit. Your bike accident story is bullshit. You think I don't know you were in a fight and that you got your fucking ass kicked?"

"Well the other kid is worse off than me," I tried to argue.

Not listening, he pummeled me everywhere else that wasn't bruised already and when he was finished, he told me if I ever lost another fight, he would beat me worse. He sent me to my room and soon returned with a bag of ice.

It was ironic, I had to admit. Fucked up, but ironic.

And yet my irony couldn't assuage the torture I started to have in regard to the onset of puberty. By the second semester of seventh grade, I had a little mustache and a couple of hair strands growing out of my chin. Actually, the chin hairs were pulled out by Tony.

As usual, he was far superior to me in the maturation process, having begun sprouting facial and body hair at nine years old. Now in the ninth grade at Hawthorne High School, Tony had been shaving for some time and it seemed that I'd never be able to join him in front of the mirror. Sometimes I did body searches on myself with a magnifying glass. Whenever I'd been dumb enough to point chin hairs out to Tony, announcing that I'd need to shave soon, he'd pretend to inspect them and then grab the sole hair or two and yank it out, laughing, "Now you don't!" The hairs took forever to sprout again.

Then there was the new phenomenon of having a lot of erections. The really embarrassing ones were at school or on the bus that I rode sometimes. In the packed bus, which was jiggling and hitting potholes and dips in the road, with books on my lap, there was no avoiding an erection just from the bouncing and stimulation. Then, getting off the bus at school with an erection meant holding the books in front of my crotch until things settled down a bit. But here again, the profusion of miniskirts didn't help. In spite of dress codes, some skirts barely covered panties. I was not the only boy dropping my pencil on the floor with regularity, but I was probably the only boy who had as many crushes as I did. My romanticism and my insecurity made puberty all the more challenging, aside from the dysfunction of our home life.

To help me out with a little guidance in this area, it was my good fortune to have Coach Sweeney as my seventh-grade P.E. teacher. This was the first year that boys and girls were segregated for P.E. We changed into gym clothes of shorts and T-shirts in a small locker room that had no showers, hurrying out into the gym with the buoyant encouragement of Coach Sweeney. A kooky guy, Sweeney looked like a marine drill sergeant, with a high and tight crew cut, and spoke in a loud voice, always referring to us by our last names. One of his goals for this class, he announced early on, was for all his students to win the Presidential Physical Fitness Award, inaugurated by the late John F. Kennedy. I was usually at the top of the class in events like sit-ups, push-ups, broad jump, ball throw, and running, but the muscularity of my lower body always gave me trouble with pull-ups. No matter how strong I would get or how hard I trained, the wiry guys would always have that over me.

Between Coach Groshon encouraging me with "Thattaboy, Vic!" on the baseball diamond and Coach Sweeney's loud "You can do it, Rivas!" I was able to cope with the probability that I was going to get a rotten report card at the end of the year. But Coach Sweeney's two-week segment on "health" (code for sex ed) was what made the year at school worthwhile.

Without changing into our gym clothes, we were ushered into Coach Sweeney's classroom and told to take our seats. What confronted us on the chalkboard was two detailed charts of the human anatomy, one female and one male, private parts included. Before too many of us could make lewd comments, Coach Sweeney grabbed a

stick and pointed to the genitals of the male chart and asked if anyone could tell him what this area was called. No one answered or
raised his hand. "Now, come on, you guys have names you use. You
won't get into trouble for telling me what they are."

A series of euphemisms were mentioned—dick, cock, one-eyed
trouser snake, balls, nuts, family jewels, and so on—as the room
erupted with shouts and laughter. Coach Sweeney then began pointing at specific areas and saying the name of the area and describing
what the function was. One kid in the back of the class kept making
smart-aleck comments. Coach Sweeney turned to him and said,
"How's your scrotum?"

The kid rubbed his chin and said, "Pretty good."

Coach Sweeney then pointed to the sac that holds the testicles.
We howled with laughter, most of it directed at the smart-aleck in the
back.

When Coach Sweeney moved over to the female genitalia the
room became still, almost reverent. He described all the changes that
a woman's body went through during puberty and pregnancy. He
told us about the menstruation cycle and that a lot of the girls in our
school were either menstruating regularly or getting ready to start.
He went into great detail about the discomforts and emotional
changes that women go through during their cycle. With his eccen-
tric and upbeat manner, he explained, "When girls or women are
having their 'periods' they have to wear belts with sanitary napkins
called Kotex."

Ay, Dios mio! No wonder everyone at York Elementary was
repulsed by my changing Genie Hotez's name to Kotex. It made complete sense to me and I felt worse for being so insensitive. Coach
Sweeney really encouraged us to be sensitive. When we got older, he
promised, girls would like us more if we listened to them and were
sensitive to their moods. Since the belts and napkins were worn
under their clothing, Coach Sweeney advised us to be nice if we saw
a girl with a little bulkier private area than the day before.

A few days later, one of the girls I liked a lot had on a pair of tight white jeans, and sure enough I noticed that she was puffy down there. Before I wouldn't have known what to say, but now I did. "How are you feeling?" I said, with concern. "Are you all right today?"

"What do you mean?" she replied.

"I was just wondering, are you having your period?"

I had no time to brace myself for the vicious slap she gave me. I was left there, holding my face, while a nearby group of boys laughed derisively. How could I explain that I was trying to show a little empathy for her possible discomfort? She ran off in tears before I could apologize.

With flirtation spreading all over campus and couples starting to hold hands, swapping Saint Christopher medals or stealing kisses in the hallways, my progress with the opposite sex continued to be hampered by ignorance. While other boys bragged about how certain girls liked them and who they got to feel up, I was mystified. What signal did a girl give that she was interested?

A tiny miniskirt wearer who sat in front of me in homeroom class seemed to be flirting. A pretty, slender blond, she had a habit of bending backward and draping her hair on my desk, giving me a free look at her modest cleavage. Oh, that was the signal, I was told by some of the boys in my class; that was the signal that she wanted me to touch her breast.

"Nah, I don't think that's what she means," I argued.

"That's what it means," one of them said. Another boy added, "If you don't touch her breast, it's an insult. She'll think you're insensitive." A third said, "I dare ya, Rivas. Don't be a homo."

Against my misgivings, after she leaned back and swished my desk a few more times, I reached around and grabbed one of her breasts. With catlike quickness, she recoiled and jabbed me in the arm with her pencil. The lead broke off and remained permanently, a reminder that adolescent boys can't be trusted as authorities on what girls really want. I apologized profusely, but she stopped talking to me.

The obsession with girls got worse when the weather started heating up and many of us began congregating at Hawthorne municipal pool, where I spent most of the time gawking at the bikinis. At last, I found that when we played chicken, because of my physical size, a lot of the girls wanted me to be their partner. In heaven, I would swim underwater between their legs and lift them up on my shoulders, and the battles would begin. It wasn't only that I enjoyed feeling their smooth feminine legs and warm, soft bodies, it was also that I was unaccustomed to being touched or touching someone in any way that wasn't combative.

But I was conscious of being respectful in every way that I could be. To my surprise, before I finished my twelfth year, I had a sexual encounter that a girl initiated. I think. An older girl from the neighborhood had borrowed a bike, and when she came to return it, she walked with me into the garage. She put the kickstand down on the bike and turned around to leave. We just stopped and stared at each other. She closed the distance between us and leaned in. Before I knew it, we started mashing our bodies against each other. The door was still open, so I pushed it closed with my foot. In the heat of the moment I can't recall how our pants and underwear ended up at our knees. I pressed against her and came instantly. I was so embarrassed that I grabbed my pants and pulled them up. She did the same and ran out of the garage. We never even kissed.

There may not have even been any penetration. But whatever it was, for the next two years we could barely look each other in the eye without turning away. Though this didn't put an end to my preoccupation with the opposite sex, other concerns definitely took precedence.

Before the end of seventh grade, we made yet another move, this time to the house on Oxford Street that was to be our last residence in California. Two blocks east of the Hawthorne Municipal Airport, the house was directly under the path of the small planes as they came in to land.

A few miles north on Prairie Avenue, the Fabulous Forum was

being built. The Forum was going to be the new home for the Los Angeles Lakers. Sometimes, I snuck out on my bike and rode over to watch the construction, less fascinated by the building process than needing to get away from the increasingly crazy shit that was going on in our house.

Dad had begun working the swing shift, from 4 P.M. to 12 A.M. That meant he was usually asleep in the morning when I left for school, but still at home, waiting to interrogate me, at the end of the school day. At the Oxford house, Dad's habit of spending hours on the toilet was ritualized to the point that we referred to the bathroom as *la oficina,* The Office. Without being told, whenever I got home from school I reported to the bathroom. Dad had bought a fifty-foot extension cord for the telephone so he could make calls from his throne. With his underwear and pants down around his ankles, he talked on the phone, read the paper, looked through the classified ads for boats and miscellaneous junk to buy, studied stacks of self-help books, worked crossword puzzles, and called out orders to Mami, Tony, Eddie, and me, whether it was to bring him more Cuban coffee, serve him his breakfast, or perform any chore he desired.

Tony and I were summoned to his side one afternoon and presented with a book by L. Ron Hubbard on the subject of "cyber cybernetics." Dad thumbed through it, stopped seemingly at random, and said, "I want each of you to read this chapter and be ready for a quiz tomorrow."

That night, after Tony read the chapter, I did my reading assignment and found myself reading the same passages, over and over again. I had no fucking idea what this book was trying to teach me.

As promised, we were called into the bathroom the next day. Dad seemed genuinely interested in our synopsis. He looked at me first, and asked, "Bictor, what did you get from it?"

"Well, I thought that, um, that, um . . ." Turning to Tony with enthusiasm, I said, "Oh, you know, what was that, ah, we were talking about?" Dad turned his attention to my brother.

Fourteen-year-old Tony said very somberly, "We both found the chapter interesting and insightful." It was clear to me that Tony was also totally baffled by the book.

Dad waved us both away, unimpressed.

In his darker moods, after he had been sitting for hours, he occasionally lifted up to show us the red ring on his white ass left by the hole in the toilet seat. "You see what you're doing to me!" he'd shout, as we gaped at his ugly butt. "You see what you've driven me to!"

Dad saw other women, including a lady he had taken with us once when Tony and I went with him to see Yosemite. I didn't mention the woman to Mami. We also knew that when he wasn't working, he'd dress up and go out on the town without an explanation. When he started to look a little middle-aged, he reacted by going on a strict diet and exercise regimen, adapting his look to include bell-bottoms and Nehru jackets, with big gaudy fake medallions and, on occasion, a kind of flattering Beatles wig. He bought an eight-track cassette player for the house with a collection of eight-tracks, including Cream, Jimi Hendrix, Brazil 66, and Nancy Wilson. Watching him dance to this music—as he danced to any genre of music—was an exercise in restraint, especially when Dad threw one leg forward and started doing a variation of the twist. After a few beats, he'd start clucking with his tongue, put one arm over his head, and make small circles, like a cowboy trying to lasso a calf. Finally, the front leg would come off the floor and he would balance on his back leg. Grooby! Grooby! Outasight! Sockitooomeeeeee!

Dad was clearly on a self-improvement kick. Besides a visit or two to the company psychiatrist at work—something I knew about only later—he exercised at the full gym at North American Rockwell and, long before the yoga craze of later eras, started practicing yoga. Everywhere. On the sand at Manhattan Beach, he stood on his head and folded his legs into the lotus position. We were not allowed to leave his side during these demonstrations. Thankfully, none of our friends walked by as Tony and I sat glumly while our dad posed for hours.

A few times, I found my father meditating in the bathtub. In an imitation of some kind of hippo, he filled up the tub and submerged his whole body, with only his nostrils above water. The time I heard him accidentally go under and swallow a good amount of water gave me a hearty laugh.

The stranger he became behind closed doors or just with the family, the more outgoing and sociable he managed to be outside our home, and he even invited some of his teammates over from the men's baseball team he joined. Sometimes he had Tony play on the team as well. If someone who didn't know what was happening stopped by on those occasions, they wouldn't have believed him capable of hurting anybody, much less his wife and children. Many of our neighbors and their kids thought Dad was the greatest. In a festive mood my father liked to round up kids from families like the Pilars, the Abrahams, and the Guerreros, all my friends, load everyone in the Impala station wagon, and treat everyone to ice cream.

It didn't seem to faze any of my friends that I rarely got to go along. When I tried to tell someone like Greg Guerrero who Dad really was, he and the others would tell me I was full of shit. They had no idea, I pleaded, while my old reputation as the boy who cried wolf or who bragged that he could play the electric guitar caught up with me.

But how could anyone really know? When others weren't around, the house was locked and the curtains were rarely opened. We had been programmed and trained not to cry, not to make a scene. Dad stepped up his assaults on Mami and on me, maybe because I had put myself in his path to stop him one too many times, or for other reasons. In several instances, he attacked her when I wasn't around, and went after me when she was gone.

If there was any punishment Mami most despised, it was being put in cold water. That was what Dad did one afternoon, not long before we got home from school, just after Mami put Barbie down for her nap. Dad fought my mother and dragged her in her clothes and shoes, threw her into the shower, and with her screams unleashed, turned on the freezing cold water. Because she screamed, he blasted her with scalding hot water. Alternating between freezing and burning, he waited until she stopped screaming and then turned off the water. When Dad saw her huddled into a squat and shaking violently, he told her that he would be right back and went to the kitchen to get ice so he could fill up the bathtub. The second he left the bathroom, Mami raced for the front door and ran down the street screaming at full volume, her wet hair and clothes plastered to her body. At a time of day when many were at work or at school, her calls for help were unanswered, until, a block down the street, she saw an opened door and ran in. An elderly gentleman was home and he called the police.

By the time they arrived at our house, my father had shaved, showered, and was dressed impeccably, as usual. Still shaking with terror, looking like a drowned rat, Mami came back inside when one of the two policemen pulled Dad onto the front porch. "Sorry, Officer," my well-groomed, charming father confided to the policeman. "As you can see she's got some mental problems. We won't disturb you again. I'll keep things under control."

The two officers exchanged glances, as though not believing him completely. This was their third call to the house. The other one warned him, "Next time, we'll arrest you."

Such was the description of events that Mami gave me later that day when I got home from school. My reaction was a physical one, a flow of anger inside me that ran like the shower he'd blasted on Mami, from freezing to burning. Why he did this to her was beyond the limit of my understanding. Mami did everything that was expected of a wife and mother and more, and brought home a paycheck. There were times when I thought that maybe I deserved the punishment that he administered, but I had always known, instinctually, that it was wrong to violate a woman. I couldn't understand why the police didn't arrest him. If they had seen the marks he had left on her chest from the steel hairbrush he had started using for beatings, they surely would have had to arrest him.

Perhaps if I went to the police they would do something to help us. This thought came at a time when I was sliding into a new helplessness, especially with the reality that the school year was coming to a close and I was doing poorly, mainly because the various stresses prevented me from concentrating. By May, a major chip had formed on my shoulder, and though I had stayed out of trouble that would have sent me to the principal's office, that changed on a day when I was undoubtedly looking for a confrontation with someone, anyone.

"That's it!" one of my teachers finally exploded. "You will not disrupt this class. Take your desk and go sit on the balcony."

Not saying a word, I grabbed my desk and stormed out angrily. Once I got out to the stretch of cement on the second-story balcony, instead of putting my desk down and sitting at it, I went to the railing and heaved the desk over it, sending it crashing to the pavement below. My reward was a trip to the principal's office, a three-day suspension, and Dad's company at home. He called in sick.

The beatings continued for two days. He took breaks, ordering me into the kitchen to make him some Cuban coffee, and he even napped between the beatings, which had to be tiring him. At twelve, not only was I his height, I was also around 160 pounds and could flex whatever part of my body he was attacking, enough so that I could take most of his body blows and barely wince. Midway through the first day, he came into my bedroom wearing a black glove, with the choke chain that belonged to our new German shepherd, Van Auckland's King Anthony, also known as King (like his predecessor), wrapped around his hand.

Obviously Dad's bare hands had begun to hurt from punching me, so this was his new technique, an implement he'd also use on Mami and my brothers. Dad was excruciatingly careful to punch me only in those body parts typically covered by clothes, and the blows from the choke chain left welts and bruises everywhere he landed them. At the end of the second day, just before it was time for the rest of my family members to come home, he ordered me into the kitchen, where he removed a steak knife from a drawer, held it over the gas flame of the burner, and placed the blade on my belly, where it burned an imprint onto my flesh.

When I went back to school, two days later, I was limping and in an incredible amount of pain. For the first few periods, I felt the waves of resentment and hopelessness battering inside me. At the start of lunch period, with no one watching me, I snuck off campus and walked as fast as I could, still struggling, to the police station.

The first detective that interviewed me appeared concerned but didn't see what he could do for me.

"No!" I argued when he started to send me away, "let me show you. I want to show everyone here what I'm talking about!"

He agreed and led me into the adjoining office, where several police officers stood by as I took off all my clothes. They seemed to acknowledge that I needed them as witnesses. As I stood there naked with huge tears of humiliation streaming down my face, I looked at their faces. They were genuinely shocked by what they saw. It was all there. The bruises, welts, cuts, scars, and a few burns. Saying nothing, I hurriedly put my clothes back on and waited to be rescued.

"That's what my father's doing to me, my other siblings, and my mother," I reminded them. Speaking urgently, I pleaded, "Now, go to my house and arrest him, he's at home right now, and get him out of there for good." That was it. The moment I had spoken those words, I felt clear, for the first time in my life. I wanted him gone.

The officers looked somewhat uncomfortable. "You don't understand how this works," one of them explained. "What happens is that you can fill out a complaint and we'll go out and have a talk with him."

"You don't understand," I came back desperately. "If I fill out a complaint and you don't arrest him, he'll kill me as soon as you leave!"

The first detective apologized, saying that there really was nothing more they could do. After all, he added, "This is a private family matter."

For the rest of the day at school and on the walk home, I searched my soul and talked out loud to myself and God. A plan of last resort had made itself known. Since I had come to the conclusion that no arrest would be made unless he killed one of us or we killed him, there didn't seem to be any alternative.

That evening, after Dad went to work, I sat down at the kitchen table with Mami and Tony. The stuttering tick of the clock on the stove was all that could be heard above my quiet voice. Mami, about thirty-nine years old, looked thinner and more exhausted than I'd maybe ever seen her, but appeared relieved and grateful when I explained what I was going to do. Tony kept his eyes down, not letting me see what he was feeling. But when I put it to both of them, asking, if I got a gun and killed Dad, "will you back me up and say it was self-defense?" without hesitation both Tony and Mami nodded yes.

In the gray days that followed, during a southern Californian seasonal disorder in late spring when the marine layer rolls in from the ocean and lasts all day, I went in search of a gun. I canvassed my friends, asking who, of their fathers, owned a hunting rifle or other sort of firearm. The idea was to find out who owned one and then to go steal it. No offspring of gun owners volunteered that information. In later eras, I could have walked down the street to any corner and bought anything from a heavy-duty handgun to an AK-47. But fortunately, though there were plenty of guns around, I couldn't get my hands on one. If I had, there is no question that I would have used it regardless of the consequences.

My focus on killing Dad became all-consuming but the image of bludgeoning him or stabbing him was too violent, too personal; a gun was the only way. Mami made a plan, not telling me, to pour gasoline on the bed and light him on fire. But every time she came close to doing it, she couldn't muster the courage to follow through with us in the house. Finally, after what she saw happening to me, my mother decided that she would kill him, also as a form of self-defense, by stabbing him when he slept. She expected to go to jail, but saw no other way to protect her children. Mami picked the date and time, did several loads of laundry and ironed all our clothes, cooked food

for a week, and readied her weapon. In Dad's latest binge of new hob-
bies, he had taken up scuba diving and had a monstrous Aqua-Lung
knife that he wore strapped around his calf so he could battle the
ocean life, or just look like a real scuba diver. A foot in length, the
knife—which later played a significant role at a turning point in my
life—weighed five pounds and had a hammer head for such tasks as
knocking off the abalone that crusted on rock formations.

At the appointed moment, as Barbie napped in her crib and Dad
slept in their bedroom, the rest of us at school, Mami tiptoed down
the hall, silently removed the knife from the hall closet, unsheathed
it, and tiptoed to the side of the bed. Mami raised the Aqua-Lung
knife, with its point targeted at the neck of Anthony Rivas, her husband and tormentor for almost fifteen years, and in the split second
before she plunged the knife into him, the doorbell rang.

"Mami!" Barbie called out from her bedroom. "The door!"

With her concentration broken, my mother lost her will. Barbie
had saved Dad's life.

A few months before that took place, we had all been at home
when Barbie either climbed or fell out of her crib and was crying.
Dad marched into the bedroom to thrash her, a two-year-old toddler.
Before he had a chance, however, Mami, Tony, Eddie, and I swarmed
into the bedroom and stood ready to attack Dad as a unit. He backed
down, shoving past Mami with a grunt, saying, "Fix that goddamn
crib, why don't you?"

Shortly after our various plots to end our nightmare had been
foiled, we came to the conclusion that the authorities would never
help us unless one of us died. My mother made an attempt on her
life, her second after an earlier failed attempt in Chicago. When Dad
couldn't rouse her from sleep one morning and found the empty pill
bottles that she had not done much to hide, he yelled for Tony and
me to come to the bedroom immediately. Mami simply appeared to
be asleep. "Bictor, go fill the tub, make it lukewarm!" he ordered me.
"And then come back here."

When I returned, Dad and Tony were pushing and tugging on

Mami, calling to her as if she was somewhere far away. "Olga! Wake up!" Dad shook her. Tony said, "Mami, wake up, wake up!"

She didn't move.

Under Dad's instructions, the three of us carried her into the bathroom and placed her in the tub, fully clothed. Her face looked so peaceful, almost smiling. Knowing nothing about the pills, I looked for marks to see if Dad had knocked her unconscious, but finding none, decided she must have passed out from utter exhaustion. Slowly, very slowly, she came around.

"What happened?" I asked, days later.

She looked away wistfully, the dark circles under her eyes not much improved. "I just wanted to rest, *mijo*," she said. Somehow, someway, she told me, she had just wanted to get away from the madness, and had swallowed all the pills that lined one end of the dresser in their room.

The sealed report card handed out on the last day of school didn't make it home with me. On the way there, I tore open the envelope to see what I feared: two D's and the rest C's. Already in a fairly suicidal state of mind myself, I reverted to something I'd done back in Chicago and ripped up the report card, disposing of it in a trash can.

With no game plan, I was met at home by Dad at the kitchen table. Dressed and ready to go to work with his photo I.D. security badge that he was required to wear at North American Rockwell, he was drinking his Cuban coffee and smoking a cigarette. For a second, I recalled the tour he'd given me of his work, and how impressed I had been to learn how Dad's company was involved in aerospace and military technology. The computers that he worked on were massive and were all lined up in endless rows in a giant building. In that setting, I remembered walking through the building with him, meeting the other men, and feeling so proud to be his son. No more.

"Where's your report card?" Dad asked.

The lie I fabricated came out of nowhere. "The school's gonna

mail it in a couple of weeks," I explained. "It's because of my participation," and I elongated this word, which I had probably just learned,
"in a special mathematics program. I heard that the grades hadn't been
tabulated yet, so the school will send them as soon as they're in. Soon."

Impassive, Dad called for my brother. "Tony, get in here."

Tony came into the kitchen and Dad made me repeat my story
about the special mathematics program I had been selected for. Tony
couldn't keep a straight face, much to my anguish. When he started
laughing, Dad joined in. This was not a case of laughing with me;
they were laughing at me. When my father had enough, he plucked
up his keys and walked out.

Tony waited until he was sure Dad had pulled out of the driveway before he turned to look at me with his big soulful eyes. He
shook his head.

"Fuck off!" I barked and stomped into our bedroom, and sat
down on my bed. I rifled through old imaginary files in search of
daydreams to transport me from this place. I had a conversation with
my imaginary jury, polling them and asking what they would have
done. I tried the game of acting out different dramatic ways of dying,
something that would come in handy later on. Nothing worked.
How was I going to last the next several hours isolated, punished,
wronged?

That night it turned out not to be hours, but only about thirty
minutes before I heard the jingling of keys and began to panic. Like
Pavlov's dog, I responded to the jingling of keys as a trigger to anticipate being hit. The same response happened when Dad removed his
watch, which was a special trigger to let me know that the interrogation and beatings that followed would not be spontaneous. They
would go on until he heard what he thought was the truth, whatever
it was that he had conjured up in his head. Rather than have him torture me at length to get whatever confession he wanted, I would
often invent elaborate tales of my misbehavior. But in this instance,
as he returned, evidence of my dismal grades in hand, I was dead to
rights. Dad saw to it that I remembered his participation in the many

days-long beatings and groundings that followed. I began another summer isolated in my bedroom, sitting on the end of my bed.

Baseball continued to be the only haven that Dad hadn't barred me from. And this summer I was in top form, close to unhittable as a southpaw pitcher, and swatting numerous home runs out of the park from my right-handed batting stance.

But on one night around this time, even the knowledge that I was scheduled to pitch the next day wasn't enough to keep me from trying to permanently escape from our war zone. This incident had begun with a tussle between me and Tony that resulted in an accidental foot in my nose. Instead of trying to stop the bleeding, I went into my room and punched myself several more times in the nose. Gushing blood, I curled up in bed and went to sleep.

I woke up, groggy and weak, with Dad shaking me. He had arrived home from the swing shift shortly after 1 A.M. and had looked in on us. Seeing that my bedsheets were soaked in blood from the waist up, he was convinced, as he later remarked, that someone had stabbed me. Dad called for Mami. Together they cleaned me up as he asked what had happened. He took my lie, that I had tripped and knocked my nose on the bathroom doorjamb, at face value. As they debated over whether to take me to the emergency room, I piped up, "I'm all right. I just want to go to sleep."

Though I woke up weak and pale the next morning, Dad insisted he take me to my game. Interestingly enough, he had been to only a couple of my games; since he so rarely complimented me but had to find lots to critique, I preferred it that way. This day, however, after I ate and put on my uniform, he assured me, as we drove to Stark Field, that he would help guide me through.

In the Office, he had recently been reading a book on self-hypnosis and had begun practicing at home. That was going to be how he was going to get me through, by putting me in some form of a hypnotic trance.

I felt light-headed on the mound and I was having trouble controlling my pitches. The parents and other fans were yelling words of encouragement, but the only voice I could distinguish was coming from Dad up in the bleachers: "One, two, three. Breathe. Relax."

I walked the first three batters and hit the fourth. Coach Groshon had seen enough. Making a beeline for the mound, he pulled me. He moved me over to first base, where I began to have trouble just standing. The crack of the bat alerted me to a grounder coming my way. I was able to bend over to catch it, but when the ball took a short hop in front of me, it recoiled and hit me in the nose. With blood spurting again and blurry vision, I left the field, done for the day. Dad drove me home, confused as to why his hypnotic suggestions hadn't pulled me through.

This debacle wasn't the last time I attempted to kill myself. On a brighter note, I returned to my next game with a vengeance that sustained me through my best season ever. Besides the trophies and ribbons that I'd accumulated throughout the three regular seasons I'd played so far, this year I was eventually selected as an alternate to the all-star team. As part of the team, I was proud to represent the Hawthorne Little League in its journey to achieve the ultimate dream, a trip to the Little League World Series in Williamsport, Pennsylvania. Though we didn't go all the way, we made it out of the Los Angeles regional and traveled up to Lompoc, California, where we were eliminated. I came home with three more trophies and a beautiful red all-star warm-up jacket, complete with my name on it, and badges memorializing the different wins that season. Nothing I had ever owned meant as much to me; I even wore it on warm southern California days.

After earning a reputation for less than admirable reasons, these awards reminded me that there was a way to earn a different kind of reputation. Other kids I knew tossed me nods and an occasional compliment when we passed on the street. Adults rolled down the windows of their cars sometimes to yell, "Great game the other day, Vic!" before driving on by.

And what I loved best about the jacket and the trophies, like my talent for the sport, was that I believed Dad could never take them from me. But I was wrong about that too.

"Victor, what's happening to you?" was the question posed to me in the middle of the eighth grade by my homeroom teacher, Mrs. Rice. She was a tall, middle-aged brunette, with a quiet, gentle disposition.

I was too afraid to answer. For the first time in my thirteen years of life, someone had finally asked me the question that I'd been praying to hear and wanting to answer. But now I couldn't.

Dad had all his bases covered. If any of us tried to run away or tell on him, he'd find us, he said, and harm us or worse; that failing, he'd harm other family members. His mistreatment of Mami was more degrading, and the violence being leveled at her was more intense than ever. He had a new tactic with me: starvation.

Starting midyear I suddenly had a substantial growth spurt. Besides my size thirteen shoe—and the joke along with it that my feet arrived in a room long before I did—I was inching taller than Tony and my father, while my thighs and butt continued filling in with bulky muscles. One afternoon when I was out mowing the back lawn, bare-chested, I was startled as Dad stalked up behind me and grabbed me by my waist. Pinching and twisting a chunk of skin, he barked, "You're getting fat. I'm putting you on a diet."

My diet consisted of one meal a day that only he could feed to me in small portions when he arrived home from work at 1 A.M. To wake me up out of a deep slumber so I could have my meal, he usually did so with a hard slap to the face, jolting me into a groggy shuffle to the kitchen. Before I could eat, I was required to pass his interrogation about whether I got into trouble at school. If he accepted my answer, I was given the plate of food; if not, I was sent back to bed with nothing. Within weeks, I began to lose weight precipitously. In a year that I had started to improve as a student and citizen, I began once more to have problems paying attention in class, even staying awake. On the playground, I had an extremely short fuse. By the end of the first month of Dad's diet, I had probably lost between ten and fifteen pounds.

Mami devised a form of subterfuge to sneak me food. At the time, as it happened, she was working at Chef's Orchid, an airline catering company. Since Dad was sometimes home when she got back from work, Mami was able to occasionally hide a small sandwich in her hairnet when she could and hand it off to me when none of my siblings were watching. She couldn't just cook me something in the kitchen, as Dad was monitoring the contents of the kitchen with Gestapo-like scrutiny. There were days when I couldn't remember if I had eaten the night before. Added to my weakened condition was a constant ringing in my ears from the open-handed boxings Dad was giving them.

Just before lunch period at school during the second month of my diet, I fainted in class. When I came to, I was on the floor next to my desk with Mrs. Rice leaning over me. The lunch bell rang and she ordered the rest of the class to go to lunch.

She walked me over to the classroom sink and wetted down some brown paper towels. Mrs. Rice had me look in the mirror above the sink as she pointed to my left ear. There was blood coming out of it and trickling down my neck. After mopping my brow and cleaning up the blood, she sat me down at a desk and took a seat at one next to it. That was when she asked me the question I couldn't answer.

"Something's going on at home, isn't it?" she repeated.

"What do you mean?"

Mrs. Rice reviewed what she had been noticing, the rapid weight loss, lack of concentration, and now the collapse she had just witnessed. She knew that I wasn't eating lunch and didn't know why.

Tears poured from my eyes. I wanted to tell her everything. But if anything got back to Dad, who knew what he would do next?

Mrs. Rice stood and grabbed a chair so she could sit in front of me. Taking my hands in hers, she looked at me with sad brown eyes and allowed me to cry. Then she told me, "I'm going to buy you a lunch ticket for the rest of the year, and you need to eat."

"No, thank you, but my . . . my father wouldn't allow it," I stammered.

"You have two choices," she said. "Accept my offer, or I'll have to call your father in for a conference."

I accepted her offer.

For the rest of the year, the aptly named Mrs. Rice literally and figuratively fed me, returning to me many pieces of my eroding self-esteem. She never forced me to talk; she was simply paying attention and offering sustenance to a boy who was on his way to being a lost cause. Mrs. Rice gave me a shot in the arm when I most needed it. Her kindness and generosity made me feel worthwhile enough to apply myself, and at the end of the year, I took home my best report card to date, straight B's.

In the interim, Dad had allowed me to start eating dinner at a normal hour. To the best of my knowledge, he never figured out how Mami with her stolen sandwiches and my eighth-grade homeroom teacher kept me and my spirit alive.

None of my classmates ever said anything to indicate that they knew about my situation. But on the last day of school, during our end-of-the-year party with cake and ice cream, one by one several of my classmates brought me their pieces of cake and set their plates down in front of me on my desk until it was covered with more than I could eat in one sitting.

The summer of 1969 was when Dad started staying home from work more often, spending more time in his bathroom office and more time with the epic struggle required to get him out of sleep and ready for work, whether it was for his later swing shift or the regular day shift, or for when he decided he needed to stay home to administer the rule of law and order. He had been doing this for years, but now it turned pathological. Two to ten hours could be spent in rousing him. And we were all recruited for the job, sometimes even Barbie.

Dad's approval of me and my improved grades hadn't lasted long.

He was impressed at first, of course. That same day when I rushed home from school with my report card and brought it to him in the bathroom, he sat on the toilet and nodded with self-satisfaction, as if he was to be credited. With a gallant gesture, he waved me outside, telling me I was off my current punishment. Fifteen minutes late coming home that afternoon, I was promptly repunished.

That left me lots of time to participate in the team effort necessary to wake Dad each day. After preparing the coffee, our next step was to congregate in the bedroom. We always seemed to take a moment to look at each other before we started, like athletes before the big game, psyching each other up.

"Papi, *levantate!*" were the words uttered by the children. "Tony, *levantate!*" was spoken by my mother. "Dad, get up!" and "Dad, wake up!" were other variations.

This typically went on for several minutes with no results. But knowing the havoc to be wreaked if we gave up, we moved to the next stage of this ludicrous exercise, best described as the laying on of hands. We would attempt to physically get him out of bed, first by precariously pushing on him ever so slightly and repeating the chant *"Levantate."* Then we proceeded to chant and lay on hands in an island rhythm. Push. *"Levantate."* Push. *"Levantate."* Sometimes the result was a seemingly unconscious slap, punch, or kick.

The next stage was to try and pull his sequoia-sized legs to the edge of the bed. That completed, we would then move to his arms, grabbing his hands and pulling him to the sitting position. While two of us held on to his hands, the others would offer the coffee, many times holding the cup under his nose in the wild hopes its aroma would have some magical effect and levitate him out of the bed and into the bathroom. No such luck. The bed acted like a giant magnet, yanking him from our grasp and back to the prone position. This ridiculous tug-of-war would be repeated several times, my father always winning the contest.

When we were too successful, Dad invented new strategies to combat us. He started grasping the underside of the mattress with his

hands and feet, showing a strong resemblance to a frog clinging desperately to the side of a mossy rock. This made him absolutely
unmovable. Eventually he would open one eye and close it, asking,
"What time is it?" In the split second that it would take us to answer,
sounding like a chorus in perfect harmony, he was fast asleep again.
Eventually he would wake up and we would receive our punishment
for our failure.

The most maddening part was that if the phone rang, miraculously
he would bolt up and reach for it, answer it with a friendly "Hello?"
and happily or formally identify himself, "Tony." We had standing
orders to throw water on him if all else failed. This was a trick, since
he'd beat the crap out of us for it anyway. I did, however, take great
pleasure in dumping a bucket of cold water on him one afternoon. The
aftermath was brutal, but it could not rob me of always recalling the
sight of him leaping out of the bed like a deranged cat.

The insanity of this ordeal was not unlike the ironic habit Dad
had of asking me to get him Bengay to rub on his sore muscles so he
could better kick the shit out of me. It wasn't funny when it was happening, but these were clear indications that something was very
wrong with my father.

There may have come a point that summer when Dad's deteriorating psychological state scared even him, perhaps one of the reasons
he sought counseling. After one of these visits, he came home and
told Mami that the psychiatrist had asked her to come in for a session. When she went, the psychiatrist strongly advised her to get herself and her kids out of the home; he hinted that her husband showed
homicidal tendencies. But when it came to helping her with resources
for how she might get away and how to support four children on her
factory wages and sparse English, the doctor couldn't help.

For the next few weeks, as though he were telepathic, Dad's congenial, easygoing behavior was a stunning exhibition of normalcy.
Even so, I was glad to be out of the house, as Tony and I were
enrolled for summer school at Hawthorne High School. My brother
was taking some honors classes in preparation for the eleventh grade,

while I was brushing up on subjects that would help me in the ninth grade the following fall.

Dad soon returned to his increased volatility and there was no question that by midsummer I was his main target. Mami once explained that my full head of hair was part of the problem. She couldn't believe that a grown man could be so jealous of his son's good looks, she said; neither could I, especially given how thoroughly convinced I was that I would never be good looking. But the best analysis, which my siblings might have later helped me to understand, was that I was Dad's spitting image. His uncontrollable self-loathing was such that he didn't want to annihilate me; he really wanted to annihilate himself.

Still, that understanding would not have helped my certainty that I had arrived at a place with him where I couldn't seem to do anything right or please him in any way. No matter what I tried to do to persuade him to see me in a different light, he would find fault. I spent an entire day mowing, edging, and raking the backyard without being asked, just to please him. When Dad walked into the yard later that day, he surveyed my effort, and then his eyes narrowed and he pointed to the back wall. "You missed that spot. If you're going to do a job, don't do it half-assed." And then he turned and walked back into the house.

I stood in the backyard with the rake in my hand, wanting to drive it through the bald spot in his head. Instead, I cried and made a decision not to go out of my way for him again. For years, I'd had the resiliency of a puppy that chews a shoe or soils the house, only to wag his tail and try to please his master.

But even I knew that if you beat the sweetest of dogs enough, fear and anger will turn him mean, not obedient. That afternoon, I put down my rake and went to pet Van Auckland's King Anthony, identifying with him.

King was from a champion German shepherd line, a powerfully built animal, with the classic shepherd coloring of black and brown and a regal white V adorning his chest just below his neck. Dad and

Tony had taken him to obedience class together, and though King was protective of our property with outsiders, he was a gentle, loving animal with family members. Dad often put Barbie on King's back and King would take her for rides in the backyard. This was where he stayed primarily, watching through the slats in the gate that led to the front. This was where the peach tree stood that King fertilized into producing such oversized fruit, sometimes from the blasts of diarrhea that shot out his rear in terror when Dad called his name. Our previous dog, also named King, had done that too; so had our collie, Duke. It was like the jingling of keys or the removal of a watch. Sometimes King was allowed inside as a treat; or if he required a beating, Dad brought him inside to the hallway between my bedroom and the kitchen, where the sounds of poor King reverberated through the house.

Like our German shepherd, perhaps, my increasing weight and size posed a training challenge to my dad. By the end of the summer, I was taller than he and Tony. The look on Tony's face told me that though he hadn't mentioned it, he wasn't thrilled when his friends commented, "This is your *little* brother?"

My father used my increasing size as an excuse to bring out the big guns. My stance of boiling defiance was that I could take whatever he had to offer. The threat to his control was so maddening, he sank to a new deviant low.

There was the evening that he caught me jerking off in the bathtub and pulled me out by my hair and ordered me to sit on the edge of the tub with my legs open. He took out the hard case that housed his Norelco shaver and drove it into my nuts, causing me to almost lose consciousness from the pain.

On another occasion, we were working in the kitchen, putting in new linoleum, and my effort was not to his liking. His creative punishment was to tie me by my wrists with rope, as he proceeded to force me onto the unfinished floor on my back and then to yank my arms over my head, my tank top revealing the small sprouts of hair under my arms. He secured the other end of the rope to the plumbing under the kitchen sink. Picking up a piece of baseboard not yet installed, he took the eighteen-inch piece of wood with three nails at one end and sharpened them with a metal file. These filed nail ends he dragged across my exposed armpits, scraping the outer layer of skin off so there was only limited bleeding. To optimize the impact of his terrorism, Dad forced my brother Tony to stand by and watch, requiring him to mask his loathing and disgust as I was writhing in agony on the floor. Tony stood dumbfounded looking at Dad and then me. There was an expression of great pain in his soulful brown eyes.

The pain of that afternoon stayed with me for a couple of weeks because every time I sprayed Right Guard under my arms, the sting would remind me of that day.

Somewhere around this time, Dad called me into the hallway between my bedroom and the kitchen, which had access to the backyard. This was also the area reserved for King's beatings. He told me to kneel down on the floor. He took out some rope and hogtied my legs and arms behind me, like I'd seen the police do to antiwar protestors on the evening news. He ordered me to lower my head and close my eyes. After I heard what I deciphered to be the sound of pants being unzipped, I felt a warm steady stream of liquid cascading off my head and down my face and back.

There was no need to open my eyes to know that this was the ultimate degradation, the final statement of my nothingness and worthlessness: I deserved to be pissed on.

He cut the rope and released me. Whatever flicker that once burned of the proud young boy who yearned so desperately to love and be loved was just about out. Numb with humiliation, I heard him say very calmly, "Go take a shower. You're disgusting."

Tony was the one who figured out that I tried to commit suicide by swallowing a bottle of Vivarin that I had shoplifted earlier in the day. It didn't matter to him that I was probably only doing it out of a need for attention, rather than a desire not to live. Seeing me jittery and sweaty, he made me go take a shower and then eat some food in the kitchen, where he came in to talk to me.

He listened to the reasons that I had tried to die, all the while making sure that I was starting to feel a little better and that I was going to sweat it out without having to go to the hospital, even if I didn't sleep for the next couple of nights.

Tony said, "Vic, you're almost fifteen, hang in there. When we're eighteen, we can leave Dad's house legally. There's nothing he can do to stop us, okay?"

It later occurred to me that my big brother had given me the attention that I'd been looking for, and a confirmation that Dad had not succeeded in dividing and conquering us. In fact, about the best thing that happened over the course of my freshman year at Hawthorne High School was being Tony Rivas's younger brother.

A member of the wrestling team, Tony had become a very handsome young man with a great physique and what I considered a striking resemblance to Sajid Khan, the star of the popular television show *Maya*. Sajid was a huge teen idol at the time, gracing the covers of various teen magazines. Tony had his own following of girls. He was also an honor student and the starting offensive guard on the football team. It was a great team with some outstanding athletes, including Scott Laidlaw, the state high hurdle champion and star running back, who went on to play for Stanford and the Dallas Cowboys.

Dad wouldn't allow me to play football. He gave me two reasons. First, he said I wasn't tough enough; second, I might injure my pitching arm. He did allow me to wrestle on the junior varsity team. I wasn't initially that excited about the sport, but it kept me out of the house in the afternoons. The atmosphere had become even crazier after Dad made Barbie and Eddie give up their bedroom so that one of his baseball teammates, John, could stay in it, along with his wife, Elsa, and their baby.

John and Elsa were a good-looking young couple with a very sick child. The baby had some type of liver ailment that required a transplant. Elsa and John argued a lot and usually about the baby. Their child was constantly being rushed to the UCLA Medical Center.

Within the first month of their stay with us, John went out and never came back. Dad started spending lots of time with Elsa, shuttling her and her baby back and forth from the hospital and taking her out to eat. He told Mami that he was consoling her. My father's relationship with Elsa was obvious to me and it became more so when he made Mami sleep on the couch. Eventually, he moved Mami out to the garage.

The shame and anger over what he was doing to my mother, turning her into a live-in housekeeper, was more painful than the indignities he made me suffer. Mami refused to escape, even though I was certain the Colemans would help her. The thought of us not having anything to eat or any clean clothes to wear kept her struggling on. Then, on December 3, 1969, after she left on foot pulling a laundry cart full of clothes, Mami didn't come home. A day passed. Another. And another. No sign or message came from her. She was gone.

For the next two weeks, while Dad preoccupied himself with Elsa and her child, telling us that Mami would be back and was just having herself a little vacation, Tony and I started to think that he had killed her and that she was never coming home. He and I tried to comfort Eddie and Barbie, but our nervousness had to be apparent. Nothing could make me believe that she would abandon us.

At the end of the second week, my fourth-grade friend Carol Coleman and her friend Gloria, a dark, sexy Latina, approached me when I was on my way to wrestling practice. "Victor, I have to tell you something," Carol began, going on to say that her mother had sent her to say that Mami was seriously ill and in the hospital. Forgetting my practice, I left immediately for the hospital, with Carol and Gloria in tow.

When I walked into the hospital room, Mami was hooked up to several machines and IV tubes. She looked so fragile and swollen.

Lillian Coleman, truly an angel to my mother, was at her side and rose to leave so that Mami and I could be alone. My attempt to smile was useless and soon I was sobbing.

She haltingly told me how she had collapsed on the street on her way to the laundromat. "A kind soul called for an ambulance," she recalled, saying that she would never know who that good Samaritan was, but that when she regained consciousness there were two policemen by her side asking questions. An ambulance arrived moments later and she was rushed to the hospital, along with the dirty laundry.

At the emergency room, the attending physician told the nurses to remove her clothing. Mami said they had to cut her out of her clothes because her body was so swollen. The cardiologist who examined her was not too encouraging. He would do everything in his power to save her, but her fate was ultimately in God's hands. The doctor said that he had never seen a case like hers. It seems that because of the beatings with the metal hairbrush to her skull and chest, she had developed a form of pleurisy, or swelling of the membrane lining the chest cavity. The doctor told her that had she not been rushed immediately to the hospital after her collapse, she would have definitely died.

Mami had not been carrying her purse when she collapsed and had no identification on her, so she had been admitted as a Jane Doe. When she came out of critical care, she decided not to give her identity for fear of what Dad might do if she did survive. "Today the hospital called him," she warned me. "So be careful. Go now before he finds out you were here."

On my walk home from the hospital, I stopped to use a restroom at a park. Since I was supposed to have been at wrestling practice, I used the sink there to get my singlet and tights wet, giving my hair a dousing while I was at it.

When Dad arrived home with Elsa, the two were in a somber mood after returning from the hospital where her baby was staying. My father contrasted the child's tragedy with the "show your mother is putting on at the hospital."

Acting dumb, I said, "Where is she? What happened?"

He told me what hospital it was, what they had told him, and that she was fine. Then he warned, "You're forbidden to visit her, do you hear me?"

Whenever I was supposed to have wrestling practice for the next ten days I went to see Mami. After what would be the last of these visits, Dad was waiting for me by the front door. He ordered me inside and yanked the gym bag from my shoulder. The house was empty. He pulled out my wet wrestling uniform and began to sniff it. "This doesn't smell very stinky."

"That's good." I shrugged, pretending to be cool. "I rinse it out after practice every day."

He started to remove his watch. "Try again, Bictor, and remember, I already know the answer."

He eventually got the truth out of me. He told me that I was off the wrestling team and had to report home immediately after school from then on.

As if Mami's nightmare was not miserable enough, Dad and Elsa went to visit her at the hospital. This visit ended in a shouting match with Dad and Elsa being removed forcibly by hospital security. They were warned not to return.

He did return on the day of Mami's release. She had been in the hospital for exactly one month. My father began to raise another stink about the cost of Mami's stay, insisting that his insurance shouldn't have to cover the cost. The hospital administrator pulled my father into his office and let him know in no uncertain terms that he would pay one way or the other.

Mami was going to stay at Lillian Coleman's apartment, as she continued to recuperate. Dad drove her there and charged her for the ride, like a cabbie.

A few days after Mami was released from the hospital, Elsa's baby died. Of course, I felt bad for Elsa and especially the baby, but I refused to show it. During my mother's disappearance and hospital stay, neither Dad nor Elsa showed much concern or compassion for her. Right after the baby was buried, the two of them began what seemed like a monthlong party. They drank every day, making out constantly and grabbing each other sexually in front of all of us. Dad changed from a man I'd never seen hug or kiss my mother to a dog in heat, pouncing over the very hot-looking twenty-two-year-old Elsa, with her ivory skin, black hair, and blue eyes, and her miniskirts. Dad actually got down on all fours, as she did, and chased her fun-lovingly down the hall.

Elsa didn't do much housework or cooking. Either we had take-out or Tony and I would make some sandwiches, soup, or whatever was in the house. Dad bitched periodically that Mami had selfishly abandoned us. The only solace from this absurdist piece of theatre was that as long as Elsa was around, Dad had little energy for disciplining us. He slapped her one afternoon and she raised her index finger to him and said, "Old man, this is where I draw the line."

As she went to pack her things, Dad did lots of crying and hand-kerchief wringing to try to get her to forgive him. But his charms didn't work and she left on the spot.

Mami recuperated at Lillian's apartment for a few days and went back to work, only to be fired. She applied for government assistance and was, eventually, granted some help, enough to be able to rent a small apartment. To support herself, she took in laundry and ironing, carrying loads many times the size of our family's laundry cart to and from the laundry area of her apartment complex. La Luchadora, she did this without complaint or self-pity, with only that spark in her that refused to be killed. Whenever I could, I snuck over for a brief visit, sometimes accompanied by Carol and Gloria.

As it happened, I had the hots for Gloria, and when she invited me to a little party she was having while her mother was out of town, she didn't have to twist my arm to agree to bring some liquor. With a background in shoplifting, I would have no problem, so I thought, stopping into Clark Drugs and sliding a pint bottle of whiskey into the lining of my windbreaker. But my days as an innocent-looking waif were apparently numbered, and I was apprehended by a store manager who gave me a choice of having my father come down to get me or going to jail. After many elaborate versions of why my father couldn't be named, due to classified reasons of national security, I eventually gave his work number. But it was too late to avoid having the police arrive and lead me, in tears and in handcuffs, out of the store.

At the city police station, I was led into a detective's office. He gave me a short lecture on the dangers of drugs and alcohol. I tried to explain that I didn't drink and that I had stolen the whiskey for a girl. That made him smile, but it didn't save me from being put into a holding cell, where I sat alone and terrified, avoiding even looking at the drunk in the next cell, for over an hour. When they came to release me, I was ushered into the main part of the station. Another detective was there having a friendly chat with my father. Dad swiveled his neck in my direction and bored holes through me with his yellow eyes. No charges were to be filed, said the detective, but if I got in trouble again they might add this infraction to my record.

My embattled sense of irony did appreciate the fact that this was the same police station where, a couple of years earlier, I had begged for protection from my father and received none. This time they were placing me into his hands.

Without a word spoken, we took the short drive home and walked into the house. The punches started landing as soon as the door slammed behind us.

But these beatings and the other sick physical batterings didn't damage me the way that his words did. The survival lesson here: Sticks and stones may break my bones, and names can hurt worse. This all came to a head on an afternoon in this time period, with Mami out of the house, when Dad had spent the better part of the day berating me for my poor performance at school, comparing my mediocrity to Tony's straight-A genius. My name and "stupid" seemed to melt into one.

Finally I couldn't take it anymore and I talked back. We stood in the living room near the shelf that displayed all my baseball trophies and game balls, the only representation in our household of the last vestiges of my worth in his eyes. Pointing up at them, I said, "If I'm such a piece of shit, then who do all those trophies belong to?"

Whatever was going to be his reaction, I didn't think would matter anymore. Certainly, I wasn't expecting a magical father-son moment with the eventual apology and hug. Maybe he would clobber me. So what? Or maybe he would just back off me. Nothing could have prepared me for what he did do.

First, he turned and simply stared. Cold, emotionless. Then he left the living room and went out the back door, returning a few minutes later with a sledgehammer and a box cutter.

Dad told me that the trophies meant nothing to him. And to prove it, he took each trophy down, one by one, and, right there in the living room, smashed the metal and marble of each and every trophy into little pieces. He turned next to the game balls, using the razor-sharp box cutter to slice through the seams of the baseballs and to rip off the rawhide covering. When he finished with all of the balls, he yelled to Tony in another room to go to our bedroom closet and bring him back my all-star jacket. With a big pair of kitchen shears, Dad cut my jacket into tiny pieces in front of me.

"Clean it up," he ordered before he left the living room.

All the remains of my proud mementos made a little pile on the floor. Everything had been smashed, slashed, and cut until nothing was recognizable, like the shards of belief that my father could love and approve of me, and the last of what had been my self-esteem— smashed into little pieces that I had to sweep up and throw away.

That night I slit one of my wrists, but failed again to die.

In late February of 1970, I trudged home from school as I had for most of my life, with every step feeling heavier and more difficult to take the closer I got to our house. Anticipating the usual reception from Dad—the hour of his undivided attention that kept him home from work with increasing regularity—I was startled when I turned the corner onto Oxford Street and caught a whiff of the familiar scent of onions sautéing in oil.

And when I scanned the block and our driveway, I could see no shit brown-gold Impala station wagon in front of our house. With an emphatic sigh of relief and a smile I couldn't withhold, I headed up to the front door. From behind it came the faint sounds of a conga drum. More wonderful smells were seeping out onto the front porch. What the hell was going on?

As I entered our house, the sounds and smells exploded: Cuban music, Barbie's laughter, and a cast-iron pan being scraped along the burner. And there, hunched over the stove, as if nothing had changed, was Mami, with my grinning little sister seated at the kitchen table.

Early that day, Dad had gone to get Mami with the excuse that Barbie was sick with a fever and was being watched by a neighbor who needed to leave. He dropped Mami at the house before driving off to work. Mami found that Barbie was not sick at all, but certainly happy to see her mother. I was too. But as much as I wanted to run and hug her, neither of us knew how to do that. Instead she smiled with love and approval, like manna from heaven, despite the sight of her missing teeth, which Dad had previously knocked out.

Though thin and weak, Mami had a calm expression that was encouraging to see. She had a certain detachment, a survival mechanism I understood. She turned away from me and said with effort, "You came to see me all those times. Even though you knew you'd be punished." That was Mami's way of saying thank you.

Refusing to leave her side, I followed her around as she washed our clothes, cleaned the house, and served us dinner. After she washed the dishes, she grabbed her purse and headed for the front door. Eddie, Barbie, Tony, and I were all hoping she'd move back in, but she said her good-byes and walked back to her apartment.

This arrangement continued off and on for a few more weeks, until Dad, arguing that her children needed her, convinced her to move back in. She could sleep on the sofa and he promised he would never touch her in any way again. Mami agreed but made it very clear: "I'm only doing this for the children, because for my children, I will do anything."

As she later told me, she was home for a few weeks before he made a move. El Caballero poured it on like it had never been poured, calling her into the bedroom, sobbing, telling her how much he had missed being with her, and that he wanted to make up for everything. In a moment of weakness and fear that afternoon, she had sex with him for the last time. She was soon pregnant with her sixth child. Mami's account of what happened next was this:

> When he found out he asked me to abort the child and I said no. He stated it would then be my problem. He did not allow me to tell the children but they soon noticed, especially the older ones. They asked me and I confirmed that I was indeed pregnant. Eddie asked me, since he was still relatively young, "Mami are you pregnant?" I had to say no, only that I was gaining weight.

When Dad started to beat her one day, Mami stopped him with a threat. She said, "Listen, you sonofabitch, you've already damaged one of my children beyond repair, you won't do it again." When he scoffed she warned him, "If you lay a hand on me, you'd better kill me, because if you don't, I'll kill you."

"You don't have the guts," he snarled.

Mami shrugged and begged to differ, warning him that she'd do it in his sleep.

To my knowledge, that chastened him so much that he left her alone until everything came to a colossal explosion on one of the last days of my freshman school year. And I was to blame.

Not surprisingly, I was on punishment, meaning Mami had to enforce the rule that I had to be inside; not surprisingly, I was prepared to bend if not break the rule and suffer the consequences. First, I went to the backyard to keep company with King. Our backyard was enclosed on three sides by a six-foot-high concrete wall, with the only opening being the wooden gate that led to the front yard. It was through those slats that King watched the small portion of the front yard that was visible.

After a while, I headed to the front, thinking I could throw the football with some of the neighborhood kids. Mami came to the front porch and warned me, but I assured her that I could see Dad's car coming down the street before he could see me. With that, my friends and I set up a game of tackle football that used the north and south boundaries of our house as goal lines. King sat behind the gate intently watching the game whenever it entered his sight line at the north goal line.

About fifteen minutes into the game, a Pesky Neighbor Kid tackled me from behind as I was running for a touchdown, right at that north goal line.

This Neighbor Kid had the obnoxious habit of climbing up on his grandparents' fence and throwing small rocks at King. The instant that I got up after he had tackled me and started to walk away, I heard two sounds simultaneously. The first was the *CRACCKKK* of wood shattering and the second was King's vicious *GROWWLLL*.

With lightning speed, King bounded toward the Pesky Neighbor Kid, and by the time I turned around, the poor guy was pinned to the ground with King on top, attacking and tearing into him with his teeth. I dove on top of King and put a choke hold around his neck and pulled back with all my strength. Useless. "King! Stop!" I yelled, while the kid wailed and King kept biting and tearing. As a last desperate measure, I punched King in the testicles. But to no avail; he kept attacking.

"KING!!!"

Suddenly, King froze and got off the terrorized Neighbor Kid. With his tail between his legs, King ran to the backyard. I turned toward the front porch and there was Mami standing in her apron. It was her voice that had stopped King's vicious assault on the kid who had pestered him for over a year.

In moments, the kid's grandparents, who lived nearby, had raced to his side. The attack probably lasted all of thirty seconds, but to my horror it left the Neighbor Kid with numerous wounds: a bullet-sized hole through his arm, a wound around his neck that required fifteen stitches, and another around his crotch, just missing his testicles, which took fifty-four stitches. Those were the bites that could be sewn up; the others had to heal from the inside out, and a couple required plastic surgery. Several bites just missed a major artery.

After the paramedics took the boy away in an ambulance, the crowd of kids and some of their parents who had gathered went back to their houses. With trepidation, I went to the backyard to find King and inspect the damage to our fence. The gate was lying in the path, a full five yards from where it connected to the fence. I didn't know if King, like Buck in Jack London's *Call of the Wild*, would begin the transformation from domesticated to primal. I found him cowering and shaking under the peach tree, his muzzle and coat stained with blood. Keeping my eye on him, I picked up the gate to try and reinstall it. King had blown it clean off the hinges, with wood splintered and splayed on the ground. The best I could do was to tie it with rope from the garage.

I went inside and found Mami sitting at the kitchen table, sorrowfully, sipping on Cuban coffee and smoking her still forbidden cigarette. She advised me to go take a shower and then bring my clothes out to her to be washed. We both knew there was a futility in doing anything to prevent the inevitable carnage from taking place when Dad got home. Nonetheless, she called him at work to tell him that King had attacked a child, knowing it could be worse if he found out in some other way.

The first target of his wrath when he got home was King. Through the window of my bedroom, I could see to the backyard as Dad went out and yelled, "King, get over here!" and Van Auckland's King Anthony cowered and then scooted on his belly with his head lowered toward my dad. He grabbed King by the scruff of the neck and threw him through the opened door of the garage. The door slammed and we could all hear the punishment he was administering to the poor dog by its mournful yelps and wails. Looking like a complete madman, Dad walked out a few minutes later, his carefully combed hair covering his face. I was next.

This was one of those times where the evidence against me was overwhelming. The Neighbor Kid was the physical evidence, and the other kids, who loved my dad, the eyewitnesses. Initially, he called Mami, Tony, and me into the kitchen. Tony was first up and promptly told him that he was still at school at the time of the incident.

Mami and I nodded in confirmation. Dad focused now on my mother. "Olga, *que paso?*"

Mami told him that she was in the kitchen cooking and she could hear the neighborhood kids playing out front, and then she heard screaming and King attacking. He asked for more details; Mami said that's all she saw.

Dad cocked his head my way. "I left you for last because, somehow, I know you're involved in this."

Like the nun with the broken kneecap, I felt responsible for the Pesky Neighbor Kid's injuries. Sure, King did the biting and the kid had pestered the dog, but I was outside playing when I shouldn't have been. Mami had warned me about going outside without Dad's permission and I disobeyed her and, more important, him. Stepping forward to take responsibility, I ventured, "It's my fault. I was outside playing football and the kid tackled me. I guess King wanted to protect me."

Assuming my stance to be punched, hands clasped behind my back, body erect and muscles tightened—like a boxer's heavy punching bag—I took the barrage of punches to my stomach, ribs, back, and thighs, not making a sound. Several times I had to pick myself off the kitchen floor with Mami begging him, "*Ya,* Tony!"

In my mind, I withstood all this out of guilt for our neighbor's injuries and, moreover, for the excessive beating that King had gotten. He didn't know any better and had only been protecting me.

Dad's smoking must have been catching up with him because he became winded and actually stopped hitting me to light up a cigarette.

A little while later when I was sent back to my bedroom, I heard Dad and Tony working on the damaged gate. In the darkness, chained to the peach tree, King was visible, shivering and shaking.

SLAP!!! I opened my eyes with one cheek burning and saw Dad towering over me. "Who told you to go to sleep?"

"No one did," I answered, as I rubbed my face where he had slapped me awake. I was still fully dressed.

"I'm not done with you. Why did you let King out?"

"What? I didn't let him out, he broke down the gate."

"Somebody let him out. Think about it and I'll see you in the morning." He left my room, but he hadn't given me permission to go to sleep.

What did he mean by "Somebody let him out"? Wasn't it clear to him that the gate had been destroyed by King's charge?

He walked back in, delivered a couple of more blows without warning, and yelled, "Didn't I tell you to go to sleep?"

"No, you said I'll see you in the morning."

"Are you that fucking stupid? Do I have to spell it out for you? Take some *initiative*." He flicked off the light and left the room for the last time that night.

The next morning I awoke and hurried around, getting ready for school. Before I could finish shoveling in a bowl of cereal, Dad stopped me. Smoking a cigarette, he leaned against the doorjamb and informed me that I was not going to school.

Once everyone had left the house except for us, he came into my room, holding several strands of rope and King's choke chain. He ordered me onto my back. He tied my arms and legs to the bed frame and hovered over me, choke chain in one hand.

He beat me with the chain, off and on, for several hours, taking breaks for food and cigarettes or to answer the phone. He stayed home from work the next couple of days interrogating and beating all of us, except three-and-a-half-year-old Barbie. After her earlier warning to Dad, Mami may have gotten off with only a slap but not the mental torture.

Underneath the onslaught in one of the bloodiest battles to take place in our war zone was his almost religious belief that *someone* had left the gate open when they took out the trash. Not only was this completely negated by the broken gate, but the other fact was that *none* of us ever opened the gate when we took out the trash. The garbage cans were accessible from the house by taking the back door. On top of that, I had already taken the blame and subsequent beatings.

When it was Eddie's turn to be interrogated, Dad began in an almost kindly, *Father Knows Best* manner, asking, "Do you know what happened, Eddie?"

My nine-and-a-half-year-old brother began to quiver, his programmed response to being in Dad's presence. Eddie wasn't even home at the time of the incident; he was at a neighbor's house playing.

"Relax, relax," my father said. "Just tell me the truth. That's all. Tell me the truth about what happened to the gate and you can go back outside and play."

Eddie's voice shook as he confessed, "Yeah, Daddy. I did it."

Dad grabbed King's choke chain and started wrapping it around his hand. He was going to beat Eddie with it, knowing full well that my younger brother, like Tony, was nowhere near the house.

Livid, I stepped in front of Eddie and yelled at Dad, "He wasn't even home! I left the gate open, all right!"

Finally, with this outburst and confession, I had given my father the information that made sense to him and no one else. For this, I received the last of the beatings Dad could mete out from this ordeal. I had been convicted several times for this crime and now, at least as far as he was concerned, it was over.

But it wasn't over for me. A smoldering tinderbox of a fourteen-and-a-half-year-old, all I needed was one careless match to be thrown and I was ready to ignite, to become one dangerous kid.

Several days later, when Tony was outside walking King in the front yard, our once proud, gallant German shepherd spotted a kid running up to the house. It happened to be Eddie but all King saw was him running toward Tony, and he lurched for Eddie in an attempt to bite him. Luckily Tony had him on a tight leash, so King missed taking a chunk out of Eddie. That was how good dogs went bad, Dad said, once they had the taste of blood.

The next day King was gone. Dad told us that he had sold King to a ranch as a security dog.

I didn't quite believe that story, just as I didn't believe Dad's story about where Mami was, that she had left us and didn't want us, when he lined us up in the kitchen on that morning of July 24, 1970, to announce he was taking us to Florida.

None of us ever used the word "kidnapped" for what was happening. But that's exactly what it was.

4
miami
(1970–1971)

Your prior actions will follow you around in life like a plague.
—Anthony Rivas Sr.
(advice on staying out of trouble)

SIERRA BLANCA, TEXAS.

In the early morning hours, eighty miles southeast of El Paso, where the intersection of Interstate Highway 10, U.S. Highway 80, and Ranch Road 1111 meets the junction of the Southern Pacific and Missouri Pacific railroads, my story almost came crashing to a cataclysmic end.

There was a quiet stillness interrupted only by the deep rhythmic breathing of REM sleep and the muffled sound of rocks hitting the undercarriage. At this literal and metaphoric crossroads, I peered one second longer out into the darkness as we inched closer to the forty-foot drop into the gully. Afraid as I was of the consequences of hitting my father for the first time in my life, forces more powerful than my own helped me make the only choice there was. Grabbing the back of the front seat with my left hand, I leaned up and across the car, hauling back with my right hand and slapping Dad flush on the face. *SLLAPPP!!!!*

Like a patient being jolted back to life from a cardiac arrest with paddles, Dad opened his eyes and automatically locked out his elbows, while an audible *GASP* of air was expelled from his lungs. The muscles and tendons of his forearms taut and bulging, Dad cranked the steering wheel hard to the left, sending Eddie sliding across the backseat to me, where I grabbed and held on to him. We were on the very edge of the right emergency lane next to the gully when we began our violent slide across the four eastbound lanes of Interstate 10. Our station wagon now sped directly toward the dividing wall of this massive roadway. Behind us, I saw the back end of the car fishtailing as our cabin cruiser/moving van leaned hard to the right, while the straps that secured the boat to the stolen trailer were audibly and visibly straining like overstretched piano wire.

And then it happened. The straps SNNNAPPPED and Dad's beloved cabin cruiser became airborne, sailing up into a stunning, gravity-defying flight before it crashed violently down onto the interstate, wood and fiberglass exploding into shards on contact. We were seconds from crashing into the dividing wall in front of us when Dad managed to turn the steering wheel to the right and slam on the brakes. No longer hampered by the weight of the boat, the car and trailer responded, stuttering to a halt. The smell of burnt rubber permeated the air. Just to my right the boat was on its side, looking like a dead fish.

With everyone very much awake, Dad checked to make sure none of us was hurt. Unbelievably, though we had worn our seat belts the entire trip, like Dad had ordered us to, this was the one time when we didn't have them on, maybe because we had been too exhausted to bother. This was one of the busiest interstates in the country, at a time in early morning when speeding eighteen-wheelers were typically out in hordes. Yet during the crucial seconds when we careened across four lanes and back, there wasn't a vehicle in sight. *Un milagro* in any language.

Mami's phrase burst in my senses. We should have just died, *pero con el ayudo de Dios,* there we sat in the shit brown-gold Impala station wagon in the middle of the freeway, shocked but unscathed. In that moment, I became certain that my mother was alive and safe somewhere and had not been separated from us by her own choice. Her vibration was almost a presence with me, as though I could feel her using her gift of sight to follow and protect us, maybe even to wake me up in time to slap my father. For a fleeting second, I could feel her—her scent, her sighs, her sad eyes watching over us—but then she was gone.

All at once, the traffic flew toward us, on both sides of the interstate. Several drivers pulled over on both sides of the road to lend assistance. A tow truck appeared seemingly out of nowhere and began strapping ropes and hooks to the trailerless boat and pulled it over to the emergency lane. Despite the tremendous torque and braking that the station wagon had withstood, it was drivable.

With the guidance of the tow truck driver, a big burly cowboy with the best beer belly I ever saw hanging over his belt, we made it to a motel in the town of Sierra Blanca, population one thousand. A much-subdued version of my father spent the next twenty-four hours obtaining the U-Haul that would replace the boat for carrying our belongings the rest of the way to Miami. Another miracle we discovered when we drove over to the tow truck driver's property and found a small graveyard of various vehicles where the cabin cruiser had docked for the night—amid swarming rattlesnakes—was that everything we'd packed inside the boat was intact. Dad paid and thanked the tow truck cowboy with the beer belly and assured him that he would return to claim his boat.

With that, we forged on, chugging back onto the interstate right at the spot where our lives had almost ended, moving now at a pace that felt less crazed than before but no less anxiety-provoking.

As we drove across the great flat expanse of Texas and dipped down into the humid July hothouse of Louisiana and finally turned south into the state of Florida, I thought a lot about an earlier trip, back in 1960, when Papi drove Tony and me from Chicago to Miami to see some of our relatives who had emigrated from Cuba.

In another stroke of Dad's impeccable timing, it turned out that when we hit Florida we just missed being blown to kingdom come by hurricane Donna. We drove through her swath of destruction, which rose from southern Florida almost up to the coast of Maine. Leafless trees were blown everywhere I looked, and to my barely five-year-old eyes, they were made even more ominous by the shadows they cast as the light from the cars hit them.

Our journey then, as now, reminded me of the tornado scenes from *The Wizard of Oz*, with Dad a wicked witch on a broomstick, flying half-crazed while the music played that sinister yet up-tempo witch's theme.

The comparison didn't amuse me in the least. And there was no mistaking the new attitude that marked me when I arrived in Miami. I was angry, fucking angry.

In late January of 1971, I arrived home from JV wrestling practice to find my father fuming as he waited for me on the front porch of our funky little place off Red Road (S.W. Fifty-seventh Avenue) and Coral Way, in South Miami.

Dad had just returned from a walk-up coffee stand where he sometimes went. A source of gossip and fellowship, this coffee stand and others like it were hangouts where Cuban exiles could congregate at any hour of the day to have a shot of Cuban coffee, play dominoes, smoke cigars, and bullshit. The men talked passionately about their homeland and their lost farms and businesses, and how, if given the chance, they would kill Castro. It seemed that Dad had gotten into a conversation with a man whose son attended the same high school as I did, and he had discovered, in this secondhand way, that I had made an important decision without consulting him.

In fact, that's what I had done, in an act of defiance that I had been building toward from the moment we had arrived in Florida six months earlier.

For starters, acclimating to Miami in August is like being thrust into hell. You feel as if you're melting; your body secretes moisture faster than you can ingest it. The bug life, spawned by the moisture and the heat, is overwhelming. There are mosquitoes with hypodermic stingers that suck your blood and leave quarter-sized welts for you to scratch, dragonflies that zip around in gangster formations, and gnats that move in armies camouflaged as huge black clouds that stick to the moisture of your body and give you the appearance of excess body hair. But what shocked and repulsed me the most was the cockroaches, in sizes and quantities that were staggering, especially the palmetto variety of flying roaches that can grow up to three inches long and makes a disgusting popping sound and gross mess when you inevitably step on one or many of them.

Not that home had ever been a refuge, but the small house on Red Road—with two bedrooms and one bathroom and only one noisy air conditioner wall unit, in Dad's room—was not the good life our father had led us to believe we would find. Without Mami around, Tony and I were responsible for cooking, cleaning, and taking care of our two younger siblings. Except for the dinners that were delivered from the cantina, an array of Cuban food that arrived in stacked stainless steel containers, Tony and I were in charge of breakfast and lunch, and the rest of the household chores.

Dad had found a job working nights at a Miami Beach mortuary. No doubt embarrassed about what we understood was a position answering the switchboard there, he seemed to have lost some of his former swagger that went along with being a computer programmer with top security clearance. Dad had always told me that the reason he tried to keep me from screwing up was that my misdeeds would come back to haunt me; and yet in California I watched him fuck up his good job because of all the missed days he spent at home punishing me.

Without word from my mother, I held on to the hope that some of our Florida relatives might help us look for her, but that wasn't the case. The only time we saw everyone was at a park in Coral Gables for a large annual reunion of *Los Spirituanos,* which included anyone originally from Sancti Spíritus and their family, bringing together two hundred of my countrymen and -women bearing food, congas, claves, and other musical instruments. Most of my Miami relatives were there and had the nerve to use the name they gave me when I was a pretty fair-skinned baby: Vicky.

Dad went around introducing us, and when he pointed to me, already six foot two and two hundred pounds, the standard comment was "Oh Vicky, you're so big!"

With a scowl on my face, each time I blurted back, "It's VIC!"

"Vicky, *dame un besito*" was the response from my aunts as they leaned their faces in for the kiss on their cheeks. For a kid who was, by this point, extremely uncomfortable being touched in any fashion, this customary peck of respect, expected by every female I met at this party, was traumatic. You had to kiss hello and good-bye; it made no difference if they were cute and young or old and reeking of perfume and smelly dentures. If I hesitated with the kiss, Dad would throw me a look and flare his nostrils.

Dad put on quite a show at this party. He played the part of the proud father and found any opportunity to boast about his kids and wrap his arm around our shoulders. He danced his hiked-up-leg dance and sang off-key to the many Cuban songs being sung, with the congas pushing the rhythm.

Father Ernesto was there, along with his sister Carmen, a Catholic sister who stood six feet tall in her black habit, and their brother Jorge, rumored to have been an operative for the CIA during the Bay of Pigs invasion. My dad's sister, the beautiful, elegant Maria Rosa, was there with her family, my uncle Jose Posa and my cousins Margarita, Coqui, and Pepe.

When we had come to Florida ten years earlier, we stayed with Maria Rosa and her family, and I had never forgotten what a warm, affectionate family they were. Margarita and Coqui, pretty teenage girls who doted on me, cuddled me all the time and showered me with kisses. At age five, I loved how demonstrative they were. But at fifteen, the memory embarrassed me.

Instead of finding the right moment to tell an uncle, aunt, or cousin about the other side of El Ciclón and to enlist their aid in helping us find Mami, I became shy and stood tight-lipped next to Tony. We did let loose eventually, ending our stay at the party when he and I stole an entire flan each and hid behind some bushes to devour them.

It didn't take Dad long to find a girlfriend. A Wild-Eyed Latina, she was an attractive middle-aged single woman who had a rental unit behind us. For some reason, however, Dad insisted on having sex with her in his bedroom at our place. It was bad enough that a curtain was the only partition between his room and the hallway, but it wouldn't have mattered if there had been a door because the volume at which the Wild-Eyed Latina screamed and cussed when they were screwing could be heard outside the house. Whenever Barbie heard them and started to cry, Tony or I would say, "Oh, Papi and his friend are playing a rough game, everything's okay."

There were other times, after Dad fell asleep, that the Wild-Eyed Latina came out and gave me suggestive looks, which just added to my overall discomfort and stress. But then, in a much-needed ironic backlash, after Dad broke things off with her (which he did despite what a "hot fuck" she was, as he told Tony), my father found out that hell hath no fury like a Wild-Eyed Latina scorned. He was tormented by her profanity-laced messages on the answering machine, which we all could hear. Tony and I, and possibly even Eddie, were shocked by the look of fear that we saw in Dad's eyes as he listened to her proclaim that she was going to cut off his balls and feed them to the dog next door. Then the Wild-Eyed Latina started coming over and demanding to see him. We had to tell her that he wasn't home, which she never believed, and we would have to hear her bellowing *"Maricón!"* and *"Hijo de puto!"* at our windows as she roused the neighborhood.

My parents' wedding day—what my mother dreamt would be a Cinderella story.
Years later my father cut himself from any picture that included my mother.

Papi as a young boy
growing up privileged in
Sancti Spíritus, Cuba. He
was always a mystery to
me; even this photo
doesn't reveal his true
nature.

My father, Anthony Arthur Rivas, was proud that his wealthy parents could afford to educate him in the United States, where he attended Georgia Military School.

Mami and a headless Papi in the limousine at the beginning of their honeymoon. My mother's nightmare would begin later that night.

In Cuba in 1955, the Rivas and Lopez families celebrated my brother Tony's first birthday (he's behind the cake). Pregnant with me, Mami kept her hand on Tony's shoulder while my father, glowering behind sunglasses, looked on.

This photograph was taken in Cuba in 1955; Tony is seated and I'm in my baptismal gown on Mami's lap. This was another memory my father later tried to cut himself out of.

In the summer of 1959, just months after Castro took control of Cuba, Tony and I (age three, on the left) visited my grandparents and played on the white sands of Varadero—my last trip to my homeland.

Me (on the right) at four years old with Tony and Mami; we're adjusting to the Windy City and a new country.

A family outing in Chicago—the fear had begun to show in our faces. Left to right: Tony, Eddie, Mami, and me (seven years old).

Taken during a picnic at one of Chicago's many parks. The notorious Rivas thighs are on display. At six years old, I was already working on my Charles Atlas Dynamic-Tension. Left to right: me, Papi, Eddie (on Papi's shoulders), and Tony.

Posed pictures hide the truth. In Chicago, left to right: Tony, Papi, and me at about five years old.

At thirteen, the smile on my face hides the fact that my father had instituted a starvation plan—he allowed me to eat only one meal a day, if he determined that I had been good that day.

1968 was a turbulent time in our country and in our home on Oxford Street. Left to right: me, Eddie, and Dad.

In front of the house on Oxford Street, Hawthorne, California—the War Zone. At age thirteen, I was homicidal and suicidal. Left to right: Tony, Dad, Barbie, Eddie, and me.

Still dark and brooding. Me as a Miami Coral Park High School heavyweight wrestler, 1972.

Lillian Echevarria (now Lillian Bethea), who became my second mom after taking a risk on me, even after being warned that I was a big bad kid from a bad background.

In my last season at FSU, when our new coach, Bobby Bowden, was about to turn the Seminoles around, my fellow offensive lineman, Tom Rushing, and I helped initiate a bold new look for the team. Tom and I were known as "the Tube and the Cube."

After being a witness and victim of the terror inflicted on Mami and on us for fifteen years, it gave me some pleasure to see him having to park his car around the block to evade her and then being forced to sneak into our house to avoid running into her. Either the Wild-Eyed Latina had exposed him as a chickenshit or he had met his match in craziness and it had really scared him.

This may have been the point at which he went on a kick blaming all our problems on Mami for leaving us, and he went through our photo albums to make sure no pictures existed of him and her together, by cutting her head off in the picture, or his. To me, it only symbolized the hole her absence left in our lives and what a maniac he was.

Of course, his reign of terror still ruled, but the frequency of his physical assaults had lessened. This was partly because he couldn't incapacitate his slave labor force and also because he was working the graveyard shift at the mortuary. By the time he got home, we had all left for our various schools.

School was a mixed bag for me and had required some adjustment. Coral Park High School was now the seventh school I had attended in my ten-year educational career, and its large student body packed into tight quarters was very different from the sprawling campus of Hawthorne High School. My first week of school, I made my first appearance in the vice principal's office, for making the comment "Oh, wow, bitchin' " in English class.

Apparently South Miamians were offended by my Beach Boys lingo. Though I explained to Vice Principal McNulty that in Los Angeles "bitchin'" was commonly used like "cool" or "neat," he still saw fit to give me a verbal reprimand. Not surprisingly, I was to become a familiar visitor to the offices of Mr. McNulty and Mr. Farthing, the other vice principal.

While it had once bothered me that Tony and I were the only Cuban kids in our schools in Illinois and California, at Coral Park it bothered me more that we were no longer the novelty. To my disdain, many of the Cuban teenagers spoke Spanish in the halls or talked in a hybrid Spanglish, saying phrases like *"La cosa estaba supercool!"* (The thing was supercool!) With a reputation as something of a loner, I didn't associate with these kids, and few knew I was Cuban, until they made some remark in Spanish about me and I turned to eyeball them.

After a couple of hallway confrontations—a hard intended shoulder slam as a group of boys who were looking to mess with me got slammed into hallway lockers, and my reaction to a wannabe tough guy who stepped on the heel of my shoe—I established myself as someone not to be fucked with. Although I made a few friends, for the most part I rarely smiled and I walked around with a major chip on my shoulder. I began noticing that as I walked the school halls, some of the students moved out of my path. Or on other occasions, I stared down those who did look at me until they became uncomfortable and turned their gaze away, like a cat can do to you.

My earlier efforts to earn above-average grades had not kept Dad from shitting on me, and so I had pretty much succumbed to apathy. Certainly, I hadn't lost my sense of humor, but I was no longer the class clown, no longer the puppy who wanted to please someone. I went to class, paid attention, and made the grades I wanted to. Basically, I was a C student and that was fine with me.

One of the few highlights of my school day was homeroom, the first period of the day, where attendance was taken and announcements were made over the P.A. system. My homeroom teacher was a lovely young woman named Miss Susi Baldwin. Unlike the teachers who dealt with me either cautiously or strictly, Miss Baldwin didn't treat me, as some did, like a big scary kid. However she did it, her kindness and interest made me think that maybe I was smart, and possibly even a good person.

The other salvation Coral Park had brought, perhaps by a fluke or mistake on Dad's part, was football. When Dad had come to school to get us registered at the start of the school year, he had met the head varsity football coach, Frank Downing. Coach Downing took a look at both Tony and me and told Dad he was impressed with our physical size. "Are your boys coming out for the team?" he had asked.

To my indescribable surprise, Dad nodded in the affirmative, saying that, yep, both his two sons were outstanding athletes and both would love to play football.

At the first practice, Coach Downing introduced Tony and me to the team as high school all-stars from California. Tony had the experience and ability to back up that statement, but I had never even put on a football uniform. That became evident during the first practice. I made the mistake of inserting my thigh pads in wrong and then hitting the ground facefirst. The outside edges of the pads were driven into my testicles. Once I got my breath, I reinserted the pads correctly.

Placed on the JV team, which was coached by Ron Balaz, I made up for my lack of experience by drawing from my knowledge as a fan—after numerous L.A. Rams and USC games in California that I had seen on TV—and my determination to do well at a game my father said I would never be tough enough to play. The two-a-day summer practices were long, hot, and muggy, freshly cut grass clinging to our drenched bodies as the south Florida humidity climbed above 90 percent. The water weight loss at practice averaged between ten and thirteen pounds. Just when our padding and uniforms finished absorbing most of our body's discarded moisture, we'd get hit with a torrential downpour and we'd be hauling around an extra twenty-five pounds by the end of practice. The gassers, or wind sprints, in those conditions were oppressive.

The best part of practice for me was hitting. Whether it was driving the blocking sled, one-on-one drills, or a scrimmage, I was in my element slamming my body into other people or objects at full throttle. In baseball, I would have been thrown out of games for making contact with another player, but in football it was legal. Initially I was so aggressive that I had trouble hearing the whistle that ended the plays. The coaches liked my aggression on the playing field as long as it didn't spill over into an off-the-field fight. When I stupidly decided to take on a senior starter on the varsity, after he punched me in the back of the helmet for besting him during a scrimmage, my ever-protective older brother intervened.

Having heard that I was going to fight this guy later that after-noon, Tony stopped me on the way into the locker room, pulling me to the side as he said, "What are you, crazy?"

I told him that his teammate hit me in the head when I had my back turned.

"So what? That's football. You need to apologize to him."

"Fuck him."

Having quickly earned the respect of his teammates for his quiet leadership, Tony had already talked to the guy and had explained that I was a little hotheaded and also new to the game of football. The deal was that if I apologized, he'd let it slide. "Otherwise, Vic," Tony warned me, "he's gonna kill you."

It took a lot of convincing, but I eventually walked into the locker room and muttered that I was sorry. The guy seemed bigger out of uniform than in one. With a hairy barrel chest and a permanent five o'clock shadow, he had the appearance of a man in his thirties, not eighteen. We shook hands and he grinned, saying, "You got balls."

That may have been true but what I also had was a brother who had stood up for me and protected me. For the first time in a long while, that day I wore a smile on the long bus ride home.

Tony and I were worried about Barbie. We were all missing Mami but she was especially in need of her mother. She had also developed a chronic runny nose that required us to constantly have tissue paper at the ready. Dad never took her to the doctor to see if she had an infection or an allergy. By the third week, Barbie developed a foul smell around her face and her mucus was a funky yellow-green color.

"Come on, Barbie, blow" had become our mantra around her. It was difficult to be close to her and not react to the stench around her cute little face; when we did, it made her cry. Finally, just before foot-ball season got really busy, when it was time to get Eddie and Barbie ready for bed one night, Tony took on the job of getting her to blow her nose so she could breathe a little easier. She snorted several times when I heard Tony say, "Oh my God! Vic, get over here."

From my station in the kitchen, where I was washing the dishes, I walked toward the two of them and looked at what he was holding in the tissue. Eddie came running too. Mixed in with Barbie's snot was a one-and-a-half-inch rusted screw. Barbie whimpered as my brothers and I tried to console her.

"It'll be okay," one of us said. "Your nose is all better now," said another. "And how did that screw get up in your nose?" somebody had to ask.

"I don't know!" she wailed.

The stench went away immediately and a couple of days later, Barbie's nose stopped running. We didn't tell Dad about the screw, doing what we thought best to keep Barbie from being interrogated and punished for being a four-year-old little girl in need of love and attention.

Even as the months went by without any information about Mami's whereabouts, I wouldn't and couldn't give up hope that she was safe and on her way back to us. At times, I had flashes of her, as I had in the car during our trip. In the meantime, my coping mechanism was to vent everything I was feeling on the football field. As I continued growing and bulking up, I was on my way to becoming a formidable young player, except when my rapid growth caused me to lose coordination. As a tight end—basically an offensive lineman who is eligible to catch passes—I made a spectacular catch in one of our JV games and started rumbling up the right sideline with no one within thirty yards of me when, ten yards from scoring my first touchdown, my size thirteen shoes came together and I tripped myself. I landed on the three-yard line without ever being touched by the opposing team. We scored on the next play but I was furious at myself and my feet for days. The real bummer is that this JV game was the only shot I'd ever get in my life to score a touchdown.

The football bug didn't truly bite me until the last varsity game of the season, when several members of the JV squad and I were invited to dress for the game. Whereas the underclassmen competed in white uniforms, the true colors of the Coral Park Rams were blue and gold. Our varsity uniforms, in fact, were an exact match to the uniforms worn by the Notre Dame Fighting Irish football team. Since Tony was a senior, this would be the only time we would be members of the same football team. We dressed together in the locker room, rode the team bus, and took the field together.

The Rams were playing the Killian High Cougars in what was referred to as the "Toilet Bowl" because both teams were perennial losers. Even so, nothing could take away from the high that it gave me to stand in the tunnel before the game, looking out to the stadium and the capacity crowd through the mist of steam coming off my teammates. In one of the crispest déjà vus of my whole life, I was convinced that I had been in this place before, but in some ancient time.

This was different from my dreams of being a tiger, which were connected to sleep and fantasy. My flashes of being a Roman gladiator felt as powerful as memories and could strike at any time, like a lightning bolt, subconsciously or consciously. As I stood in this tunnel with the fans in the stadium screaming and stomping their feet, I knew that this was my game, the sport that allowed me my need to make physical contact, that gave me a structured outlet for some of the rage that boiled inside me, and that, perhaps best of all, fulfilled my desire to be acknowledged as a warrior.

I never got into the game that night. But once it was clear that the Rams were going to win, an upperclassman walked by and barked, "Keep your chin strap on." Code for "Get ready to rumble."

As the delegated leader of the underclassmen, I helped lead the charge just after the two teams met in the middle of the field for the handshake and I saw the fight break out. Unable to spot Tony, I dove in, swinging at anything attired in Killian green and yellow. Coaches began brawling and fans spilled out onto the field. The riot lasted for a few minutes until the police got it under control.

We boarded the buses for the short but glorious ride home. Once the coaches went down the aisles, confirming that there were no meaningful injuries, we began our victory celebration, chanting and singing the whole way back to Coral Park.

Dad had never come to see me play in my JV games; to my knowledge, he never went to see Tony play in his varsity games. Yet he maintained with certainty that my game was baseball and that I would never amount to anything on the football field.

There was a different kind of darkness setting in at home. Dad was still hitting us, but he seemed to be focusing on psychological warfare. His voice could make Eddie shake or Barbie cry. He used threats to our younger siblings to control Tony and me, on top of us being overwhelmed by housework and substitute parenting. What was starting to scare me most wasn't what Dad might do to us. At moments, I was more afraid of what I was going to do if pushed to the edge.

Staying out of the house was one of the reasons that, when football season was over, I signed up for the JV wrestling team, as a heavyweight. Besides that, the football coaches recommended it as a great conditioning sport and my goal was to be a starter on the varsity the next year. The heavyweight division started at over 185 pounds but had no limit on the upper end of the scale, so that I went on to face several wrestlers who exceeded three hundred pounds. By January, though I had won only about 50 percent of my matches, I was getting into better shape on a daily basis, my chest and arms expanding and becoming rock hard. Also valuable for me, hotheaded as I was, were the mental skills of patience and strategy required for choosing what takedowns and holds to use to defeat an opponent.

The information that Dad had heard at the coffee stand—which he presented to me upon my return home after wrestling practice—was that this fellow he had met had been boasting that his son at Coral Park had made the JV baseball team after some grueling try-outs.

Dad sat in a chair on our porch, smoking and glaring down at me on the lower step. "I told him that wasn't possible," my father continued, "because my son hadn't mentioned a thing about tryouts to me."

Impassively, I didn't speak, giving my father nothing. Staring up, I looked at him in his tank top and cutoff army pants that he rolled up to show off his large Rivas thighs. His right midthigh had a pronounced jagged scar that he claimed was from a childhood accident with barbed wire in Cuba.

"What do you know about that? There's another set of tryouts, right?"

Without too much effort, switching into defensive gear—legs shoulder width apart, soft knees, stomach tightening into rope cords, and schoolbooks protecting my balls—I looked him in the eyes and said, "No. Tryouts are over. I'm not playing baseball this year."

Dad's face became flushed, his jaw dropped, and the rest of his face had a quizzical, incredulous look. He flicked his cigarette and stood up, glaring down at me. In the cutoffs and tank top he appeared somewhat soft and chunky, something I hadn't noticed lately. He hadn't been working out or doing yoga much either.

"Get inside."

I moved around sideways, never taking my eyes off his hands and feet, until I went inside, where my eyes adjusted to the dark.

"Tell me again about baseball."

"I don't want to play this year. I want to concentrate on football."

"Who the fuck are you to decide about anything? You do what I tell you to do." Dad threw a couple of punches to my midsection. I shifted my weight to that side, tightening my oblique and abdominal muscles. The blows landed but with very little effect. Rubbing his wrist from discomfort, he hissed, "You're going to try out for baseball."

"Tryouts are over."

Two more punches landed as I took a step in to meet them. For years, he had controlled these moments with confidence and terror, ordering us to inch our way to him, sometimes with our bodies shaking. I had just closed the distance on him willingly. Dad took a step backward and cocked his head, like a primordial lizard, trying to make sense of what had just happened. "You better get yourself a try-out, because if you don't play baseball, you won't play any other sports. Oh, and by the way, you're done with wrestling." He snatched up his keys and wallet and stormed out, never looking back.

I watched him walking to the car and fantasized about slamming a knife into the middle of his back. Why was it that all of the men I admired growing up, John and Robert Kennedy, Martin Luther King Jr., had been killed by assassin's bullets, but some assholes could move through life untouched?

The next day at school, first thing, I talked to Coach Kirkpatrick, an assistant wrestling and JV football coach. A great guy with a couple of idiosyncrasies, Coach Kirkpatrick had a horrible stutter and wore a heavy layer of zinc oxide on his lips when he was outdoors. During football season, players hated when Coach Kirkpatrick would grab one of them by the face mask and pull him in to have a face-to-face conversation. He would start stuttering and soon the unfortunate player was spotted with zinc oxide.

Coach Kirkpatrick wasn't encouraging. "V-v-vic, tryouts are over. Coach Hertz has very strict rules and I doubt he'll make an ex-ex-exception."

I begged, pleaded, cajoled, and finally convinced Coach Kirkpatrick to see what he could do. At the end of a painfully suspenseful day, I was back to learn the verdict.

"Hey there, V-v-vic. Coach Hertz said . . ." Coach Kirkpatrick just paused, stuck on the next word, with his eyes opening and closing, for what seemed like an eternity, before he said, "th-th-that he's going to make an exception because of your situation." My tryout was not the next day, or the day after that. It was to take place immediately.

Changed into an old baseball uniform that barely fit anymore, cleats on and glove in hand, I raced to the field behind the school. Coach Steve Hertz was a former professional ball player with the Houston Astros organization. Handsome, well dressed, and a no-nonsense guy with just a speck of arrogance, he let me warm up my arm with one of the reserve catchers before taking the mound. Coach Hertz came to life after my first throw, and then he watched me throw another four pitches. He stopped me and asked his starting catcher to get behind the plate. Several members of the team gathered behind the backstop and watched with curiosity. I threw another ten pitches, rearing back and letting it go.

"Okay, that's enough! Come on over." Coach Hertz waited until I was closer before he asked, "How old are you?"

"Fifteen."

Coach Hertz told me to report the next day at three-thirty. Obviously, I had made the team. Acting cool, I asked who the JV coach was. That's when Coach Hertz informed me that I had just made the varsity.

As a change of pace, I flew home in record time so I could give Dad the news. When I arrived he was on his way out and his response to my excited "Hey, guess what? I made the varsity!" was a smirk. He merely said, "You're lucky," and left, slamming the screen door behind him.

Two weeks into practice, I stepped off the late bus that brought me home each day, which stopped on Red Road a few blocks from our house. The doors of the bus closed behind me and the roar of the engine muffled any other sound and left a trail of black oily smoke. As the smoke cleared I was about to turn to begin the short walk home when my attention was caught by a sight across the street, on the other side of Red Road.

Across the four lanes of busy Miami traffic, I saw a woman pushing a baby carriage. The woman reminded me instantly of my mother. But this happened all the time. Obviously, the tall Latina lady just coincidentally looked like Mami, or did so because of my desire for it to be her. Still, when the woman saw me looking in her direction, her face lit up with a brilliant smile. Then she waved at me. Was this a mirage? A fantasy?

My first impulse was to turn around to see if she was waving at someone behind me. No, I guessed not. I looked back and saw her motioning for me to cross the street toward her. Zigzagging across Red Road's busy four lanes, I never took my eyes off her, and by the time I was standing on the yellow dividing line, I knew that it was her. It was Mami!

Once on the other sidewalk, I ran to her, afraid she might disappear like an apparition in the movies. Inexperience be damned, I grabbed her and hugged her on the spot, clumsily leaning down to give her a peck on the cheek. Careful not to squeeze too hard, I just wanted to hold on and never let go.

Mami knew that she couldn't keep me long and hurried to fill in the gaps of what had happened since the day she disappeared seven months earlier, a version of which she eventually put into written form. She recalled that the day my father threw her out of the house in the early morning hours, July 24, 1970, happened to mark the date of her seventeenth wedding anniversary. She was four months pregnant by then and Dad threatened her and us if she dared make a scene, ordering her to get her things.

> He shoved me out the back door and I left with a small box of items and my Saint Barbara statue and a few dollars in my purse. He dropped me off in a small motel. . . . I went to a local market and bought bread with strawberry jelly and that is what I had for breakfast, lunch, and dinner. Next to me was a hamburger stand and the smell drove me crazy. Plus, being pregnant, I was hungrier than normal. I called several friends asking for help but they all turned me down, saying that it was too much responsibility to take on. I became very anxious in that small room not knowing what I would do next.

Mami then called a Peruvian couple, who came to pick her up and brought her home to stay with them for a few days. Out of gratitude, my mother spent that time cooking, cleaning, and helping take care of their four children. By the end of the week, she was able to get a ride to our house, only to find all of us and everything vanished without a trace. Neighbors informed her that her husband had taken her four kids and left in the car. Someone had heard a mention about Florida as the destination and passed that on to her. She immediately wrote to Dad's family members.

> I wanted them to know both versions of the story and knew he had been telling them his version only, which was a lie. Indeed I was right. He told them that I had a nervous breakdown and was being treated in a hospital. . . .
>
> It goes without saying that I spent many months crying over the loss of my children. Only a mother could understand this pain. I again had to ask for government assistance since I was receiving prenatal care and my due date was fast approaching.

In her own inimitable fashion, Mami struggled and juggled, finding work and a few kind friends and strangers. She never forgot one penny that she earned in the many odd jobs she took on; she never forgot any act of generosity. One old friend she found was shocked to see her, saying she had heard that Mami had been in a mental institution. That friend organized a garage sale among neighbors to raise money to throw a baby shower for her and Carmencita.

When I first saw the baby in the carriage with Mami, I had completely forgotten that she had been pregnant. In fact, I asked my mother if she was working as a nanny for someone.

My mother laughed. "No, this is your baby sister, Carmen."

The moment I looked closely at Carmen, it was clear she was a Rivas. Born at the end of November, she was a gorgeous, sweet-faced infant who looked a lot like Mami and Tony, although there was some of Papi in her too. Once she was born, my mother had taken on even more work to raise the money to come to Florida to find us. She had arrived about two weeks prior to our reunion and was staying with an aunt and uncle for the time being.

She never told me exactly how she had tracked us down. But for the past few days, Mami admitted, she had stood in this very place for hours, waiting and watching all the kids come off the different buses, just to catch a few glimpses of me.

Before either of us could break down, she urged me to hurry home and not to raise any suspicion with Dad. Giving me the phone number at her aunt's house, she promised that I would see her again soon. I leaned down and gave my new baby sister a kiss on the cheek, and then placed another peck on Mami's cheek. Again, I started to choke up. Her eyes were dry, however, and smiling. She said, "You know, I can't cry anymore. He took all my tears away."

Mami later said that our reunion out on the street was one of the most unforgettable moments of her life.

Shortly after it, Dad was served with divorce papers, and after seventeen years of her nightmare, she got her day in court. She was able to tell her story, even though Dad denied everything. But she won and was granted the divorce she sought, along with ten dollars a month for Carmen's child support. Unfortunately, because she was on public assistance, Dad retained custody of those of us kids still living with him. The court granted her only one visitation day a month to see the rest of us and required it to be held at a neutral location.

Dad dropped us off at our first meeting, which was arranged near a fountain at a park in Coral Gables, letting us know he'd return in a couple of hours.

Mami did what she had always done and made sure that we ate something. She had made sandwiches and a flan, and had brought us sodas. We ate in a kind of awkward silence, no one really saying anything that could become a conversation. How could we? Those normal family exchanges had never happened before; why should they now?

After we ate, we clustered around Mami and Carmencita, not

knowing what to say or do, each of us mostly staring at the ground. It reminded me of TV shows that I'd seen where family members got visitation time with loved ones who were in prison. Only, in our case, my brothers and sister and I were still in lockup; Mami and my baby sister had already been paroled.

Eddie and Barbie, eventually, ran off to play on the playground equipment. Mami asked some basic questions about our new high school and the different sports we were playing. There was so much I wanted to say about how much we all missed her and loved her; my siblings no doubt felt the same way. But again, we were all handicapped when it came to showing affection.

Dad drove up and parked the Impala station wagon a hundred yards away. As Tony, Eddie, and Barbie began the slow march back into his custody, I waited, not wanting to leave Mami's side.

At the last minute, making sure that Dad was watching, I leaned down and gave Mami another kiss on the cheek.

I could hear him yelling at me in my mind, "Who the fuck are you to love? You do what I tell you to do!"

That had been true for fifteen and a half years. But it was about to change.

The shit was always hitting the fan in our house. But the day the inferno was finally lit in me, the shit was literally to blame. Dad's question, "Who left the toilet lid up?" set everything that would dramatically and irrevocably change my life into motion.

He had been wound up tight from the minute I walked in the door late from baseball practice for no special reason other than that the bus was late dropping me off.

"Why are you late?" Dad challenged as I swung in the door.

I stopped and answered, "The bus was late."

Quickly surveying the scene, I concluded that Tony—who had stayed home with a terrible cold and high fever—was asleep in the small bedroom he and I shared in the back. Eddie and Barbie were in the living room on the floor in front of Dad, quietly watching television. They were probably hungry, I realized.

Dad wasn't done with me. "Why were you late? I want the truth."

"I just told you, the bus was late."

Reacting as if my tone was not to his liking, with maybe a little too much attitude, he rose from the couch and squared off on me. Not intimidated, I dropped my books and baseball gear, preparing myself for his assault. He stood and stared at me, narrowing his yellow eyes. I matched his stare and waited.

Dad jutted his chin up and nodded toward the kitchen. "Go make me *un café.*" He turned and walked down the short hall to his room.

Something had just happened between us but I wasn't sure what. Had he just backed down from the same mad-dogging that I used to intimidate other kids at school?

Not pushing my luck, I made Dad's *café* and carried it into his room. He took a sip and before I could slip out through the curtain, he stopped me. "*Este café tiene sabor de mierda.*" This coffee tastes like shit. "Go make some more."

Back in the kitchen, after my younger siblings announced that, yes, they were starving, I started another small percolator of Cuban coffee and worked on some peanut butter and jelly sandwiches. The *café* I made as before, first adding a couple of drops of coffee to the sugar, and stirring it to create the foamy, syrupy liquid that was then added to the rest of the espresso. After I handed off the sandwiches to Eddie and Barbie, I returned to Dad's room with the second cup of *café.*

Dad sat at the end of his bed, half dressed, tying his shoes. When I held the coffee out to him, rather than take it, he stared at me for several moments, forcing me to stand and wait, holding the small cup out. At last he took it, now not looking, and drank it in one long sip. "That's more like it."

Back in the living room with my younger siblings, I sat down on a chair near the front door and the two of them took seats on the couch. I had just started my homework when I heard the sound of bed springs uncoiling in his room. The sound told me he was standing up. Next came the sounds of his feet going into the bathroom and running water from the bathroom sink. Almost immediately, I could hear him shut the faucets and his presence coming closer. A coiled cobra, he stood at the entrance to the living room just blazing as he stared at the three of us, moving his eyes to each of us. There was no question that when he next asked who left the top up on the toilet, that person was going to suffer his major wrath.

We all looked up at Dad but it was Eddie, his body beginning to shake and his face twitching, who had been in there last. Barbie sat next to Eddie, frozen.

"I said, who left the top up on the toilet? The place smells like shit." He waited for the answer that was becoming clearer with every spasm of my little brother's body. Dad took a step toward Eddie and asked again, his rage coming to the surface. "Who left the fuckin' top up?"

Like a shark zeroing in on its prey, Dad had his eyes locked in on Eddie as he walked toward him slowly. As he was about to take that last step before striking Eddie, I dropped my books and stood up.

The sound of my books hitting the floor turned his head in my direction.

My voice exploded from my core. "I didn't put the fuckin' top down on the toilet! So what!"

The minute the profanity flew from my mouth, something I'd never used in responding to him, I knew he would come for me. But what more could he do? I was already a walking recipe for a disaster of his making. Beyond my short fuse, my talking out loud to myself, my constant thoughts of killing myself and killing him, I couldn't forget anything he had ever done to me. What was left? Whatever he had waiting, I could take it. He wasn't going to beat my ten-year-old brother for taking a shit that smelled. He wasn't going to make me insane like him anymore.

Dad didn't take a step toward me. But he looked at me, flaring and constricting his nostrils with every breath.

Summoning the guts, despite my absolute terror, I flared and constricted my nostrils right back at him. And with every intake of air, I expanded my six-foot-two-inch frame for all it was worth.

For a second, my father flinched. He shifted his eyes and saw the weapon he was looking for, the Kirby upright vacuum next to him. Without any hesitation, he grabbed it and flung the twenty-five-pound machine at me. The vacuum hit me in the chest, but before it hit the ground, I was able to grab the base with one hand and the handle with the other. I bench-pressed it right back at him.

Time and space moved quickly and slowly, and expanded and constricted, all at the same time. Out of order and rhythm, Dad pushed the vacuum aside, lowered his head, and charged at me. I took a step to the side, thrusting my left arm through his armpit and around his back. With my right arm, I reached across, grabbed his shoulder, and then torqued my hips into him and slammed him to the ground, driving my body weight into his chest. During my brief wrestling career, this was my best move. A whizzer with a hip throw.

The force of the throw combined with my body weight had knocked the air out of Dad. All of the hurt, anger, and humiliation that I had endured and witnessed for the past fifteen years exploded in a flurry of punches. Instead of fighting back or defending himself, he curled up in a fetal position and covered his face with his arms. None of my blows did much to his face, but his torso must have felt the ferocity of my attack.

When I backed off him, drenched in sweat and drooling saliva, I stood up and saw Eddie and Barbie traumatized, with slack jaws and terrified eyes.

Then I looked back down at Papi. This was the man who had terrified our entire household for years, now cowering and crying beneath me. I felt no pity for the pathetic sight that I now towered over. But neither did I feel any satisfaction for the well-deserved punishment that I had inflicted on him. He crawled away in the direction of his room and pulled himself up to standing as he reached the hallway.

Dad was crying audibly in his room. Still standing in the same place, I cried quietly. Eddie and Barbie didn't move. My brain tried to come to terms with the reality of my options. Should I run screaming into the street, asking a neighbor for protection?

Before I could even consider this course of action, Dad reappeared, crazy-eyed, strands of his baby-fine auburn hair covering one side of his face. My eyes caught a glint of metal near his right hand and then, like a catcher picking off a runner trying to steal second base, he snap-threw the object at my head. I had no time to react. Just inches from my right ear, it crashed into the wall. I looked down and saw Dad's Aqua-Lung knife.

The foot-long thick stainless steel blade beckoned to me. I picked up the knife and looked back at Dad.

"Kill me! Kill me!" he yelled.

A deep guttural pain moved its way through my body and exploded in a loud sob. The knife fell from my hand as I started crying.

He begged and bullied, shouting, "Come on, kill me!"

But I couldn't. "You're my father."

What looked almost like disappointment flickered on Dad's face. Then he turned and stalked back down the hall, emerging moments later with his keys, and giving us one last look before he left the house.

Convinced he would return with a gun, I started packing, stuffing a few articles of clothing into a brown paper grocery bag. I moved through the house grabbing any coins that I saw and emptying the contents of my siblings' piggy banks into my pockets. In our bedroom, where Tony had managed to sleep through everything, I grabbed my baseball gear.

"Tony," I began loudly, not sure why I wanted to wake him, but maybe to say good-bye.

He opened his bloodshot eyes and moaned.

"Dad wants me to go buy him some cigarettes. I'll be right back."

"Could you get me some orange juice?" His voice was dry and raspy. "There's some change on the nightstand."

"Yeah, sure," I lied, grabbing up the change. Then I told him that I'd be back soon.

Eddie and Barbie got the same story too. They were still too dazed to question me. For a moment I hesitated, wondering if I should say anything else, with no idea what would happen once I walked out the door. But something else inside told me not to linger.

After checking for any signs of my father's car or him, I began to run. My pace was moderate at first, with my head on a swivel, making sure Dad was nowhere lurking in shadows. The farther from my house I traveled, the faster I ran, cutting across less-traveled streets, hiding behind cars. I ran and I ran and I ran.

Sweating and sobbing as I ran, I fled the war zone, a refugee running from an enemy that, when given the chance, I couldn't kill. Because he was my father. Because I loved him. And all I wanted was for him to love me. But I had learned one of the truest survival lessons of my life: Love should never hurt. No matter what he said his reasons were for brutally punishing us, that he was making us strong or making us better, because he loved us, that wasn't love.

I ran until my lungs felt like they were going to explode, and then I ran a few blocks more, collapsing against an old six-foot-tall mildewed brick wall. There I sat, panting, still crying, but starting to laugh. Aware that I was too much in the open, I stood and looked over the wall onto what would be my home for the next few days. It was an old cemetery.

Hopping the high wall, I landed in the grass and headed toward a tree, careful to step around the burial plots. When I made it to the tree, I sat down again and leaned my back against its wet bark. Whatever fear I may have felt about sleeping in a graveyard soon dissipated with an overwhelming exhaustion and the knowledge that my tough assignment was over.

part two

exodus

5

rescue

(1972–1973)

It takes a village to raise a child.
—African saying

IN THE EARLY 1970S an emerging movement, pioneered mainly by women activists, created a new breed of advocates who would in time radically transform the landscape for families like mine. This movement, which sought to end violence against women and their children, had already begun to establish safe houses and shelters in some cities, while also promoting awareness that abuse was no longer a "private family matter." Buoyed by the peace movement that was bringing an end to the Vietnam War and by Dr. Martin Luther King Jr.'s values of nonviolence, advocates for women and children had begun to send the message that the right to be safe at home was a fundamental human right that ought to belong to every citizen of the world.

In years to come, I often wondered how different life would have been for my family if we had been able to get the kind of help that later became available in a growing number of communities across the country, or if we had at least known that there were advocates out there. At the same time, and much to my unending surprise, a series of unofficial advocates, champions, and true angels, sometimes in the least likely form, began to step out from the woodwork on my behalf, almost from the moment that I left my father's house.

The first of my rescuers, a small Wiry Kid from school whom I barely knew, found me not far from the cemetery, near S.W. Eighth Street (also known as the Tamiami Trail) and Forty-third Avenue, about two miles from my house. After just about forty-eight hours on the lam, I wasn't so sure I could handle a third night of sleeping in the cemetery. The night before had been pretty terrifying, not like the first night, when the victory of my escape may have given me a false sense of courage. Or maybe, I thought, the spirits of the dead decided to give me a pass the first night but came back to haunt me the next. When I climbed over the wall and made a dash for the tree that second time, the markers and headstones looked as if they had been raised higher than the night before, and were maniacally daring me, like land mines, to get by them. Lowering my head, I crisscrossed and hurdled over the uneasy dead, until I reached my tree of shelter, out of breath. Though it was a warm, balmy Miami night, I trembled as if the Chicago winter winds were whipping through me. What little sleep I did get was nightmare-ridden, with images of hands reaching up through the ground and trying to pull me under.

When my classmate spotted me late the next afternoon, two days of homelessness had left me hungry and starting to smell rather ripe. Ashamed, I wasn't sure what to say or do when he called my name.

The Wiry Kid had a high-energy way of talking. He ran over and started asking questions at a rapid-fire pace. Where had I been? What happened to me? Did I know that everyone was looking for me?

"Who?" I asked, warily.

"Everybody, man, I mean, the school, you know. Oh yeah, the cops too. And your dad."

I hesitated, not sure whether I could or should trust him. That was my training. My own brother had been forced to turn over information given to him in confidence. As much as I'd talked to my friends and neighbors in California, even the police, nobody had ever believed me or was ever able to do anything to help me. But my new friend was willing to listen, and I, relieved to be talking to somebody other than myself, was more than willing, my eyes brimming and then overflowing with tears, to tell him about what had happened, in as much of a condensed version of my life as possible. Being not only Cuban but having spent my formative years in the Windy City, I couldn't help a certain degree of long-windedness, besides the fact that I had my first-ever captive audience, as we walked and I talked, and talked, and talked. By the time I finished, it was dusk.

The Wiry Kid had listened the whole time with a look of shock and disbelief on his face but the first thing he said, when I allowed him to get a word in edgewise, indicated that he had no reason not to believe me. He didn't just believe me; he wanted, even *insisted,* that I go home with him and tell my story to his father.

There were many angels, as I couldn't help but call them, who were being sent, I was sure, to help guide me out of the long dark night of childhood. That Wiry Kid was most definitely an angel. And so too was his father, who also happened to be a lawyer.

With his quiet, thoughtful demeanor, he could have been a double for Ward Cleaver as he listened to my story. This time, I told it with even more detail than I'd given his son. He not only believed me but he told me that what Dad had been doing behind closed doors wasn't a private family matter; it was in fact a crime. My mind reeling, I listened as he picked up the phone and began making calls to inquire about how soon a hearing could be scheduled with a judge.

Although I was somewhat nervous to impose on my mother, knowing that Dad could easily come there to threaten me and her, my classmate's father assured me that once the judge ruled on my case, that wouldn't be a problem. Unsure as to how he could be so certain with the madman I had for a father, I called Mami next and she arrived shortly after that with her aunt and uncle, and baby Carmen. Ironically, it turned out that their house was less than two blocks from the cemetery.

The hearing at court took place within days, thanks to the Wiry Kid's father. But from the minute I arrived at the courthouse, with Mami at my side, my optimism that it would turn out in my favor drained away. As God was my family's witness, Dad's acting abilities could snow anybody. El Caballero, or El Ciclón? The Gentleman, or the Cyclone? Who was going to show up this morning? When an armed, uniformed bailiff came to escort me and Mami into the judge's private chambers where the hearing was to be held, I tried not to show my mounting nervousness. We were seated on one side of the room and informed that the judge would be with us momentarily. Before my father was allowed to come in, I was to be first given a chance to tell my side of the story.

On the judge's desk were a few framed photographs of an attractive middle-aged blond woman surrounded by what appeared to be her children. As I was looking at the pictures, the judge entered the chambers, the same woman in the photos with her children. Seeing that the judge who was going to decide my fate was a woman, and that she had children of her own, I instantly knew that I would be safe. She listened carefully to my more concise version of the events that had precipitated my disappearance earlier in the week.

Then she signaled to the bailiff to escort my father in. Looking more like a dashing movie star than ever, Dad stepped into her chambers elegantly attired in one of his expensive suits, with a crisp white shirt and conservative tie. With a respectful, almost statesmanlike demeanor, he walked to his seat on the opposite side of the room from me and Mami, smiling warmly at the judge. Before he sat, Dad turned and smiled lovingly at me. Of course, that twinkle in his eye might have been seen as fond and friendly to the untrained eye; but I knew that twinkle well, and it was dangerous.

The judge had me repeat my accusations with him sitting directly across from me on the other side of the room. Close to the end of my account, just after I described his throwing the Aqua-Lung knife at my head, she stopped me and turned to Dad. "Mr. Rivas, did you throw a knife at your son?"

Dad straightened up in his chair, adjusted his tie, and smiled charmingly at the judge. "Well, Your Honor—"

"Did you throw a knife at your son?"

"Well, you see, Your Honor, um . . ."

"Answer the question! Did you throw a knife at your son?"

Dad kept trying to explain away his behavior in his most congenial tone but couldn't come right out and deny that he had thrown it.

That was all she had to hear. "That's enough," the judge began, and when Dad tried one last "Your Honor, he is—" she shut him down. "I said, that's enough! If you get within a hundred yards of Victor, I'll have you arrested and thrown in jail. Is that clear?" He balked, still arguing, until finally he nodded yes. She had made it clear.

That was it. All my father's power and control over me had been dissolved. By a woman no less. Eyes shifting, he rose and left the room, followed by the bailiff. The judge kept me and Mami in chambers, just chatting with us for a few minutes, waiting to make sure that we gave Mr. Rivas a head start to leave the courthouse and vicinity. She had issued a restraining order against him (what was then known as a peace bond); if he violated it, he would be in much more trouble. Somehow I didn't think he would. To my great embarrassment, I had realized in my own confrontation with him that, like most bullies, he was a coward who only oppressed those who couldn't fight back. It occurred to me now that I had never seen him take on anybody his own size. But even though I was probably safe from him, I couldn't ignore worries about my siblings. As a rationalization, I tried to reassure myself that because the three of them were so much better behaved than me, they would be okay. Maybe I was having survivor's guilt.

The bailiff returned and went around to the judge's side of her desk before leaning down and whispering in her ear. The judge nodded. With a serious expression she looked at me, as though double-checking to make sure she had made the right decision, and then said, "You're free to go. Good luck to you."

Mami and I walked out, side by side, mother and son, fellow refugees. I was free, I was free. What a country, America! Justice had smiled on me.

What stands out most in my memory was what it felt like to step outside the courthouse into the warm, humid Miami air and to look up into the white billowy clouds and breathe.

A stranger in the strange land of freedom, I was ill prepared for the tests and temptations that leapt out of the woodwork right along with my rescuers.

My biggest problems? Me, my lack of self-esteem, and my inner five-hundred-pound gorilla of anger who had been rattling his cage just waiting for this day. Any sociologist could have explained what it meant to be an at-risk youth.

In my case, it meant that it took me less than two weeks before I was on my way to smoking dope and joining a gang. In the service of honesty and fair reporting, however, let me point out that I got a better buzz from *café con leche* than Miami pot in 1971, and that in those years the gangs, or what we politely referred to as our "club," fought with fists, not with knives or guns.

After a week away from school, when I returned there was a noticeable change in how others seemed to perceive me. Walking the halls, I was greeted by respectful nods of acknowledgment from many of the guys and coy smiles from a lot of girls. In my homeroom, a handful of students surrounded me to ask questions about my disappearance. How did it happen? How far had I traveled? What happened when I was captured? Uncomfortable with so much attention and not sure how I felt about my elevated bad-boy status, I clammed up, telling them, "I don't want to talk about it." That only served to reinforce the rumors and my mystique.

On my first day back to school, I hurried to baseball practice, concerned that my absence might have put my standing in jeopardy. In retrospect, even though I hated how Dad forced me to try out, I needed baseball, both as a physical outlet and as something that made me proud of myself. I didn't want to disappoint Coach Kirkpatrick—who had helped me pull strings to get the tryout—or Coach Hertz, who had enough faith in my talent to put me on the varsity. I would never forget how after that last-minute tryout, when I went to the locker room the next day, one of the lockers was labeled with my name. And inside it had been a brand-new practice uniform with "Coral Park" emblazoned across the chest.

The reality that my talent was being taken seriously became evident a week or so into the season when a scout with the Miami Orioles, a farm team in the Baltimore Orioles organization, approached me after practice. Since Coral Park was known for its high level of baseball talent, there were often plenty of scouts for college and professional teams stopping by practice. With their notepads and stopwatches and rudimentary radar guns, they were pretty obvious. After I finished my pitching practice and stepped off the mound, the scout that approached asked, "Jim?"

My lack of response caused him to say, "You're Jim Pacheco, right?" He had mistaken me for a senior pitcher with a whip of a throwing arm.

"No." I shrugged. "I'm Vic Rivas."

He quickly asked me what grade I was in. When I told him I was a sophomore, he was a little disappointed, but then asked my age.

"Fifteen," I said, knowing by now that I towered over most of my team.

"Vic, do you have any idea how hard you're throwing?"

Nah, I shrugged again. "But I have a pretty good fastball."

"Pretty good?" He held out the LCD readout to show me. His radar had timed me at ninety miles per hour.

From then on, I'd notice other scouts checking me out at practices and games. In the meantime, I seemed to have also proven myself to Coach Hertz. As a pretty tough drill sergeant, he emphasized top-notch conditioning, and I had learned that pitchers had to be the best-conditioned players on the team. I had to perform drill after drill with intervals of sprinting. Though I would be drenched with sweat at the end of a practice, I thrived on working hard and proving that I could meet challenges on the ball field.

Much to my relief, I didn't have to explain to Coach Hertz about where I'd been the last week. In general, he tended to show a little more patience with me since I was the only sophomore on the team. But he was probably aware that I had run away from home and was going through a difficult transition.

Living under the same roof as Mami again was wonderful. But because she and Carmen were already guests in the home of her aunt and uncle, being one more mouth to feed felt like an imposition. Tia Gloria and Tio Tata were generous, making sure I didn't go hungry and buying me a few clothes, and I tried to be gracious by helping out with chores—the trash, dishes, the lawn. Mami did everything else, as far as I could tell. Cooking, cleaning, laundry. It bothered me to see her aunt treating her as something of a servant. I had to hold my tongue the afternoon that Tia Gloria, lounging in her recliner and watching one of her *novellas,* practically ordered Mami to bring her something to eat and drink, and when my mother patiently brought her a beverage and a snack, my great-aunt merely pointed with the long manicured nail of her index finger at the TV tray. Tia Gloria didn't deign to thank Mami or even look up at her.

Instead of saying anything, I tended to spend less time in their house, avoiding returning home. A lifelong habit. My new friendship with Gil, a football buddy, gave me other places to go.

A year older than I, Gil had an easygoing yet still focused manner, and he happened to be the president of the Deucalions, a fraternity-styled gang. He started keeping tabs on me, not pressing me but just making sure everything was cool. Pretty soon he was walking me down the halls and buying me lunch in the cafeteria, more or less taking me under his wing. Good-looking, with long brown hair parted in the middle, a nice set of biceps on him, and a disarming smile, he didn't need to know my story to know that I was starved for the sense of belonging that he and thc club could offer. But when he invited me to hang out at his house, after a couple of visits and some lightweight marijuana to loosen my tongue, I spilled my guts. Gil listened intently and I was sure his eyes welled up a couple of times.

When he brought up the Deucalions, if I hadn't shown so much interest, he probably wouldn't have pushed the idea. But I was all for it. To get in, I had to be nominated, and I was eager to be part of a fraternity. From what I could tell, the emphasis wasn't on violence or lawlessness; it was more about upholding a code of honor, about protecting your fellow members, your turf, even your school campus.

My initiation took place behind a municipal building at Coral Estates Park, a recreation center near the high school, on a Friday night. Amid pot smoking and drinking, there were fifteen members present, as well as a few girls there for the partying. But when my moment came, the atmosphere was suddenly very serious as Gil got up to begin a process that was an odd combination of parliamentary procedure and an ancient tribal rite of passage. After the first test was over, I had been paddled by the barrel of a baseball bat that had been sawed in half to give it a flat hard surface. Each member gave me three whacks on my behind and I went three rounds, enduring 135 swings at my ass that would have made Sister Ernie Banks, and every principal who ever took the wood to me, cringe. Nobody in the history of the Deucalions had ever withstood that many swings. The other members were blown away, not so much at what I'd endured but that I'd done it with barely a flinch. Though I was bleeding and swollen, it was almost nothing compared to what Dad could do to me.

The second test, known as the bull run, gave me a chance to redeem myself from the humiliation of Red Rover back in Catholic school. Holding trash can lids and some cans, the members formed a small menacing circle around me. The object was to fight my way out, using any means necessary. The only advice I was given was not to end up on the ground. I lowered my head, swinging wildly, looking for a path to escape from. It took me several beats to realize that this was a bluff. Nobody struck me. It was a test of nerve. Immediately, I was engulfed in a communal bear hug by the mob. Laughing, Gil yelled, "You're in! You're in!" as several others congratulated me.

Barely conscious, I collapsed and was taken to someone's house to spend the night before staggering back to Tia Gloria's house. When I told Mami that I had fallen backward down the stairs at school, she believed me. But the Cuban doctor who examined me at the local clinic probably didn't. Cleaning me up and sending me off with a pair of loaner crutches, he warned me to be careful.

Despite whatever badge of pride my swollen and bleeding ass and crutches represented to me, Vice Principal McNulty had gotten wind of what had happened and was ready for me first thing Monday morning, escorting me back to his office and interrogating me. Staring at me over his glasses, his bushy eyebrows dancing up and down, he listened to me tell my made-up story about my injuries and then launched into a lecture about the pitfalls of gang life. "It's a dead-end street," he insisted, in almost the same language I had heard on Bowery Boys films I'd seen on TV. Making it clear he didn't think much of me, he also had to add that gang life would certainly ruin whatever "limited" opportunity I had to succeed in the future.

This felt like Dad all over again, and it pissed me off. Who was he to lecture me? I didn't know what he was talking about, I said, repeating my lie: "I fell down the stairs."

"Wait here," he told me, and left his office. A few minutes later, the door opened and McNulty returned with Tony. My brother and I hadn't talked to each other since the night I had left the house. Whenever we passed in the halls we looked at each other uncomfortably, as though we now lived in such different worlds that we didn't speak the same language. That was how we greeted each other in Mr. McNulty's office.

The vice principal made me stand up and show Tony my injuries. With the same sad, soulful brown eyes that Mami had, my brother watched me undo my belt and lower my pants. A nasty sight, I was sure. His eyes filled up but no tears spilled. I looked at him and he just shook his head sadly.

Of course, Tony would never join a gang. He was the First Son, not the eternal fuckup like me.

Mr. McNulty dismissed us. Tony left first, then I hobbled out on my loaner crutches. In the hours that followed, I convinced myself that I didn't care what he thought, but I did. I missed him. I missed the patient way he listened. He was my brother and I loved him, as foreign a concept as that was. My impulse was to try to find Tony later and say something, but the thought that he might reject me stopped me.

A week later we had a different conversation from what I had in mind.

That particular Monday my injuries had healed enough that I was able to resume baseball practice. After the final bell rang, as was my routine, I hurried out the back doors of the school to the cement corridor that led to the athletic locker rooms. After walking into the dark, musty, mildewed locker room, early enough for there not to be many other players there yet, I set my books down on the bench to free my hands for the combination lock.

My locker was empty. All of my baseball gear was gone. Uniform, cleats, gloves, hat, even my jock and cup. Maybe Coach Hertz wasn't putting up with my missed practices due to a questionable injury; maybe he'd heard about my getting jumped into the gang.

"Coach Hertz?" I called, knocking on the door to his office.

Coach Hertz appeared a few seconds later in a pair of shorts and long baseball undershirt.

"What happened to my stuff?"

"Your brother came by and took it." He said this as if I ought to have known.

"What do you mean, he came and took it?"

Coach Hertz described the note that had been written by Dad, instructing my coaches to turn my equipment over to Tony. The note informed the coaches that I was done with baseball for the season because I needed to get my grades up and be better behaved.

The blood in my ears felt like it was boiling. My fists were balled up so tightly that my fingernails were digging into my palms.

"I don't live with my dad! He has no right to take my stuff! Why didn't you call me out of class?"

"Look, Vic, I think you should take some time off and get your life in order. Come out next year."

"I don't need to take any fucking time off. I'm getting my stuff back!"

I turned and bolted out of the locker room, leaving my books behind. I had to get out to the school bus stop before Tony got on the bus. Every step there, I gnashed my teeth, crying and cussing; several students got out of my way.

"Hey!" I shouted the instant I spotted my brother. Not, "Hey, Tony!" Just "Hey!"—the same guttural bark our father used to summon us. Tony turned and we locked eyes. I was still fifty yards away but closing fast, almost sprinting. "Where's my fucking stuff?"

"I don't have it." He said this matter-of-factly, not smugly.

"Bullshit, you took my stuff. Coach Hertz told me."

"I don't have it. Dad came by and I gave it to him."

There was a split second where I could have let loose on him. I'm not even sure what kept me from trying to pummel him in front of a gathering crowd of students. But no matter how much I hated him in this moment, I knew very clearly the control Dad had on all of us. The look of shame and sadness on Tony's face I'll never forget.

"Keep your fuckin' hands off my stuff and stay the fuck away from me!" was the best I could do. I turned to walk away, and then the gorilla leapt out, and forced me to add, "You tell that chickenshit that if he has something to say, say it to my face."

I spent the rest of the afternoon alone in the far corner of the athletic field behind Coral Park, bawling my eyes out. Tony and I had very few days left on the same school campus and our confrontation at the bus stop that day was to be the last contact we had for the rest of the school year. A month later, Anthony Rivas Jr. graduated from Coral Park High School with honors at age sixteen. For reasons that had less to do with Tony than with Dad, Mami and I were not invited to attend his graduation ceremony.

In between spending much of the summer swimming at the YMHA, I continued to flirt with the dead-end road of gang life, with the occasional functions, as we called our rumbles, that gave me a license to brawl. My sense of irony did enjoy the rough function we had just outside the Children's Hospital. To say that we could have walked our injuries in was no exaggeration.

But then, in no way connected to the Deucalions, I started to dabble in a much more serious form of criminal behavior. What was scary, for a kid like me who never had money of his own, was how profitable it was. Nothing I ever did in my life left me with more shame.

It started happening after a couple of times when I was hitching rides home from the YMHA. Two middle-aged men, clean-cut fatherly types, who picked me up started their conversations with almost the same dialogue: "How old are you? Wow, fifteen! You're a big kid."

The first man who picked me up asked me if I did any modeling. Like for the Sears, Roebuck catalog?

"No," he said, and pulled the car over. He led me to the back of his car and opened up his trunk. Inside were numerous magazines with cover shots of young men dressed scantily in underwear or leather. Without further ado, I split, darting into the first store I saw.

The other man, in a suit and tie, really looked like he could have been one of my Cuban uncles. His compliments were flattering; he asked if I had a lot of girlfriends. I lied and said, "Yeah, lots."

"You must be really big." He smiled.

"I'm over two hundred pounds," I admitted.

He shook his head and said, "No, down there." Without warning, he reached over and put his hand on my crotch while he continued driving the car.

It took me a couple of moments to get over the shock and then I reacted. I punched him in the face, which drove his head into the driver's door window as I yelled for him to pull over. He was crying and begging forgiveness.

In a rage, I almost hit him again. Instead, I blurted out, "Give me your wallet!" When he refused, I threatened to call the cops, and he relented. I pulled out a wad of cash, threw the wallet in his face, and exited his car, feeling filthy from this encounter. But I was ninety dollars richer.

The next few times the same kind of fatherly types tried to pick me up, either when I was hitching or on the street, I kept their credit cards too. More pity for them if they happened to remind me of Dad. What really scared me was to think I could become like him, without a conscience.

Each time, even after I bought things for myself, or for Mami and Carmen, I couldn't shake the devil voice of Papi inside: *Fucking* ladrón. But there was another voice that kept asking me, *What are you doing? This isn't who you are. You're better than this.* I wasn't so sure I believed that either.

The only thing I was sure about, as summer came to an end, was that I needed to do the righteous thing and get a job to earn some money, not just for extras and to save up for a car, but so I wouldn't be a burden on Mami. Always resourceful, always juggling, she had managed to move us to a small apartment in the northwest section of Miami. It was tiny, basically a converted garage with Carmen's crib against the wall next to the kitchen counter and two twin beds that lined the other wall, where Mami and I slept head to head. In the bathroom, the miniature shower, toilet, and sink were so close that I could sit on the pot, lean forward, and shave at the same time.

My mother magically filled the humble abode with warmth and the delicious smells of her cooking. She never complained, but I knew we were barely making the rent and eating. And I was aware that Mami sometimes went hungry to feed us, on top of the fact that I was fifteen going on sixteen, six foot two and over two hundred pounds, and an eating machine. If I didn't get a job to supplement Mami's income, I could easily eat us out of house and home. Of course, once school started, a part-time job would require me to quit sports, something I dreaded.

There was one other problem. Our apartment was directly across the street from Miami High School and seven miles from Coral Park High School. If anyone in the Coral Park administration found out, I'd be required to transfer, and for all kinds of reasons, I didn't want to do that. That meant keeping my living situation secret from almost everyone.

By the time the summer two-a-day football practices started in August, as I showed up early after taking the city bus and then returned to Mami's on it late in the afternoon, I hadn't come up with a practical game plan yet. The more I practiced and got a sense of the team that we had shaping up, the more depressed I became about the idea of having to drop out. The varsity had a new coach, named Carl Mosso, a short, tough, middle-aged Italian with the middle and fourth fingers on his left hand missing. There were several spurious rumors about the missing fingers. One was that Coach Mosso was a Korean War veteran whose fingers were blown up by a grenade; the other was that he was mob connected and had crossed the wrong guy. Not that I cared either way. What mattered was that he was a great coach and that he liked me. At the beginning of the second week of two-a-days, he announced that I was the starting tight end on offense.

In our starting lineup, I played next to Randy Clark, affectionately known as the White Whale. The White Whale was a three-hundred-pound behemoth with such fair skin that some kids thought he might be an albino, but no one ever asked. He was laconic—you could barely get a word out of him—but on the field he was quick, strong, and aggressive. The White Whale and I had awesome potential to be a dominant blocking partnership with our over five hundred pounds of mass and strength.

We also promised to have an improved season, I thought, because of our quarterback, Marvin Wheeler. A senior, Marvin was an average-sized quarterback with a decent arm and good footwork. But what looked to set him apart was that special quality that only a few QBs have: his cool under pressure.

"Coach Mosso," I heard myself asking on the last day of the second week of practice, "I need to speak to you later."

He nodded, and told me to stop by the office after we were done that day.

My stomach was in knots when the time came. Sitting down, I told him and the assistant coaches, for starters, that I had to be honest with them about where I lived. They knew, as I did, that I could get the team in a lot of trouble if a rival high school or the district office ever found out. But there was more, I went on, and then becoming visibly upset, confessed that it was all moot because I was probably going to have to quit school and get a job to help my mother financially.

This short, tough Italian football coach with two mysteriously missing fingers and his fellow assistant coaches were unwittingly about to earn their wings. Coach Mosso agreed that my situation could be a problem, but asked me to give him a couple of days to work on it. "In the meantime," he said, "keep coming to practice. I'll let you know what I figure out."

It took Coach Mosso only a day to get back to me. His proposition was this: during the school year I would live, more or less, as a foster kid with a Coral Park family. The high school booster club would pitch in with an allowance to cover added living expenses.

Warning me, he said, "You'll have to abide by the family's rules, stay out of trouble, and keep up with your schoolwork, do you understand?"

I understood. Deep down, I couldn't imagine what or how I had deserved his vote of confidence. My insides were jumbled up with gratitude, and worry that I would mess up this unbelievable gift. Somewhere the words "Thank you" got swallowed, but maybe he saw what I was feeling on my face.

"There's one other thing, Vic," he reminded me. "You have to get permission from your mother."

That night Mami listened as I related not only the offer that had been given to me but how it had evolved and why it was unfair for me to be a burden on her. Before she said anything, she studied me long and hard with her ever-familiar sad brown eyes. We had been through a war together that was over for both of us, though our wounds were hardly healed. We had never been allowed to express affection, but our love for each other was not ever in question. Mami would have done anything for me, and that night she made the toughest sacrifice imaginable. She let me go. And she gave me her blessing.

Mami put it this way, speaking slowly in Spanish: "You do what you need to do for yourself. I don't have a lot right now and you deserve more than I give you. You've suffered enough." For a second, she looked like she might cry, as I gulped and blinked, trying not to break down. Then, rising to the occasion, La Luchadora, always practical, asked, "Do you need me to write a note for you?"

"No, Mami," I said, "I don't think so." And then I took her hand and said, *"Gracias."*

When I left the next morning, clothes and toiletries packed in an old pillowcase, Mami held baby Carmen on her hip as she came to see me off. We saluted the future, when she would be holding down a good job and could move us into the Coral Park district and we could live together. Soon, soon. Probably we both knew that within the two years I had left in high school, that wouldn't happen, and that I would never live with her again. Even so, I promised Mami I'd come to see her all the time; she wasn't able to afford a telephone yet.

My pillowcase slung over my shoulder, I gave her and Carmencita last hugs and kisses, and then ran the ten blocks to the bus, never once looking back, only imagining her sad face watching me disappear from her view.

Home, they say, is a place where, when you go there, they have to take you in.

In the course of the next two years, I was taken into at least seven homes. Seven different families, along with nights spent here and there with a handful of others, decided that, despite my violent upbringing, they were willing to give me a chance.

Loving families, I learned, came in all shapes and sizes and backgrounds. Out of the seven pseudo–foster homes where I lived—the Echevarrias', the Varonas', the Wahrburgs', the Gablemans', the DiBernardos', the Robertses', and the Wheelers'—two families were Cuban-American, two were Jewish, one was Italian-American, one was Southern Baptist, and another was basically a middle-class all-American household. Some had lots of kids; others had only a couple of children. There were happy marriages, single parents, and strained marriages. All families, I learned, had their own shit to work through, though it was possible, I also saw, to do so without violence.

After about sixteen years of having everything good that I ever received taken away from me, like my trophies that Dad had smashed, it was almost impossible for me to be able to trust my wonderful fortune. At every step of the way, I was sure someone would say that they had changed their minds or, more to the point, that I had screwed up. But that never happened. I just kept pinching myself to make sure that I didn't wake up and find this had all been a dream. How lucky was it that the first family who took me in was none other than that of Marvin Wheeler, our star quarterback? It was all the more remarkable that he was an upperclassman, a year ahead of me in school, and that we weren't close friends.

Miraculously, however, his parents, Jay and Joyce Ann Wheeler, agreed to be the first family to let me stay with them, along with their three sons, Marvin, Brian, and Steven. The Wheelers' ground rules were reasonable and even somewhat loose. Adjusting to this relaxed atmosphere was easy, especially with football season occupying my spare hours.

If I was going through a positive transformation, so too were the Coral Park Rams. By the end of the season, we went from being a lousy team with one victory the previous year to a state title contender. We had several players who earned all-city honors, including Marvin and his favorite receiver, Rick Zeller. Throughout my football career, I went on to play with many incredible pass catchers, but I never played with a receiver like Rick Zeller. Oppositions typically double- and triple-teamed him, and he still managed to catch the ball. One rival high school feared his ability so much that they sent some thugs to our cafeteria to injure him before the game. Big mistake. They didn't lay a finger on Rick, got their asses kicked by us, and then got arrested. On game day, Rick ripped up their secondary and we won the contest handily.

But we were not so confident when we faced South Dade High School in a home game and found ourselves down by twenty points with 1:48 left in the game, not to mention the torrential downpour we were playing in that had sent most of our loyal fans fleeing the bleachers. In true gladiator mode, Marvin came into the offensive huddle, inspired us not to quit, and called a deep pass route for Zeller. As envisioned, Marvin hit Zeller deep down the field for the score and the momentum shifted our way, but we had very little time left on the clock. We onsided the ensuing kickoff, recovered it, and scored! And then, as South Dade reeled in shock, we did it again.

Although there were few witnesses to our incredible comeback, little could diminish our elation that we had just scored twenty-one points with under two minutes to go and won the game. A monumental football and life lesson: There is always hope.

My days of thuggery were numbered. Not that I had embraced the Victor in me, but I didn't feel so hopeless anymore. At the end of the season, I was aware that I had established myself as an above-average player, but I was not expecting what Coach Mosso called me into his office to show me days after our last game—my first college recruiting letter.

And there were more to follow. They arrived like migrating birds, first one by one, then in little groups, and before long en masse. Overwhelmed, feeling still that I didn't deserve them, I stashed them in a shoe box, afraid they might fly away, and waited to make any decisions.

By now it was the end of 1971, the most tumultuous year of my life, and I had moved on to the home of Richard Wahrburg, one of the senior kickers on the football team and one of the funniest guys at our high school. A lot of us assumed that Richard, a slightly overweight Jewish kid with frizzy brown hair and braces, was wealthy. After all, he seemed to have an endless supply of cash and often picked up the tab at restaurants, whether he wanted to or not. What he was, I discovered when I moved in with him, his mother, and his younger brother, James, was a hardworking, natural-born entrepreneur.

Mrs. Wahrburg was the owner of a Chinese restaurant called Won Ton, which was next door to a movie theatre in the Westchester shopping center. She was a glamorous, always fashionably dressed, attractive middle-aged woman, who drove around in a Cadillac. As it so happened that she had just finished converting their garage into a guest bedroom with its own bathroom, I was fortunate enough to stay in that comfortable setting. I even had my own phone line. Though I rarely used it, I felt almost spoiled.

Since Richard worked part-time at Won Ton, I tagged along to be helpful whenever I could, packing to-go orders or pouring tea. Before long, Richard took me on as his apprentice in a brilliant and profitable undertaking that he conceived. Typically business at Won Ton went crazy whenever shows let out at the movie theatre. But from the instant that Francis Ford Coppola's *The Godfather* opened, we all witnessed a phenomenon that had never happened before. Moviegoers were willing to wait for hours, their lines traveling down the sidewalk in front of the stores and around the block. Richard looked at these lines and saw opportunity. He convinced his mother that Won Ton could turn a nice profit by selling egg rolls and soda to the people waiting to get into the next showing of the movie. Mrs. Wahrburg sold us the egg rolls at her cost and the soda sales were ours to keep. The weekend crowds were massive for about a month, and we would walk down the line with our trays of hot egg rolls and ice cold soda. We did a brisk business and I was able to put a little money away, which I later used for some new clothes and my first shag haircut at an upscale Miami salon.

Since Richard was an upperclassman with his own set of friends, when he wasn't around I spent time befriending his younger brother, James. A bona fide genius, James had a room filled with complicated electronic and scientific projects he had designed and built himself, including a very cool system of lights he had rigged to his stereo that could pulsate to the beat of the music. Whenever I hung out with James or stopped into his room to listen to psychedelic music and watch the light show, I waited for any opportunity to talk to him about the bandage of tape and gauze that he wore to cover his left hand. As I understood it, he had lost all his fingers and most of his thumb in a serious accident the previous Fourth of July, after an explosive that he was building blew up early. For some time Mrs. Wahrburg had been trying to get her son to remove the bandage, but James was still too self-conscious to show his mangled hand.

I related a lot to James, and understood what it was to keep a hurt covered up. There were people throughout my life who didn't want to see my hurts; but I was learning that there were also others who would like me all the same. Instead of trying to say that to James Wahrburg, in my own industrious way I eventually was able to finagle a tryout for him with the football team.

"But James, there's only one thing," I told him matter-of-factly before the tryout, "you have to take off the bandage. It doesn't matter. You gotta show 'em what you got in your heart." Then I might have mentioned that Coach Mosso had some missing fingers of his own.

James Wahrburg took off his bandage, went to the tryout, and made the team.

Same lesson: There is always hope. I was glad to pay it forward.

In early January of 1972, I waited to talk to Miss Baldwin after the homeroom bell had rung and the last of my classmates straggled out the door.

One of the most important members of the village that was raising me, Miss Susi Baldwin, by some great stroke of fortune, was my teacher for a second year in a row. Young, energetic, and always available if I needed to talk to her, she had the added advantage of being really cute, with her long blond hair, knee-high boots, occasional short skirts, and a buoyant smile that revealed a slight overbite that I found irresistibly endearing. That smile diffused the powder keg inside me many times.

Over the holidays, Miss Baldwin had helped me get a job working on preparations for the Orange Bowl parade, allowing me to earn a little money to buy Christmas presents for Mami and Carmen. Now she had another "opportunity" that she wanted to discuss with me before trying to pull strings on my behalf.

There was a new program in its very first year called Close Up, she explained. The Close Up program brought high school students from around the country to Washington, D.C., to allow them to experience a total immersion into how our government works. Was that something I was interested in?

Flashes of JFK went off in my brain. "Sure!"

She smiled her slight-overbite smile. Miss Baldwin's next step was to figure out how to get me into the program. There was only one scholarship available, and heavy competition for that spot from much more studious kids than me.

This was not the first or last time Susi Baldwin went to bat for me. Apparently, in a report I got much later, the opposition to my getting the scholarship was ugly. In spite of my scholastic improvement and high marks from my coaches, my reputation as a Big Tough Kid from a Bad Background made me undesirable, said many, to be part of Coral Park High School's delegation of its best and brightest to Washington, D.C. But whatever she said or did to change some minds, two weeks later I stopped by to check on any updates for the umpteenth time and all she said was, "Better pack your suitcase with some warm clothes. You're going to Washington, D.C., next week."

"Oh my God! I got in? Oh, thank you, thanks!" I wanted to pick her up and hug her. But then I realized something.

She saw it register on my face. Reading me very well, Miss Baldwin asked, "Do you have a suitcase? Do you have any winter clothes?"

Oh sure, I lied. Then, not wanting to be untruthful, I told her not to worry about it, I'd borrow some clothes and a suitcase.

What a country, America! I returned from my week in Washington, D.C., convinced that if more kids and adults in the country had a chance to experience something along the lines of Close Up, we could solve so many of our national problems. There was plenty of reason for cynicism, of course, especially in those waning years of the Vietnam War, on the eve of Watergate. But Close Up also made me appreciate the honor that accompanies public service, and the true greatness of our democracy and our institutions. As a boy who had never had a voice, I was inspired by the American ideal that every individual can make a difference, no matter their background. History came alive for me as we toured the national monuments and were given access to restricted areas in and around the capital. We met with many of our leaders in Congress, including Senators Claude Pepper and Lawton Chiles from Florida, along with many other representatives in the House. Meeting the very young and handsome Senator Ted Kennedy from Massachusetts was a highlight for me, as it was for many in our group. I sincerely wanted to reach out to him and let him know what his brothers had meant to me, how much I loved and admired them, but I just stood, quietly, in awe and respect.

My experience at Close Up fueled my desire to be a more active member of my community, outside of sports as well, and to start breaking out of my shy exterior. There were no girlfriends yet, but I had a wonderful friendship with a girl, an adorable perky cheerleader named Roberta. Bert had a terrific sense of humor and seemed to appreciate my quirky joking too. To really crack me up and impress me, she insisted on giving me piggyback rides down the halls of the school. She may have been a little thing but she was unbelievably strong. Through Bert, I was given entrée to her group of friends, who called themselves the Boppers.

Mostly jocks and cheerleaders, they were energetic, preppy, and peppy, and sometimes annoyingly nice to the point of syrupy. There was still a part of me that couldn't relate, and I found myself more at home with my fellow troubled youth. In the spirit of bipartisanship and equality, I decided to be friendly with everybody and learn to live with my lack of belonging.

The inciting incident that caused me to officially leave the gang occurred when an older member pulled a gun during a beef with another member. Several members were able to wrestle the gun away before any shots were fired. The next day I caught up with Gil and submitted my formal resignation. "I'm out, man," I said.

He wanted to know what had made me change my mind. Normally, leaving a gang is not as easy as dropping out of a club.

" 'Cause I'll fight anyone, and usually I'll kick their ass," I confessed. "But a bullet will win every time."

Gil accepted my resignation without much of a discussion. He told me that my future was in athletics and that if I stayed out of trouble, I would have numerous scholarship offers. I was never harassed by any of the other members, and in fact, some of them were my biggest fans.

So as it happened, my stint as a badass gang member was fast and furious. Meanwhile I found there were other clubs to join, as I continued to get more and more involved with school activities. There was football, baseball, wrestling, and I competed in the shot put in track. I was in the pep club, the Fellowship of Christian Athletes, and I was elected to the student council. People began to seek me out not just for my athletic ability or fighting skills but for my friendship and opinions.

My self-esteem was slowly being rebuilt, one step at a time. In my life, I had been a tiger, several types of puppies and dogs, and a gladiator. In this era, I was reminded of an episode I'd once seen on *Mutual of Omaha's Wild Kingdom* in which Marlin Perkins and Big Jim Fowler nursed an injured and broken-down bald eagle back from the brink of death. Through their love and kindness, the eagle's wings and body mended, but more important, it got its spirit back; and then, at last, the eagle was ready to take its place back in its own society.

That was happening to me bit by bit. I had my detractors, especially our vice principals. To them I was a bad seed beyond repair. But there were several Marlin Perkins and Big Jim Fowler types who, through love and kindness, were helping me mend my wings.

Toward the end of my junior year, I confided in Miss Baldwin that I wanted to enter my name as a candidate in the upcoming elections for senior class president. "But I'm nervous," I admitted. "I mean, do you think anyone will vote for me?"

She assured me that I was a lot more popular in school than I gave myself credit for.

And so, with her encouragement and support, I launched my campaign. Much to my surprise, a wave of friends from many diverse groups, including many of the most popular girls, helped with a massive grassroots effort, complete with posters, pin-on badges, and flyers that simply said: VOTE FOR VIC.

Even more surprising was that I won by a landslide.

Mami made each of my visits to see her, which were once or twice a month, a special occasion. On one Saturday night, her friend was over visiting and Mami cordially invited her to stay for dinner. A Sexy Young Woman, Mami's friend was a *cubana* in her early twenties, and obviously had much respect for my mother. "Talk, talk," my mother encouraged us, setting up folding chairs outside, bringing us beers ("You can have *one*, Victor") as she hustled in and out of the little apartment, the aroma of *arroz con pollo* and *plantanos fritos* wafting through the Miami evening air. We ate outside on paper plates as day turned to night. Mami seemed content. She had a new factory job with a better wage, a son who loved her cooking, and a new, interesting friend.

When it came time to catch the bus back to the neighborhood where I was staying at the time, the Sexy Young Woman offered me a lift. Thinking nothing of it, I accepted, gave Mami and Carmen a good-bye hug, and hopped into her four-door Impala sedan with statues of her various saints looking back at me from the dashboard. In Miami in these years, the Chevy Impala was referred to as the Cuban Cadillac, whereas the Ford Falcon was the Cuban Vette. The Sexy Young Woman and I spoke briefly in Spanish until we arrived at my stop. As I turned to thank her, she pounced, kissing, tonguing, and biting me so aggressively I could taste blood on my lips.

She reached back with her left arm to the steering column to throw the car into park. She had me pinned against the passenger door, kissing me and grabbing my hands and placing them on her breasts. Though I was turned on and panting, my erection throbbing and smashed against my zipper, I had to stop and breathlessly explain that I was a guest in these people's house and we couldn't make out like this here.

"Take me where you take other girls!" she moaned.

Well, clearly, there were no other girls. But since I had heard of other friends parking behind the high school, I suggested we go there.

Behind the wheel of her Cuban Cadillac, she cooed, *"Vamos."*

As soon as we parked behind the school, we jumped into the backseat—after she threw her folded laundry into the front seat— and we closed the doors. Silently thanking all those saints on her dashboard and all other religious entities who came to mind, I enjoyed the best, hottest sex I'd had up to that point in my life. True, it was either the first or second time I'd ever gotten laid, but it was better than all the fantasies combined. It was "The Star-Spangled Banner"—rockets' red glare and bombs bursting in air—complete with fireworks.

The two of us were sweating profusely as we got dressed and threw the laundry back onto the backseat and climbed into the front. Moments later, the interior of the car was illuminated with a bright white light and a hint of red. All the windows of the car were fogged, but I could see the outline of the cherry top of a cop car.

Great, I freaked out, I finally get laid and I'm going to be arrested for it!

The patrol car, carrying two policemen, pulled up alongside us and its horn tooted. The Sexy Young Woman rolled her window down.

Staring inside the car toward me, the cop in the passenger seat said, "Everything all right?"

Not understanding, she didn't answer. "Say yes," I whispered through clenched teeth.

The Sexy Young Woman gave him a curl of her shoulders and a breathy "Oh, jes!" That pretty much answered their question.

Thank God for that spirited introduction to sex. Thank God I was fortunate to come of age in the free-loving, freewheeling 1970s.

On July 9, 1972, my brother Tony turned eighteen and, as planned long ago, began his official odyssey out of Dad's house. He had actually left within six months of my departure, after beginning his undergraduate education up at the University of Florida, in Gainesville.

Back in town for the summer, Tony was playing baseball in a local men's league and called to ask me if I was interested in coming to watch him play. He had tracked me down at the home of my friend Mary DiBernardo, where I was staying that summer.

Mary was a jewel, an extremely attractive, incredibly graceful young lady; she wore a constant angelic smile and had only positive things to say about others. She was also a top local gymnast and synchronized swimmer. There were six boys and three girls in her large Italian family, and they were all, as well as her parents, exceptional individuals. For me, the DiBernardos epitomized the philosophy that there was no limit on the amount of love available. They welcomed me to an extra seat at dinner on what was two long picnic tables pushed together and found me an empty bunk with three of the older boys in a room that had wall-to-wall bunk beds. Two of the DiBernardo brothers, Bruce and Fluff, as we called him, both talked in their sleep. Oh, and not only that. They talked to each other in their sleep. It was all gibberish, but it was a conversation that went on for hours.

Tony had gotten the phone number at the DiBernardos' from Mami, no doubt. Without hesitation, I told him it would be great to see him and to come to his game. He came to pick me up in none other than the old shit brown-gold Impala station wagon.

Instead of driving straight to the game, he needed to change into his uniform back at Dad and Mecca's house in North Miami. Mami had kept me up-to-date on the news that over the past year and a half since I'd been gone, Dad had remarried. He, Eddie, and Barbie were living at Mecca's home, along with her kids, Charlie and Elena. I remembered them well from El Club Cubano in Chicago. According to my mother, who thought very highly of her old friend, Mecca wouldn't take shit from El Caballero, as Mami called him with more and more sarcasm as time went by.

"You can visit Eddie and Barbie for a few minutes while I change," Tony said. What he really meant was that this had been planned so I could run into Dad.

Fine, I thought, I can handle it.

Eddie and Barbie were both out on the front lawn when we pulled up. Both had grown so much since the last time I had seen them. Barbie, going on six, was lean and tall for her age, with wavy brown hair and a beautiful olive complexion. She ran up to the car, smiling the sweetest smile with identical dimples in each cheek, before I could open the door. Bouncing up and down, she shouted, "Bic! Bic!"

Eleven-year-old Eddie, also tall and lean, was somewhat stand-offish, as I could understand. Behind the glasses he had started wearing—the cheap, sturdy, dorky frames Dad probably insisted on—he was becoming a handsome kid. Seeing my younger siblings made me feel suddenly guilty again for abandoning them to the madman. One look at Eddie and I knew he feared the inside of his home.

A vivacious blond with thick lenses in her spectacles, Mecca waved us inside. It was a spacious, nicely furnished three-level house, much nicer than anywhere we'd lived when Dad was the provider for our family. It was obvious that Barbie was getting lots of nurturing from Mecca, and that made me happy. Maybe she had helped tame the beast, who had yet to make an entrance. After all, there was always hope.

"*Mi casa es su casa*," Mecca told me before hurrying off to her beauty salon for a customer. "The blue-hairs," she quipped, "they keep me employed."

Tony checked the time and ran to change his uniform. The moment I was alone in the living room, in walked El Caballero. Dad was barely recognizable from the dapper man who had swept into the judge's chambers to try to charm her into believing his story over mine. He had stopped dyeing his hair and beard and had put on fifteen to twenty pounds. In an old white T-shirt and khaki army pants, Dad looked like a chubby, disheveled old man, not the movie-star-looking cad I remembered.

Whatever apprehension I was feeling dissipated at the sight of the person in front of me. He smiled at me as he walked over, and I had almost forgotten about the large gap between his two front teeth. He extended his hand.

I hesitated for a moment, remembering the many times he had

asked us to pull his finger so he could fart, and we would be required to laugh at this stupid gag, and if our laughter wasn't calibrated to his liking, we would get slapped around. I extended my hand and took his.

As we were having our handshake of reconciliation—or whatever it was—Tony reappeared in his baseball uniform, apologizing. "Sorry, listen, Vic, we gotta go."

Dad didn't look at Tony. Keeping his eyes on me, he said, "I want to talk to Vic for a few minutes."

Tony knew the control game Dad was playing and, as a survivor in his own right, wasn't going to be taken down that road. "Dad, we don't have time right now. I gotta get to my game."

In the friendliest, most accommodating tone, Dad volunteered to drive me over, promising to get me there before they hit the field.

"Dad, really. We have to leave now."

"I want to talk to my son. I'll take him over. Is that okay, Vic?"

So now it was on me. Dad's eyes pleaded with me. Tony, clearly frustrated, shot me a warning look. This was old power stuff. I settled it by saying that Dad could drive me over after we talked.

Dad invited me to sit on the couch with him, as he lit a cigarette. "So, how's it going?"

"Fine."

"You look good. You've put on some muscle. How's your pitching?"

Even though I had dropped out of baseball when Coach Hertz told me to take some time off, I had played well my junior season and would play my senior year too. But I wasn't going to give that satisfaction to him. "I'm focusing on football, right now."

"Yeah, but, you know, baseball's your ticket."

"Really? Well, there are a lot of people who think football is."

"Football is a tough sport. You're more suited for baseball."

We headed into the old argument. He had found his opening. Pushing it, I asked him what exactly he was trying to say.

"I'm just saying football's a tough sport and you're not tough enough to play it."

Hairs stood up on the back of my neck. Dad's appearance had changed, but nothing else. I smiled back at him and said, "You don't even know me."

"I know you been running around with a gang, probably doing drugs, and living like a hobo at people's houses."

He kept talking for some time, but I had shut him out, my anger building up inside of me, heating up my body. But at the same time, I wasn't letting him see me sweat. That was until he found my button, the soft underbelly of love he could stick his knife in. His tirade began, "This is all your mother's fault. She never could control you and now she's ruined you. Worthless whore!"

I shot up off the couch and stared down at him. He backed up against the armrest of the couch, looking cautiously back at me.

"You will not talk about Mami that way!" I had fooled myself into hoping for a couple of hours that we could establish a different relationship or redefine it somehow. Forgiveness. I wanted to forgive and love him. But all I wanted to do now was beat the shit out of him. Whatever hope had been mustered spilled from me like ashes from his cigarette.

On this, one of our last conversations ever, I told him he was an asshole and to apologize to Tony about his game. When I left the house, I waved good-bye to my little sister and brother, and hurried away.

Angry, talking to myself, in tears, I began hiking back in the direction of the DiBernardos', twenty miles away. After two miles or so, I stopped at a pay phone and called Bruce DiBernardo and pleaded with him to come pick me up. Bruce wasn't happy about it, but he said he was on his way.

We drove back to the Coral Park area without saying a word.

My life as a hobo came to an end in August of 1972. It was two days before summer football practice was set to start and I had run out of places to stay.

After returning from a week in the Blue Ridge Mountains, outside of Asheville, North Carolina, at a camp sponsored by the Fellowship of Christian Athletes, I stopped by to visit my coaches and to see if they had any ideas. As we were talking, a junior named Rocky Echevarria overheard our conversation and, unbeknownst to me, hurried home to see if I could stay with his family.

A month earlier, as vice president of the school chapter of the FCA, I had been responsible for filling six scholarship spots for the camp trip to Asheville and had been able to fill only five. Brian Wheeler, at whose house I had first stayed, suggested, "What about Rocky Echevarria?" I knew Rocky was one of the backup quarterbacks on the football team, but I didn't know much else about him. We were leaving the next day and I didn't want to waste a scholarship, so I told Brian to give him a call. Rocky accepted immediately.

Rocky, a tall, good-looking, sweet-natured Cuban-American teenager, was waiting outside his house when Mr. Wheeler swung by to pick him up the next day and take him with us to board the bus to North Carolina. Standing with him to see him off were two of his family members, an attractive younger brother, I assumed, and a gorgeous sister.

Rocky said his good-byes and climbed into the car. He was so psyched to be going, he said, and he couldn't thank me enough for giving him the spot.

"Hey, no problem." Figuring it was worth a try, I said, "I'll tell you what. You want to thank me, when we get back, set me up with your sister."

Appalled, Rocky quickly corrected me, "That's my mom!"

Ooops. He accepted my apology and agreed that his mother, Lillian Echevarria, looked much younger than a woman who was the mother of two teenage boys.

When Rocky—or Steven, his real name—came home to talk to his mom about me staying there, she didn't really object except for asking, "Well, where is he going to sleep?"

Rocky shrugged. "On the floor." That was where other friends slept when they came to spend the night, he reminded her.

Lillian was used to both fifteen-year-old Steven and her thirteen-year-old son, Ernesto, bringing home all sorts of stray animals. But she was ill prepared, she later admitted, for the Incredible Hulk to walk through her door, a well-meaning but testosterone-pumping sixteen-year-old with rage lurking just below the surface.

Rocky led me to understand that it was all settled. With a bag of my belongings and about twenty hangers of clothes, I arrived at the Echevarrias' house the next morning and followed Rocky inside through the front door. At the entryway, without indicating whether or not I should follow him, he made a hard right and disappeared down the hallway. Awkwardly, I stood in the open foyer, looking out the sliding glass doors behind a dining room through which light poured and bathed the interior of the house in a golden glow. Outside, their backyard had a pool with a giant palm and a mango tree standing guard, and just beyond that a small, glittering lake with houses bordering the circumference. It looked like a dream of the perfect backyard. The house wasn't a mansion, but it appeared to me to be the home of nobility.

The rustling of newspaper moved my gaze away from the lake to the table.

Sitting behind the newspaper, wearing a pair of reading glasses that were perched on the end of his nose, was a handsome bear of a man in a T-shirt and underwear. He looked at me standing there, frozen, with my twenty hangers slung over one shoulder and my bag in the other hand. "Hello?" he said in a deeply accented yet articulate voice.

"Hello," I ventured.

He started to raise the paper, stopped, and lowered it again, peering at me over the glasses. "Who are you?"

"I'm Vic."

"Ah . . ." He paused, not sure if that was supposed to mean anything to him. He tested me by introducing himself. "I'm Bebo." This bear of a man just told me his nickname; translated from Spanish to English, it meant Big Baby. When that didn't provoke me to say anything more, he asked the question that was on his mind. "What are you doing here?"

"I'm moving in."

Bebo registered his obvious lack of knowledge before he bellowed, "LILLIAN! LILLIAN! *Pero que coño esta pasando aqui?*" What the hell's going on here?

Not knowing what to do next, I turned and darted back in the direction where Rocky had last disappeared. I found him in the bedroom that he shared with his brother. His mom stuck her head in the door for a moment, smiling at me and whispering, "Hello!"

Then she vanished, obviously heading to the living room as Bebo unleashed a barrage of questions in Spanish about the big stranger that just walked into his house. Who is he? Where does he come from? Who does he belong to? What is he doing here? In her musical, lilting voice, she answered each question patiently, only slightly humoring her husband. I felt as if I had walked into a scene from *I Love Lucy*, and Bebo was a 250-pound Ricky Ricardo.

When I asked Rocky if he had forgotten to ask his dad about me moving in, it turned out he had done so on purpose. "Trust me, it's better not to ask in advance," Rocky explained. "This way, he doesn't have time to think about it and then say no."

The argument in the other room died down to a discussion and finally a conversation, with Bebo occasionally saying, "But, Lillian . . ." She kept calming him with her melodious voice.

I heard his footsteps coming down the hall until he stopped at the door where we were. Bebo covered the door frame with his girth.

Standing comfortably in his underwear, he asked, "You're on the football team?"

"Yes."

"Are you any good?"

"Yeah, Dad. He's one of the stars!" Rocky interjected.

"Tu eres cubano?"

"Sí, como no."

"Okay." He turned and left the room.

Lillian then made her appearance to make a formal introduction. She was petite, with a full mane of dark wavy hair. She was wearing little or no makeup and was still stunningly beautiful. She asked the universally important question: "Are you hungry?"

Rocky and I followed her into the kitchen, where, like a sorcerer, she whipped up the most delicious egg sandwich I ever tasted, with cheese oozing out the side and sweet ham. Soon I met Rocky's younger brother, Ernie, a seventh-grader at the local junior high, when he joined us. He was a very handsome, well-built kid with a great smile. There was something very familiar about him. He recognized me immediately from an earlier stint I had done guest-coaching with the Kiwanis Youth football team.

Ernie welcomed me to his house, saying, "Hey, Coach Vic."

The Echevarria family consisted not only of Esteban (Bebo), Lillian, Rocky (Esteban Jr.), and Ernesto (Ernie), but also a menagerie of animals. There were dogs, cats, a Spanish-speaking half-moon parrot, and eventually a capuchin monkey named, in homage to the Pink Panther, Minkey. Almost all of their animals had been taken in as strays and were given the same love and attention as family members.

On my second day at their house, I got violently ill with a twenty-four-hour stomach flu from drinking tainted ice water at practice. Great, some houseguest I was turning out to be. On my way out to the hallway bathroom, I ended up puking all the way down the hall. Poor Lillian followed me around cleaning up my mess. I was so embarrassed for myself. But not wanting to make me feel bad, she did it with a smile on her face.

Before school began, Lillian, who I was now calling Mom, took us shopping for school clothes. She didn't discriminate between her biological sons and her new ward. If Rocky and Ernie got new jeans, I got a pair of new jeans. It was my instinct not to trust this kindness and generosity, but with each purchase and each bag that was handed to me, there were no strings, no warnings that if I messed up it would all be taken away. In the other homes where I was taken in, I had been well treated as a guest. All of a sudden, for reasons I didn't know if I deserved, I was being treated as another member of their family. Pretty soon Rocky and Ernie started to introduce me as their brother; I was proud to do the same.

Later I learned that Mom was warned against taking me in by several parties in the community. To them, I was dangerous, pretty much a bad risk. But she was willing to take that risk, to try to make a difference in my life. She was the embodiment of the belief that there is always hope, and her sons had the same infectiously warm and upbeat personalities. And my new family members not only made their house my home, they also gave me a space to tell my story—to talk, and to talk, and to talk. There were times when I realized that they didn't always believe some of the extremes that I had been through. But over time, when they actually compared the different stories, they acknowledged that they were never adapted or embellished, and all fit together. They also shared their stories and rich family history with me.

Mom taught kindergarten in the Little Havana section of Miami, where many of her students were low-income Spanish-speaking kids. I visited her a few times at her school and saw firsthand why she would later be honored with the Teacher of the Year Award for Dade County.

Bebo and I had the least amount of close communication. But we did talk in a way, so different from what I knew, that was respectful of my opinion and my intelligence. He could talk sports and he could really talk politics, especially the passionate politics that burned in the heart of every Cuban exile. He was a commercial pilot with a big appetite for life and learning, always reading his newspapers and books, mainly military and spy thrillers, planted, as he was that first day when I arrived, at the dining table, in his underwear and reading glasses.

One of the things that Rocky had also forgotten to tell me was that I was supposed to stay at their house only until another family could be located to take me in. Mom did ask Rocky on occasion if I was still looking. Both he and Ernie chimed in, "Why?" Rocky said, "He's not getting into trouble." Ernie added, "And Dad seems to like him."

"Guess who's coming to dinner and staying?" became the family joke, and now that I was part of their family, I didn't care that the joke was on me.

In the two years since I had walked out of the judge's chambers, liberated from Dad but an emotional toddler when it came to love, the prospect of having a girlfriend had become more and more remote. By the fall of my senior year, I had dated a few girls, but nothing serious. I had never held hands or snuck a kiss in the halls. And then, providence smiled on me and picked the sweetest, prettiest, most soulful young woman, Kim Smith, to be my first love.

A striking blond with brown eyes and a stunning figure, she was bright, funny, sexy, and extremely talented as an artist. Conveniently, she lived three blocks away from the Echevarrias, which made getting together easier. Over the course of our relationship, she helped guide me through some very tough waters, first just by convincing me that I was attractive and lovable, next by nudging me along to express affection verbally as well as physically, and finally by trying to get me to face a serious jealousy problem that it turned out I had.

Early in our relationship at Coral Park, I spotted two guys looking up her short skirt as she walked by them in the cafeteria. I walked over and grabbed them by the hair and smashed their faces into their trays of food. My actions had made it abundantly clear to them and most of the other students in the cafeteria that Kim was my girlfriend. Kim was appalled by my show of force and told me she could take care of herself. As time would tell in our relationship, I had a lot to learn in the love department.

My seventeenth birthday, on October 1, was undoubtedly the happiest birthday of my life. I was safe in a loving home, a cocaptain of the football team, president of the senior class, doing well in school, and I had a girlfriend. Who would have ever thought it possible? And then, as a gift to myself, with fifteen dollars of my savings, I bought myself a car. Not just any car. This was a 1947 British-made Ford Anglia that was the color and shape of a lemon. It had broken motor mounts, no radio, and a stick shift with a hole in the boot that allowed exhaust fumes to fill the car, but its get-up-and-go was impressively peppy.

For the next six months, my Anglia served me like a loyal steed, as long as I kept the windows opened at all times so as not to faint from the fumes and made sure that I slowed down around turns. The first time I made a hard, fast turn, coming out of the school parking lot, the car tipped over. But not right away. It tipped and teetered—like Arte Johnson's *Laugh-In* character, who dwarfed his rickety tricycle—in suspended animation for another block until it finally plopped over on its side. A group of young boys playing in the street gathered around the fallen Anglia as I emerged from the opened window and climbed out, unhurt. The car was so light that I was able to grab the door and hoist it back upright onto all four wheels. The boys stood in the street slack-jawed. "Wow! Batman!" cried one of them as I drove off. Since there was no horn to honk, I reached my arm out of the window and pumped my fist for Anglia power.

Inevitably, my steed took one dip too hard on my way to school; that, along with the broken motor mounts, caused the engine to fall out and burn its way into the asphalt. I got out, saluted it for service rendered, and walked the rest of the way to school on foot. Later, when I passed by, there was no sign of the car, and even the asphalt had been repaved. After that, I started saving my bucks for a motorcycle. There were still, unfortunately, several traits inherited from El Ciclón that would crop up in many ways in the years to come.

Had it not been for Bebo, who showed me a much different side of what it meant to be a father, I could never have come through several challenges. Ironically, for a long time I didn't know where I stood with him. This was despite the fact that he took an immediate parental role with me, particularly as a sounding board in my difficult decision about where to go to college. He took every sport I played seriously, showing up and cheering for me, never criticizing without also encouraging.

The football team my senior year had a quarterback who wasn't of Marvin Wheeler's caliber, often underthrowing the ball with an arm that was suspect. In one poorly thrown play, I had to leap up at an angle that allowed a defensive back to take my legs out, causing me to flip over and land on my head, knocking me unconscious. I woke up in the stadium's field house, staring into the face of Fluff DiBernardo, who asked if I was all right. Just over his shoulder, a very concerned Bebo was standing by as the ambulance arrived.

At the emergency room, where they ran several tests and found no discernible damage, I was given a thick foam neck brace and released, Bebo leading me out to his car and driving me home. He turned me over to Lillian, who made sure I ate something, naturally—and ordered me to lie in Rocky's bed for the night. Before I fell asleep there was a rap at the window that turned out to be Mary DiBernardo and some of her friends, and then a slow trickle of more than thirty other high school classmates, many of them in tears. The rumor was that I was dead or crippled, and they had come to pay their respects. Overwhelmed by the attention, pretty soon I asked everyone to leave because I didn't want them to see me crying. When they did go, I let the dam burst, falling asleep in my new brother's bed. That night, and in the week that followed, when I saw that news of my untimely death brought much of the student body and many of the teachers running up to me with big beaming smiles, many an old wound healed. I was no longer the same boy who wished himself dead so people would pay attention and love him.

Mami was spared the details of my getting knocked unconscious. Previously she had come to see me play and hated it. Afterward, Mami said to me that she had cringed every time I hit someone or they hit me. Please, *mijo,* she said, invite me to other places, but not to football games. Kim and my mother got along famously, despite the language barrier. Mami's approval of my girlfriend was important to me. With her gift of sight, I saw, she continued to read people and their intentions very well. Mami was also happy that I had found a safe, supportive second family. Certainly there was a part of her that mourned not being able to raise all of us under her roof, but it never diminished her wanting the best for each of us. It was great that I was living in a house where I could swim in a swimming pool and water-ski in a lake whenever I wanted and eat three large meals a day, at least. But what she liked best about the Echevarrias, she later wrote, was that they understood my complexities and were still able to nurture me.

Although Bebo seemed genuinely proud of my accomplishments, he was not overtly affectionate with me the way that Lillian, Rocky, and Ernie were. In his bearish way, he did get annoyed with a household that took in so many strays. But even though he barked about it, he was not threatening in a physical or hurtful way. Mainly, he channeled his angst into long, passionate, and sometimes hilarious rants about the communists and Fidel. His fondest fantasy was that we would all grow up and join the air force so we could go drop bombs on Castro's head.

The night that he revealed how he really felt about me came after I'd been living at their house for several months. On a school night when he was supposed to be out of town for the rest of the week—flying one of the many cargo and charter flights he flew in this era—someone had the bright idea to visit a cemetery and an old abandoned haunted house, and to borrow some of Bebo's prized antique weapons, such as swords, shields, battleaxes, and maces, so that we could defend ourselves. In a collective effort, Rocky, Ernie, and I managed to quietly take the valuable items that Bebo had collected over many trips to Europe and elsewhere, without Mom finding out, and setting off in a car driven by Jimmy Miranda, the one-hundred-pound high school state wrestling champion (who later became a well-known jockey).

We had a ball scaring ourselves silly. We were just starting to calm down, a little after midnight, when Jimmy pulled back into the Echevarrias' driveway and we started unloading the battle gear. Suddenly, the front door burst open and there was Bebo standing in his underwear and T-shirt.

Oh shit. He was obviously home early. Glancing down at all the medieval weaponry at my feet, I murmured to Jimmy, just under my breath, "Take all this shit home. I'll get it tomorrow."

"*Coño!* What's going on here?" Bebo's voice was two octaves higher, which meant he was REALLY ANGRY. It was after midnight, with school the next day, and we had taken Ernie, then only in junior high.

While Bebo read the riot act to Rocky and Ernie, I went back to our bedroom and sat glumly on the bed, thinking that I should walk back and volunteer to take responsibility for the night's event. But I didn't think I had the right to interfere. Moments later the underwear-clad Bebo appeared in the doorway, filling it with his size as he had on my first day at his house. This was it, I thought, he was finally going to give me my walking papers.

He immediately pointed his finger right at me, as though continuing the speech he had given in the living room. "And you? You are the oldest! You should know better. You're supposed to be in charge!"

He had paid me the highest compliment I had ever received. He was treating me as he would have his own son. I kept my head down, looking at the floor, feigning shame, trying to disguise the fact that I was smiling. I was now a true, full-fledged member of the family.

Bebo, Mom, Rocky, and Ernie seemed to take family pride in the volume and intensity of the recruiting efforts being made to court my interest. By the time the football season came to an end, I had added to my desirability with several athletic honors, including the citywide recognition that I was one of the top offensive linemen and tight ends in Miami. Whenever the college recruiters made personal visits to promote their programs to me, Bebo loved to sit in on these meetings, during which he freely boasted to them about my talent, toughness, and determination. But when it came time to make a decision, although he was glad to offer an opinion, he respected that it was going to be mine alone to make.

Out of the 150-odd recruiting letters, the schools and the football programs that most interested me were Memphis State, Iowa State, University of Miami, Florida State, Princeton, University of Pennsylvania, the Citadel, and a few lesser-known military schools. The latter were appealing because I could see myself pursuing a military career after football. The Ivy League programs were also flattering. Even if their teams weren't the strongest, just the thought of Dad having to chew on that made me want to sign up immediately. Taking a wait-and-see stance, however, I decided to postpone my choice until after I'd gone on the many recruiting trips that had been scheduled for me. By early December I had already visited Penn, Memphis State, the University of Miami, and Florida State when I knew that I had made up my mind and insisted on canceling the rest of the trips. There were so many factors to consider, including the availability of scholarships, the atmosphere of the campus, the cost of travel, and, of course, the football personnel. But the most influential factor in my ultimate decision to attend FSU, aside from the likelihood that I could receive a full four-year scholarship there, was the very gracious reception I was given by what were then known as Seminole Seekers.

The picturesque campus in Tallahassee, the state capital of Florida, was most inviting, dotted by redbrick buildings and surrounded by beautiful green rolling hills, lakes, and pine forests. I was also excited by the fact that head coach Larry Jones was there and that FSU was a top twenty program. Another draw was Cash Hall, the off-campus private dormitory that housed the football and baseball teams, complete with its own cafeteria and pool. When I attended a game, wearing the garnet-and-gold Seminole game jersey, at Doak Campbell Stadium, which was filled to capacity with over fifty thousand diehard fans, I knew that this was where I wanted to play. Seeing FSU win easily likewise made me feel that I wanted to be associated with a winning program.

But the clincher was the astonishing amount of beautiful female students that I saw and, most of all, the special charms of the Seminole Seekers, a battalion of gorgeous young ladies and obvious football enthusiasts who made me feel very, very wanted. Converted to the cause, I knew that I wanted to be a Seminole.

And so, on December 9, 1972, with Mami and the Echevarria family present, I signed my national letter of intent to attend Florida State University on a full athletic scholarship, along with approximately fifteen other players from Miami who also signed early. This event was covered by the *Miami Herald* and various local television stations. The image of Dad watching me defy his every worst prediction did give me some satisfaction. Who said I wasn't tough enough?

But the following day when Bebo mentioned, "Your father called. He wants to have a meeting with us," that didn't sound good to me.

"What for?" I panicked. "Why does he want to talk to you?"

"Yo no se."

Dad arrived the next night absolutely transformed from six months earlier. No longer old and unkempt, he was once more well groomed and fashionably dressed as he walked in carrying a businesslike attaché case.

"Hey, Vic." He smiled ever so charmingly when he saw me seated on the sofa in the living room. Not saying a word, I stared back at him, expressionless.

In an Academy Award performance, his polite and soft-spoken demeanor seemed to take Bebo and Mom by surprise. They offered him something to drink; he declined graciously. Bebo suggested they go sit on the pool deck; he acquiesced willingly.

Jittery, and sure Dad had come to sabotage everything, I watched Bebo, Mom, and Dad take seats on patio furniture. Dad set the attaché in front of him as he talked and opened it. He pulled out some forms that he kept referring to. What were those papers? What did he want? Had he managed to get a court to give him custody back?

The conversation lasted only a few minutes. Bebo's quiet but firm "No" reached me in the living room. Dad packed up his paperwork, shook hands with Bebo and Mom, and they marched back in. Dad never looked at me as he made his way through the house and out the door.

"What did he want?"

"It was nothing. It's over," Bebo stated. Then seeing my face, he reassured me, "You're fine, don't worry about it."

No matter how much I asked, neither Bebo nor Mom would answer why he was there. Much later on, after many more cataclysmic events had taken place, Mom admitted that my father wanted them to sign papers that would affirm he no longer had financial or legal responsibility for me.

The Echevarrias didn't have to sign anything to prove what they had given to me unconditionally. They would long remember how I flinched when anyone touched me in any way when I first arrived in their home. But touch by touch, hug by hug, kiss by kiss, kindness by kindness, that was definitely changing.

Nonetheless, during the days leading up to Christmas, as I saw several gifts accumulating for me under the tree, for reasons I didn't understand, I began to have an irrational fear that all this good that was coming to me would vaporize once the holidays were over. This didn't hit me on Noche Buena, during the traditional Christmas Eve festivities that were enjoyed with unparalleled revelry at the Echevarrias, as tons of friends and relatives packed the house with music, food, drink, conversation, and stories overflowing.

But on Christmas morning, when everyone else was up and waiting for me in the living room, ready to open presents, I was in no hurry. Every ghost of every Christmas past had haunted my dreams, with images collected from years of getting just underwear or socks as punishment. After Ernie called yet again to say that they were still waiting, I shuffled to the bathroom, where I caught my frightening reflection in the mirror. My eyes were swollen almost closed.

Mom noticed them immediately, as did Kim when she arrived a short while later carrying even more presents for me. It finally occurred to me that I had been making myself sick every Christmas of my life so that I could get out of being disappointed and feeling unworthy. Now, instead of being disappointed, I didn't know what I had done right to deserve the present after present that had my name on it.

With each gift I opened, my eyes became more irritated and swollen. The looks of amazement coming from the group and even Sally, the German shepherd, made me run to the bathroom to have a look myself. I looked like a mutation between the Incredible Hulk and a frog! Bebo loaned me a pair of sunglasses so I could return to my pile of presents. Tears flowed uncontrollably down my face and onto my shirt.

Rocky asked, "Vic, are you crying?"

"No, man," I said sternly. "It's my eyes."

For six months, I'd been sitting on a dam of emotion that wanted to break, but hadn't until now. I didn't want to come off like Dickens's Scrooge, when I actually felt like Tiny Tim. I was happy, I was safe, and I was loved. God bless us every one.

Despite the genuinely miraculous transformation I had made since the time I arrived at Coral Park in the fall of 1970 as a brooding, combustible boy destined for trouble, by New Year's Day in 1973 there were still major hurdles for me to overcome in order to make it to graduation. It wasn't just that the vice principals seemed to be looking for any chance to expel me, it was also the fact that with my hot-headed tendencies, my intolerance for bullies, and the lurking specter of violence that continued to dog me, I was on my way to becoming the master of my own undoing.

There had been a brawl outside our local hangout, Lum's Restaurant on Southwest Eighth Street, when a gang from Miami High went after some of my buddies. This badass gang, primarily Cubans, many of them distinguished by their high-styling large afros, had a reputation for traveling out of their area and jumping students from other schools. They traveled in large packs and almost always outnumbered their victims. After they showed up at Lum's and baited two of my friends, bloodying them with steel pipes, my sense of injustice was so inflamed that I stupidly stepped in, taunting them all, "Come on you chickenshits, come get me!"

Sirens approached and the fight was broken up, but my verbal challenge made its way back to Miami High, making me a target for retribution for the rest of my senior year.

There was another group of disco-styled Cubans at Coral Park who were picking on a quiet kid from my English class on the way to a senior assembly one day. Just as they surrounded him, dressed flamboyantly in polyester and platform shoes, I walked up and in a noncombative, very low-key manner said, *"Dejalo."* Leave him alone.

The apparent ringleader of this group turned his attention to me and shifted his body into a karate pose, what I knew from kung fu movies was called a horse stance.

The rest of the guys GASSSPPPED as if I was in for big trouble. In a chorus they pleaded with their leader, "No! Karate, no!"

The second he brought his hands up, I dropped him with a short but powerful left hook. He hit the ground and covered up, much to the disappointment of his cohorts. They repeated the same line, once more in unison, this time in a woeful, embarrassed cry: "No. Karate, no."

Reports of these confrontations gave vice principals McNulty and Farthing ammunition to argue with my champion, Susi Baldwin, and my coaches that they had given me far too much credit for having improved. The next incident gave the vice principals cause to proceed with my expulsion.

In this instance, the person being picked on was female. Carol, one of the sweetest, prettiest girls in school, was six foot two, and was often picked on for her height by certain idiots. After school one day, on my way out of the weight room to get some air, I spotted a guy backing her up into a corner. Though she tried to defend herself, he pointed his finger in a scolding, bossy fashion and began to lunge at her, reminding me instantly of how my father used to close in on my mother.

Without hesitation I barreled in their direction. The guy froze, seeing me in my tank top, shorts, and tightly cinched weight-lifting belt. With my muscles bulging, I probably looked like all I needed was a cape flapping behind me. The guy took off running as I gave chase, Carol calling after me, "Vic, it's okay!"

In a rage, I pursued him into the boys' locker room and cornered him, slamming him against the wall as I lifted him up to eye level and barked in his face, "We don't hit girls!"

With that, I let him go. After he scampered to his feet, almost leaving skid marks with his sneakers on the way out of the locker room, I assured a worried Carol that I hadn't hurt him but had only given him a warning. From her reaction it was apparent that the guy had been tormenting her for a long time.

My heroics were not viewed as such by Vice Principal McNulty, who summoned me from Miss Baldwin's class to inform me that when I slammed the kid against the wall, I broke a bone in his forearm. That was it, the vice principal said; grounds for expulsion. This would be the cancellation of everything I had accomplished and my dreams for the future. Graduation, the FSU scholarship, maybe even my standing with my new family. It killed me to see McNulty so smug. He waved me away, saying he and Farthing would make their decision by the end of the day.

When Miss Baldwin heard the news, for once she looked very concerned for me. She promised to do what she could but I had the impression that she might have spent the last of her capital on me in previous incidents.

Word travels fast on a high school campus. Over the course of the day as I became more and more upset, several students approached me to say that the guy whose arm I broke was a menace. Kim had been in an art class with him and he had taken a razor blade to several students' canvases. By the end of the day, several teachers went down to the office to protest a decision to expel me, informing Mr.

McNulty and Mr. Farthing about this student's behavior. The assistant principals admitted they knew very well that he was a real troublemaker. Nonetheless, they said, that still didn't give me the right to take matters into my own hands. Finally a compromise was reached when the kid's parents decided they wouldn't press charges. I would have to serve after-school detention but I was not going to be expelled. Miss Baldwin informed me that several teachers agreed with the statement that one had made to the vice principals: "If we had more students like Vic Rivas on campus, we'd have a lot less bullying and kids getting hurt."

With graduation a couple of months away, I vowed to avoid confrontation and try to find a more diplomatic road to solving differences. Well, at least I thought about trying. The problem was, the minute I heard of somebody weaker or younger being threatened by someone stronger or older, I became a hurt little angry boy all over again, but with the body of a seventeen-year-old lineman.

That happened toward the end of the school year when a junior high school friend of Ernie's started getting harassed by a high school kid. The friends I had made through Rocky and Ernie meant a great deal to me. As an outgoing, charismatic kid, Rocky was a magnet for both males and females, all of whom became another circle of friends for me. Ernie, finishing up the eighth grade, also had lots of good buddies with whom he proudly shared me, his other older brother. One of his best friends was a kid named Adolfo, who had been threatened by an older kid, the state judo champion. Don't worry about him, I assured Ernie and his friend, I'd have a little talk with the bully.

What began as a diplomatic effort on my part quickly turned combative after I tracked the judo champion down in the cafeteria, letting him know that if he persisted in threatening Adolfo, he'd have to deal with me.

The guy may have been the state judo champion, but he was half my size. He looked at me very calmly and said, "If you touch me, you'll have at least three gangs on your ass!"

Unfazed I countered, "Go ahead, bring your pussy gangs if you want, but leave the kid alone." Valiant? Perhaps. But not smart.

Within days, gangs started showing up and there were sightings of the Afro-wearing Cuban gang I'd challenged in the Lum's parking lot. The police were called whenever they showed up, but the gang members weren't there when they came. At one point, Mr. McNulty suggested that I recruit a few of the football players as bodyguards. To my surprise, when I asked if he would let me carry a bat on campus, he went for it.

Now, ruing my braggadocio, I had to travel through school with my own personal posse of friends and fellow athletes, my bat in hand. I put up a tough front, but on the inside I was scared; besides that, Kim was endangered.

Though I seemed to be winging it okay so far, my delayed emotional development often left me unprepared for dealing with confrontation and disappointment. This became evident after something that happened at home with Mom on the day of Grad Night, an event I'd been eagerly anticipating. As senior class president, I'd helped organize our class trip up to Disney World, where the park was to be shut down to the public, admitting only high school seniors from around the state who would rule the night.

Though Mom had promised to wake me up shortly after midday from the nap I took—before it was time to board one of the buses scheduled to make the four-hour drive from Miami to Orlando late in the afternoon—when I awoke, the room was dark. My heart was pounding, my pulse speeding. The clock said 7:30 P.M.

When I stormed into the kitchen, getting angrier with every step, I confronted Mom. "You were supposed to wake me up! What happened?"

Mom looked at me with a little anger of her own. "I tried to, but when I touched you, you started swinging and yelling and you almost hit me."

This wasn't the first time something like that had happened in their house. During football season, when I took a nap, since alarm clocks were useless, either Rocky or Ernie would get me up. After my first violent sleeping outburst, they learned to use the end of the broomstick to poke at me until I was awake. They appeared to understand that I had been violently awakened so many times as a child that this defense mechanism became built into my sleep. It wasn't Mom's fault, obviously. But I was so upset about missing Grad Night, I couldn't let it go. "Goddamnit. Why didn't you use the broomstick?"

Mom wasn't going to argue with me. "Look, Vic. I'm sorry I didn't get you up, but you're not going to hit me." Changing the subject, she suggested I hurry and get dressed, even offering me her new Pontiac Trans Am to drive myself to Orlando.

It was too late, I mourned tragically, and stomped back to bed, sulking under the covers. The disappointment took some days to wear off. But something positive came out of what had happened between me and Mom and what was the first and only time that I had an outburst of anger and disappointment with her that could have also hurt her feelings. Instead of it creating a rift or a problem in the household, it changed nothing. She still loved me, warts and outbursts and all. People who loved each other unconditionally could get mad at each other. It happened. But love could withstand such passing storms.

Miss Baldwin certainly must have had moments when she was disappointed and upset with me, but on the evening before the graduation ceremonies for Coral Park High School's class of 1973, when she invited me out to dinner at the 45th Air Squadron, a World War II–style restaurant that overlooked a runway at Miami International Airport, she expressed only her immense pride.

As president of my class, I had the honor and challenge of delivering a commencement speech the following night, and she was going to help me work on it over dinner. But first Miss Baldwin wanted to remind me of my accomplishments that went beyond grades, test scores, or scholarships. Despite being a kid who once thought nobody liked him, I had recently been voted Most Popular—an incredible feat (even though I was kind of hoping for Funniest or Most Athletic). As the boy whose father had told him he wasn't tough enough for football, I was proud of my title as captain of the football team and also proud of having competed on the state champion wrestling team. I had a healthy, loving relationship with a wonderful, talented girlfriend, and, above all, I had been welcomed into seven different homes and had now been unofficially adopted into a family.

Thanks to Miss Baldwin, I had also been inspired by my experience with Close Up to do community service by volunteering to clean up public parks, guest-coaching at area schools, and working for a program for developmentally disabled adults—which provided the impetus that revived my need to find my brother Robert.

More than anyone, she was the person I felt was most responsible for my being made a Silver Knight nominee by the *Miami Herald,* a prestigious award "to recognize the outstanding seniors in Dade County high schools for unselfish service to their schools, church, community and fellow man."

She and the other members of my extended family, my angels and advocates, everyone at Coral Park High School, even my critics, had helped me walk out of their doors, guaranteed a college education for the next four years, as long as I did my part.

I had arrived into this community as a perfect stranger, a lost and wounded boy, a time bomb waiting to blow. Even with opportunity after opportunity, this village never gave up on me; even when I stumbled or took advantage of someone's kindness or generosity, I was taught to accept love and to love in return.

Much of this we recalled with laughter and a few tears over dinner. The speech I was making the next night was a combination of football-laced metaphors and an emphasis on service to community à la "Ask not what others can do for you but what you can do for others" and a little bit of "Hell, if I can do it, anybody can!" Not totally original but authentic, and it would come straight from the heart.

At the end of our dinner, she presented me with a gift. It was my first suitcase, for my new adventure as a student athlete at FSU. We walked out to the parking lot, into the balmy Miami night. The lights of the airport and incoming jets danced around us. We hugged and I leaned down to kiss her on the cheek. She stood looking at me with pride, her long wisps of blond hair blown across her face. I knew that probably after graduation, I might never see her again. She turned to go, got into her car, and backed out, turning and driving off. I sobbed like a baby as her car's taillights vanished from sight.

The Echevarrias drove me to the auditorium in Miami Beach where the commencement exercises were being held. Rocky determined that I should no longer go by my nickname Vic. "It's Victor for victory!" he sang, his motivational line to me for years to come. It was gratifying to know that they would be out in the crowd, along with Miss Baldwin and most of the families who had taken me into their homes. But this night belonged to Mami, who attended my graduation with her friend the Sexy Young Woman and two-and-a-half-year-old Carmen. This was my mother's victory. No one cheered louder than Mami when I received my diploma or applauded more after my speech. She was never prouder, she said, because though I had started by reading from my three-by-five cards, I had laid them down and just spoken from my heart. My favorite part was getting to ask the entire senior class to stand, grab their tassels, and move them from one side to the other, signifying our transition into adulthood. The entire auditorium erupted with applause, cheers, and hats flying everywhere. Euphoric madness!

After the ceremony, Kim and I met outside the auditorium, found our families, and took tons of photographs. We dashed off to the big senior blowout held at a sprawling dirt parking lot that belonged to a student's family. She and I hadn't even had our first beer when a classmate came running over to us, out of breath, and said, "You gotta go! Right now! They're here!"

From a distance, an undulating wave of Cuban Afros was heading our way, out for my blood.

"Kim, get in your car," someone yelled. "Vic, get down in the backseat!" Kim was led out a back gate and sped off.

In hiding the next two days, I called the coaches at FSU to see if I could still take them up on the offer to come up early and begin training for the upcoming season. When I heard, "Come on up," I was on a Greyhound to Tallahassee, toting my new suitcase, sitting low in my seat until I was well outside the city limits.

My sense of irony did not fail to observe that three years before, I had been brought into Miami in secrecy, and was now leaving it in the same fashion.

6

the madcuban
(1973–1979)

We are all born mad. Some remain so.
—Samuel Beckett

IN THE SUMMER OF 1978, I died and went to heaven. When I got there I found myself seated in the back of a classroom at Biscayne College, where the Miami Dolphins held training camp. The room bristled with the presence of football legends I had idolized as a teenager in Miami. Next to me were all-pro offensive linemen Jim Langer, Larry Little, and Bob Kuechenberg. A few rows up sat Vern Den Herder, Tim Foley, Bob Matheson, and Curtis Johnson, members of the No-Name Defense. In the front row were Garo Yepremian and Bob Griese. And there at the podium was the illustrious jutting jaw of the Football God himself, Coach Don Shula.

The *Miami News* had proclaimed that my ascension to this heaven, which made me the first Cuban-American rookie ever to attend a Miami Dolphins training camp, was the story of "the longest of long shots." And they didn't know the half of it.

The truth, as crazy as it made me to admit it, was that Dad may have actually been right about the fact that baseball was the sport I should have pursued. He was wrong about my toughness, of course. The real problem for me as an offensive guard—the position I played for the Seminoles—was my size. It turned out, after so many years of seeing myself as this big, hulking kid, that I needed to beef up.

This was the first thing I learned upon my arrival in Tallahassee in June 1973, when Coach Frank Debord, the big, jovial southerner who was the equipment manager, looked me over and sent me straight to the weight room, telling me, "Looks like ya need to put some meat on your bones."

The lone athlete in the weight room that day gave me a crash course in college-level weight training. A senior linebacker named Phil Arnold, he was just under six feet tall, but sculpted and ripped like a Greek statue, with arms the size of my thighs. Watching him load forty-five-pound plates, one after the other, onto the bar over the bench press, I thought he was kidding when they totaled ten, until he proceeded to bench-press this amount ten times with ease. I was benching about 225 pounds at the time; he had just benched 450 pounds. It so happened that Phil Arnold was considered to be the strongest football player in the nation. Meanwhile, I thought this was par for the FSU course.

Between the weight room, the cafeteria at Cash Hall, and various summer jobs clearing brush and loading trucks with rebar, I packed on fifteen pounds of bulk by the time the two-a-day practices began in August. With the temperature of ninety degrees and the 90 percent humidity creating a heat index of over one hundred, together with the speed and size of the other athletes, which made the hitting that much more ferocious, I thought nostalgically of those high school practices that seemed like romps in the park. Red ants were always villainous in Florida. But here at practice, there were many days when, if I crouched into my stance and put my hand down, it would be right on a red ant hill. Not permitted to move as an offensive lineman, I would have to endure the biting, stinging, outraged ants flying up my arm. My great friend and college roommate, Doug Dane, and

I had to take turns pulling each other out of bed in the morning because of muscle stiffness, cramping, bruises, and bug bites.

But the main hurdle my first year wasn't the demands of training. It was my nemesis, Coach Mac, who oversaw the training of the offensive line with all the intensity and intimidation of a military commander. A former All-American guard for Florida State, he spoke through his teeth while he gritted them and never looked away from you when he spoke. We were destined to clash. In his defense, he had a tough assignment: the previous spring, a rash of top players had quit over personnel changes. That meant there were positions that needed to be filled on the varsity from our freshman ranks and there was a lot of competition between us for those spots. His job was obviously to separate the boys from the men. To do so, his militant approach was to rid us of our individuality, and that touched off a nerve that reminded me just too much of Papi. The way I saw it there was no question that I could play for the man, but I didn't have to like him.

Our first face-off occurred on October 1. I had been trading time between practicing and playing with both the JV squad and the varsity. During a brutal scrimmage when I delivered a hard hit against the defense, I got knocked out cold and ended up with my face in the mud. The offense went back to the huddle as a teammate ran over to lift me up, moments before I came to. "Get back in the huddle!" Coach Mac yelled and motioned, while my teammate protested that I had been knocked out.

"He looks fine now. Let's go!" Coach Mac hollered in his Kirk-Douglas-as-Spartacus voice.

I lined up for the play and blasted off the line, hitting my opponent with everything I had. The play ended, but according to the report I heard later, I remained on top of the defensive player, beating him with my fists and forearms as Coach Mac furiously blew his whistle and motioned for the other players to pull me off. When they did, my teammates said I looked psychotic, and the next thing they knew my eyes rolled back into my head and I passed out. An ambulance was called and I was rushed to the campus hospital.

The verdict that I had suffered a concussion during the initial play and compounded it on the next play was related to me when I woke up in a hospital bed, four hours later, wearing a paper nightgown and blinded by a killer headache. When the nurse came in to fill out paperwork with general information from me, she paused after I gave her my birth date. "Well, Victor"—she smiled—"happy birthday!"

Moments later Kim rushed in tearfully and helped me to celebrate turning eighteen years old as best she could. The headache and the fog I was in put a damper on any party plans we might have had.

After a battery of tests was run the next day, all negative, I was released late in the afternoon. When I called to report what had happened to the Echevarrias, Bebo said, "You don't sound like yourself! You sure you're okay?"

In subsequent conversations, Bebo became very concerned about my state of mind and called to speak with one of my JV coaches.

"Oh, Vic is fine," he was told. "We're giving him a couple of days off and he'll be traveling with us to the JV game on Saturday."

Bebo exploded. "What are you, fucking crazy? I talked to him last night and he doesn't even know who he is. He is not making any sense."

"Sir, they ran some tests on him and the doctors cleared him."

"I don't care! He sounds crazy to me!"

Bebo insisted that the school fly me home to have more tests. The next morning, Bebo picked me up at Miami International Airport and drove directly to Baptist Hospital, where he had arranged for me to be examined by one of the country's leading neurologists. My headaches had become excruciating and I could barely open my eyes from the pain and brightness.

The doctor, in his melodic Indian accent, explained that I had suffered a serious concussion and that I was done playing for some time. He prescribed several medications, including painkillers for the headaches, and prescription Ray-Ban sunglasses to be worn night and day for my light sensitivity. When Bebo drove me back to the airport to return to Tallahassee after a few days' rest and wonderful meals made by Mom, I couldn't find the words to thank him and tell him that I loved him. To be protected by him, as he would have protected one of his own sons, gave me an enormous sense of security. Rather than saying what I felt, I reached out and shook his hand, saying simply, *"Gracias."*

Coach Mac never came to see me. He didn't inquire about how I was doing. My conclusion was that my injury was an excuse to weed me out of the program. After weeks of struggling with a drug-induced fog and debilitating headaches that caused me to scream into a pillow and didn't help my academic work, I forced myself to get back to practice. My morale wasn't great and neither was the team's. The varsity hadn't won a game all year. Many of us nursed our flagging spirits in local watering holes and discos, often staying out well past the football team's lights-out curfew of 11 P.M. Most of the coaches looked the other way, probably wishing they could join us. But not Coach Mac. Out to clean up Dodge, he went on a raid of our dorm and dragged us out on the field the next morning, alcohol raging in our veins, to make us run stadiums.

A stadium is a measure of distance in the football lexicon that requires you to run up the steps from midfield to the top of the stadium and back down them. Coach Mac went down the line of players, starting with the seniors, who were given fifteen stadiums each. The rest of the players were given ten stadiums to run. He left me for last. As all the other players took off running to the top of Doak Campbell Stadium, Coach Mac barked, "Rivas, you give me fifty!"

"Fifty! Why fifty? All the other freshmen got ten!"

"Okay, sixty."

"That's not fair. I should get the same punishment as the rest of the guys."

"Okay, a hundred. You want to keep going?"

"No."

"No, what?"

I knew what he wanted me to say, but I refused to give him the pleasure of having me address him as "sir." I looked him dead in the eye with a hatred I had reserved for one other person in my life. He was trying to run me off. The head injury hadn't done it, so now he was going to break my spirit.

My spirit fought back stupidly and crazily as I repeated myself with another smart-assed "No." I turned around and began sprinting up the steep steps to the top, eighty-five of them in all.

My reward for that remark was that for the next four days I had to run ten stadiums before school and ten stadiums before practice. By the end of the third day I could barely walk, let alone run. My already large thighs looked and certainly felt swollen. Coach Mac personally supervised these sanctions, relishing each time I bent over to gasp for air.

On the fourth day, I had run the stadiums in the morning, showered, and gone to class. Suffering from severe cramps and muscle spasms, I left my second class to go back to the field house and into the training room, where the trainers gave me salt and potassium pills for the cramping. As I was leaving, Coach Mac walked out of the showers with a towel wrapped around his waist. We locked eyes.

"Rivas, let's go run some stadiums."

"Nope. It's not time."

"What was that?" He closed the distance between us with a few quick strides, his nose to my nose. He could smell my rage and sense my involuntary clenching of my fists. "You want to hit me?"

Heat rose into my ears. My heart banged on my chest. The beast rattled its cages. I stood my ground.

"Go on, I'll give you the first shot." He said it calmly, but his wild blue eyes were dancing around in their sockets.

I called him on his bluff, reminding him that if I hit him, I would have my scholarship taken away from me.

He laughed, and then, through clenched teeth, swore to me, "As long as I'm here, Rivas, you're never gonna play a down of football."

Now I was the one to make a prediction. "You know," I seethed, "I may be around longer than you."

With that, Coach Mac grabbed the front of my shirt and I could see his other hand, balled in a fist. "What's that *suppo*se to mean?" His *p*'s caused spit to splatter on my face.

I was ready for him to hit me, so he could lose his job. "We're oh-and-seven; haven't won a game all year. The players don't get fired." I smiled back at him.

He held the front of my shirt, his face trembling, and then he let go, ordering me to the office of Head Coach Jones after practice.

A little smiling devil who looked like Papi leapt on my shoulder and whispered, "You always know how to fuck up a good thing."

Two hours later Coach Mac led me into the inner sanctum of the head coach. Coach Larry Jones was sitting behind his desk, head lowered, writing on a pad. He looked up, smiled, and said, "Hey, Vic Rivas. I hear we have a little problem."

Coach Jones asked me to tell him about the incident in the locker room. I explained to him what happened and also told him that I thought it was unfair that I received such a severe punishment for the same infraction the other players had committed.

Coach Jones patiently listened and then said, "Son, I understand your beef, but that doesn't give you the right to put your hands on your coach."

"What? I never touched him! He's the one that grabbed me!"

"You know what you did, Rivas," Coach Mac barked back. "Own up to it."

I sprang out of my chair and leaned hard against the desk, yelling back at him, "You're a liar!" Tears rolled down my face as I accused him of being exactly like my father, whom I hated. We once again came nearly to blows until Coach Jones broke it up, ordering Coach Mac out of his office.

"We think it's best if you leave the team." He smiled his best fatherly smile back at me, as he continued. "You're becoming a bit of a distraction to the other players right now."

"I don't understand. I've done everything that's been expected of me. I took my punishment like a man. I came here to play football."

When I reminded him of all the other schools I'd turned down to come to FSU, he had the nerve to offer to contact them on my behalf. No, I pleaded, I was a Seminole.

It was clear-cut. If Coach Mac wouldn't coach me, Coach Jones couldn't make him. But I was now fighting for my college life. They couldn't take my scholarship away if my grades were fine and I hadn't been arrested and hadn't struck the coach. The subterfuge was obvious. For them to get rid of me, I had to quit; I had to voluntarily relinquish my scholarship. I wasn't budging.

Coach Jones resolved it his way by kicking me off the team and out of Cash Hall. My scholarship was to remain intact. The death of all my dreams sent me out to the stadium and under the bleachers to vent my anguish alone. But as if Dad was somewhere orchestrating these abysmal events, there was more to come. That evening when I went back to my room at Cash Hall to get my things, I was greeted by a loud commotion and the sight of my clothes being thrown out of my room and onto the floor of the hallway. Frozen in disbelief, I looked up from my clothes and saw Coach Mac standing over them with a crazy smirk on his face.

"Get out, Rivas. You're not welcome anymore. I don't want you polluting your roommate." In his left hand was one of my jerseys. "This belongs to me now."

Flashing in my brain was every penny my father ever stole from my paper route savings, every trophy that he smashed as he made me watch and then made me clean up, and my slashed all-star warm-up jacket. My Seminole football jersey was the one piece of material I valued most and I wasn't going to let him rob me again. Who knows what I would have done to Coach Mac if my fellow players hadn't intercepted me in my stampede toward killing this guy. I wanted to kill that motherfucker. And because he wasn't my father, my own flesh and blood, after all, I just might have. Coach Mac turned and left. True to my prediction, he was long gone by the time I returned to the team next season.

An old school lesson: History repeats itself. I was starting to be aware that many of the scenarios from childhood in which I'd found myself battling the forces of injustice were repeating themselves in my adulthood. But when I found myself spending another birthday in the hospital, under somewhat similar circumstances the very next year, I got spooked.

Well, the good news was that after suffering a horrendous 0–11 season, FSU replaced its entire coaching staff, and by the end of my freshman year, I was back in Cash Hall and glad to welcome the new coaches, who had their work cut out for them to get us in shape for the fall.

How bad were we? When a fight broke out between a group of football players, including me, and the ATO fraternity guys, who outnumbered us two to one, and we kicked their asses, it became the top story in the media from Tallahassee to Miami and beyond, with headlines like "FSU Football Team Wins First One! Seminole Football Now 1–11!"

This was the sorry state of affairs that faced Dr. Darrell Mudra, the new head coach, who was a look-alike and sound-alike for Peter Falk's Columbo character. He held a doctorate in psychology, had been a national badminton champion, and was a funny, intellectual little man with a stellar career of turning losing football programs around. In his crumpled clothes with his badminton racquet in hand, Coach Mudra had quite the gift for mixing metaphors and snippets of oddly assembled bits of philosophy. He also had the unorthodox and controversial practice of coaching from the coaches' box above the field and not on the sidelines.

He hired an eclectic staff of assistant coaches, including my new coach, Bob Harbison. A former coach for the Seminoles, Coach Harbison had been brought out of retirement. Somewhere in his sixties, maybe, he was a tough, cantankerous man who loved to stuff tobacco snuff between his lower lip and gums. He had his own home-spun sayings and his voice had a soft, grandfatherly purr when he was egging me on, like the time I was hitting Big Bertha, the hanging five-hundred-pound rain-soaked bag: "That's it, Rivas! That's the way to hit it! It should sound like a big fart out of an old sow's ass!"

These were just the guys to give me that second chance to prove myself. A new day, a new dawn. The liberated feeling I had inside me was, coincidentally, epitomized by a new craze that was sweeping the country: streaking! Florida State was credited with being the site of one of the first mass streaks in the nation, with over ten thousand stu-dents running naked across the campus. The mass streak was orga-nized and announced on the news by a bearded student whose moniker was Rasputin. Hundreds of local residents of Tallahassee descended on the campus that night with lawn chairs and coolers while our Buford Pusser sheriff arrived ready with his horse-mounted troops.

At Cash Hall, the football team got in the mood with a keg of beer, dressed in our gray practice shorts, knee-high garnet-and-gold tube socks, and sneakers. When we made our way down to Landis Green, the huge grassy area in the middle of campus, I couldn't believe my eyes. Naked people were dashing to and fro, most of them male. But a few females got into the act, and with each woman that I saw deciding to rip her clothes off, I also saw a throng of men follow-ing behind her, worshipping and protecting her as if she was the statue of Venus.

In a spontaneous burst, while the naked band arrived and broke into the Seminole fight song—"Paa, paa, paa. Paa, paa, paa. Paa, paa, paa. F-L-O-R-I-D-A S-T-A-T-E. Florida State! Florida State! Florida State! Whoo!"—the football team was at the center of a mass of people parting for us like Moses at the Red Sea. Chanting at us, the crowd commanded, "Streak! Streak! Streak!" and without any hesitation, I dropped my shorts, along with my teammates, and began what by def-inition was "the nonsexual act of running freely." Everywhere I looked or streaked there was a naked wave of humanity. It was not the nudity that was fun, it was the nudity while running, because the moment you stopped running, you were, well, NAKED. And that's how I was when one of my new coaches was relaxed enough to say hello and suggest that I get on back to Cash Hall. Good thing, since some of my other teammates were arrested by the fuddy-duddy sheriff.

In fine spirits and health, I began my sophomore year ready to make up for lost time off the field and to be part of the new and improved Seminole team. Our first game was against the Pittsburgh Panthers and their star running back, Tony Dorsett, scheduled as a night game under the lights at Doak Campbell Stadium.

We eagerly gathered around Coach Mudra in the locker room to hear what promised to be a stirringly motivational speech and listened intently as he started by asking us, "Have you ever heard of the exponential motivation factor in Pavlov's dog?"

We scratched our helmeted heads, trying to unriddle this one, but it was clear no one understood what the hell he was talking about.

"You know, the stimulus of the bell and the salivation?"

No response from the players. Many of us began looking at one another, in case one of us had the key to this foreign language.

"Well, you know, it's like that old saying, 'You can lead a horse to water but'—oh, that kind of reminds me of my wife . . ."

We burst into laughter at this point, and he sputtered, "Well, all right, let's get them!"

The team left the locker room in a state of confusion. That quickly changed in the tunnel, with the percussive beat of the tom-toms from the Florida State Marching Chiefs. We played like the FSU team I'd signed up for, and I had the pleasure of playing about half the game. Although we were tough, holding Tony Dorsett to under a hundred yards, we lost the game 9–6. Still, between this game and the next one, which we lost by only a touchdown, we were starting to play like winners. Now it was time for the scoreboard to reflect that.

We next traveled to an away game in Lawrence, Kansas, to play the University of Kansas Jayhawks. Away games always brought out the gladiator in me; I enjoyed traveling to the enemies' arena to take on their gladiators with their bloodthirsty fans screaming. We came prepared, fitted with special shoes to play on their new Astroturf field. During pregame warm-ups, I had the honor of shaking hands with the Jayhawks' athletic director, Hall of Fame running back Gayle Sayers of the Chicago Bears. And that's basically all I remembered about a game in which we got our butts kicked, 40–9, other than a miserable first half that was coming to a close when our quarterback threw a pass into coverage and Kansas's linebacker Steve Towle intercepted the ball with lots of open field.

The only way to catch him was to take a pursuit angle and hope that I judged the point of collision correctly. The geometry looked predictable. I took off after Towle, up and across the field, while he ran straight toward our goal line. Our point of impact—forty yards straight for Towle and thirty yards that I had sprinted at an angle—happened near the sideline. Just before the collision, I opened my arms, like a bird of prey expanding its wingspan, and began lowering my helmet, targeting the middle of his chest. Perfect. Except for the damn shoes that, we later learned, were experimental. Their rubber tips had been getting stuck in the Astroturf throughout the pregame warm-ups, preventing slips but causing stumbles. I lurched forward and instead of my head driving through his chest, his knee drove right into my helmet at the temple. The violent impact sent both of us crashing to the turf.

In the hospital back in Tallahassee, where I woke up the next day, the report was that after I was knocked unconscious and landed on my back, with both arms splayed to either side of my body, I lay motionless for a second or two, and like a zombie in *The Night of the Living Dead,* my body sat up for a moment and then slammed back to the surface. Apparently I was out for twenty minutes but, most fortunately, didn't suffer any spinal cord damage. Still, I was disoriented for the plane ride home and upset to spend not just a night but a week in the hospital undergoing extensive neurological tests to determine the short-term and possible long-term damage from this second major concussion. All the tests came back negative. My angel of a girlfriend, Kim, came to visit me every day, including my nineteenth birthday. She arrived with a cake and a few of my teammates. They joined together with the nursing staff in singing me "Happy Birthday."

I went straight to the football field house upon my release, where Coach Harbison gave me the bad news. I was off the team, again. But this time it wasn't because they were out to get me. It was for my own good.

"Son, I've been doing this for twenty-five years," Coach Harbison said. "I've seen a lot of injuries, but I've never been so scared for a player in my life. My God, I thought you were dead!" Over my pleadings, he insisted that he and Coach Mudra had talked and it was agreed that if I stayed in school, I could keep my scholarship. He chewed on his tobacco, watching me fall apart in front of him before admonishing, "Get your education, son. Forget about football."

Nothing I could say or do, no amount of wailing and raging, could change his mind. Storming out of the field house, I could hear my dad starting up again. No, no, no! Fuck them all. I would prove them all wrong. Maybe.

For once, instead of acting on my rage, I opted for a somewhat creative solution. I went to the defensive coaches and asked if I could try out for a position on the other side of the ball. They agreed, but made it clear that I would have to start at the bottom of the depth chart. I was excited and nervous to be given the opportunity to play again.

As it turned out, the Miami Dolphins star running back, Larry Csonka, had also suffered from a series of concussions and had been using a newly designed helmet, called a water helmet. The Dolphins equipment manager had sent one of his older water helmets for our team to try out, and fortuitously I was selected to give it a trial run. The exterior of the helmet looked the same as any other helmet, but the interior was lined with small pads that were filled with a liquid. The helmet was extremely heavy and made a squishy sound when you made contact with another surface. For the first week I had to strain to keep my head up in my stance. By the second week, I was using it as a battering ram.

The defense employed me well by making me a member of the scout team for the offense, meaning it was my job to simulate the opponent's defensive schemes. My priority was to prove Coach Harbison wrong and work my way back to the offense. I spent the first two weeks delivering some of the hardest hits of my football career. I wasn't concerned about my defensive responsibilities. Basically, I was firing off the line and driving the offensive lineman backward. After an extremely vicious hit, I would pop up from the ground and look at Coach Harbison. There's no question I had his attention. By the third week, I was back with the offensive line.

Unfortunately, our season hadn't done much to change FSU's numbers. A sports lesson relearned: Losing is as contagious as winning. The football program had lost its luster and was becoming the butt of many jokes, locally and nationally. In the personnel switches that followed, Coach Harbison departed and a new offensive line coach came in. A big man from the Midwest, Coach Grouwinkle had a voice to match his name. A real character, he growled a lot, but there was always a twinkle in his eyes; he reminded me of Bebo and I thought highly of him.

During preseason spring training, Arthur Jones, the creator of the Nautilus exercise machines, designed and monitored a conditioning program for our football program. We were pushed to the limits of exhaustion and pain, but the results were phenomenal. As a whole the team set new strength records, with more than thirty players bench-pressing over three hundred pounds and a few of us closing in on four hundred.

Just as I was about to end the year on a high note, I got myself and my roommate into trouble for having a bag of marijuana in our room. No matter how much I protested that it was mine, that he was completely innocent and had nothing to do with it being in our room—where I had hosted an impromptu party—Coach Mudra and Coach Grouwinkle hauled us both into a meeting with all the other coaches.

"Rivas, I don't understand," charged one of the defensive coaches. "You seemed to be one of the most dedicated players, and certainly one of the best-conditioned athletes on this team. How can you be addicted to marijuana?"

God only knows what possessed me to try to explain that the weed we smoked was less potent than a couple of cocktails and to let them know that I was far from alone in my cannabis indulgence. Ooops. My roommate could have killed me in a glance. The coaches then wanted to make a deal, asking us to name names. When we refused, a meeting of the team was called at which Coach Mudra announced, "It's been brought to our attention that we have an epidemic of drug use on this team." He went on a five-minute ramble about drug use that made about as much sense as his Pavlovian pregame pep talk. Not only was I now the scourge of the team, but the following day, Mudra called my roommate and me in to say that the coaches were leaning toward kicking us off the team and taking away our scholarships. He decided instead that we had to sign a contract that we would relinquish our scholarships if we got in trouble again. Both of us were demoted to the bottom of the offensive line depth chart.

With three weeks to go until the end of spring practice, I was sixth string. I worked my butt off, hustling and leading the offensive line from one drill to another. By the end, I was alternating with the first team.

Although football was all-consuming, there were certainly other active parts of my life in these years. As a student, I had begun the slow but satisfying discovery that Dad was absolutely wrong about my intellect. I wasn't so stupid after all and was possibly even smarter than the average bear. Moreover, I had taken to heart the advice given to me in my freshman year by Chris Griffin, a senior defensive back and one of FSU's top students. Chris had been a straight-A student during his time at Florida State, an elected officer of the school, and an athlete. He told me, "Don't miss a class, take good notes, and you're guaranteed a C."

My relationship with Kim in some respects had run its course. She was sensing the same thing, and, earlier on, had been the one to attempt to do the breaking up. I went berserk and behaved so dramatically—as if I had been abandoned—that she reconsidered and soon called off the calling-off. She had put up with a lot from me—including my intermittent infidelities and a ridiculous double standard that made the mere thought of her being with anybody else unbearable. When we tried to break up at one point back in high school, I had actually followed her out on a date one night, scaring her and the guy by dropping out of a tree as they made their way home.

Kim didn't talk to me for a few days after that, and when she did, I apologized, promising never to do it again. It turned out to be a valuable lesson about how intolerable stalking behavior like that could be and I tried never to repeat it. Another time, during a heated argument, I had thoughtlessly grabbed her by the arms and pushed her against the wall. The second I did it, I let go of her and backed off, seriously afraid that I could possibly do what I had promised myself I would never subject a woman to. Though I hadn't hit Kim, I had physically restrained her against her will. "That will never happen again," I promised her. And it never happened again, with her or anyone else.

One of the things I loved and admired most about Kim was her independence. While she was obviously proud of my accomplishments and my status as a big man on campus, Kim made it clear that she had her own academic goals and career aspirations. As time went on, this was a quality that became more important to me in the opposite sex. For the time being, however, I simply found everything attractive about the opposite sex.

Whenever she accused me of sleeping around, I'd bark back, "Prove it!" She never actually caught me in the act, but she tried. My indignant reactions were shameful, as were my temperamental outbursts when I punched a wall or two to make a point with her. The fact that she loved me enough to put up with me was one of the other reasons I didn't want to break up.

I was really torn over what to do. Break up, or continue being dishonest? I spent the summer pondering that question as I slept around, remaining up in Tallahassee.

There were a few trips to Miami that summer when, as usual on holiday breaks, I stayed at the Echevarrias' house. Quick visits to see Mami and other friends were also on the agenda. Besides the hospitality that Mom and Bebo offered during these breaks, I was often able to get off-season work through Bebo and his sister Yolanda, as both were in the airline business. In various jobs in and around Miami International Airport, I worked in security, the cleaning and maintenance of aircrafts, loading baggage and cargo.

As vice president of a cargo company, Bebo had hired me as well as Rocky to work loading and unloading everything from Dutch tulips to exotic fish from the Amazon, cattle, wild animals, and fruit from all over the world. Once I even helped load Flipper from the Miami Seaquarium onto a plane headed for South America. During Christmas break in my freshman year, Rocky and I were at a jet's cargo hold when the forklift driver missed the doorway with the pallet of cargo. From the doorway of the cargo hold, we watched the crate travel fifteen feet to the tarmac below and splinter on impact, liberating a dozen baby capuchin monkeys, which scattered and scurried for freedom. Before we could be lowered to the ground, the little monkeys disappeared into the Miami night.

Three days later, Rocky discovered one of the monkeys behind a box, shivering, scared, and hungry. And like all the other strays, including myself, it was brought home to the Echevarrias', adding to the menagerie of animals that already included a dog, several cats, and a Spanish-speaking half-moon parrot named Cotiqa. Cotiqa terrorized the other animals in the house and sometimes human house-guests. Cotiqa had the run of the house and liked to hide behind the tall frame of a painting and swoop down on unsuspecting visitors, especially one female friend of the family. This woman was always dressed to impress and dolled up with a little too much makeup. Cotiqa waited quietly on her perch until this woman made her entrance, and then came dive-bombing down, shrieking, *"Puta! Puta!"*

But compared to Minkey, as Rocky and Ernie named the orphaned capuchin, the half-moon parrot was tame.

"Sir, do you have a pet monkey?" was the question put to me by a female police officer when I arrived home at one holiday break to an empty house.

"Yes, we do."

"Step outside." She pointed to the roof of the house. Minkey was on the roof, holding a rock in each hand and jumping up and down, screaming. Our house was on a slow curve, where cars had to reduce their speed to five miles an hour. Minkey had apparently escaped from the long chain leash that was padlocked to his waist, had climbed on the roof, and was throwing the decorative rocks from the roof at cars going by. He had actually hit a couple of cars. The officer ordered me to get him off the roof and gave me a citation.

Minkey had already bitten the ear off a huge Doberman down the street. I arrived to find the dog cowering in the corner with a bloody ear and Minkey screaming at it from a tree. Another time, during one of Minkey's many escapes, he had made his way to another neighbor's house, where the teenagers hanging out thought it would be funny to get the monkey drunk. Minkey, in a drunken stupor, climbed the telephone pole and started swinging on the wires, until he hit a live one. The kids arrived at the house with a fur-singed, unconscious Minkey wrapped in a towel and handed him to Bebo. In a gesture that looked like CPR, Bebo laid him down on the dining room table and began pushing on his chest. Minkey regained consciousness and suddenly stood on the table and screamed at the kids, who went flying out the door.

Later Minkey traveled across the Tamiami Trail to the city of Sweetwater, where he spent the afternoon terrorizing the entire police force until Bebo was able to come and pick him up. When Bebo arrived at the station, the desk sergeant warned, "This monkey's crazy and violent. He's a menace."

Tough big bear of a man that he was, Bebo promptly responded, "No, he is *bery* sweet." Minkey screamed and proceeded to bite Bebo on the thumb. "See?" Bebo showed them. "It doesn't hurt."

Later Bebo told us it hurt like hell. "It's fucking killing me!"

In yet another instance of mischief, Minkey tried to jump into a ski boat just as the driver gunned its engine. He missed the boat but landed on the ski rope, held on, and was dragged around the lake, skimming and bouncing wildly on the surface. We were able to get the driver's attention and get Minkey back before he drowned.

Eventually, Minkey did go crazy. Bebo was trying to feed him a banana when without warning Minkey attacked and bit through one of Bebo's wrists. Bebo lost a lot of blood and suffered from a nasty infection for several weeks. An animal psychologist was called in to evaluate Minkey's increasingly violent and erratic behavior, especially toward Bebo. The doctor explained that capuchin monkeys tend to get schizophrenic over time and that the males take one mate for life. Obviously, in our house that mate, in Minkey's mind, was Mom, and Bebo was his rival. The psychologist advised them either to have Minkey defanged and castrated or to set him free in the wild.

The family deliberated. It was decided that it would be cruel to deprive him of his manhood. Soon after that, he was adopted by a man who lived in the Everglades with his own menagerie of exotic pets, including an alligator.

From time to time I wondered how Minkey was doing living closer to the wild. Was he still crazy, giving hell to the gators? Or had freedom given him back his sanity?

* * *

In the middle of the football season during my junior year, I almost went really crazy myself. But instead of being turned loose in the wild, I earned the nickname "the Madcuban," which would mark me for the rest of my football career.

Training camp started in the oppressive heat of August. I was back in the starting lineup. I had convinced the coaching staff that I was dedicated to the team and I had kicked my "marijuana addiction."

Near the end of training camp, at one afternoon practice, a massive black cloud approached the campus, littered with lightning strikes. Coach Grouwinkle didn't understand the weather in Florida. On several previous occasions, ominous thunderstorms had approached with lightning, but when we encouraged Grouwinkle to call practice off, he growled, "Come on, ladies. It's just a little rain."

We knew better. The practice fields were out in the open, with six towering sets of goal posts that surrounded us and a metal coaching tower. The tallest structure was a hundred yards behind the field. It was a circus tent pole. For many years, Florida State University was the only school in the country that offered a circus curriculum, and the big top was right behind us with its towering poles.

When the sky turned dark with the approaching storm, Grouwinkle ignored it, keeping up with the drills he was running us through. The rumblings of thunder grew in frequency and volume; the long skeletal fingers of lightning now traveled in every direction above us.

I piped up, "Coach, we need to get in, right now!"

He growled something back at us, but all we heard was a massive boom and we were blinded by an explosion of light. When our eyes cleared, we discovered that we had been blown off our feet by the lightning strike that hit the circus tent pole. We looked around to make sure everyone was all right, and then we turned our attention to Coach Grouwinkle, awaiting his decision. Grouwinkle was a hundred yards away, sprinting to the field house. We followed him, with many of us yelling at him, "Come on, Coach. It's just a little rain."

When the season kicked off, our team was very competitive. But again, our record didn't reflect that. Most of our games were very close, within a touchdown or two.

On a personal level, I was having a good year. I was playing well and my head injuries seemed to be behind me, thanks to the water helmet. During an afternoon practice, after striking someone and cracking the shell of my helmet, I felt a warm liquid trickling down my forehead and face. Was it blood from a cut? Nope; by the taste of it, which made me gag, it turned out to be antifreeze in the water helmet. Made sense for cold weather.

Academically, I had moved into my degree field of criminology. Although my first choice had been to pursue a theatre degree at FSU's excellent theatre program, the team's academic adviser convinced me that I wouldn't have time for productions with my football load. Since I was contemplating a career with the FBI after college, a criminology major wasn't a bad choice.

Going into our fourth game of the season, against Clemson— with permanent war wounds I'd earned in games we'd played at Georgia Tech, the University of Florida, and Auburn—I finally got my comeuppance from Kim. Boy, were my ego and double standard in for a shock. What started as a rumor that she was seeing someone else, told to me by a loyal friend who thought I should know, was confirmed by Kim. She wasn't just seeing someone else. She was seeing Clyde Walker. She had cheated on me with Clyde Walker!

Clyde Walker? Oh, thou murderess of my heart, I wanted to moan in Shakespearian outrage, get thee to a nunnery! Clyde Walker? Not the blond-haired, blue-eyed starting quarterback of the football team. Not the player who commandeered the offensive side of the ball. Not the leader who called the plays in the huddle and led our marches down the field. Not the one player that I and my fellow offensive linemen would protect and defend at all cost.

I *ROARED*. I *hy-per-ven-ti-lat-ed*. I WEPPPPT. And then I charged out to kill the motherfucker. When I got to Clyde's door, his roommate answered it, fortunately. "If you see him, tell him I'm looking for him," I hissed.

My first acting job was on the movie *Semi-Tough*. I'm number 60, kneeling behind Burt Reynolds, another FSU alum.

A Christmas visit to Miami in the early 1980s. With everything that we'd been through together, my mother and I could always make each other smile.

At the 1978 Hall of Fame Game in Canton, Ohio—the Miami Dolphins against the Philadelphia Eagles—I was the "longest of long shots" and fulfilled a lifelong goal not only to play professional sports but to wear the uniform of my dream team.

1979. My father, Tony Rivas Sr., nearing the end.

July 1987. My journey to overcome the demons of my childhood took many turns, including this pitfall at one of my lowest points.

My wedding day in April 1991. On a bluff in Malibu overlooking the Pacific, my transformation from wounded boy to loving husband was formally celebrated.

A celebration of survival—Christmas 1991. After everything she had endured, Mami was now surrounded by her children, their spouses, and her numerous grandchildren. (Olga Rivas seated between Barbie, left, and Carmen, right; I am flanked by my brothers, Ed, left, and Tony, right.)

July 1994. The moment I held Eli in my arms, I knew I could never hurt him the way that my father hurt me.

My journey of unconditional love begins. Elias Kennedy Rivas and me.

Family bliss in Hermosa Beach, California. Left to right: Mim, Eli, and me.

At the age of five, Eli asked to join me in speaking out against domestic violence and child abuse. Here, at age nine, he speaks at a conference on victims of crime in Sonoma, California.

Mother's Day 2004. A little older, a little grayer, I was never happier. (Seated, left to right: Tony, Carmen, and Mami; standing, left to right: me, Barbie, and Ed.

Back in my room, I cranked up the stereo to songs about love gone wrong, lit a joint, and started guzzling Old Milwaukee beers, then dragged a chair outside my open door to wait for Clyde's return. My buddies Doug, also an offensive lineman, Ed, our tight end, and Jeff, a running back, returned from class and tried to console me, but I was beyond help.

Jeff said, "There goes our quarterback."

Through my anger and sadness, Jeff's comment reached me. If I unleashed my rage on Clyde, the chances of him playing the remaining four games were slim. And besides, that would be the end of football for me, and the end of my scholarship.

With an hour to go before practice, I was drunk. Doug advised me to sit this practice out and cool off. All three of them understood my disappointment with Kim and the betrayal by a teammate, but showing up drunk would only make it worse. Besides, there was that contract I had signed. Even in my drunken fury, in a passing flash of clarity, I realized that if I remained on campus I wouldn't be able to stop myself from going after Clyde. The only thing to do was to get my crazy ass out of town.

Unbeknownst to my friends, that's what I did. Roaring off on my brown Honda 500 cc motorcycle, which I'd proudly bought earlier that year, I had no idea where I was headed or what I'd do when I got there. The sign said I was traveling south on U.S. 27. With spattered bug juice and tears streaming down my face, I sped into the night, desperate to get far away from FSU as quickly as possible.

Three hours later, in my Seminole practice jersey, I found myself in Gator country, of all places, flying through the University of Florida campus, in Gainesville. Gators and Seminoles were hated rivals. I had to be crazy.

"You've got to be crazy!" said Marvin Wheeler when I showed up at his dorm, knowing he went to school there. His family had been the first to ever take me in. Now he took me in again and let me crash in his room.

For the next twenty-four hours, I drank, smoked pot, cried,

passed out, and repeated the same cycle. At one point, I talked to a very concerned Doug on the phone and told him where I was.

Several hours later, Doug, Jeff, and Ed came through the door at Marvin's.

"You're coming back with us!" Ed announced.

"Okay." The truth is, I was too exhausted to argue with them. They loaded my motorcycle into the back of Jeff's white Dodge van and lifted it through the back doors, strapping it down for the three-hour ride north to Tallahassee. To my surprise, the offensive coaching staff had said, "Go get Vic," and had given them a gas credit card and some cash for meals. The coaches understood my anger and disappointment with my girlfriend, but even more so with Clyde. Everyone was pissed off at Clyde, especially the coaches. Coach Grouwinkle told them to come and get me and to let me know that there wouldn't be any discipline for my absence. What really surprised me was Grouwinkle's assurance that I would be starting at the Clemson game.

But Jeff was worried about what might happen on the field. "What are you gonna do to Clyde?" he asked with dread.

"I'm not going to do a thing, right now. We got four games left. I can wait, because if I do get ahold of him, I'm going to fuck him up good. That's why I left. There's no need for the rest of the team to suffer." I spoke this like a mighty warrior island king, thinking more of his tribe than his own need for face-saving vengeance. For the time being.

Doug was relieved. He confessed that they had brought a bat in case they had to subdue me. "I know I wouldn't ever wanna make you mad," he said.

" 'Cause you's the Madcuban!" Jeff chimed in.

Ed completed the statement. "You the Madcuban exile now!"

We all laughed hard the rest of the way home.

I was the Madcuban for sure, remaining angry for the rest of the season. In every huddle, I had to look into the eyes and read the lips of the prick who reminded me of what a jerk I had been to the woman who was my first love. My opponents suffered the effects of my hostility from huddle to huddle, play to play.

But I also took away from this explosion and this season the realization that I had found an identity and sense of belonging that I'd always wanted. The team was a brotherhood of over one hundred young men from disparate places, backgrounds, religions, and ethnicities. This brotherhood changed from season to season with graduation, injuries, or those who opted to return to their real families. With each scholarship class, we adopted thirty more boys and watched as they became men in a short amount of time. Most of us acclimated quickly to the demands of living on our own, schoolwork, and training, each with the dedication and desire to be a major college football player.

My core group of guys—we had arrived in our teens in 1973—came to the end of our third year at FSU in the spring of 1976 knowing we had survived many things. Many had just missed the draft as the Vietnam War was coming to an end; Watergate had exploded and Richard Nixon had resigned in disgrace; a peanut farmer from nearby Georgia was campaigning on our campus; rock 'n' roll had been replaced by disco.

We were certainly a cast of characters: Rudy T. from Quincy, Florida, the black running back who talked in the third person so quickly that sometimes the only thing we understood was "Rudy T." Bruce Harrison, "Bullet Head," the offensive guard with a lisp, who shot himself in the head with a .22 caliber bullet by accident (it remained lodged in his skull) and who ate lightbulbs. Ed Beckman, the moody tight end, nicknamed "the Edge of Night." Joe Goldsmith, affectionately known as "Goldie" because of his curly blond hair, always spewing southernisms ("Could it be any hotter for ya?"). Phil Jones, the "Horse with No Name," who once held the entire team hostage with his hunting bow and arrow because he was mad about a practical joke. Willie Jones, the incredibly gifted defensive end, who once hurdled me in a scrimmage. Bobby Jackson, "BoJack," a dead ringer for Muhammad Ali and a defensive back who later played for the New York Jets.

Randy Coffield, "Coma," the tough linebacker-end with the walrus mustache. Joe Camps, destined to become Dr. Joe Camps. Tom Rushing, "Tube," the barrel-chested offensive tackle from Blythe, California. Leon "Neon" Bright, running back, who soon became the rookie of the year in the Canadian Football League. Larry Key, the black sculpted statue-of-David running back who followed Leon as rookie of the year, and who inspired fans to shake their keys after he had taken off on yet another yardage-winning run. We were all a little crazy. Football is crazy.

This was a fairly healthy family. And after I became the Madcuban, I realized that when you're part of a large family, there are going to be members you like and those you dislike or just can't stand. But when push comes to shove you try not to hurt your own family members, and you'll defend those same members whenever they're in trouble.

After the rumors had become reality at the end of the season with the firing of Coach Mudra and his entire staff, the administration and key alumni had gone on a search for that special man who could take all the talent and resources we had and really turn our program around.

In the spring of 1976 he arrived at FSU without a lot of fanfare or media attention. After notices for a team meeting were posted at our apartment complex and at the football field house, we soon assembled to meet the new head coach in the spacious gymnasium that doubled as our cafeteria during training table meals.

Without much buildup, the athletic director introduced the forty-seven-year-old Alabama native, who came with successes at Samford and West Virginia—not exactly well-known or respected college programs. Then again, after we had won only four games in three years, we were considered by many to be one of the worst in the country.

He was a short man who stood straight, with his hands on his hips, and looked you square in the eye, but with a twinkle. Before he even spoke his first words, I had a premonition that this man was the football messiah. Mami had endowed me with her gift of sight for this moment, and the vibe I got was powerful. Something about this man made me sit up straight, wanting him to notice me. With his presence filling the room, he said, "Hi, I'm Bobby Bowden."

College football history was about to be written.

One of the first problems Coach Bowden confronted was our living situation. After the first year, when we had basically trashed Cash Hall, we had been moved to Nob Hill, a huge complex that housed students other than football players. In quick order, Bowden convinced the school administration and the Seminole Boosters that we needed our own apartment complex, so by fall we were in a housing facility behind the stadium that was just for the team. With limited distractions—including other students, parties, and, of course, girls—we were ready for him to guide us on the healing process for a team with low self-esteem and very little discipline. Coach Bowden instituted a code of conduct and guided it with a firm but caring hand.

He addressed the various racial, cultural and socioeconomic differences that caused problems for us in the past by making it clear that what mattered most to him was "the size of your heart, not the color of your skin or who your daddy is." Coach Bowden never talked in circles. Direct to the point, he said, "I don't care if you're green. If you follow the rules and give me everything you got, you'll play for me."

We had a terrific spring practice. We lost some players who either couldn't remain eligible academically or couldn't conform to the rules. Some players had lost the desire to play and just wanted to be students. Coach Bowden didn't judge them or put them down. He and his staff made every effort to guide all of us during this transition. Bowden made us listen and believe with a down-home oratorical style that borrowed freely from the Bible and from great thinkers and generals throughout history. By the end of spring practice, his confidence in us as individuals and as a team was contagious, even if we couldn't quite see it yet ourselves. We would see, he promised: "The cream always rises to the top."

Indeed, by the end of the spring I had risen to the top of the depth chart for the offensive line. I was the starting right guard for the upcoming season, slated to be my last at Florida State and Bobby Bowden's first. After three years in which I'd tried to pack on the weight, Coach Bowden sent me home for the summer with the request that I return at 235 pounds, fifteen pounds lighter than the previous season.

Instilling me with my higher calling, he explained, "I need you quick and lean to lead our backs on the sweeps."

Ensconced again at the Echevarrias' for the summer, I began my rigorous training program immediately. Sometimes Lillian and Bebo worried that I was pushing myself too hard, especially when I trained in summer heat with my heavy helmet and shoulder pads on. One afternoon, after a grueling run, I walked into the air-conditioned house and fainted. Bebo was home and didn't know what to do; he ran to Lillian's vanity and grabbed a bottle of her expensive perfume. Apparently trying to use it like an ammonia capsule, when he placed it under my nostrils his finger slipped on the bottle top and half its contents went up my nose. The scent lingered in my nose for over a week.

In addition to training, I obtained a summer job at Flamingo Park in Miami Beach as a recreation leader. The kids in my charge were a mix of Jews, African-Americans, Indians, Jamaicans, and Cubans. They were all good kids in my opinion but there were a handful of young boys who challenged me daily with their surly attitudes and disrespect of others. The hardest part was that I saw a young me in each of them. My ace up the sleeve, fortunately, was being a major college football player; that was something that they respected. And when I had their attention, I told them the story about my violent upbringing and about the good people who influenced and ultimately saved my life. They asked tough questions. You got into trouble? How bad? When did you stop getting into trouble?

There were three boys in particular who shadowed me all day, desperately looking for guidance and protection, yet also giving it back to me. Rather than leave my side during lunch, they stuck around while I trained for the upcoming season, cheering for me and even manning the stopwatch while I ran wind sprints and various football drills. When I returned each morning, they made sure to ask if I had done my evening run and lifted weights at home. I was bench-pressing over four hundred pounds, becoming one of the strongest players on the team. My three young friends promoted this fact to the other kids with personal pride.

On the last day of my summer job, the kids at the park gave me a little going-away party. Saying good-bye to all of them was emotional, especially my three guys. "Stay out of trouble," I reminded them. "Go to school!"

After everyone left, I walked out to the field, laced up my cleats, and began my strenuous sprint workout. I had run a few sprints when I felt a short, sharp pull in my groin. I stretched it out and tried to run another sprint. The pain in my crotch exploded. Driving my motorcycle the twenty miles back to the Echevarrias' was a struggle, especially shifting gears. Mom called the family doctor and got me an immediate appointment.

The doctor was a young, handsome Cuban. He spoke perfectly fine English but insisted on speaking Spanish. I described to him what had happened and the area of discomfort.

"Vamo pesarte." Let's weigh you.

I got on the scale wearing only shorts; it balanced out at 235 pounds. I was right on my playing weight!

"You probably have a hernia," he said in Spanish. "And no wonder, because you're obese."

"Obese?" I looked over to Mom, whose face was contorted in confusion.

The doctor reached into my shorts, just inches from my testicles, and pushed in. I jumped back in pain.

"It's a hernia, all right. Let's schedule surgery for next week."

"I start football practice in two weeks. How soon will I heal?"

"You're done playing football. At least this year." The doctor made this statement in a cold, callous manner.

Beads of sweat burst forth on my forehead; the room began to spin. Stunned, I reached for the examining table and slumped back on it. When Mom walked me back to the car, my reaction kicked in. I cried like a little boy all the way home. The minute we walked in the door, I ran to our room and threw myself on the bed that I didn't fit on and covered my head with a pillow.

After a while, Mom came in. "Vic," she said gently, "maybe you should call Tallahassee."

Dreading the call, I went ahead and made it, knowing there was no other choice. My call to the football field house was put through to Don "Doc" Fauls, our earthy, much-loved head trainer. Sadly, I began my tale of woe, about the pain and the diagnosis and my upcoming surgery. Before I could get to the horrific news that I was out of football for the year, he interrupted me in midsentence. "Get your ass on a plane and get up here!"

Cut to: Tallahassee, the next day, in the office of the team doctor. Tall and amiable, Dr. Henderson strolls into the examining room as I once again recount my tragic saga of a football career cut short.

"Drop your shorts," Dr. Henderson says immediately. I do so and look down at my privates. The golf-ball-sized bulge protrudes menacingly from the right side of my crotch.

"Oh, yeah," Dr. Henderson says, eyebrows raised, pushing on the area with two fingers. "Spread your legs." As I open my stance, he reaches under my testicles, touching along the inside of my upper thighs. "Here, feel this." He reaches up and grabs my hand, placing it on the growth. "Okay, now, feel this . . . and this . . . and this." He guides my hand all around my groin. There are several bumps around and under my testicles.

Dr. Henderson: "Vic, you don't have a hernia. Your lymph glands are really infected and that's why you're in such pain. I'm going to give you some antibiotics to take for a week and you'll be fine."

Me: "I don't need surgery?"

Dr. Henderson: "No. Get out of here! I'll see you in a couple weeks for the team physical."

Me (with a range of expressions from shocked to relieved to overjoyed): "Oh, my God! Thank you, thank you!"

Had my shorts not still been down at my ankles, I would have hugged him. Instead, I pulled them up as I backed out, spewing my thanks to Dr. Henderson all the way out the door and into the humid Tallahassee afternoon, where I praised God and all the saints and angels and deities I could name. Hallelujah!

In celebration, after a few or more beers with my good friend Tom Rushing, aka the Tube, we arrived at the idea that we needed to do something symbolic to commemorate my survival of yet one more roadblock and to show our dedication to the Seminoles and the season ahead. As a formidable and sometimes inseparable duo, we were affectionately known as the Tube and the Cube (the shortened version of the "Madcuban").

So what was the symbolic act that we chose to undertake? We shaved our heads. But not completely. Any punks could shave their heads. We wanted to do something that reflected the transformation of the team and went along with the new look our game uniforms would have. This was the year that our helmets were going to be emblazoned with spears, or what were known by Native Americans as coupsticks. For some Native American tribes, the coupstick was a way to announce to your enemy the number of men you had defeated, each feather representing a kill. So instead of shaving our heads completely, we left one pointed spear down the middle of our heads that pointed forward at the top of our scalps. With our milky white shaved heads, tan faces, and dark spears, we were very intimidating. And we were uh-uh-ugggly.

Imagine the heads we turned that night when the two of us strode into Stonehenge, a hopping two-story nightclub in the shadow of the state capitol, in the heart of downtown. One of those heads was a green-eyed goddess named Christy Jernigan, although what I thought she said was "Jergens" when she told it to me over the roar of the crowd. She had given me her father's first name and said that they were in the phone book. "Like the lotion?" I asked, yelling to make sure I got it right. She didn't hear me but nodded yes. For the next two weeks I went on a frantic chase and talked about the elusive beauty to all my teammates so much that they named her Christy Love. Miraculously our paths crossed yet again and she became my girlfriend a short while later, then a great love, and by the end of the year, the woman I planned to marry.

The first reaction of our teammates to our new look was horror. They called us aliens. But then by the end of the night, one of the players joined us by shaving his head and leaving a spear down the middle. By the next day there were five of us, by the end of the week twenty. By the time the season got under way there were more than sixty of us.

Coach Bowden didn't have a problem with our statement of commitment, or at least never said so. Nor did he say anything about having caught wind of the stunt we pulled on the incoming freshman players.

First, as upperclassmen, we required the freshmen to shave their heads, whether they wanted to or not. They were absolutely intimidated by us. A couple of the freshmen offensive linemen actually called me "sir." Traditionally, seniors were expected to be treated with respect and accorded certain privileges—like showering first after practice—and in our new, well-disciplined sense of protocol, this was even more the case.

At the end of the first week of practice, there were about fifteen of us seniors in the shower when we heard the trotting and tapping of cleats on the locker room floor that sounded the return of the underclassmen from practice.

When a large throng of them passed by the open entrance to the showers, they froze en masse, and GASSSPPPED. With the fronts of our bodies facing forward, we paid no attention to them, yakking away with one another, lathering up with soap. They wore terrified, confused, and embarrassed faces as they all stared at our privates. We had pulled the old vagina trick by tucking our genitals down behind us and closing our legs over them. None of them said a word but by their expressions it looked like they were thinking, Oh shit, first we shave our heads and then we become eunuchs! Every single one of them backed out and left the shower area. We laughed ourselves into a stupor.

Coach Bowden's leadership and his coaching staff—enthusiastic, knowledgeable, and fair—brought us an unprecedented level of confidence. There was a buzz out there. When training camp came to a close with the annual picture day, for the first time it was well attended by both the media and the fans. Our shaved-and-spear-headed hairdos dominated the coverage.

We lost our hard-fought first game in Tennessee against Memphis, but by only two points. Coach Bowden not only reviewed what didn't work; he focused as well on what did work, accentuating the positive. As a new policy instituted in the Bowden era, tomahawk decals were awarded to players for plays that made a difference in a game—a big hit, great block, touchdown pass, or run—that were then worn permanently on our helmets. For the first game, Coach Bowden selected me as offensive player of the game, along with our tight end, Ed Beckman, an incredible honor for me or any offensive lineman. Three tomahawk decals were given to me to place on my helmet. The next game, I was honored again by being named a team captain.

Coach Bowden always had time to talk to you, even if you were a scout team member. I don't remember talking to him about my childhood, but somehow he knew to throw his arm around me and reenforce my positive contributions on and off the field. When I stepped out of line, he would pull me aside, express his disappointment, and then pat me on the back and say, "I'm counting on you, Vic," or "Go get 'em, Vic. Be a leader." Bobby Bowden was a father of five and yet he always had time for one of "his boys."

For the first time in my life, I started to understand how to tap my madness in appropriate ways, with boundaries, often using it to psych me up before hitting the field. Athletes have many unusual pregame rituals. Mine was to get fully dressed and stuff myself inside my locker, using the claustrophobia of the small space to further increase my madness, as I thought about the opposing team and my assignments for the day. Opposing players admitted that there was no more frightening sight than the charging face and form of the Madcuban coming down the field in their direction.

Though it was regrettable that I didn't get to study theatre, getting to play football was sometimes like performing in a great Shakespearian drama, or an action-adventure movie, or a suspenseful thriller, or a burlesque comedy, or a *Peyton Place* soap opera. On the field with every move of the ball were games within games, ploys within ploys. The stars, of course, were the quarterbacks and the guys who scored. There was much less glory for the linemen, who took the toughest beating on the field and without whom the stars couldn't do their jobs. Still, there was also a freedom and nobility, as far as I was concerned, in being a journeyman player, a craftsman in the art and science of football as Coach Bowden approached it. I couldn't have been prouder or happier to have arrived at where I was.

But there were days, as there will always be days, when everything that could go wrong went wrong. The game in Miami against the Hurricanes, another major rival, was one such debacle. The Seminoles were the better team but the harder we tried, the worse it got. We were debased and demolished, losing with a final score of 47–0. Beforehand I had been so thrilled knowing that my two families were there, including Mami, Eddie, Barbie, Carmen, Bebo, Lillian, Ernie, and Rocky. After the game, I crawled back in my locker and brooded, the sound of my father's derisive laughter taunting me.

But as soon as I exited the locker room, I realized that their excitement and approval had nothing to do with whether we won or not. They gathered around me, applauding, smiling, and looking thrilled to know me, their big football star coming out of the locker room doors at the Orange Bowl. Once I was back on the team bus, all

I could think about when I looked out the window at my two families, standing side by side, was how lucky I was.

When we traveled to Norman, Oklahoma, to play the University of Oklahoma Sooners, the reigning national champions, coached by Barry Switzer, I witnessed a brilliant strategic move on the part of Coach Bowden as the team stood in the visitors' tunnel. Instead of letting us take the field before the home team—as is traditional—Coach Bowden restrained us. I was near the front of the line and everyone behind me was pushing forward, wanting to charge the field. By now, the Sooners were gathered in their tunnel on the other side of the field. Coach Switzer was motioning for us to go.

Coach Bowden turned to us and shouted, "Look out there, fellas. There's over seventy thousand Oklahoma fans out there. A sea of red. Let's pretend they're our fans. Hold on."

We stood like wooden soldiers looking across at the confused Sooners in the other tunnel, watching Coach Switzer's frustration level rise. It was a standoff. Coach Switzer gave in first and with a fist pump implored his team to take the field. Their charge was led by the Sooner Schooner, a covered wagon pulled by two horses. The stadium erupted with a deafening roar. Now Coach Bowden raised his hand and moved it forward. We charged the field with Oklahoma, their fans seemingly welcoming us with a thunderous ovation. The teams crossed each other at midfield, elbows flying, shoulders lowered. It was an incredibly ballsy thing for Coach Bowden to do, but it worked. We were so fired up that we stayed with Oklahoma for three quarters, until their team speed took over and won the game. But the lesson for me about making an entrance was worth the price of admission: Never be afraid to steal thunder.

We traveled to Boston College to play the fifteenth-ranked Eagles as forty-point underdogs. We were insulted and outraged that the media thought anyone was forty points better than we were. They were a physically huge team, but we beat them up and down the field. By the last quarter, their coaches were putting in their second- and third-string players, because their starters had failed to stop us. This game had been designated a sod game, which meant that if, on the longest of long shots, we won, we got to cut out a piece of their field and bring it home. Back in Tallahassee there was a small graveyard in a corner of our practice field, complete with brass grave markers with game scores on them, and buried below the field surface lay the sod of our defeated opponents. We had a formal burial ceremony for Boston College.

My last away game as a Seminole was to play North Texas in Denton. We arrived in mid-November on a beautiful fall day, practiced, and went to sleep. The next morning, I woke up and pulled back the curtains in our hotel room and was shocked to see that the ground was covered in a foot or more of snow. Several players were already outside playing in it. For many of our southern Floridians, this was the first time they had witnessed snow firsthand. When I stepped outside in my sweat gear, it was freezing. "Could it be any colder for ya?" No! This freak blizzard was not anticipated by anyone, and our team had traveled with the wrong equipment. We had mesh jerseys and cutoff T-shirts for the game.

Our equipment manager, Frank Debord, ran out to several stores in search of warm clothes. He came back with a handful of jackets, some long underwear, a bunch of white gardening gloves, a huge box of panty hose, and several rolls of cellophane.

During pregame warm-ups, I had refused the items that Coach Debord offered me. I returned to the locker room before the game, begging him for anything he had. The only thing left was the panty hose and cellophane. I swallowed my pride and slipped on the panty hose. The cellophane was used to wrap our feet, to try and keep the moisture out.

The snow fell throughout the game, making the goal posts the only discernible markers on the field. We had to dig out the goal line to see when either team scored. There was a constant playful snowball fight on the sidelines going on with the few fans who showed up for the game.

We won the game 21–20 with a late fourth-quarter touchdown

pass that covered ninety-five yards, from Jimmy Black to Kurt Unglaub. I saw the pass travel high over my head while I was pass protecting. You could barely detect the ball with the heavy snowfall. I looked upfield and watched as the two defenders who were covering Kurt both slipped and fell. There was no one within thirty yards of him as he dashed gingerly to the end zone, trying not to slip. The players from our team trailing him were yelling, "Don't fall!"

He scored, and in our jubilation, we leaped onto our stomachs and slid the remaining ten yards into the end zone, some of us crashing into the six-inch cement barrier surrounding the field that was buried in the snow. Henceforth, the game was affectionately called the Snow Bowl. It was undoubtedly the most fun, before or after, that I ever had playing any sport. Coach Bowden later recalled it as one of his favorite games in his long and storied career.

At the end of the season we had won five out of eleven games, more wins than during the three previous seasons combined. In our hearts and minds we had become winners. The team had turned a corner. Florida State was soon to become a football dynasty and Bobby Bowden the winningest coach in Division 1-A history.

We seniors who played on Bowden's first team at FSU carried a lot of pride away with us because we had gotten the ball rolling, not to overuse the metaphor. His influence on me, even after only one season, remained profound in the years to come. Much later on, I was honored when he named me to his All-Miami team. No matter how much time was to go by, his door was always open to me or any of his players, whenever we needed his advice or guidance. In fact, in August of 1977, not long after graduation, I called to ask for a favor and he said yes before I even told him what it was.

Though I was still mourning the death of Elvis Presley that week, and still in shock over the fact that I was never going to play football again—I had cried like a jilted lover when I said good-bye to the Tube and some of my other teammates—I was glad to tell Coach Bowden that I was in high spirits about my life and where I was headed. Christy and I were talking about marriage plans already. She and our relationship had taught me much about fidelity and sensitivity. As Christy's dad was a high-ranking air force officer, through his advice and her support I had decided to pursue a spot in the air force's Officer Training School. Christy's father believed I would be able to gain valuable experience that would serve me later in my quest to work for the FBI. He was convinced I would make a great officer and eventually branch into intelligence.

That was the reason for my call to Coach Bowden. I had strong letters of recommendation from Christy's father (a retired lieutenant colonel), from a full bird colonel, from a general, and from Congressman Don Fuqua. But none of them knew me, I suspected, as well as Coach Bobby Bowden. He was happy to do it, he said, and soon sent the following:

> Victor M. Rivas was a starting guard on the 1976 Florida State University football team. I feel he would be excellent officer material for our armed services.
>
> Vic's physical ability is unquestionable—big, strong, and alert. He is a fighter and will take you on anyway you want it. He has adapted to life as well as any young man I have coached. He has had a very tough life, having to be on his own since early childhood. Football and education have saved him from the pitfalls that besiege most youngsters with his background. He fights to be the best in whatever he does.
>
> Again, I feel he would be excellent officer material and I would not hesitate to fight alongside him.

The last months of 1977 flew quickly. My mistake was that I assumed that my acceptance into OTS was a given and that I would be at Lackland Air Force Base, in Texas, within a month or two. There were several tests, both written and oral, and even a pilot aptitude test. After that, there was a series of interviews. Sometimes I could hear Dad's voice telling me that I was being stupid, that I had put all my eggs in one basket. What if I wasn't tough enough or good enough?

Those feelings surged through me when I actually saw Dad in person for the first time in five years. The occasion was a wake for my grandfather Abuelo Chucho. As I told Christy, "I should go pay my respects to my grandfather. And to Dad."

She knew this could be a minefield but encouraged me to go.

In Miami, as usual, I stayed with the Echevarrias and spent time getting caught up with many family members. Rocky, soon to be known as Steven Bauer, had majored in theatre at the University of Miami and was on his way to becoming a huge star in Miami with the success of *Qué Pasa, USA?*, a PBS bilingual situation comedy that would help send him to Hollywood. Getting to see him star as Lenny in *Of Mice and Men* at the University of Miami, along with his classmate Ray Liotta as George, was an unforgettable experience. Both their performances blew the roof off. I was so proud of my brother, seeing how gifted he was and how he disappeared onstage, becoming a totally different character. Offstage, Rocky had grown into his handsome good looks and had big-time sex appeal. Ray, a friend of Rocky's as well as a fellow thespian, had other qualities that were mesmerizing on- and offstage. He had a well of emotion and intensity that seemed to lie just below the surface, something I could relate to, that made him bristle with energy and presence. Certainly they made me think twice about the path that I had chosen.

My brother Ernesto was college-bound and had chosen to go to FSU. Ernie was an avid sports and news aficionado, like Bebo, and had closely followed my journey as a Seminole. On the Rivas side of the family, my younger brother Ed was also headed to FSU. Now six two and over two hundred pounds, as a senior at Hialeah High School, Ed wrestled and played baseball and football (he was an offensive guard like his older brothers). He had paid tribute to me by choosing to wear the number 70, the number I wore as a Seminole. We never talked about what the years had been like after I left the

household, followed next by Tony. From a few conversations, however, I was aware that Dad had continued to terrorize Eddie and
Barbie, though to what extent I didn't yet know. At age fourteen, Ed
had left after his own confrontation with Dad. Besides the hurts and
humiliations, and his slave labor in the Rivas & Sons painting business, which required Ed to do all the work and Dad to take all the
money, my younger brother left home when he learned the truth
about our brother Robert. Even when Ed confronted Dad about the
lies he had told, our father denied them and made up new stories
about the cause of Robert's brain damage and about abandoning him.

Ed moved in with Mami and the man she had married sometime
earlier. Antonio Maestegui was a short, dapper *cubano* with a pencil-
thin mustache. He had challenging mood swings but treated my
mom only with great respect and adopted my sister Carmen, giving
her his last name. My littlest sister, now age seven, was pretty, smart,
funny, and tough. She had been spared growing up in the home of El
Caballero but had dealt with other stresses, not the least of which was
her outsider status. Perhaps because Mami wanted her not to grow up
in the shadow of her ex-husband, she had decided not to tell Carmen
who her real father was. It was implied she was a Maestegui daughter,
while we, in her understanding, were her half siblings.

While I was able to see Barbie during a few visits, because she was
still living with Dad and Mecca in North Miami, our contact was
limited. At eleven, she was gorgeous and sweet, but if I had looked
closer into her eyes, I might have better seen the hurt and fear in
them. Even so, she seemed also to have created her own survival
mechanisms. We all had them. Somehow we had all made an unspoken pact not to be sick and crazy, despite what was done to us. We all
had more of La Luchadora in us than El Ciclón.

Tony had to bear maybe the most complicated burden, of having
been the First Son, the golden one, expected not only to live up to the
impossible standards of perfection Dad demanded of him, but also to
be so good as to redeem our father's tainted soul. That would make
anyone crazy. But in his quiet, nonconfrontational manner, my big

brother refused to have that trip put on him. He made his own choices, carving out a path to create a loving home built on faith and laughter, after he had married the love of his life, a nurturing *cubana* beauty named Nieves for her snowy white complexion. Together they were now living in Houston, Texas, where Tony, an architectural engineer, was the project manager in charge of building several major office buildings in the city. That's what happens when you're a kid who reads instructions for Lincoln Logs.

My grandfather's wake, at what was ironically named the Caballero Funeral Home, in Little Havana, was a strange reincarnation of the atmosphere at El Club Cubano in Chicago, a loud, festive gathering of family and friends, with my grandfather visible through the cigar smoke, lying in an open casket. Here lay my father's father, a man I hardly knew and had rarely seen in the years gone past. A fallen Cuban exile, Victoriano Rivas had once been a proud, tall man, a provincial magistrate, a prominent rancher and landowner in Sancti Spíritus. Lying in his casket, he looked so little. His long mane of silver hair was now short and sparse. Unlike Mami's parents, who never got out of Cuba, my father's parents had escaped Castro's regime and made it out with nothing left of their former wealth. En route to Miami, they were waylaid in Mexico City. There, in 1969, days before their U.S. visas had come through, my elegant Abuela Maria died, leaving Abuelo Chucho brokenhearted for the rest of his days.

This was the only time since the *Spirituanos* party at the park seven years earlier that I had seen my relatives on the Rivas side of the family. A few things had changed as I went around the room and saw many gawking at me. At 250 pounds—thirty pounds of which I had to take off for my air force OTS program— with a twenty-inch neck and thirty-two-inch thighs, I was the biggest man in the room, towering over most of the crowd.

Many of my aunts and cousins used the same line they had used before, cooing, "Oh Vicky, you're so big!" but now I only grinned. My response to "Vicky, *dame un besito*" as they leaned in for a kiss on the cheek was different too, and I was happy to oblige.

Then I looked around and spotted Dad, the charmer, holding court with a group of men I didn't know. He looked up and saw me with my entourage of admirers and turned back to his group, bragging big and loud as he nodded over in my direction, *"Tu ves ese animal? Es mi otro hijo."* You see that animal? That's my other son.

Reactions of "oohs" and "ays" followed as he added even more proudly, "He's a big college football star."

The acknowledgment, though not spoken to me directly, lit up my heart like a comet in the dark. After all his pronouncements that I would never amount to anything, he was over there boasting about my accomplishments. In my mind, the script for a reconciliatory dialogue between us unrolled like a regal banner. The past would be the past. We would start again. Despite my rottweiler appearance, I was a puppy all over again, happy to please my old master, ready to wag my tail and bow my head for a loving scratch around my neck.

"Hey, Vic," my brother Ed said in a voice low in pitch and volume, as he walked over from the side of the room where Dad was standing. I greeted him with a smile, noticing the same sad brown eyes Tony and Mami had as he exhaled before saying, "Dad asked me to come over and tell you that he said to stay away from him."

It felt like I had been slugged in the stomach. "Go tell him to fuck off!" Ed blinked hard with my statement. "Go tell him!" The messenger had been shot.

That was the only contact I had with my siblings that night. My eyes followed Ed's labored walk across to Dad. He leaned in and whispered. Dad turned and glared at a distance. But those yellow reptilian eyes with their sparse lashes had no power over me. I glared right back with the green-eyed gaze of the Madcuban. My father looked away.

Out of respect for my grandfather, I left immediately and didn't attend his funeral. I never saw my father again.

* * *

The phone call from George Young, director of player personnel for the Miami Dolphins, came in around late March of 1978. It was so out of the blue that I caught it like an errant pass, thinking there had to be a mistake.

The call I had been waiting for, of course, was from the air force. The long, drawn-out process had been more trying than I'd anticipated. To meet officers' standards, I was dieting and working out rigorously, trying to whittle myself down to 220 pounds. My test scores had come back, and while I scored very highly on the pilot's tests—thanks to exposure to flying from Bebo and some lessons I'd taken on a small aircraft he co-owned—it looked like my other scores were only average. My interviews, on the other hand, were pretty good. Apparently the jury was still out and all I could do was wait.

That was my state of mind when George Young called. After I made sure that he had the right Vic Rivas, I listened and tried not to HY-PER-VEN-TI-LATE as he asked if I was interested in attending a three-day minicamp tryout for the team. "This would be strictly a look-see situation," he emphasized, "and it doesn't guarantee you'll be invited back to training camp in the summer."

Without deliberating, I said yes to the minicamp and agreed to come down in five weeks. That was exactly how long I had to try to put back on the weight I'd lost and to psych myself back into my Madcuban mentality. When I stepped on the scales I was shocked to see a scrawny 215 pounds. To even think I could walk into a tryout at that weight was a joke.

Christy didn't understand why on earth I was putting myself through the five-week torture and even taking the trip down to Miami. Wasn't I done with football? Didn't I want to get on with life? What about the air force? What about our wedding plans?

"But this is a chance of a lifetime!" was all I could say to her. And just because I was going to show up and give it my best shot for three days in May didn't change my ambition to be an officer and didn't change my desire to be her husband.

It *was* the chance of a lifetime. Christy's mixed feelings didn't deter me from managing to bulk up to 238 pounds, still puny by any stretch for an NFL lineman, by the time I arrived at the tryouts. The minicamp was held at Biscayne College in North Miami, a small, unglamorous, and smack-in-the-middle-of-nothing-special campus.

Rated second best in strength among the hopefuls at the tryouts, I compensated for my size with my conditioning and my passion. What I lacked in terms of blazing speed, I made up for with agility and quickness. "He moved pretty well," was the report of offensive line coach John Sandusky, quoted by local newspapers. "He had good foot movement . . . and he showed pretty good determination in the twelve-minute run. He was a shade light at 238, but he said he could put the weight on."

At the end of the three-day camp, I was summoned to George Young's office. I was offered a free agent contract to return in July for training camp. This meant that I would train all summer as a Miami Dolphin and play in preseason games. Depending on how I did, I would either earn a place on the team in the fall or not be invited to continue on. This was beyond even my wildest dreams, which were typically pretty wild! At the same time, I tried to bear in mind that it was still a major crapshoot. My size was my worst liability.

Though I reminded Christy that I could very well return in the fall with all of our plans back on track, she was not happy. This was my dream, not hers. When the press started calling, she was more upset. For my part, I was rather bewildered by all the attention. As an offensive lineman, a position that goes virtually unnoticed by the public and the media, I was unaccustomed to it. Many times at FSU I read stories in the paper that named, for example, "running back Larry Key," who had scored a three-yard dive over "the right guard," and I had to shout at the paper, "The right guard's name is Vic Rivas! Can't you print that?"

But now, suddenly, the fact that this was the first time in the thirteen-year history of the Miami Dolphins franchise that a Cuban would be in training camp was noteworthy in Miami, with over a half million Cubans living in South Florida. Even though I had been dubbed the Longest of Long Shots by the English-language press, the articles and broadcast stories in Spanish-language media just called me one of their own.

These were heady, heady days. Fellow Seminole Mike Shuman, a superlative wide receiver who battled back from an injury and other obstacles, was also headed to training camp and we flew down from Tallahassee together. We were surprised to be joined on the flight by Earl Morrall, former quarterback for the Baltimore Colts and Miami Dolphins. Now working with the Dolphins organization, he made us feel like royalty as the three of us sat together chatting and he signed autographs for many of the passengers on board. None of us missed the trophy he was wearing, the Super Bowl ring from the 1972–1973 "perfect season," when the Dolphins became the only team in NFL history to go undefeated for an entire season. That had been during my senior year in high school, when I was living with the Echevarrias and we all followed every game fanatically. In the fifth game of the season, future Hall of Fame quarterback Bob Griese broke his ankle, and the then thirty-eight-year-old Earl Morrall steered the offense the rest of the season and into the AFC championship, when Griese took over again.

Back at the campus of Biscayne College for training camp, I barely had a chance to say hello to the other rookies who reported at the same time, as did newly acquired veterans from other teams and players who were on the bubble from the previous season. We hit the ground running, literally, doing Shula's famed twelve-minute run in the oppressive summer swelter of south Florida. I improved upon my distance from the minicamp, finishing among the leaders of all the linemen. All of my strength tests took big leaps, including bench-pressing 405 pounds. And I had reported at a lean and quick 245 pounds.

Meetings began each day at 7:30 A.M., followed by the morning practice, which focused on the running game, offense and defense. The afternoon practice was devoted to the passing game. The rest of the day was devoted to studying my playbook and receiving treatment for any injuries that were sustained. The evening concluded with meetings from 7 to 9 P.M., more individual study, and finally lights out. A monastery for footballology.

During the first week I held my own, but that all changed with the arrival of the veteran players, who showed up in a fleet of customized BMWs and Mercedes while we were practicing. Football was a game for big boys that, when played well, brought big toys. I didn't know whose car to envy most. Welcome to the NFL!

During our first practice with the vets, I got an eye-opening sense of demographics. There were behemoths whose sheer size would intimidate the average person. There were several defensive backs who were the size of linebackers; and linebackers the size of defensive linemen. But it was the speed and quickness that clearly defined the difference between the college game and professional football.

Coach Shula now became a more visible presence at practice, moving from one drill to the other. My focus was on excelling in general but also finding that right moment to impress him. It came at the end of a morning practice during a scrimmage with the defense. It was my unit's turn to run a play. Quarterback Don Strock called a sweep, my favorite type of running play. In college, I used my quickness to lead the running backs out on a sweep and then blast most safeties or cornerbacks into the sideline, stand over their prone bodies, smile, and then return to the huddle.

As we broke the huddle, I glanced over my shoulder to see where Shula was standing. Perfect! He was right behind the offensive unit. I exploded out of my stance, pivoting my body to the right, taking short, choppy steps, looking for my target. There he was, number 41, Norris Thomas, right where I needed him. I closed the distance quickly with the running back on my right hip. Thomas squatted down for the impact as I exploded into him. He was five eleven and 190 pounds, and I didn't move him. It was a stalemate. Welcome to the NFL!

Training camp opened with eighty-five players trying to make a squad of forty-five. The competition was fierce. It was abundantly clear from day one that after any practice, if the Turk tapped you on the shoulder, you were gone. A great guy but with the onus of being the Grim Reaper to hopefuls, assistant coach Carl Taseff was the Turk. The sight of him lurking about the locker room after practice was a sure bet that a player was about to be to cut; sometimes several. If a player went down to injury in your position, it meant one less player to worry about. The Dolphins kept eight offensive linemen on the roster. They had their five starters: Wayne Moore, Bob Kuechenberg, Jim Langer, Larry Little, and Mike Current, with Ed Newman as an alternate. Six of us were competing for those other two spots. Every play, every drill, every sprint after practice could determine your survival and extend your stay another day.

The competition made it difficult to establish friendships in your position, but I did make friends with players in other positions. There was Witt Beckman, a wide receiver from the University of Miami and brother of our tight end, Ed, at Florida State; Bruce Hardy, a tight end from Arizona State; and, of course, Mike Shuman from FSU. My closest friend and kindred spirit was fellow rookie Doug Betters, a six-foot-seven defensive end from the University of Nevada, Reno.

Doug reached out to me during the first week of practice because he needed my services as an interpreter. "It's the maids," he explained. Apparently, the maids always started their rounds with his dorm room first thing in the morning. Now, after he shouted, "Get out!" at them a few mornings, they were refusing to come back in, not even to give him clean towels or sheets.

Since I had been getting so much coverage in the Hispanic press, with much of the Spanish-speaking community following my daily fate at training camp, the housekeepers were very happy with the autographs I gave them to give to their kids. Needless to say, my room was spotless, with lots of extra towels and soap, sometimes even Cuban food. After I talked to them about Doug Betters's room, they compromised by dropping off towels and sheets while he was at practice.

A pivotal event took place during an afternoon pass protection drill against the defense. Vern Den Herder, the six-foot-six defensive end and charter member of the No-Name Defense, was head up on me. As I dropped back to pass protect, he grabbed me by the front of my jersey, picked me up, threw me on my back, and then left his cleat marks on my chest as he made his way to the quarterback. He tossed me aside as if I didn't exist! I popped up quickly and tried to get back and protect the quarterback, but it was too late. To add to my humiliation, Shula was watching. As Den Herder walked back to his huddle he gave me an added whack to the back of the helmet. I exploded in rage and started swinging wildly at him. The fight was immediately broken up.

Fuming, I wasn't going to take shit from anybody. This caught the attention of some of the veteran offensive linemen.

"Hey, Cuban Kid. Come here." All-Pro offensive guard Bob Kuechenberg, a big personality with blond and gray speckled hair and a beard, beckoned me to his side. Six foot two and 250 pounds, he was the prototype of the Dolphin offensive guards and centers of this era. Standing next to him were future Hall of Fame members: Jim Langer, our mustached center, with his thick limbs and huge hands, and on the other side, guard Larry Little, as wide as he was tall, with dark ebony skin. Good guys.

"Cuban Kid," said Kuechenberg, repeating my new nickname, "that's gonna happen to guys our size. Here's what you need to do when you feel you're going on your back. Reach out and grab their jersey. Pull it in tight." He explained, however, that if my arms were extended, I'd get caught for holding. "So don't let go, and take him with you to the ground. Now, he'll beat the shit out of you on the way down, but he won't get to the quarterback."

"Thanks," I said, still glowering, wondering when I could try that one out. Nonetheless, as the Cuban Kid, I'd gotten the attention of the veterans, and that was a start.

Later that day, I got even more attention. I was at the training table that was set up in the school cafeteria and Kuechenberg shouted, "Hey, Cuban Kid! Let's hear it!"

This was one of the training camp rituals, which took place at almost every meal. The way it worked was that a veteran could call on any rookie and put him on the spot. The rookie was required to stand on a chair and sing his college fight song. If you refused, you were immediately grabbed by the nearest players, taken outside, and thrown into a slimy, stinky, moss-filled pond. (Only one player that I saw refused to sing.) You had to sing in a clear, loud voice or they'd make you start again.

Climbing up to stand on my chair, I suddenly panicked. I had no idea what the words to the FSU fight song were.

A chorus of veterans yelled: "Let's go. Come on. You got three seconds!" Now I was to be the second rookie to be dunked in the slimy pond.

By divine intervention, I opened my mouth and sang. And what came out was a country-western tune by the Outlaws. By the time I choked out the first line, singing "put another log on the fire," the laughter began. Then the rhythmic clapping started. More laughter soared. Encouraged, I added a country twang.

Several offensive linemen were soon on their feet clapping, and Kuechenberg was doing a bad variation of a clog dance.

Applause, applause, applause! Then—by the time I finished—a standing ovation.

How cruel an irony it was that I had chosen to sing that of all songs, given the fact that a Dear John letter was waiting for me in my room. Christy Jernigan, the woman that my teammates at FSU had called Christy Love because I had hunted for her high and low after meeting her in the bar and thinking her name was Jergens, like the lotion, was leaving me because of "stupid football," when she had wanted to marry "an officer and a gentleman." This she wrote before the movie had ever come out.

Devastated, I cried for the next two hours until I had to go to a meeting. Coach Sandusky took one look at me and asked, "Are you all right? You don't look so hot."

I lied. "I ate something that didn't agree with me."

Doug Betters tried to calm me down and talk me out of quitting stupid football. Even if I didn't feel like training, he reminded me that just going through the motions would be an opening for the tap from the Turk; worse, it could lead to serious injury. With the first preseason game coming up at the end of the week, I had only four more weeks of camp, if I didn't get released first. Although my heart was broken, I thought about the little Cuban boys waiting by the fence after each practice who wanted my autograph or some soggy, soiled piece of my equipment as a souvenir. I rededicated myself to living out my dream and maybe their dreams, too.

My first preseason game was in Canton, Ohio, at the Pro Football Hall of Fame. The Dolphins were playing the Philadelphia Eagles in the nationally televised Hall of Fame game. ABC Sports, along with Howard Cosell, Don Meredith, and Frank Gifford, was covering the game and the inductions of five new members to the Hall: Lance Alworth, Weeb Ewbank, Tuffy Leemans, Larry Wilson, and one of my all-time favorite players, Ray Nitschke of the Green Bay Packers.

There was a mythic moment in Canton when I went to look for my locker and found it by spotting my pristine Dolphins game jersey hanging there, and just above the number 93 was my name, RIVAS, in bold lettering. After many weeks of wearing sweaty practice jerseys, this was the first time I would don the uniform. My fantasy, spun from years and years of wild imaginings, had become real. This was a religious experience. Like a priest preparing for mass, I carefully and meticulously put each part of my uniform on.

Then came the *nerves*. I sat by my locker shaking like a leaf, something I'd never done before playing a game. Langer and Kuechenberg sat down on either side of me.

"You nervous, Cuban Kid?" asked Kooch, as we called him.

"Yeah!" The word exploded a little too loud from my throat.

Langer put his hand on my shoulder. "We all get nervous, kid. If I didn't get a little nervous before a game, I'd be concerned." He took out a pack of Marlboros. "You wanna smoke?"

I took a cigarette, a foreign concept, and lit it, choking on the first puff. Kooch and Langer shook their heads, patted me on the back, and went back to their lockers.

To continue the weeding-out process, the coaches played the rookies a great deal in this game. With the very first snap that I was in the game for, my first ever as a Dolphin, backup quarterback Don Strock called a pass play. As I sank into my stance, I looked up and saw the snarling bearded face of the Eagles' perennial All-Pro linebacker, Bill Bergey. The ball was snapped and I took my first step back to pass protect. Bergey was coming hard on a blitz. He drove into me and I could feel my legs buckling; I was going on my back! Kooch's advice rang in my ears. I reached out, grabbed a handful of number 66, and yanked it hard to my body as I fell backward. Bergey was cussing up a storm and punching me in the helmet, but he didn't sack Strock. Welcome to the NFL!

Later in the game, just as I was getting my groove on, I got called for holding. As I ran off the field, Shula met me on the sideline and launched into a barrage of profanities that had something to do with *when was I ever going to* gain *the [expletives deleted] fifteen yards I'd just cost the team in a penalty* and ended with *"Sit your fat ass on the bench!"* The football god with the stoic profile who reigned as the King of Calm during practice became a raging, cussing maniac in the heat of a game. I felt like a little boy who had disappointed his father and was being sent to his room. I had to fight back the tears as I was made to sit out a couple of series.

"Rivas, you're back in," Coach Sandusky finally barked.

Another chance! I charged onto the field. We drove the ball down the field with running plays and then a pass play was called. The pass was intercepted. Speeding off downfield in hot pursuit, I had a nice bead on the defender and was just starting to unload on him, when the rest of the pile hit me from behind, sending me over the top of it and onto my neck. Then the weight of the pile landed on me, crushing my face mask onto my chest. I had been bent in half with at least a thousand pounds of NFL football players on top of me. But the worst and eeriest part of it was that I couldn't feel a thing. Wide awake and numb at the same time, I stared up into the sky, and then I saw Witt Beckman's face looking down at me.

"You all right?" he said as he reached down to undo my chin strap, probably on reflex to help me breathe and lighten my load.

"Don't touch him!" A green shirt appeared in my sight line. The pile had landed near the Philadelphia sideline, where one of their trainers bellowed at Witt.

I remained motionless for a very long thirty seconds before I felt my toes and fingers tingling; the rest of my body came alive moments later. Our trainers arrived and kept me in a prone position for several minutes, while they ran a few tests.

Back home in Miami, my brother Ed was in the living room, watching on TV while Mami was in the kitchen cooking. "Ah, shit!" my brother moaned, as the camera came in for a close-up on me lying there on the field, surrounded by trainers and emergency medical specialists.

"Qué paso?" Mami asked with concern, making her way back to the living room.

Ed yelled out, "Don't come in here."

Howard Cosell, in his own inimitable announcing voice, was telling my brother and the rest of the viewers watching this preseason game, "It's number 93, the young Cuban lad from Miami," when I stood up. "He's okay, Mami," Eddie called to her with relief.

The diagnosis was a pinched nerve in my neck or back that caused the momentary paralysis. Spared, I lived on to fight another day. Neither the holding penalty nor the injury brought out the Turk for my shoulder tap.

We geared up for the next preseason game. Part of this process involved meetings in which we were divided up into groups according to our different positions. We also gathered as a whole team to study footage of our opponent in action, focusing on special teams and kicking reels.

As the blue-collar workers of the football team, we offensive linemen often called ourselves "mushrooms." Why? Because "they feed us bullshit and keep us in the dark." This was true even in these film sessions, when the offensive line was always seated in the back of the room. And when the lights went out, the farting began.

Sitting in the very back, I could see the oversized silhouettes of players straddling the students' desks, which we dwarfed, their bodies leaning left or right, lifting the opposite butt cheek to release gas. The side-to-side movement in front of me reminded me of the dancing hippos in Disney's *Fantasia,* and the sounds emanating from their butts were reminiscent of the French horn section of an orchestra, warming up. Berrrup. Brrep. Berrup. After a few short minutes, the room smelled like a barnyard.

The veteran offensive linemen, led by Kooch, kept saying two words after each stinky outburst: "Consequential?" or "Inconsequential." It was like a call-and-answer gospel song, like a "Well?" and a "Nah." This ritual had been going on since the veterans arrived and I had no idea what they were talking about.

For some weeks I had been holding my gas politely but simply could not on one very gassy afternoon. It burst from me in a classic silent-but-deadly bomb and it almost knocked me out. With the air-conditioning blowing behind me, it quickly traveled around the room. Players began fanning themselves and you could hear shouts of "Oh, my God!" "Pheww!" and "Oh, man. Who died?"

It reached Howard Schellenberger, the offensive coordinator, who ran the film projector. Coach Schellenberger, who had a gravelly voice and wore a big curled mustache, barked, "Jesus Christ!" He shut off the projector.

Shula stood up and yelled, "Take five."

Everyone began a stampede for the doors. I could hear Kooch, Langer, and Newman screaming, "Consequential! Consequential!" as they evacuated.

I now knew what "consequential" meant. It was a Room-Clearing Fart.

When I went out for five minutes to get some air for myself, I could hear Kooch polling other players to see if they were responsible for the evacuation.

As one of the first players to return to the meeting room, I was sitting at my desk when Kooch walked in, stopped, and stared at me. He walked suspiciously over to my desk. "Was that you, Cuban Kid?"

The straight face that I stretched across my cheeks fell off and I cracked up. The smell was still so heinous I could only laugh. With a serious expression, Kooch thrust out his right hand. For a moment, I thought he was going to hit me, but he was extending his hand to shake mine. I extended my hand and we shook vigorously as he said, "Goddamnit, son! You gotta claim those, you're an offensive lineman. That's a proud moment!"

By now, the rest of the team and the coaches were making their way back into the room. Kooch yelled over to Coach Sandusky, "Hey, John, it was the Cuban Kid!"

Coach Sandusky, an ex–NFL offensive lineman, strode up and towered over me, extending his hand. "Goddamnit, son! You're an offensive lineman, you gotta claim those. That's a proud moment!"

With everyone sitting, just before the lights were turned off to continue the film study, Sandusky stood up. "Don," he said, stopping Coach Shula from taking a seat, "hold on a second. Rivas, stand up."

I stood up, nervous again, facing Don Shula with the rest of the room looking at me.

Coach Sandusky said, "That was Rivas who cleared the room. We just wanted to claim it."

Coach Shula's eyes narrowed and he jutted his jaw at me. "Rivas," he warned, "if that happens again, you'll be on the next plane home."

"Yes sir."

Shula held his menacing stare a few more seconds and then, with a thespian's flair, leaned his head back and HOWLED with laughter. I almost peed my pants. I thought he was serious.

It hit me like a wave, sitting there in the room, watching the film as the Dancing Hippos and the French-horn farting *BRRPP*s began amid the sweet soulful gospel call-and-answer of the offensive linemen singing "Consequential?" and "Inconsequential," that games were what children played. As I looked around the room, at many of the men that I had idolized as a youth, some with graying hair and arthritic knees, I realized they were a bunch of overgrown boys. Like me.

I was bent over, putting my socks on in front of my locker, when the Turk tapped me on my shoulder.

"Coach Shula would like to see you in his office. Bring your playbook," Coach Taseff said quietly.

As I walked down the hallway to Shula's office, I held my head up high and puffed out my chest. I had nothing to be ashamed of. I had arrived at camp as the Longest of Long Shots and had lasted longer than some of the high draft picks, making it to the next-to-last cut. I played in three NFL preseason games, wearing the uniform of my favorite team and playing alongside several future Hall of Famers. Once again, I was taken in by a family and given love and protection. A very large family of over a half million south Florida Cubans, who kept me focused, even when I was heartbroken. I had reconnected with my roots, my people, and my island.

Coach Shula sat behind his desk with the straight-backed posture he always had. He stood up to greet me and shake my hand. He asked me to have a seat. "I'm sorry I have to do this. I've really enjoyed having you in camp." His eyes and his voice backed up the sincerity of his statement; I had earned his respect.

"Don't be sorry, Coach. I was honored to be here. Thank you for the opportunity."

We chatted for a few minutes about my plans for the future. Coach Shula stood up, shook my hand again, and said, "Good luck, Vic. Stay in touch. Let us know what you're doing." Prophetically, as I walked out, he left the door open.

Mounting my Kawasaki 1000, I took one last look at the practice fields of Biscayne College. There were two voices talking in my head.

One said, "Not tough enough, you never were." The other said, "Stay in touch."

I popped a wheelie down the long driveway of the college and I heard another voice, my own, saying with certainty, *I'm not done yet.*

Ten months later, I was back. The first time they had come to me with the once-in-a-lifetime chance. This time, I went back and asked for another tryout. Some chances come twice in a lifetime. I was twenty pounds heavier, topping the scales at 265 and bench-pressing 480, the second strongest on the entire team. I was listed as a one-year veteran; I knew the system and what was expected of me.

During the minicamp, Coach Sandusky advised me to learn another position or skill to enhance my chances on an already loaded offensive line. I taught myself to deep snap the ball for punts, field goals, and PATs, and I was learning the center position. My deep snapping was fair at best, but it was center that gave me the most difficulty. I had played my whole career in a left-handed stance, but with a right-handed quarterback, you have to snap the ball right-handed.

The second training camp and preseason brought with it old and new friendships and adventures. The media hounded me again that year, but for another reason. The Dolphins had reacquired future Hall of Fame fullback Larry Csonka from the New York Giants. Zonk was my all-time favorite player from the Dolphin Super Bowl teams of the early seventies. I had never noticed this, but I could have been his twin, except for my straight nose; Csonka's nose had been broken many times from his battering-ram style of running.

Though I was the Madcuban to a few old-timers with ties to FSU, I continued to be the Cuban Kid to most of the players. But a few of the guys began calling me Baby Zonk. The press picked up on the story and even ran our pictures side by side. Whenever I walked out of our locker room at Biscayne College or wherever we played during the preseason, fans mobbed me with cries of "Larry Csonka!" and requests for autographs. Initially, I tried to inform them that they were mistaken, but they kept shoving a pen and paper or Csonka's picture at me.

"Okay." I'd give in and sign my own name, smile, and watch them walk away staring down at the autograph, going, "Who the fuck is Vic Rivas?"

Csonka picked up on this and after we played the Vikings in Minnesota, he did a double take at seeing me swarmed by a hundred crazed fans seeking his autograph. One woman even had me sign her breast.

I survived through the last week of training camp, making it to the very last cut, before the Turk tapped my shoulder.

As I sat with Coach Shula in his office, he made it clear to me that I was capable of playing in the NFL. "Unfortunately, we have four All-Pro players in your position. I'm sure with another team, you'd have a better shot." He offered to recommend me if there was any-where that I wanted to go.

A tryout with the 49ers was even in the offing. The reality, how-ever, was that the days of the three-hundred-pound-and-over, six-five, behemoth offensive lineman were coming down the pike. If I wanted to beef up another forty pounds, maybe my size wouldn't be such a liability. At the same time, when I was on my back in Canton, Ohio, that day, thinking I'd broken my neck, I had started wondering if maybe I was pushing my luck.

Coach Shula asked about any other plans. Well, I told him, I had a brother out in Hollywood who was getting his start in show busi-ness and I had been thinking about going to California to check it out. He told me that he expected to hear good things about me and to know that if every player on his team played with my heart, he'd never lose a game.

With that, I said good-bye to Shula and to football, the sport that had given me so much. This breakup of a grand love affair was leav-ing me without any permanent injuries or hard feelings. No, I never got to come home with a Super Bowl ring of my own, and there was that Second Son in me that felt I should have gone further. Yet I had competed at the highest level and held my own. I had earned the respect of the two winningest coaches in college and professional football. These memories were my trophies that replaced the old ones that had been shattered.

I could hear my buddy Kooch saying to me, as I drove away, "Goddamnit, son! You gotta claim those, you're an offensive lineman!"

They were all proud moments.

7
hollywood
(1979–1989)

Tell Victor . . . my deepest love to him, he was always #1 with me. . . .
Well, you read about some people coming out of the closet for this and
that, but I had to be different, I'm going into the closet and goodby.
> —Letter to Tony Rivas Jr. from Dad,
> February 21, 1980

T HE GOOD NEWS about coming to Hollywood as yet another
Longest of Long Shots was that I was in fine company. Show business
was like football in that respect. You had to be a little crazy to want to
play the game, and even more crazy to stay in it.

It was also the 1980s. These were the days of excess, high-rolling
and partying times, with lots of distractions and temptations for anyone without a strong sense of self or a strong sense of direction.
Paradoxically, my background in overcoming obstacles made me a
good candidate for gaining some kind of foothold, while my background as a wounded boy was to set me up for taking the worst fall of
my life.

At first, I approached my pursuit of an acting career as I might
have chased after a hard-to-get woman, pretending that I wasn't so
interested. The truth is that I was smitten, but didn't want to be
rejected. Yet the ability to handle rejection is a prerequisite for any

actor, one of the most important tools to have in the Hollywood survival kit that I soon set about creating. But first, I had unfinished
business to address.

It was on my mind from the moment I finished saying my good-
byes to the various members of my families and boarded a charter
flight to Las Vegas. In the cargo hold was my gleaming steed, the
Kawasaki 1000. In the pilot's cabin, flying me partway on my journey
west, was Bebo Echevarria. In Las Vegas, I said my *gracias* and *adios* to
him before making my way down to the cargo hold and climbing on
top of my motorcycle. Much to the surprise of those at work at the
airport, I rode my bike right off the loading platform and onto the
tarmac, speeding away to the freeway, then across Death Valley
toward L.A.

The ghosts came out to welcome me as I entered the city limits,
riding sunburned and wind-bitten past the spires of downtown that I
had last seen nine years before when my father stole us away under
the cover of night. In Hawthorne, I had seen and endured the worst
of Dad's abuse and violence, to the point where I had become homicidal and suicidal. And it was there too that a little soul, my brother
Robert David Rivas, had been abandoned.

The day after my arrival at Rocky's place in East Hollywood, I
mounted my motorcycle and headed south. Like a homing pigeon
returning to its roost, I was soon parked in front of the house on
Oxford Street. The house that loomed in my memories and nightmares looked so small, so ordinary, so harmless. I knocked on a few
doors, finding only one neighbor still living on the block from my
childhood. We chatted for a while and then I rode back to
Hollywood, with no new revelations and without having exorcised
any past demons. That was when I got around to picking up the
phone and dialing information, recalling the visual memory of that
envelope that had arrived from Fairview State Hospital.

After being transferred from one department to another, I was
connected with record keeping. "I'm trying to locate my brother," I
explained, and gave his name.

"I'm sorry," the clerk replied, "that information can be released only to a parent or legal guardian."

"I understand," I lied, and probably not well, "but my mother and father were killed in a car accident so I'm his only next of kin."

To my great surprise, she said that would be fine and read me the information she had on record. Robert David Rivas had died on November 12, 1971, a little over a year after we left L.A., as though he had given up his final hope of rescue. He was only nine years old.

At the time of his death, brought on by his deteriorating physical condition and pneumonia, Robert was on leave from the hospital at a Compton foster-care group home for children with severe developmental disabilities. That comforted me, knowing my brother had been living in the 'hood, where I had faith he had received the kindness of strangers, and that for his short time on earth and in his last days, Robert had been in the care of angels, like those in my community who had given me shelter, love, and protection.

Yet the more grateful I was for those advocates and those agencies that care for children like Robert, the angrier and more enraged I became at Dad. I now grew more tortured than ever by the image of his assault on Mami and the terror I had felt as a six-year-old jumping on his back and trying unsuccessfully to stop him. All over again, I wanted to kill my father, to make him pay for every cruelty he had ever wreaked on us, and in the most violent way imaginable. I murdered him in my dreams night after night. But he just wouldn't die.

Then, in February of 1980, only a few months after my arrival in Hollywood, I got the news that someone else had actually killed him for me.

Fragments of the story continued to come together like pieces of a puzzle over the years to come. The main puzzle piece eventually came from Barbie, an eighth-grader at the time. During the years he was married to Mecca, from outward appearances Dad's violence had been held in greater check. Mecca's son, Charlie, a likable yet tough young man, probably helped to keep the peace. Or "piss," as Dad said it—one of those other words he still had trouble pronouncing. But when Mecca was at work or Charlie wasn't around, Barbie was left unprotected. A photograph taken in this era of Dad with his arm around my sister, his thirteen-year-old daughter, revealed a hint of what that might have been like. Standing in a hot tub in front of tropical foliage, my father, in fairly good shape at age forty-nine, had his arm over Barbie's shoulder. Possessive. Barbie, the little Kewpie doll with the curly hair I had last seen, was now a tall, slender, brown-skinned, gorgeous Latina. Both faced the camera, neither smiling. Her expression was fearful, his inscrutable.

She, like all of us, had planned his death many times in her mind. Dad had found ways to terrorize her as he had my mother, my brothers, and me, but through violence he had threatened, controlled, and owned Barbie in a way that even I believed he wasn't capable of doing. My sister had been living with what Dad called "our little secret" and the certainty, as he promised, that if she told anyone, he would take her away from Mecca, and from everyone she loved, so far away that no one would find them. This couldn't have sounded like an empty threat to a girl who had been kidnapped once already from her own mother.

At her Catholic junior high school, in the middle of the day on February 21, Barbie had felt a sudden jolt to her chest as she walked across the parking lot to the cafeteria for lunch. She flashed instantly on a dream she had dreamt a week earlier in which she saw herself looking down at Dad in his coffin. After school, she got on her bike and rode home. Something felt different, strange. Two blocks from the house, she could hear Dad's stereo blaring with the music of Brazil 66. Several thoughts cluttered her brain, including the image of Dad ordering this stereo from an ad in *Reader's Digest*. What kind of a music lover would own a damn *Reader's Digest* stereo in the first place? Brazil 66 told her something else. This was what Dad liked to hear, he said, when he was seeking "piss of mind." And it was blasting through the neighborhood at top volume, playing over and over and over.

Barbie knew what had happened even before she put her bike away and strode up the front steps, with the deafening music that caused her to hurry inside and close the door behind her. She knew even before she read the note hanging from Dad's bedroom door. My sister stood in the living room, not sure what to do. Turn the stereo down? Get in trouble for changing it because that's the way he wanted it? Then she read the note that answered everything: *"Barbie, don't wake me up. Have Mecca do it. Dad."*

Nothing else was necessary for her to understand that she was free. Barbie recalled that as a calm came over her that she had never known, she went over to the *Reader's Digest* stereo and turned it off, then went into the kitchen and took out a Farm Stores carton of cherry vanilla ice cream. Those two acts of free will, which when Dad was alive she would have never been allowed, followed with a third as she sat down at the dining room table and slowly consumed the full carton in peace, knowing that he was gone and could never hurt her again.

Mecca came home a few hours later, found the mess he had left behind, and sent Barbie to the neighbor's house. For the next several hours, Barbie watched as the house became a crime scene. In the ultimate act of self-loathing that he had often projected onto us—maybe causing my sister and me to endure the worst because we had the audacity to look so much like him—Anthony Rivas Sr. had at last stared into the cesspool of himself and couldn't bear what he saw. He planned his suicide as meticulously as the tortures he had inflicted on us, writing suicide letters, sticking the note on the door for Barbie not to come in, putting Brazil 66 on the record player at top volume and set to replay over and over to mask the sound of the double-barreled shotgun that he used, after he went into the closet, put it to his chest, and pulled the trigger.

When nineteen-year-old Ed heard the news over the phone from Tony, he had been studying for a test at Osceola Hall on the Florida State campus. Ed hung up and forced himself to cry for the next half hour because, he figured, it was the right thing to do. But then it dawned on Ed that Dad's supreme act of cowardice had deprived him of the opportunity to take his diploma and "stuff it up Dad's ass" after graduation. Lately our father had been boasting to those who still saw him as the most charming guy in the world that Ed was now his third son to go to college, despite the fact that El Caballero never shelled out a penny to help put his boys through school. I was fortunate with my full athletic scholarship, but Tony and Ed paid their own way at major universities.

In a small apartment in Hialeah, Mami sat nine-and-a-half-year-old Carmen down at the kitchen table to deliver a series of bombshells, starting with the announcement, "Your brothers' and Barbie's father killed himself."

This came at a time when Mami and her second husband, Antonio Maestegui, had recently separated, a difficult period for Carmen, who believed that he was her father. She was not aware that earlier on Antonio had legally adopted her and had given her his last name after Dad signed paperwork disowning her as his daughter. Very precocious, Carmen was sad that her papi and mami were divorcing, but she understood that his severe manic depression had taken a toll on the household. She loved him and was comforted by the knowledge that he loved her and would remain a father figure to her, even helping with child support.

But then Mami revealed the secret she had been keeping. Antonio Maestegui wasn't Carmen's real father. Reeling, Carmen could never have expected the next revelation. Her real father was the man who had just killed himself, whom she knew as the father to her half siblings, Tony, me, Ed, and Barbie. She had visited his home a few times but knew very little about who he was, bad or good. Except for one time when they were playing some card game and he cheated to win. The *cabrón*. He had to cheat at cards against a little girl. Now she had to grapple with having been cheated out of the knowledge that she was every bit our full sibling and that he was gone before she knew he was her real father. Maddeningly, even though she had not grown up subjected to Dad's insanity, he managed to haunt and trouble her life for years to come. But like all of us who had elements of La Luchadora in us, she came through with her own sanity, humor, goodness, and loving nature intact.

When Tony called me in California to give me the news, he was sobbing on the other end of the line. Sitting down in the stylish Hollywood Hills apartment I shared with Rocky (who went back to Steven, his real first name, and used the last name Bauer, a family name on Lillian's side, because nobody seemed to be able to pronounce Echevarria in the movie and television industry), I listened as my big brother, the First Son, haltingly related the discovery made by Barbie and Mecca.

After several long beats, I responded with, "Wow, really?"

That was not the response that my devastated brother was looking for. My muted reaction surprised even me. Always the responsible one, Tony wasn't angry with me, and he promised to send copies of the suicide notes. He made the same suggestion that he had made in his calls to Mami and Ed, that we arrange some kind of a memorial, perhaps to dispose of Dad's ashes, the expenses for which we would share, and got the same definite "No way" from me that he did from our mother and Ed.

A short while later, Steven came home and found me sitting alone in the dark hallway between the two bedrooms of our Canyon Drive apartment. "What's wrong?" he asked at once, and when I told him about Dad's suicide, he slowly and thoughtfully replied, "Ah, Vic. I'm sorry."

"What's really wrong," I confessed, "is that I've been sitting here for a couple hours trying to cry and nothing comes out."

Steven nodded and sat down next to me, leaning against the wall. He had a soulful compassion and sometimes understood me better than I knew myself. Explaining what he thought was really wrong, he said, "You have no more tears left. He beat them out of you." These words reminded me of what Mami had said long ago about having lost her tears as well.

It took me five and a half long years and a Bruce Springsteen &

the E Street Band concert during the 1985 *Born in the USA* tour—in honor of my coming thirtieth birthday—to reclaim them for myself. Nothing in Dad's long, rambling suicide notes that I had read over and over had helped to burst the dam. Leave it to the Boss.

From early on in his career, I had been a huge Springsteen fan and had even met him at concerts backstage as a tagalong with Steven and Melanie Griffith, the sexy beauty and gifted actress Steven married after the two met while working on a CBS TV pilot. Bruce was also a familiar fixture at the Hollywood YMCA where I worked out, always showing up to lift weights by himself. There was something about his concerts that took on an almost religious experience, not only because of the power of the driving rock 'n' roll, his ferocious performing ability, and the subject matter and lyrics of his songs, but also because of the poetry of his spoken monologues that laced throughout the concert.

High up in the nosebleed seats of the Los Angeles Coliseum, I was mesmerized as Bruce sat alone onstage and told a story about not being able to talk to his dad about a girl he loved. I finally had my catharsis, a very public one. The E Street Band played the intro of "I'm on Fire," then Bruce began, without even taking a breath, to sing, "Hey little girl is your daddy home," and what I heard was the words in the last message my dad sent to me in his note to Tony:

> Tell Victor I love him and I just wasn't equipped or threw away my fatherly equipment somewhere, but I know he loved me and the feeling is mutual over here, please forgive our differences and problems, I can't rewrite history but I wish I could wash and rinse it, like we do our clothes and freshen them up a bit. Give my deepest love to him, he was always #1 with me.

Ironically, as I sobbed uncontrollably, allowing the flow of tears to rage with abandon, everyone up in the seats around me turned and smiled at me in awe, as if I was at an old-fashioned revival and had caught the Spirit. They lit up their lighters in the dark, cheering me on, as they sang their praise to the preacher onstage, chanting, "Bruce! Bruce! Bruce!"

I got my tears back, all right. But it was going to take more than this catharsis for me to fully exorcise the demons.

My Hollywood survival tool kit wasn't too different from the collection of survival lessons that had helped me escape the war zone of childhood and navigate the years of my refugee status.

On a macro level, these tools could be viewed under the general headings I eventually saw as *Keeping the Faith, Telling the Truth, Finding a Support System, Using Imagination,* and *Having Physical and Emotional Outlets.* Faith in a higher power, whatever its name or denomination, helps to stave off hopelessness; faith in oneself as an individual or as an artist with a meaningful calling is absolute sustenance for the days of struggle until it's feast time. For me, being able to truthfully tell my story and to be heard, however many times I needed to tell it, was the greatest act of liberation anyone ever gave me; as an actor I tried to look for that emotional truth and authenticity in my approach to characters. Angels and advocates that had been my support system in my growing-up years were as important to me as ever in my Hollywood journey; having a village, or community, of fellow artists made the bumps a lot easier to get over. It was also helpful to have friends outside of show business to help keep a perspective. The power of imagination that I had employed to entertain myself during those many years when I was punished and alone now became an even more important tool, not just in being an entertainer for others but also in being creative for opening doors that would otherwise be closed to me. Finally, the daily requirements of being able to laugh and to cry and to have the kind of physical outlet that sports had always given me are vital for all human beings; a sense of humor, pathos, and the use of one's instrument—body and voice—are the building blocks of an actor's craft.

Of course, on the micro level, there were all kinds of other lessons to be learned. It also took a lot of trial and even more error to feel that I understood the game and could claim any sort of victory.

Many of the old clichés turned out to be true. Exhibit A: *Do what you love and love what you do, and success will follow.* With Dad no longer alive, I obviously didn't have to prove anything to him anymore. Now I had the tough assignment of defining myself without him as my adversary. Before I got into the game seriously, however, I had to ask myself if this was really what I wanted to do, enough to put up with the inevitable ups and downs that would come. The answer was yes.

As it happened, I had already gotten a taste of the process when I worked on a movie as a glorified extra not long after my senior football season was over. Burt Reynolds, an FSU alum and former football player, had been in Miami making a movie called *Semi-Tough* and needed a few players to round out his team in the film. Along with three of my friends and former teammates, Danny Greene, Bob Jones, and Bobby McKinnon, I got to block and hit and run all day for the cameras. Danny, a graduate of South Miami High School, had been a fierce opponent on the field during our high school days, but later we got on the same side of the ball at FSU. Interestingly enough, we were both bit by the bug and landed in Hollywood to pursue acting careers.

Exhibit B: *Luck and connections are essential.* At first, being impatient, I took for granted how lucky I was. In fact, I had a good luck charm in Rocky. Just being Steven Bauer's brother opened doors and connections that I would never have had otherwise. He was likewise generous and Bebo-like with practical advice, giving me a jump start on some Hollywood do's and don'ts. Among the do's was the gathering of basic supplies, like headshots and résumés. Since I had a place to live with him and a set of wheels in my motorcycle, I had the necessities of housing and transportation covered.

Some of his other recommended do's: *Study your craft. Get cast in a play. Get a day gig.* One of his don'ts: *For God's sake, Vic, don't scare the nice casting director!*

Steven took me to his acting class, taught by the extraordinary actor and teacher David Proval, who ran a very cool workshop. There was an open-door policy that enabled actors to drop by unannounced. I walked in on more than one occasion and found Jon Voight, Meg Tilly, Robert De Niro, and other established names sitting in our class.

David worked with me on dropping the macho façade (which was scaring the nice casting directors) and revealing the wounded boy underneath. The first time that I gave myself permission to let go, I nearly fainted. David grabbed a chair and sat next to me onstage, guiding me through a painful but ultimately cathartic experience. His next bit of advice, spoken in his Italian tough-guy accent, was, "Victor, you need to take a dance class." My wary look caused him to add, "You move around stage with as much grace as a cornered bull."

David Proval sent me to a ballet class taught by veteran actress Betty Garrett, then a regular on *Laverne and Shirley.* In my tights, standing at the ballet barre next to the other students, mostly actresses, I looked like an oak tree surrounded by saplings. But much to everyone's surprise I soon tapped the feline grace still in me from my early days of being a tiger and now became an unusually graceful oak tree.

In a hot comedy improvisation class, I used my ballet to develop one of several comedy sketch characters, such as a former thug turned street-crime fighter who uses dance moves instead of violence to overcome his antagonists. The class was taught by one of my much-loved champions, Bill Hudnut, who was a protégé of the legendary improv teacher and comedian Harvey Lembeck. After Harvey died, his son and daughter—actor-director Michael and actress Helaine—took over teaching his workshop, a class I later attended. During the 1980s, however, Bill Hudnut's class became my true proving ground, where my social life also thrived.

Connections also flowed through this network and helped with finding agents, managers, and film and TV work, including my first guest star role, on the hit show *Benson*.

Steven's advice to get cast in a play had ultimately helped me to overcome every aspiring actor's toughest Catch-22, getting my SAG card. After a year of sporadic acting classes, I was cast in an ensemble of thirty-one actors in a production of *Marat/Sade* (written by Peter Weiss and Peter Brook, its full title is *The Persecution and Assassination of Jean-Paul Marat as Performed by the Inmates of the Asylum of Charenton Under the Direction of the Marquis de Sade*). As actors, we played the mental patients who enacted roles in the plays within the play. The production was well reviewed and attended by full houses almost every night. In the role of an oversexed, deaf and dumb prison guard assigned to watch over the inmates, I never left the stage, even during intermission.

After the show, I was approached by the head of MGM Studios casting, who was kind enough to say, "I know you never said a word, but you have an incredible presence onstage."

"Thank you," I said, careful to get myself out of my intimidating macho character and smile warmly at the nice casting director.

"Who's your agent?"

Telling the truth, I admitted that I didn't have an agent and that this was my first play. He gave me his card and told me to call him on Monday. By the end of the week, I was working on a short-lived Robert Blake series called *Joe Dancer*, as a street drug pusher. In order to join the Screen Actors Guild, you have to speak and be visible on camera. On cue, when my one-word line came up as Robert Blake's character walked down the street, I leaned forward to swallow as much of the camera lens as possible as I said, "Speed?"

My SAG card soon led to my getting an agent, and I felt that my acting career was off and running. Actually it was another ten years before I could make my living strictly as an actor.

During that time, while I worked at several different part-time day gigs and night gigs, my biggest stroke of luck was connecting with a group of friends who became the family that most helped me grow into manhood. The pillar of this "orphans" community, as we sometimes called ourselves, was a friend I had met my second day in Hollywood, when there was a knock at the apartment door and I opened it to meet a pair of electric blue eyes staring back at me as the pronounced smell of patchouli permeated the air.

"Hey there, I'm Joe Cartwright," he announced, and before I could say, "You've got to be kidding, right?" he looked me up and down. The next thing he did was to ask me to help him move his furniture in from the van parked out on the street. That was forward. His look was also quite bold: a knee-high pair of bright green tube socks over the biggest pair of calves I'd ever seen, purple Dolphin running shorts that couldn't have been any shorter, a pink, midriff-length tank top, and a colorful bandanna wrapped around his head, babushka style.

Out at the truck, I met David Plakos, a big, handsome fellow, dressed in completely normal attire, I might add. He and Joe, a Minnesota boy, were moving to Hollywood from North Dakota to pursue careers in media other than acting. David was a cameraman, on his way to becoming one of the most in-demand cameramen for major concerts and award events on television, with so many Emmys of his own that he used them as doorstops. Joe had just been hired by L.A. station KHJ to sell advertising time. The most engaging human peacock of an individual, Joe drew women in droves, including Kathy Nunez, a Latina knockout. Joe chased her, as Kathy would say, until she caught him, and the two were later married, becoming the figurative parents to the orphan brood. Joe had that rare gift of salesmanship—like actors who make acting look easy—that you never knew when he was selling. He didn't have to sell, it was his zest for life and his confidence that overflowed from him. His motto, "Don't postpone joy," was one he shared with all of us lucky enough to dwell in the rarefied air where he lived.

One joy for me in these days of adventure and struggle came on Sunday nights, when a core group of us actors and musicians got together at our apartment for the poor-boy omelet gathering. Except for Steven, who was having incredible success, the rest of us were struggling financially and might miss a meal or two here and there. So besides the camaraderie, we really looked forward to the poor boys.

Our apartment supplied a dozen eggs. Everyone else brought the filler: onions, vegetables, a can of peas and carrots, canned tuna, whatever they could afford or had left in their kitchen cabinet. Andy Garcia, a graduate of Miami Beach High School, who was starting to become known around town for improv performances at the Comedy Store, was the chef. Instead of frying the omelets in a skillet, he baked them in the oven, making them fluffy and several inches thick; it gave the illusion that we had more to eat.

We spent the rest of the night talking and playing music. Out in Hollywood now was Steven's best friend from Coral Park High School, Jim Petersen, who was my friend as well. Jimmy, who, like Steven, was a year younger than I, had been a tough linebacker on our high school football team, had attended FSU, and was now pursuing music and screen-writing. With his Dutch boy haircut and angelic voice, he sang while Jim Youngs (one of the stars of *The Wanderers)* and Steven played guitar. An accomplished percussionist, Andy brought his conga drums and claves. Ray Liotta listened in his intense, intent way, and I, like a balletic oak tree, entertained the others with my silly interpretive dancing.

Steven was almost so lucky as to be too lucky. It was unheard of, especially without having any relatives in the business, that only three days after stepping off the proverbial bus in Hollywood, he could be signed to a retainer by one of the studios until they cast him in a project. The fact that he didn't have time to grow into his stardom with sacrifice and struggle but found himself so immediately in its throes meant that he never had to get a day gig and faced little rejection early on, something that made it much harder later. At the same time, I benefited from his help and from getting to watch him take his ride, seeing how, with his incredible magnetism and talent, he landed opportunity after opportunity, including a regular spot on the short-lived TV series *From Here to Eternity* and then, not too much later, his breakout role as Al Pacino's sidekick Manny in *Scarface,* which earned Steven a Golden Globe nomination.

It was outrageously fun being a fly on those walls, going out on Monday nights to roller disco at the private events organized by Helena Kallianiotes, the malcontent hitchhiker from the movie *Five Easy Pieces.* We skated with the likes of Joni Mitchell, Jack Nicholson, Anjelica Huston, Teri Garr, Harry Dean Stanton, Kareem Abdul-Jabbar, and Jim Brown, as well as countless other movie stars and rock and sports legends, mixed in with wannabes and groupies and up-and-comers. We befriended Joni Mitchell and ended up inviting her to dinner at our humble abode because she loved Cuban food. That same night she picked up Steven's guitar and played us something that was coming out on her next album. Unreal!

The adventures at some of my various day gigs were equally memorable. One of the first of these jobs was for a fledgling moving company, called Starving Students, that Andy Garcia had heard about. When we showed up to apply, the supervisor said, "Who can drive a truck?" I raised my hand and was quickly thrown some keys and an address, with Andy following me dubiously.

"You can drive this?" he asked, as we climbed up into a thirty-foot moving truck with a manual transmission.

I had driven a pickup before, not a monster like this. Plus, the first moving job was in the Hollywood Hills, on a small winding street with no room for error, and on a curve. After fifteen minutes, with the customer watching from the window and the smell of a nearly burnt-out clutch in the air, we knocked on the front door. The customer had to ask, "Do you guys know what you're doing?"

"Sure!" we answered enthusiastically.

It was incredibly hard work. Our customers usually felt sorry for us and almost always asked, "Are you guys *really* starving students?"

With our best Oliver Twist faces, we answered sadly, "Yes," which was typically followed by a very generous tip.

Another job, procured with the help of Jim Youngs, was as a doorman-bouncer at the legendary Rainbow Bar & Grill on the Sunset Strip. During my interview, my Kawasaki was stolen and I had to hitch rides for the next year until I could buy a car. The life on Sunset Boulevard in the early and mid-1980s was a scene to end all scenes. Next door to the Rainbow was the Roxy Theatre, with Lou Adler's private club, On the Rox, above it, and the Whisky a Go Go was two blocks east. Every night at the two-story Rainbow there was a parade of sex, drugs, and rock 'n' roll, with all the tiers and circles of the record business and entertainment industry. And I was the gate-keeper known as the Wooden Indian, because of my impassive demeanor. One night I might usher in Rod Stewart and his band, Faces; Ozzy and Sharon Osbourne; and the Who's bass player, John "the Ox" Entwistle, all regulars. Another night, it might be guys like Robin Williams and John Belushi.

One of the greatest comic geniuses of our time, John was the example that made me add the "don't" about hard-core drugs to my list of guidelines. I partied along with the best of them, but after watching him on his downward spiral, I made a promise to myself that I would never go over the edge as he had done. He was at our club almost every night in the last month of his life, including his last day, literally bouncing off the walls, in such an altered state that he was beyond reach, I thought, determined to take himself out. What had stardom done to him? How had it gone wrong? You strive to be the best in what you do, you struggle for years pursuing your dream, and when you get there, you snort it all away or pump poison into your arms? His death came as a senseless loss that I took personally.

But it wasn't just the extreme examples of talented artists burning out young. The binges of the eighties were evident everywhere. People were spending huge amounts of money on cars, homes, personal grooming, and style. Corporate and personal greed flourished, as did the prevalence of the caffeine of this decade, cocaine. With every other handshake, a vial of coke was passed. Lucky for me, at least for a while, I was still struggling too much financially to overindulge.

Lots of other lessons emerged in this period. Exhibit C: *Don't count your acting jobs until they hatch*. I was cast in *Scarface* as a member of Tony Montana's gang. Thrilled to say that I was going to be working with Al Pacino, I told everyone the big news. When the film went way over budget and past schedule, my scenes were omitted before I stepped on the set. From then on, I followed the secrecy rule and rarely talked about what I was in until I wrapped.

Despite this disappointment, I was delighted to get to visit the set and spend time with Al Pacino and Steven. At one point Steven and I organized a football game on the campus of Pepperdine University and got Al to come out and play with us. By the luck of the draw, he ended up on my team and I was able to throw several touchdown passes to him because no one wanted to get close enough to him, for fear of bumping or hurting *Al Pacino*.

When Steven and Melanie were married, I considered her part of the extended family that was my support system. She dubbed me "Victoire" (pronounced "Victwah"), which she spoke in her perennially girlish yet smoky voice. Melanie was responsible for helping me book a small part in my first feature film, *Fear City*, directed by Abel Ferrara, in which she starred. As her brother-in-law for the years she was married to Steven, I was really honored to meet and visit her enchanting mom, actress Tippi Hedren (famous for her haunting role in Hitchcock's *The Birds)*, and also to visit Shambala, the rescue preserve for lions, tigers, and elephants she owns and runs. Tippi noticed immediately that I had a connection to the tigers and she wasn't nervous, as others were, when one of them approached me and put its paws on my shoulders.

Melanie and Steven became Hollywood's young "it" couple and earned all the trappings, good and bad, that came along with nonstop adulation and scrutiny. There were times when I stopped by their apartment to find a star cluster inside. One day I found myself in the kitchen with Melanie, Madonna, Cher, and Demi Moore. What a country, Hollywood!

Melanie gave me the priceless gift of introducing me to her longtime best friend, Heidi von Beltz, a champion hot-dog skier and former stuntwoman, who was devastatingly injured in a stunt gone bad on the film *Cannonball Run.* This stunning five-foot-eleven athletic beauty had been told she wouldn't live or speak or eat, but had defied every doctor's predictions, doing all those things and more. As a quadriplegic with a foundation called Follow Your Heart, Heidi refused to accept that she would never walk again and was determined to seek an alternative medical approach to spinal cord injuries, which later enabled her to stand for hours. Her indomitable spirit to live life to its fullest and her incomparable sense of humor were to inspire me always. She is a living lesson in faith if there ever was one.

Some of the faithful poor boys in our Sunday night group had seen their careers start to take off, including Andy Garcia. Along with his dry, understated sense of humor and his layered acting work that I saw get better with every performance, Andy went out of his way time and again to help friends and artists he admired. In an act that certainly fortified our friendship, he recommended me for a job in *8 Million Ways to Die,* which was directed by Hal Ashby, of *Harold and Maude* and *Being There* fame.

Andy was the lead antagonist opposite Jeff Bridges in a story about good and evil, decadence and sobriety. When he called to say that Hal Ashby was looking to add a member to the movie's drug cartel, only for a day's work, if I could be there that day, I jumped in my VW 412 fastback and raced downtown to go to work. What was supposed to be a one-day job turned into five weeks. Jeff Bridges was a prince. Another actor who makes the incredible work that he does look easy, in person he was funny, kind, and charming.

On location in Beverly Hills, where we had been shooting a party scene in a house on Rodeo Drive for several hours, we were released for twenty minutes for a lighting change. I took a stroll for air with one of my fellow gang members, the late Fred Asparagus, a three-hundred-pound comedian and actor. We went out to the alley behind the house; on the other side of the alley was the back side of a

Catholic church and a parish hall. There was a large group beginning to congregate in the hall. I spotted an attractive woman I knew and pointed her out to Fred.

"Let's go talk to her, brother," he said in his East L.A. homeboy purr.

We sauntered into the hall and noticed that people were scattering in front of us. The woman I knew approached me cautiously, asking, "What are you two doing here?"

I explained to her about the filming of a wild cocaine party scene in the house across the alley.

"Oh, thank God!" she said. "I didn't want to say anything but the two of you have coke doughnuts around your noses."

Fred and I had totally forgotten that we had been snorting crushed vitamin B_{12} from the prop department as part of the scene.

Then she added, "The guns don't help either, guys."

Ooops. Touching my right armpit, I felt the butt end of the prop department's Ruger Black Hawk .357 magnum with the six-inch barrel that was sheathed in the leather shoulder holster. Fred had an Uzi stuffed into the back of his pants.

The grand irony of this moment was that we had walked into an AA meeting. Fred and I could just imagine our characters announcing our names, "Hi, we're Filete and Mundo, and we're drug addicts and dealers," and then hearing the group respond in unison, "Hi, Filete. Hi, Mundo."

My comedy film work got a leg up from Zane Buzby, who attended an evening of Bill Hudnut's comedy-improv class and cast me in the film *Last Resort,* which she was directing. It was a low-budget film that we shot for a month on beautiful Catalina Island, just off the coast of Los Angeles. We had a ball shooting this film. It was like going to summer camp and being paid for it. In addition to smart and funny Charles Grodin, the cast consisted of a lot of young actors unknown at the time, among them Jon Lovitz, the late Phil Hartman, Mario Van Peebles, and Megan Mullally.

With luck, with friends, with champions, with my own tenacity, just when I thought I understood the playing field, I faced another lesson. Exhibit D: *Show business is unfair.* After so many years railing against injustice at home and outside it, I refused to accept there was no law and order in the way that decisions were made in Hollywood. Talent was only one of many criteria upon which actors were judged, many of the others as superficial as "I don't like his haircut" or "He's great but he'll dwarf the leading man" or "We love Victor but the role's going to the producer's nephew." Unjust! Unjust!

Steven, as well as Joe Cartwright, brothers and counselors, tried to explain that protesting these injustices wasn't going to help my cause. Earlier, I had been in contention for a role in *Quest for Fire* as one of the apelike early humans. Director Jean-Jacques Annaud had selected me along with a group of other actors to work with a coach for three weeks to develop primate movement. But when it came time for his final selection, he called me into his office and said he regretted having to tell me, "I'm sorry, I really like you but you have no acting experience."

"Oh, yeah," I couldn't refrain from saying, "like the other actors have had experience playing a fucking ape before?"

In a brief interlude, I took a year off from the business and, along with my brother Ernie Echevarria, went to New York to work for Bebo's charter airline company, known as Arrow Air. As an airline steward, I walked the aisles more like a bouncer at a rock 'n' roll club, and found myself on charter flights between New York and Puerto Rico, as well as transatlantic flights to Europe, that gave me comedy material to last for the rest of my life. The stint living in New York gave me a perspective on the acting world of the other coast, and fueled my desire to get back into the Hollywood game.

But back in L.A. I faced a new hurdle, the stereotyping of Latinos, African-Americans, and women, which made me really crazy. One of the interesting things that happened in my development as an actor was that in embracing all parts of myself and my humanity, I had started to see that the true bullies of the world were the bigots, homophobes, and misogynists. To work in Hollywood, where minorities thrive, typically individuals with those attitudes need not apply. But you wouldn't necessarily know that from the many stereotypical roles being written for minorities, which were insulting. I had decided to become an actor in order to play individuals from all walks of life, including backgrounds other than my own. Yet many times I was sent away from an audition with the promise to bring me back when a Latino role was being cast. In an effort not to be stereotyped, I changed my name to Victor Rivers.

Let's see. In a career that really kicked off toward the end of the eighties, I went on to play an array of movie bad guys. Latino convicts, Latino drug lords, Latino bank robbers, and Latino gang members. And Zorro's brother. (Melanie Griffith, later married to Antonio Banderas, my film brother Zorro, was so excited when she found out that I was playing the role. Go, Victoire!)

Playing mostly Latino villains had the upside that I was able to make a living at it and that I was able to use Dad to draw from. Also, because good usually triumphs over evil in movies, I soon developed a forte: dying frequently on-screen in ways that were as imaginative as those dramatic deaths I used to act out in my room when I was being punished.

In coming years I could boast of having been blown up, shot to death in *Fled* by Laurence Fishburne, and—as if I wasn't dead enough—run over by a motorcycle ridden by Stephen Baldwin and skewered through very slowly with a sword by Djimon Hounsou (in Steven Spielberg's *Amistad*). I even had my head chopped off and stuffed into a jar in *The Mask of Zorro*.

It never escaped me, however, that the beauty of the movies was that all this was make-believe, unlike the violence that I had known growing up. As early as 1986, I really thought that those scars had, for the most part, healed. I had been involved in several loving, passionate relationships with women who taught me as many lessons about myself as I had been learning about Hollywood. Usually it was I who broke it off. This was the eighties, after all, and I was commitment-phobic. But by now, along with forty pounds I had shed from my playing days, I had begun to lose my armor and my misconceptions about who I was. Underneath I'd discovered a handsome leading man with deep feelings and a need for companionship and acceptance. I was ready to trust, I thought, to commit to love, and even to a home and family.

Dad sat with his back to me on the end of my bed, dressed only in his briefs and a tank undershirt.

It was late 1988, and back in Miami, I had just dozed off after returning home from a long evening as a doorman at a Coconut Grove nightclub. For much of the last year, I had been living in the upstairs room of Mecca's house. One level down, in the master bedroom closet, my father had put a shotgun to his chest and pulled the trigger almost nine years earlier.

The downward spiral that had brought me to this place, despite my vows never to let drugs get the better of me, had me beating myself up with cocaine and alcohol for being a failure at love. Now Dad was haunting me again. Literally.

My friends had been quite taken with the very attractive, very wealthy young woman I'd met and married within months, but Steven hadn't shared their sentiments. He became even more concerned when I began putting less time into pursuing my acting career and more time into fixing up the fancy house with the swimming pool that her parents had bought for her in an upscale part of the Hollywood Hills. Like Mami looking at the trappings of Dad's wealth and status, I rushed into marriage without really knowing this woman at all. Somehow I believed that I could reclaim that lost glamour of the lifestyle my mother never had. In my own mythology as the son of the fallen heir of my grandparents' ranch in Cuba, it seemed to me just the Charles Dickens kind of ending to my journey that I should be rewarded for my trials and tests in this way, not unlike how my dignified grandfather Victoriano, my namesake, had married my grandmother and come into the ownership of Las Minas.

This was my unwitting way of trying to act out the story ending that my dad had never stopped thinking would resolve his inner torture. He had written about it in his suicide notes, how he had never found that bag containing $100,000 that would have cured him. There was still a part of me trying to prove to Dad that I could do it, that I had found the gold when he couldn't. The woman I married had her own illusions, apparently, about how my extended family of successful, talented friends would elevate her in a way that money couldn't. There was also a rebellious part of her that appeared to be entertained by bringing home a bad boy from the wrong side of the tracks. But it didn't take long for her to get bored of the novelty. Suddenly, the clock struck midnight and I was no longer the enchanted prince in a fairy tale but standing with my pumpkin and mice. Clearly, fairy tales didn't happen in real life. With little warning or clues, I had called from the gym to ask what she wanted me to pick up for dinner and she made her request, saying that she'd see me when I got home. I walked in to find her gone. The note of explanation said only, "I have the dogs. Sorry." I was dismissed. Like a house servant.

Every slap, kick, hit, punch, humiliation, and debasement from my own father rose up in my senses, and the one sensation that I couldn't shake was of being two years old and falling backward helplessly in my high chair, over and over, never hitting the floor. No one in my life other than Dad had ever come so close to breaking me as she did. Trying to numb the pain caused by allowing myself to be blindsided, I turned to drugs and alcohol. I moved in with a good buddy of mine, Tom Miller, a character and world traveler, with whom I'd worked at the Rainbow Bar & Grill. Tom tried desperately to raise my spirits and get my mind off the dissolution of my marriage. But I was a mess, swiftly descending into a bloated, depressed recluse. Cutting myself off from my friends and family, I made occasional appearances but was inebriated or high when I did. The late drunken entrance I made at Joe and Kathy Cartwright's wedding was an embarrassment for everyone.

Nobody could talk to me, nor did they want to after a while. I was snorting around a gram of cocaine a day and sometimes a lot more, depending on supply. Then I needed to cut the edginess with alcohol. Vodka was my drink of choice, but I could consume anything that was available. I ballooned from 220 to almost 260 pounds. Slamming back the drugs all night, I began each morning as I peeked through the blinds to see the sun rising out of the east. A vampire with a day pass.

My acting career became nonexistent. I canceled so many auditions that my agents stopped calling. Some survival instinct kept me from ever taking a meeting with a producer or director while I was high. Hollywood is a small world and the word travels fast about an actor in trouble.

After nine months of decadence, I was ready to give up. I never made a conscious decision to kill myself, but there was no question that my self-destructive path would eventually do me in. My friends in California and my extended family that had taken me in for many years sent out the red flags, but this time it was my first family who came to my rescue.

Tony and Ed became very concerned about my lack of communication and made the decision to bring me home to Florida. I put up no resistance.

In December of 1987, Ed and I climbed into the barely running BMW 2002 with no radio or heater that Steven Bauer had given me, and we made the long painful trek across the country. Broken and ashamed, I endured the three-day ride to Florida and my body's withdrawal from the alcohol and cocaine with my little brother calling the shots. Ed had to put up with one snarling, abrasive asshole, but he was patient with me.

We drove Interstate 10 from west to east, the same exact route our dad had taken in the shit brown-gold Impala station wagon with the boat and stolen trailer. Driving through Sierra Blanca, Texas, I had a flashback of the events of the day that almost ended our lives. At some point, I caught an image in the side mirror and froze at what I saw. It was Papi's face looking back at me. At thirty-two, my resemblance to him was uncanny, and in that moment what I had suspected about why he singled me out was verified. The man was definitely trying to beat himself out of me. Shivering and sweating, I wondered if he had done the opposite and turned me into him.

Along the road, the forces of resistance rose up in me to banish him. They began to ready me to be healed, not by a false fairy tale, but by authentic love. My brothers, their wives and children, my sisters and their partners and children, and Mami were waiting for me. They were pained by what I was doing to myself and to see me in pain; they put up with my self-destructive behavior that invaded their peace and didn't end right away. But they gave me the home that, as Robert Frost described, is a place where, when you have to go there, they have to take you in.

Staying both in Clearwater with Tony and Nieves and their two beautiful sons, Robert and Michael, and then later in Pembroke Pines, a northern suburb of Miami, with Ed and his lovely wife, Miriam, and their two beautiful sons, Alexander and David, I discovered that it wasn't the ranch at Las Minas I wanted to re-create. Both of my brothers had created beauty and serenity in their surroundings, but most important to me was creating the kind of loving, safe home each of them had established, as later my sisters—both terrific businesswomen and mothers—also built.

Unlike those families who love one another but can say and do hurtful things to one another, there was an unspoken rule that Dad had inflicted enough hurt on each of us and we would never intentionally bruise one another's feelings. Yet it made talking about the past that we had never discussed very difficult. Over time, both during this period and others, we did start to broach some of the thorniest memories.

At one point, Tony and I sat on his dock and he broke down, mourning the times that he had to tell on me to Dad, remembering when I had stepped in to take the punishment for something I didn't do. He asked for my forgiveness and I let him know that there was nothing to forgive. I always knew how much he loved me. What I did say was, "We should hug more."

He gave me an embarrassed look.

"We need to hug," I repeated, pointing out that it was normal in greeting each other and in saying good-bye that I hugged and kissed my Echevarria brothers. "Tony, you and I have never hugged."

The next time I was leaving and it was time to say good-bye, I nervously put my bags by the door and came toward Tony, opening my arms. Instead of hugging from the front, we made a quick adjustment and ended up putting one arm around a shoulder and the other arm across the front of our chests, hip to hip. It lasted a second or two, at best, but we hugged. There is always hope.

Eventually, I went on another kick of suggesting that we all start telling one another "I love you" more often. Ed, a star in the insurance business and later as director of human resources for a national manufacturer, had blossomed into a tall, dashing Little League coach and father figure for lots of kids other than his own. To them and to his boys and to his effervescent, articulate wife, Miriam, he was extremely affectionate verbally and physically. But in his deadpan low volume, his "I love you" to me was very strained initially. Tony at first was worse, often saying a faint "I love you" at the end of a phone conversation, usually after I'd almost hung up.

Mami and I were even more awkward in the beginning, sometimes not looking at each other when saying loving things.

The truth is that during the time I was back in Florida trying to get myself together, I avoided seeing Mami. Besides my shame, she didn't deserve any more hurt and disappointment. In fact, even though I was soon working and seeing the light at the end of the tunnel, I tended to feel the same way about staying with my brothers, who had put up with my sorry ass enough.

Though Lillian would have welcomed me back as a returning stray, I would have been a trying presence in her home. She and Bebo had divorced in the intervening years and had each remarried. Lillian and her new husband, John Bethea, as well as Bebo and his new wife, Suzelle, were still family, but I couldn't impose on them.

Mecca came to the rescue. She had a spare bedroom in her big house and welcomed me to stay for as long as I wanted. Mecca was always affectionate and generous, and her son, Charlie, and I were kindred spirits. Being a big fish in a little pond meant that I was able to book film and TV work in Florida, which was great. But when I wasn't working there were parties. Miami's cocaine culture of the 1980s was still going strong. Because I was free to come and go as I pleased, it wasn't long before I was once again a vampire with a day pass. The second problem, and one of the reasons I was busy numbing myself, was that I was back in my father's house again, a failure, with his heavy vibe everywhere, as though mocking my fumbles and flailings. It must have been difficult for Mecca to see me come and go, a younger version of the complicated man that she had married and loved, and had tried to tame.

When the first visitation happened, in the dark, early hours of morning after I'd come home from my job as a bouncer at a Coconut Grove nightclub, I thought it was a drug-induced hallucination.

Later I learned that Dad had been showing up for years. Mecca heard about my experiences in the upstairs bedroom and looked at me calmly, through her thick glasses, shaking her stylish, thick gray bob, and said with a slight Cuban-Chicago accent, "Are you kidding? Of course, it's haunted." She had a friend who needed a place to stay and Mecca gave her that room. Her friend stayed for less than two weeks and left screaming. "She said somebody was moving around the room and sitting on the bed and stuff."

Parapsychology wasn't a foreign subject to me. In my logic, it made sense that spirits could become trapped in the astral plane, waiting to be freed by a loved one or family member. The spirits of those who died suddenly or tragically, or without a chance to resolve earthly matters, understandably might lurk about waiting to have a chance to say good-bye or wanting to pass along a message. Two nights spent sleeping in a cemetery at age fifteen had certainly caused me to think about these different planes of existence.

Mami, with her gift of sight, could always feel the presence of ghosts. For many years after he died, Dad had shown up on a regular basis at her three-bedroom trailer. Once she woke up and found him in bed with her, in an amorous embrace, but usually his spirit was angry and trapped. She eventually called in a priest to say a mass and a spiritualist to cleanse her and her home.

The old lithe spiritualist picked up my father's energy from the moment she walked into the trailer. Having never met this woman before, Mami was amazed as the spiritualist transformed immediately and began to channel Anthony Rivas Sr., speaking in his voice, his inflections, and his expressions. And then the spiritualist began to cry. As she cried, she began to wring her hands together as if she was wringing out a handkerchief, and wiping her brow, repeating, *"Perdoname. Perdoname."* My father wanted my mother's forgiveness. He was begging for it. His old trick, handkerchief and all. What was Mami to do? Forgive him? "Better free him," said the spiritualist. Before leaving, the old woman cleansed the trailer and instructed Mami to keep a fresh glass of water at the highest point of her home. From then on, she has never failed to do so, washing and refilling that glass on a weekly basis.

Tony's visitations came in sleep, in epic battles with Dad. Though he had forgiven Papi maybe more than any of us, he couldn't reconcile his love with the fear that the sound of the jingling of keys shot through him, even when it was one of his sons returning home from a date. We all remembered the keys in the door as a signal that we were going to be hurt.

Even my baby sister, Carmen, who had met Dad on only a few brief occasions, was contacted by him. Once during a near-death experience, Carmen saw him standing by a bright entryway, inviting her to join him.

Papi's ghost had the consideration never to visit Ed or Barbie, but he obviously had unfinished business with me, his prodigal son. This first visit, I was awakened by the weight of someone sitting on the foot of the bed and the distinctive sound of his voice.

"Hey!" was all he said. Bolting up, I sat looking in the direction of the voice and the sensation at my feet. Nothing. Except his smell. Dad's clean, polished scent, with just a hint of tobacco. It was hard to get to sleep after that—reminiscent of the way I had learned to sleep as a child, ready to be awakened by a slap any time. For just under two weeks, I slept the old way. On alert.

Then again, as I was drifting off to sleep after work not long before dawn, his "Hey!" came first and was followed by the pressure at the end of the bed, and a wave of his scent. Instead of sitting up quickly as before, I opened my eyes slowly, testing to make sure this wasn't one of those nightmares that hovered in limbo between conscious and unconscious thought. Then I saw him, his back to me, in his underwear and undershirt. His hair was perfectly combed, including the comb-over of the bald crown at the back of his head. I sat looking at him for several seconds and realized this was the Dad or Papi of my childhood, not the bloated version of El Ciclón who had, in the room below me, made his own cowardly transition out of this world.

By now I was sitting up. Waiting for him, with more curiosity than fear, to do something. To say something. But he hardly moved and didn't speak. So I did, forcefully, asking with all my being, *"WHAT DO YOU WANT?"*

And with that, he was gone. He didn't go up in a plume of ethereal smoke like the genie in Aladdin. He didn't disappear in the blink of an eye. He faded like an old-fashioned television tube; he seemed to just drift out of focus. The only thing that lingered after this visit was his scent, although it was somewhat soured.

Dad never visited me again in the North Miami house. That didn't mean that I had slain the dragon, although it seemed I had struck a soft spot and had him on the run.

Somehow the ability to pick myself up off the floor, after being knocked down by a woman I had married but barely knew, came to me in the moment that I confronted my father and sent him on his way. My strength returned, but stronger than before. Different. My spirit turned out not to be so broken, after all, just bruised. But I could handle it.

I was the Madcuban, goddamnit! An offensive lineman in my heart, I still had a team that loved me, believed in me, and was counting on me to go back and pick up where I left off—something you can't always do in life but sometimes can in the movies.

Within a couple of weeks, I was back on the road, roaring across the California state line at Blythe in my 1970 Buick Riviera with the 454 engine, gaining strength with each mile.

8
repatriation
(1989–1994)

Life at its best is a creative synthesis of opposites in fruitful harmony.
—Martin Luther King Jr.

WHO SAID THAT FAIRY TALES can't happen in real life?

"We're seating cute petite brunettes in this section," I announced as I invited Mim Eichler to follow and join me at my table. She had just walked into the funky Japanese restaurant and karaoke bar in the Gower Gulch shopping center, at Gower and Sunset in Hollywood, an after-class hangout.

Mim, short for Miriam, was a longtime classmate of mine from the Bill Hudnut comedy workshop class. She was all of five feet tall, with a thick head of curly brown-auburn hair that framed a pretty face, almost impish in quality. We had worked together in comedy improvs over the years. She was quick-witted, good with dialects, and had a winning delivery. Improvisation is like an interpretive dance and she made a great partner. We were such opposites, both visually and stylistically. I was a caged tiger looking for prey; she was a songbird. I was a hot-blooded Latino, a cannon waiting to explode. She was an intellectual with southern charm and soul, like a character from a Tennessee Williams play.

Our classmates were scattered around the different booths, with Bill holding court in one, the sound of his booming, staccato *"Ha!"* soaring above the noise. At our table, I had spontaneously begun to entertain Mim with my many stories. This was not just the telling of stories, but the reenactment of stories that required me to stand up and act out the different scenes, something I'd done since childhood. Mim was a captive audience, listening and laughing for an hour.

The bar began to empty out. Several classmates stopped by to say good night. A few of them didn't hide their raised eyebrows. We were an unlikely match, I suppose, if that's what they were thinking. Through the years, I dated many of the women in class, and Mim had been involved with some of the guys. But we had flirted with each other, in and out of class. She had told me some years before that she had a thing for Cubans. Ironically, even though many of my girlfriends had been tall blonds, I had a thing for petite brunettes.

"I was thinking about getting something to eat. How about you?" I asked, not wanting our evening to end.

She seemed to think that I was asking if she was hungry and quickly answered, "Not really." But when she read the disappointment on my face, she said, "Sure, that sounds great."

We drove individually to a Denny's on Sunset Boulevard, only a mile west from Gower Gulch. We sat in a large red leather booth, staring into each other's eyes, squinting, actually, under the yellow glare of the bad lights, and began to talk easily about our life aspirations. Mim was excited about her burgeoning career as a writer. She had trained to be an actress, with a theatre major from the prestigious Sarah Lawrence College in Bronxville, New York, but had studied writing; one of her professors was E. L. Doctorow, author of *Ragtime*. She had been raised in Oak Ridge, Tennessee, a government-created oasis in the middle of the rural countryside that had been started for the Manhattan Project. Her late father, Eugene Eichler, Ph.D., had been a noted nuclear physicist and her mother was a classical pianist and visual artist. Mim spoke about her family with such love, and her eyes welled up when she spoke of her beloved father, who had died at forty-six from a brain tumor.

She asked me about my background and I responded honestly. I had known her for ten years and spoken only a few words with her, here and there, but in less than an hour, I felt safe with her. She wasn't aware of my time away in Miami, or that I had been back in town for only less than a month. For different reasons, we were both in a similar place, focused on career and not looking to couple up. For me, there was still a residual sting from the divorce that had been finalized a few months earlier. She too was drama weary and therefore in no hurry to get involved. Well, it was the last thing on my mind, yet I found myself telling Mim about my dreams of the house with the white picket fence and the children playing in the yard.

My turkey club sandwich arrived. It remained on the table, untouched by either of us. I paid the bill and followed Mim to her apartment a few blocks away. We broke all the rules of a first date that evening. I never left.

My official move-in date was a week later, in the middle of March 1989. As fate had it, Mim's roommate, musician and writer Jane Ford, was moving back to Canada, and Mim needed someone to share the rent. Her place in Hollywood was much more convenient for me than the apartment I had down at the beach. Jane's twin sister, Katie Ford, a writer and producer formerly on the Michael J. Fox TV series *Family Ties,* had given Jane and Mim a small Jack Russell terrier puppy named Pokey. Katie fell in love with the JRT when Pokey appeared in one episode as "puppy in a basket," and she took her home, only to find her landlord didn't allow dogs. Hence Pokey became Mim's dog when Jane left for Canada.

Though I'm pretty much a big dog kind of guy, Pokey had an infectious personality I couldn't resist. She not only looked just like the dog in the illustrated children's book *The Poky Little Puppy,* she also poked around into all my stuff. Then she ate the back end of every expensive Italian loafer and every other shoe I owned, and when

I scolded her, she simply cocked her head, wagged her tail, and appeared to smile at me. Pokey had superpowers I had only yet begun to fathom, which surfaced during a trip Mim took.

During the week she was away, I was busy filming on location as a series regular in the Michael Mann cop pilot for NBC, *L.A. Takedown*, later a very close facsimile of the script for Mann's movie *Heat*. One of the women on the film crew had been flirting from the first day of filming, but I had refused her advances. This happened to coincide with thoughts I was having during Mim's absence that perhaps I had jumped into this relationship too quickly. All of a sudden I had major doubt about making any kind of commitment.

Living together had pointed out how opposite we were. She had gone to an artsy, elite liberal arts college that she was pretty sure had no teams, although if they did, she wouldn't have known since she knew nothing about sports, much less about football. She spent all day trying to learn more by studying games on TV, even taking notes, and then asked me, "So, am I correct that there are different players for defense and offense?"

She also had a problem with how I looked. "You're too good looking," Mim said, saying that she had never had good luck with handsome guys in the past. What she was looking for now, she explained, was a balding, paunchy, bespectacled Jewish head of a movie studio.

"Wait," I promised her, "I'm an actor. I'm versatile. I can do short and balding."

I was anal retentive about my surroundings; she was not. She wasn't naïve, but had a tendency to see only the good in people. I looked through people, searching for something just below the surface that might hurt me. Mim was trusting. Whenever a writing job ended or money got tight, she remained calm, confident that something was just around the corner. I was the most distrustful when it looked like I had won something, like an acting job; I kept thinking it was going to be taken away from me or someone better would come along.

Just to remind me that maybe we were mismatched, there were also a leering husband and wife who worked for the apartment's landlord; they often sent Mim disapproving looks and made sure that I noticed. In a bizarre set of coincidences, the husband—who was a gardener at our building on Gardner Street and who looked like Chauncey Gardiner (Peter Sellers in *Being There*)—was Cuban, from Sancti Spíritus, of all places, where he had once worked on my grandparents' ranch.

As soon as she learned of this coincidence, his wife showed up the next day with pictures of their three eligible daughters who were excellent housekeepers and would never make me do my own laundry the way that American girl did.

Of course, I had no issue with doing my own laundry, and part of what I loved about Mim was her independence and commitment to her career. Frankly, it wasn't our differences that concerned me as much as the timing. Was I ready?

Mim picked up on my feelings of hesitation on our phone calls while she was traveling. "Whatever you have to figure out, take your time," she said. "I'm not in a rush. I'm not going anywhere." She told me that as far as her heart was concerned, I was the man for her. That scared me even more and opened the door for the woman on the film set. We flirted and then she called the apartment a few times, eventually inviting me out to join her and others in the cast and crew. I kept thinking about Mim and saying no. On the fourth or fifth call, I said yes. Though it was a group thing, I knew that if I stepped out of the apartment, I was going to step out on the relationship.

When it was time to get ready I headed to the bathroom, where the first thing I spotted on my way in was a spilled bottle of hydrogen peroxide on the floor. Next to that was Pokey, collapsed on her side with yellow bile foaming out of her mouth.

"Oh my God! Pokey? Pokey, are you all right?"

She looked like she was dying. I ran back to the phone to cancel my date. I told her my dog was poisoned and I needed to rush her to the vet.

My almost date yelled back at me over the receiver, "Your dog's sick? Oh, fuck you!" She hung up on me.

I ran back toward the bathroom to get Pokey, but before I got there, she was prancing out with her tail wagging. She was fine! She didn't throw up again or get ill. When I called the vet, he said to watch her and to bring her in should her condition change. It didn't.

Pokey had kept me from going out with another woman. The funny Jack Russell—who watched TV when we went out and one night must have heard the news that Lucille Ball had died and put on red lipstick in tribute, getting it all over the cream-colored carpet—had saved a love that was deepening as the months went by.

On November 18, six months after we had moved in together, on Miriam's birthday, I proposed and she accepted. For the next year and a half, I began to purge what I suspected were the last of my demons. But I did it in a most unusual fashion—in my sleep. Whatever was happening with my psyche, I apparently now felt safe enough to embark on this process, knowing that, our differences aside, love was here. I talked, I cried, I writhed as I reenacted horrific scene after scene from my life in vivid detail, with Mim at my side.

The first nightmare began with me thrashing around and cowering. She woke up to see my body convulsing, gasping, and choking, as I took hit after hit. Early on, when I talked in my sleep, she explained, I had a little boy's voice, Cuban accent and all, a voice that said, "Please, no! I'm a good boy. Please don't hurt me."

Another night I reenacted in my sleep the entire scene when Papi had Tony and me eat a cold can of asparagus, complete with gagging. She watched me try to scamper up the wall in terror, and when I woke up, she was sobbing.

The nightmares continued almost nightly until the week of our wedding, when they became laced with humor. During this time, my voice had grown up, as my narrative had unfolded, often sequentially. After she endured many sleepless nights, watching me jolt awake, wide-eyed, looking lost, then reassuring me until we both went back to sleep, I started to invent characters like Lenny Jerusalem, a kid down the block in one dream who was also an agent in another dream, and tales in which I was now a proud Yaqui deer dancer while others were mere stage props. After so many mornings when I awoke to see her shell-shocked but I had no memory of the nightmare, we were now waking up laughing and smiling.

Our wedding, on April 6, 1991, was an eclectic lovefest, a celebration that many remembered as the most romantic and beautiful wedding they had ever attended. Besides Pokey, we had several other wedding angels without whom the day wouldn't have happened— including Heidi von Beltz, who, when she heard about our limited budget, insisted that we get married in Malibu on a hill in her backyard overlooking Zuma Beach and the Pacific Ocean.

The village of friends and family at the wedding came from all walks of life. Catholics, Jews, Buddhists, Christian Scientists, and people from many other religious denominations, gay and straight, young and old, black, white, brown, from all around the country. One of the stars of the wedding was the mother of the groom. Mami commanded the dance floor, with a line of dance partners waiting to dance with her. Andy Garcia, unable to be there, had made a tape of Cuban music that set the tone, although we also used the theme from *The Godfather Part III* in his honor, for the wedding procession.

We unintentionally broke every rule that day. We were married by a reformed rabbi under a chuppah on the Sabbath on the last weekend of Passover, and served Cuban food that included a traditional *lechón* (pork) dish. During the ceremony, on a sparkling clear southern California day, the wind was howling off the coast, causing four of our friends to hold the chuppah poles throughout the service. They were affectionately called "Chuppahs-R-Us" for the rest of the day. My brothers Tony and Ed were groomsmen along with David Plakos and Tom Miller. My dear friend Joe Cartwright was the best man. We waited for the bridesmaids to make their way out of the ranch-style house, each wearing a different ivory-colored suit or dress. In tow were Heidi, Mim's sister, Margrit, Ingrid Bauer, Cheryl Perriera, Kathy Cartwright, and Betsy Jasny, the maid of honor. There at the end of the aisle was the most beautiful sight I had ever seen, a veiled angel with a thirty-foot train trailing behind her. The winds suddenly whirled and picked up and her train was lifted into the air. She looked as if she was about to become airborne herself, and as though to catch her, just about everyone in attendance guided and held the train as she made her way up the aisle to me.

As I said the vows to Mim that Rabbi Jerry Fisher had me repeat, I felt a sudden downward blast of wind that slammed the top of the chuppah onto my head. I took it as a warning from Mim's beloved father, Eugene, that I had better take care of his daughter. I smashed the wineglass, and with a "Mazel tov" and a kiss, we were one.

Almost as soon as we married, I thought I had lost her. We were scheduled to drive up the coast in a rented Cadillac and make several overnight stops along the way on our honeymoon.

Our first stop was Pismo Beach, a small seaside town famous for its sand dunes. Over the course of the drive I became increasingly ill, possibly from a vicious bug or something bad I'd eaten at a highway snack stop. By the time we checked in to our hotel room, my fever had crept so high that my vision was impaired. From our room, I could see a 7-Eleven a block away. Weakly, I handed her the keys and said, "Would you take the car and go get me some crackers and ginger ale?"

She said she'd rather walk and off she went; I crashed out on the bed. An hour and a half later, my eyes popped open.

Something was wrong, terribly wrong. In my fevered state, all I could think about was when I was living in Tallahassee and the serenity of FSU's campus was shattered when two Chi Omega co-eds were found bludgeoned and strangled to death in their beds; three other women were attacked and left for dead that night, but survived. The killer turned out to be Ted Bundy, who was soon captured, but not until after he'd kidnapped and murdered another victim, a twelve-year-old schoolgirl in Lake City, Florida. In the years since, I had read extensively about the kinds of sociopaths and drifters who hit resort towns and how they lure their victims.

My wife, my bride of not many hours, was the most trusting of targets. She had gone to run a ten-minute errand. Why hadn't she taken the car?

I jumped out of bed, reeling and unsteady, with severe stomach cramping, and stumbled out to go find her. With the sun starting to set, throwing a blinding light against my already blurry eyes, I got behind the wheel of the Caddy and sped the one block to the 7-Eleven, leapt out and raced into the very busy store *screaming* and gesturing wildly about my missing wife. The attendant confirmed that a woman fitting Mim's description had been there an hour earlier.

I bolted out of the store, jumped in the car, and peeled out of the parking lot, weaving as I raced through town. No sign of my wife.

HYS-TER-I-CAL, I stampeded into the hotel lobby, insisting, "Call the sheriffs! Call the sheriffs! My wife has been abducted!"

In a strange coincidence, the woman at the front desk had on a name tag reading "Miriam." She suggested calling the room. When she asked what my wife's name was, I pointed tragically at her name tag.

It was my worst fear, repeating itself, that everything and everyone I ever treasured was destined to be taken from me. My fairy tale had seemingly been shattered, like the trophies that Dad had smashed in front of me.

But fate had a different plan. When Miriam at the front desk called our room and my wife Miriam answered, worried about where I was, the unfunny comedy of errors revealed itself. Obviously, as I flew up to our room and into her arms, we both figured out that I hadn't heard her say that she was going to browse around town before she came back.

Although the honeymoon had gotten off to a harrowing start, by the next day, I was feeling well enough to take a hot tub with her out on our hotel balcony. Within minutes, the phone rang and it was from my agent, hunting me down to discuss the terms of a major film deal.

Stomach flu and near abduction notwithstanding, Mim and I felt that this really was a Hollywood fairy tale come true. Lounging in the hot tub, on our honeymoon, negotiating my next movie contract? We toasted all our angels, our cups overflowing.

I had yet to tell Mim about the incident with Pokey. That would have to wait.

I was fingerprinted, photographed, had an extensive background check done, and was required to sign a no-hostage policy before I walked through the gates of San Quentin, the maximum security prison in northern California.

For the next six weeks, I spent twelve to sixteen hours a day filming in the prison population without the comfort and security of private bodyguards. The script for Taylor Hackford's *Blood In, Blood Out* (also released as *Bound by Honor*) was written by Jimmy Santiago Baca, an award-winning Chicano poet who taught himself to read and write in prison. The film followed the story of two Chicano brothers, played by Benjamin Bratt and Jesse Borrego, and a cousin, played by Damian Chapa, all from East L.A., whose lives take different paths after a violent gang incident in their youth. The cousin ends up doing time in San Quentin.

Part of the power of the film for me was the combination of the authenticity of Jimmy's writing and the realism of the prison sequences. As in the film story, we actors were physically separated into the three main factions of prison society, the Chicanos, the blacks, and the whites. When we left the makeup trailer that sat in the middle of the prison yard, we could no longer associate with one another for fear of the friction it might cause. Delroy Lindo and his small group of African-American actors joined the black gang,

Billy Bob Thornton and Tom Towles joined the Aryan gang, and I, along with Damian Chapa, Enrique Castillo, Geoffrey Rivas, Danny Trejo, and Jimmy Santiago Baca fell in with the Chicano gang.

My character, Magic Mike, was a prison warlord in the hierarchy of a fictitious Chicano gang known as La Onda. From the leaner 215 that I had been weighing, I had bulked up to 245, wore a menacing mustache and soul patch, and had my entire upper body covered in jailhouse tattoos. The tattoos took up to three hours to apply with stencils and then were filled in by some of California's leading tattoo artists, including Gil "the Drill" Monte. When I walked out of the makeup trailer into the prison, I left Victor behind and became Magic Mike, dangerous, violent, ruthless, but a soldier in an army that operated with a code of honor, lethal though it was.

As I talked with some of the inmates, it was soon evident that almost every one of them had been a witness to domestic violence or had been a victim of child abuse in his past. (Some statistics say it's as high as 99 percent.) Children aren't born violent and aren't born criminals; violence is a learned behavior. Looking out over the prison yard every day, watching some of the most formidable cons interacting, I realized, There but for the grace of God go I. Without the intervention that helped me break the cycle of violence, I could have very easily become Magic Mike.

There were several prison counts daily. If any of the inmates came up missing, everything shut down, including our filming, until he was accounted for. San Quentin was originally designed to house twenty-five hundred prisoners. In 1991 there were over five thousand men there. Tension is already high in a maximum security prison; adding the element of overcrowding makes life unbearable. When the men are released from their cell blocks in the morning for their various activities, the pent-up energy is audible, like the electricity buzzing off a live wire.

I heard and saw things that a day visitor or young juvenile offender on a Scared Straight field trip will never see. There were at least four stabbings with homemade shanks while we were there, one that I witnessed. There were several lockdowns, a few suicide attempts, and the moans of pain and cries for help from the rape victims were stark reminders of the brutality that men are capable of. The clanging shut of the cell doors at night haunted all of us who were fortunate enough only to be acting in the roles of convicts. So much lost human potential.

Working with a great director like Taylor is like serving under a great military commander or football coach. Taylor helped me tap the Madcuban for this role while Jimmy talked to me about evoking the sensory movement of the jaguar. I've had many extraordinary experiences as an actor, but none of them has affected me or influenced me like my time served in Taylor Hackford's *Blood In, Blood Out.*

Ready for some comedy, I was very gratified that my next big gig was on director Jonathan Lynn's *The Distinguished Gentleman,* starring Eddie Murphy as a con man who gets elected to Congress based on name recognition. As one of his sidekicks, Armando, I had fun improvising scenes with Eddie and also developing bits for my character's journey from con man to congressional staffer. It was a different twist on what they had in mind back at Close Up, but later it gave me an icebreaker when I traveled to Washington, D.C., to lobby Congress and was able to say with conviction, "It's great to be back on the Hill."

In February of 1994, Mim and I went to see our ob-gyn for a determination on how our fourth pregnancy was progressing. We had been through three emotionally upsetting miscarriages, with none of the pregnancies lasting past the first trimester. Each time, the ultrasound had shown that the baby's heartbeat was not present. We were certainly on pins and needles for this one. Mim and I looked away from the monitor as Dr. Scott Serden applied the gel and then the ultrasound paddle. The incredible sound of our baby's heartbeat filled the examination room. We both burst into tears at the sights and sounds on the monitor. The baby was healthy and everything was functioning normally.

Unfortunately, Mim had morning sickness for the entire pregnancy. She had a wretched time and threw up blood but managed to double her weight. Despite her misery, she and I were both ecstatic when she had an amnio and we learned that the baby was doing great. We had tried for the surprise but his penis showed up right on the monitor. Attaboy! Our miracle child, prayed for and long awaited.

Toward the end of the second trimester, I was driving in West L.A., coming home from an audition, when I had a sudden piercing pain in my chest. At first I thought it might be a spasm in my pectoral muscles. But then I had difficulty breathing and my vision became impaired. Of course, my first thought was that I was having a heart attack and needed to pull over and stop driving.

Instead of calling 911, I called Mim, who was busy working against a publishing deadline on a celebrity book she was co-authoring.

Pulled over to the side of the road, looking at the activity of the busy street through tunnel vision, I told her, "I'm scared. I feel like I'm gonna die. You better get here soon."

Mim arrived after what seemed like hours and she drove me to our doctor's office. Dr. Joshua Trabulus gave me a thorough examination and could find nothing wrong with me, except that I was a little anemic. My symptoms dissipated soon after my arrival at his office. It was a mystery.

A couple of weeks later, I was working on a comedy Western TV series called *The Adventures of Brisco County, Jr.* when the symptoms returned. I was on horseback in the middle of nowhere when I suddenly felt faint. It was hard to breathe. Each time I had the impulse to get the set nurse, I fought it, not wanting to be fired or be some kind of hypochondriac.

I tried to will away whatever was happening. The more I tried, the worse I got. My fellow guest star Ely Pouget, on a horse next to mine, kept looking over at me. Between each take, I collapsed over my saddle until the director yelled "Action!" Then I sat up, moved my horse to its camera mark, pointed my revolver, and shouted out my lines. With the word "Cut!" I collapsed back onto my horse. We shot that same scene over and over again for various reasons until we were done for the day.

As Ely and I walked back to the trailers, I confided in her that I had been collapsing on the horse to keep from fainting.

"Wow," she said, "I thought it was some new acting technique."

I made the long drive back into town, more scared than ever, and called Dr. Trabulus's office for an appointment the next morning.

After a barrage of tests, a full physical examination complete with a heart echogram, EKG, full blood workup, and finally, a treadmill stress test, Dr. Trabulus announced, "There's nothing wrong with your heart. It's as strong as a bull's!" He told me to get dressed and meet him in his office.

"Are you having baby anxiety?" Dr. Trabulus asked, calmly and kindly. Seeing my confusion, he went on, carefully, "Are you worried about being a father?"

His question made me sit back in my chair and take a defensive posture. "No! I'm very excited. I've already painted his room and moved in some furniture. I'm ready!"

Dr. Trabulus eased gently into questions about my childhood and upbringing. He seemed deeply affected by what I briefly told him. "Victor, you're having anxiety attacks." He prescribed some medication to help get me through them, but recommended I definitely talk to somebody before the baby was born.

Mim arranged for me to see her therapist, Dr. Barbara Kobrin. I had never been to see a therapist, but I wanted to get to the bottom of what was going on with me and FIX IT.

Barbara made me feel comfortable as we sat across from each other, smoking cigarettes in a quaint little house in Hollywood where she then had her practice. During my first visit I talked for most of the hour about Dad and what had gone on in our home. At the end of our session, Barbara asked me if I understood that I had endured the most extreme form of abuse.

She went on to explain to me that individuals who endure this type of physical and emotional abuse many times suffer from post-traumatic stress syndrome. I had heard that term used with Vietnam veterans and other war or disaster refugees. Dr. Kobrin was the person who first compared what we had lived through to a war zone.

Though it was a relief to understand that my anxiety was normal and though Barbara assured me that I was going to be fine, in some ways our three sessions made me more fearful than I was before. Now my panic focused on whether I had really banished Dad after I confronted his apparition. Maybe as he faded, his evil had come to roost inside me, needing a live host. I put on a happy face for Mim, but deep down inside I wondered if the monster that was my father lived inside me.

The answer arrived on July 27, 1994. Mim's water broke at 2 A.M., ten days before the C-section we had scheduled because our baby was breech. Since Dr. Serden was out of town, his partner, Dr. Arthur Allen, was going to deliver the baby, still by cesarean unless the baby managed to flip. We made it quickly to Cedars-Sinai hospital and by 5 A.M. we were in the operating room.

The room was awash in bright lights with monitors everywhere. Mim was flat on her back, numb from the waist down, feeling no pain. The anesthesiologist had put together a tape of the most incredible opera arias I had ever heard. Tears rolled down my face as I stroked Mim's hair and watched Dr. Allen calmly go about his business.

"I'm going in." With his announcement, I stood up and looked over the sheet partition that was erected at Mim's shoulders, shielding her view of the surgery being performed on her lower abdomen.

Dr. Allen reached into Mim's abdomen and grabbed one of my son's unseen legs. "This kid is not seven pounds! He's big!"

With that proclamation, he pulled my son out by the ankles up to his waist. The baby immediately christened the room with a long stream of urine from his erect penis. Attaboy!

Suddenly, Dr. Allen pushed the baby back in and made an adjustment. The cord was wrapped around his neck. A second later, our
bloody, blue baby was out, but before I could admire him, I heard Dr.
Allen utter one word, "Resuscitate!"

Through her fog, Mim weakly said, "What? What's going on?"

Oh, my God, I prayed, please make him be okay. Please.

One of the nurses grabbed a suction bulb and stuck it down the
baby's throat and squeezed. The room was filled with a gargled wail
and my child turned pink in front of my eyes.

Dr. Allen invited me to join him and the nurses. They handed me
a pair of surgical scissors and guided me as I cut his cord.

I followed the nurses over to a warming station, where they
cleaned him up a little and weighed him. Moments later, my swad-
dled son was placed in my arms.

"What's his name?" someone asked.

"Elias Kennedy Rivas," I announced as I looked down at the tiny
miracle of life who was calmly sleeping in my arms. Born at 5:29
A.M., weighing eight pounds, thirteen ounces, and measuring twenty
and a half inches, he was so beautiful!

A son. He looked like me. He looked like Mim. He looked like
Eli.

I held him against my body, wanting him to feel the unconditional love that I would always have for him. I wanted him to feel my
strong body and know that it would always protect him and never
hurt him.

All of the anxiety and fear I had carried with me for thirty-nine
years washed away in those first private moments, between *this* father
and his son. Eli would have a home that he would want to come
home to and never fear.

I was at peace. I was home.

epilogue:
peace

Peace is a daily, a weekly, a monthly process, gradually changing opinions, slowly eroding old barriers, quietly building new structures.
—John F. Kennedy,
United Nations address, September 20, 1963

I GAZED OUT THE LEFT SIDE of the aircraft and saw a perfect rainbow that started at the tip of the wing and continued over the top of the plane, where it disappeared out of view. I looked across the aisle and to my amazement saw the continuation of the most magnificent rainbow I had ever witnessed. The half-empty plane that had traveled across a mourning nation from Los Angeles was making its final approach over water before landing in Baltimore, Maryland.

It was October 1, 2001, less than three weeks since the tragic events of September 11. Many of us on this plane were traveling for the first time since our world had been so shattered. I wasn't the only nervous and vigilant passenger on this flight and didn't mind that the handful of passengers sitting with me in first class watched me every time I got up to go to the lavatory outside the cockpit door.

The half halo of muted color framed the top of the plane, all the way until the wheels skidded down on a runway at BWI Airport. The rainbow felt like an arc of protection, or so I prayed.

I was on my way to Washington, D.C., to join Senator Paul Wellstone, his wife, Sheila, and others at the Wellstones' annual event to kick off National Domestic Violence Awareness Month.

With the birth of my son, Eli, the jury was no longer out. The cycle of violence had truly been broken. The idea to use my story to make a difference had been stirring in me for a while when I learned about an organization called the National Network to End Domestic Violence, a Washington, D.C.–based network of statewide coalitions working to end violence against women and children. My friend and publicist Dick Weaver called the NNEDV and spoke to their executive director, Donna Edwards.

Dick told Donna that he had a client who would make an outstanding national spokesperson for the NNEDV.

"Great," Donna said, "who is she?"

"It's a *he*." Dick laughed and then gave Donna Edwards a brief synopsis of my story. She was intrigued enough to set up a meeting with me in Los Angeles.

What I liked about the NNEDV was that it was a national organization working with Congress and the White House, with its finger on the pulse of all of the issues, on funding and legislative actions being addressed on local, state, and national levels.

Like Donna—who had the vision and courage to make a man the national spokesperson for an issue that's still seen as primarily a women's issue—her successor at the NNEDV, Executive Director Lynn Rosenthal, kept me on as spokesperson and looked for ways to expand my role in the area of public awareness. As my story underscores, the connection between domestic violence and child abuse must be addressed as these are issues that touch everyone.

Before I began speaking out, I wanted to get permission from my family. My siblings generously gave me their blessing. I left Mami for last. Retired for several years and living quietly in south Florida, La Luchadora lives surrounded by her children and numerous grandchildren and visits me often in California. One of the most joyful visions of my life was the day that I came into my living room and saw my young son cuddled up with Abbi, as he calls his *abuela*. She was stroking his hair and he had his arms around her neck. That was something she was never allowed to do with her own sons. It was beautiful.

If Mami, a private person, had said no to my telling her story, I would have respected that. I barely got the first sentence out when Mami stopped me and said, "If you can save *one person* from being subjected to the torture that was our life, then whatever loss of privacy we experience would be worth it."

When I was getting started in my role as spokesperson I had more than a couple of friends make the same comment when I told them that I was speaking on the issue of domestic violence. They would say, "So are you for or against it?"

And they'd laugh to let me know it was a joke, because, of course, who would actually admit to being for domestic violence?

The fact is that the vast majority of people can agree on being against domestic violence. That's the good news. It is truly a bipartisan issue. But what I get a lot of times from people when they make remarks like that is, "Domestic violence—why should I care about it? Why does it affect me? Do we really have to talk about this?"

Here are some very simple answers that cut across all cultures and economic strata. Domestic and sexual violence affects one in every four women: your sister, your daughter, your mother, your friend, your coworker, you. Domestic violence shatters lives in your community and costs $3 to 4 billion each year to businesses alone, due to workplace absenteeism, turnover, medical expenses, and lower productivity. Child abuse is estimated to be fifteen times more likely to occur in those homes where domestic violence is present. Between 3 and 10 million children each year witness domestic violence. Each year, two thousand children die from abuse.

I chose to break my silence and share my love story as a way of thanking all of the angels and advocates who helped to guide me out of my darkness and heal my wounds. To all of those courageous, caring families that took me into their homes in high school against the warnings of other parents in the community, my eternal gratitude. To many people, I was a big, tough, scary kid from a bad background, but as Lillian Echevarria said, taking me in was something that her family had to do, to try to make a difference in my life.

If I've learned anything in my journey from victim to survivor, and now as an activist, it's the belief that violence is preventable and that an ounce of prevention goes a long, long way.

Angels and advocates of the movement to end domestic violence not only have served victims and survivors but have begun to create programs for batterers, not just with treatment but with intervention and prevention. Whenever I have spoken to batterers' groups, the men often ask me whether it would have made a difference if my father had sought help. Without question, if my father had been willing to seek help, I would have held his hand every step of the way. The point is that no woman, child, or significant other should be left helpless and hopeless. The movement has established shelters, hotlines, counseling services, legislation, training for law enforcement and health care providers, along with public awareness campaigns that have begun to get the message across that love should never hurt. That's the good news.

The bad news is that domestic violence continues to be the most underreported crime in America, what's known as "the quiet crime" because it thrives in an atmosphere of shame, denial, and silence.

Another reason I wanted to use my story publicly was to give a voice to those victims who never had a chance to speak out, like my own brother Robert David Rivas. I hope to send the message not only that domestic violence touches everyone, but also that there is a connection between the issues of domestic violence, child abuse, sexual assault, and any form of violence. In fact, I believe there is a connection between those violations and the violence we fear on our school campuses, on our streets, and in our world.

What connects all of this is one of the most fundamental civil rights every citizen of the world ought to have—*the right to be safe*. I know that's something that dominates our national consciousness with our continuing concerns about terrorism and instability around the world. But there is another kind of terrorism we need to confront, and it is homegrown, in families and in relationships, where most violence is learned and bred.

My journey as an activist has been blessed by Mim's activism as a board member of the NNEDV Fund and by having Eli travel with me to lobby members of Congress and even to meet President Bill Clinton in the Oval Office. Eli asked to join me at the podium and share his thoughts on the issue when he was five. He's been speaking out ever since.

In 2002 our country lost two of its greatest advocates and public servants, Senator Paul Wellstone and his wife, Sheila, in a tragic plane crash. Together they had helped to raise the public's awareness regarding the complexities of the issue of domestic violence and were the staunchest allies in the fight to end it. After my 2001 attendance at the Wellstones' domestic violence awareness event, my family and I were able to visit them that following June in Senator Wellstone's Washington office, where we talked about how we could get more men involved in the movement. At the end of our meeting, I asked Senator Wellstone if he would take a picture with my son. He walked Eli over to his beautiful wooden desk with an oversized leather chair and said, "Go ahead, sit down."

Eli was a foot away from the chair when he stopped dead in his tracks and turned around and looked at Senator Wellstone and said, "You know, I might want to run for president."

Senator Wellstone leaned back and burst out laughing and we joined him. That's how I'll always remember him and Sheila, who were never too busy to stop a meeting and give students a personal tour of the office. He was a man who, with the guidance of his beloved wife, always voted with his heart and his conscience, not just with his party. After learning of their tragic deaths, I rededicated myself to trying to make the world a safer place to live in.

There are other personal angels no longer with us who made my personal world infinitely safer and happier. Our dear teacher Bill Hudnut, in whose home of laughter Mim and I met, died in 1992 from AIDS. My best friend, Joe Cartwright, fought an aggressive cancer that ended his life in 2003.

In their memory, and to all of my coaches, teachers, and members of my extended family who didn't give up hope in me, and to all the advocates in the trenches in the movement to end violence, I honor you by sharing this private family matter and by telling the story of the Madcuban, now at peace.

domestic violence resources

If you or someone you know is, or may be, a victim of abuse, please call the National Domestic Violence Hotline: 1–800–799–SAFE (7233)

If you would like to become more active in creating communities that are safer, more peaceful places to live for all of us, here are four suggestions:

1. **Break the Silence:** Whether you are a victim or a witness to any form of violence, talk to someone. Don't stand by silently.

2. **Practice Peace:** Make a pledge to yourself and the people you care about to resolve conflicts with diplomacy instead of war. Make a pledge to treat others with respect, even when you don't especially like them.

3. **Teach Peace:** If you want to take more action, volunteer at a hotline, drop off food at a women and children's shelter, or find an organization working for peace that you can support.

4. **Contribute to Peace:** Make a contribution today to a local, state, or national program working to save lives and end all violence in our homes, our neighborhoods, our nation, and our world.

For more information on the National Network to End Domestic Violence and its sister organization, the NNEDV Fund, please visit www.nnedv.org, or call 1–202–543–5566. You can join the NNEDV Fund's Acts of Love Campaign and become a supporter of our frontline efforts to end violence. The campaign helps bring resources to local domestic violence programs, supports the accomplishments of survivors, and honors the efforts of those who have dedicated their lives to creating peaceful homes. Your tax deductible contribution to the NNEDV Fund will help to raise public awareness about domestic violence and its causes, impact, and solutions:

NNEDV Fund, 660 Pennsylvania Ave. SE, Suite 303, Washington, DC 20003.

additional
acknowledgments

In my journey as an actor and an activist, I am proud to be part of an incredible community of advocates to whom I am forever indebted. There isn't enough space to thank everyone, but I would be remiss if I did not include these additional acknowledgments. Without the encouragement of the following people, this book wouldn't have been possible.

A heartfelt thank-you goes to Senator Joe Biden, a national hero in the fight to keep all of our citizens safe at home and in the world. Thanks to everyone at the Office on Violence Against Women; to those legislators in the United States Senate and House of Representatives, along with governors, state and local legislators, leaders in social and health services, in the courts, in schools, and in law enforcement, who, despite budget crises, refuse to turn back the clock on protections for all those affected by domestic violence; special gratitude to the Congressional Caucus for Women's Issues and the Congressional Hispanic Caucus for the welcome and support you've given me in Washington, D.C.

For championing me in my work as a spokesperson for the NNEDV, my enormous appreciation belongs to Fernando Laguarda and everyone at the firm of Mintz, Levin, Cohn, Ferris, Glovsky and Popeo, and to Shannon Flint Eusey of Beacon Pointe Advisors. For extraordinary personal and philanthropic generosity, a special word of thanks goes to David Geffen—an early inspiration to me to try to make a difference—and to everyone at the David Geffen Foundation. My fondest admiration belongs to Carol Black, Meredith Wagner, Mary Dixon, and to everyone at Lifetime Television for your unswerving commitment to your campaign to end violence against women.

Without the leadership and support of private and corporate foundations, countless lifesaving agencies in this nation would cease to exist. I am especially grateful to my friends Diane Eidman, Diana Echevarria, and everyone at the Altria's Doors of Hope program. Immense thanks also go to Anne Crews and everyone at the Mary Kay Ash Charitable Foundation of Mary Kay, Inc., with personal gratitude for underwriting *Breaking the Silence: Journeys of Hope*, along with more appreciation to its filmmakers, Dominique Lasseur and Catherine Tatge. Great gratitude is due to the Byron family, Marcia Roth, and everyone at the Mary Byron Foundation, along with everyone at Appriss involved with the VINE program. To Dianne Mooney, Jennifer Jacquess, and everyone at Southern Living at HOME and the Cut It Out program, I am so thankful.

There aren't enough words to say how awed I am by the tireless efforts of all the member state coalitions of the NNEDV. For inviting me to your states and making me feel so much at home, my ongoing thanks go to Mary Lauby and everyone at the Wisconsin Coalition Against Domestic Violence; to Cheryl Howard and everyone at the Illinois Coalition Against Domestic Violence; to Mary Keefe, Kathy Hagenian, and everyone at the Michigan Coalition Against Domestic and Sexual Violence; to Sherry Frohman and everyone at the New York State Coalition Against Domestic Violence; to Tiffany Carr at the Florida Coalition Against Domestic Violence; to Sandy Barnett and everyone at the Kansas Coalition Against Sexual and Domestic Violence; to Agnes Maldonado and everyone at the New Mexico Coalition Against Domestic Violence; to Carol Post and everyone at the Delaware Coalition Against Domestic Violence; to Colleen Coble and everyone at the Missouri Coalition Against Domestic Violence; to everyone at the Louisiana Coalition Against Domestic Violence; to Ellyne Bell and to everyone at the California Alliance Against Domestic Violence; to Carol Gundlach at the Alabama

Coalition Against Domestic Violence; and to Rose Pulliam and everyone at the Vermont Network Against Domestic Violence and Sexual Assault.

My ongoing respect and gratitude goes out to those national allies who are part of the movement to end violence in our homes and our relationships: Sheryl Cates and the National Domestic Violence Hotline; Deborah Tucker and Vickie Smith of the National Center on Domestic and Sexual Violence; Rita Smith and the National Coalition Against Domestic Violence; Adelita Michelle Medina and everyone at the National Latino Alliance for the elimination of Domestic Violence (Alianza); Dr. Nora Baladerian and everyone at Arc Riverside's annual International Conference on Ending Abuse of Adults and Children with Disabilities; Dr. Robert Geffner and everyone involved with the annual International Conference on Family Violence; the National College of District Attorneys; and everyone at MANA, A National Latina Empowerment Organization.

Permanent gratitude is due to fellow spokespeople who use their artistry, their celebrity, and their stories to raise awareness around the world: Eve Ensler and everyone involved with V-Day; Heidi Joyce and all the comediennes of Stand Up Against Domestic Violence; choreographer Donald Byrd for his contribution of *The Beast*; Connie Mae Fowler; Don McPherson; Michael Bolton; Jackson Katz; and all the artists, poets, actors, singers, authors, playwrights, storytellers, TV writers, filmmakers, and journalists who refuse to treat domestic violence and child abuse as private family matters.

Thank you, thank you, thank you to every advocate, volunteer, and contributor, and all those on the front lines serving battered women and their families at local shelters, programs, and agencies across the country. For the hospitality given to me in your communities and fields of work, I send gratitude to: Felicia Collins-Correia at Tulsa's Domestic Violence Intervention Services; Judith Wills and everyone at Mid-Cities S.O.S. of The Women's Shelter in the Arlington, Texas, vicinity; Candy Perez and everyone at Houston's La Rosa Family Services; Lieutenant Colonel Peggy Emington and everyone at the Kentucky Association of Chiefs of Police; Casey Gwinn and everyone at San Diego's Family Justice Center; everyone at CASA in St. Petersburg, Florida, including my big brother, Tony Rivas; everyone at The Spring of Tampa Bay in Florida; everyone at SafeNet of Erie, Pennsylvania; everyone at New York's Northern Westchester Shelter, the S.T.A.R. program, and Pace University; everyone at Napa Emergency Women's Services; the California District Attorneys Association; the Sonoma County District Attorney's Office for their work on behalf of all victims of violence; the Michigan Osteopathic Association; the University of Wisconsin; and Sylvia Heller and everyone at the Rachel Coalition in New Jersey.

Here in my backyard in southern California, I am thankful every day for lifesaving advocates in my own community. For ongoing leadership and inspiration, thank you Patti Giggans and everyone at the Los Angeles Commission on Assaults Against Women. Heartfelt thanks go to: Sister Judy Molovsky for lifelong leadership in creating peace; everyone at Mount St. Mary's College and sponsors of the Youth Summit on Peace; Sister Ann and everyone at the Good Shepherd Shelter in Los Angeles; Dr. Robert Splawn and everyone at California Hospital; Lieutenant Mike Hertica with ongoing appreciation; everyone at 1736 Family Crisis Center; Dorothy Courtney and everyone at Richstone Family Center; January Wiggins for courageous work at Torrance's Men's Domestic Violence Batterer's Treatment Program; the South Bay Family Violence Council; everyone at the Interagency Council on Child Abuse and Neglect; East Los Angeles College; El Camino College; and everyone at A Place Called Home in south central Los Angeles.

Special thanks to my career support system, which helps me juggle acting and speaking work: the multitalented Hillary Carlip for the extraordinary website design and upkeep; my wonderful agents, Ann Geddes and Richard Lewis at the Geddes Agency; and the inimitable Dick Weaver, PR maverick and dear friend, for getting the whole ball rolling.

about the author

Victor Rivas Rivers is a former college and professional athlete; a veteran actor with leading roles in over two dozen films, including Eddie Murphy's sidekick in *The Distinguished Gentleman*, Antonio Banderas's brother in *The Mask of Zorro*, and Magic Mike in the cult hit *Blood In, Blood Out;* and the national spokesperson for the National Network to End Domestic Violence. Victor was born in Cuba and now lives with his family in Hermosa Beach, California. Visit his website at www.victorrivers.com.